ANGEL OF THE EUCHARIST

Angel of the Eucharist

The Life & Spiritual Writings *of* Marie-Eustelle Harpain

Translation, introduction, and notes by
J. STEPHEN RUSSELL

English translation based on the 1883 edition of
Recueil des Ecrits de Marie-Eustelle,
née à Saint-Pallais de Saintes le 19 Juin 1814,
morte le 29 Juin 1842

Angelico Press

First published in the USA
by Angelico Press 2026

For information, address:
Angelico Press, Ltd.
169 Monitor St.
Brooklyn, NY 11222
www.angelicopress.com

Ppr 979-8-89280-183-6
Cloth 979-8-89280-184-3
Ebook 979-8-89280-185-0

Book and cover design
by Michael Schrauzer

O my only friend, whom I adore and contemplate
Spouse divine, O Jesus, my hope!
Before you in this temple, why can I not
Pass my days, until my final night.

If your love so moves me by its charms,
Ah, permit me to respond to these fires:
I want now to love you in the crosses, in the tears,
As I wait to see you in Heaven.

CONTENTS

INTRODUCTION

O, my good friend, if only I could place in your heart what Jesus has placed in mine![1]

IN THE SMALL TOWN OF SAINTES IN SOUTHwestern France, Marie-Eustelle Harpain was born on April 19, 1814 and died on June 29, 1842, at 28 years of age. Despite her best efforts at self-erasure, at her death she was already "l'ange de l'Eucharistie," "the Angel of the Eucharist," a beloved figure in her village, renowned for her humility, piety, and her extraordinary devotion to the Holy Eucharist. Writing about twelve years after her death and echoing the recollections of her bishop, Clément Villecourt, Eustelle's biographer, Edward Thompson, recounts the days immediately after her passing:

> Scarcely had Eustelle breathed her last, when the news spread through the town of Saintes, as of an event in which all must take the deepest interest. There was no talk but of her virtues, and although prayers were offered for her in accordance with the spirit of the Church, a much greater inclination was felt to implore her patronage before the Throne of God. Her friends were meanwhile hastily dividing the scanty but precious spoil she had left — those few otherwise valueless things which had belonged to the votary of poverty. A little contention occurred about her rosary; and then there was displayed that pious eagerness which is usual in the case of persons who have departed with the reputation of high sanctity, to bring medals, pictures, beads to touch the venerated body. Eustelle had injured her knees from her continual posture of adoration; a kind friend had consequently nailed down a little cushion at the spot where she was used to pray. This was speedily removed, to be preserved, no doubt, by some pious family as a dear relic of the departed. Scraps of paper

---

[1] Eustelle to her friend, Sister Anastasia; see Claudius Maria Mayet, S.M., *L'Ange de l'Eucharistie, ou Vie et Esprit de Marie-Eustelle Harpain, d'àpres les documents le plus authentiques* (Paris, 1863), 103–4: "O bonne amie, si je pouvais mettre dans votre cœur ce que Jesus a mis dans le mien!" Translations from Mayet are my own.

> with her handwriting on them were eagerly snatched up; and even the leaves which she had pasted in her books of devotion, and upon which she had written a few words, were torn out and greedily appropriated.[2]

While all of this was going on, Eustelle's bishop, Clément Villecourt, put a plan in motion, a plan he had formulated years before her death. He ordered Father de Laage de Saint-Germain, Eustelle's parish priest, and others to collect as many of her letters as they could find, knowing that a great many of these would end up as treasured relics tucked into a bible or kept reverently folded up in a drawer. Bishop Villecourt did this for two reasons, which he explains in his letter reproduced below: he did this, first, to preserve Eustelle's words for the people of the diocese and of France, and, second, to serve as evidence in what he assumed would be an investigation into her possible canonization as a saint.

About a year after Eustelle's death, in 1843, these collected letters were published under the direct auspices of Bishop Villecourt with no other editor, curator, or intermediary mentioned.[3] This two-volume work, the *Recueil* or Collection, comprised:

- an introductory letter by Bishop (later Cardinal) Villecourt;
- an autobiographical memoir written by Eustelle at the instruction of her spiritual director;
- 176 of Eustelle's letters, written to various correspondents, whose names were withheld;
- 14 poems or *cantiques* (songs) composed by Eustelle;
- a series of imagined "dialogues" between Eustelle and an interlocutor named Angelique.

This present book is an annotated English translation of the complete *Recueil*, excluding only the dialogues.[4] To the fourteen

---

[2] Edward Healy Thompson, *The Life of Marie-Eustelle Harpain, the Sempstress of Saint-Pallais, called "The Angel of the Eucharist"* (London, 1868), 371.

[3] *Recueil des Écrits de Marie-Eustelle, née à Saint-Pallais de Saintes le 19 Juin 1814, morte le 29 Juin 1842* (La Rochelle, 1843). This book is the French source for the translations in this book. The birth month in the subtitle is incorrect.

The work would be reprinted in 1848, 1855, 1860, and later. It is presently available in French via Google books and, again in French, as an historical reprint through Amazon.

[4] The dialogues purport to expand on Eustelle's thoughts and spiritual insights; these dialogues were explicitly presented as imagined conversations, and it was later established that they were actually written by Bishop Villecourt. As they do not represent Eustelle's words or even thoughts that

cantiques included in the *Recueil* are added two other bits of verse included in two of the letters. Four letters added in later editions are included. As the *Recueil* did, this book begins with Bishop Villecourt's letter to the diocese of La Rochelle, which served as the introduction to all of the French editions. This letter, dated only eight months after Eustelle's death, is a vivid testimony to the effect Eustelle had on friends and acquaintances, even (or perhaps especially) her bishop. The letter also loosely sketches the sequence of events that produced the French *Recueil.* Following the bishop's letter are Eustelle's *Memoir*, the 176 letters, and 14 *cantiques* or songs. The translation also reproduces the original chapter heads, letter headnotes, and footnotes that appeared in the French editions. Together, these pages constitute, as far as we know, the "collected written works" of Marie-Eustelle Harpain,[5] for whom, at this writing, an active cause for beatification is underway in her diocese of La Rochelle-Saintes.

EUSTELLE'S LIFE

Materials for the life of Eustelle are limited and, in different ways, problematic. The first source is Eustelle's own memoir of her life, written, grudgingly, at the direction of her spiritual director, Father Joseph Briand, and Bishop Villecourt, At their urging, she began the work in October 1840 and left it incomplete, probably in early 1842. [6] The work is a moving but factually uneven account of her life from her earliest memories until about 1838. She broke off the narrative at this point, no doubt in part due to her failing health, but also, as she suggests, that a narrative of these final, peaceful years, touched by illness but graced with divine favors, would be prideful.[7]

Eustelle is very hard on herself in this memoir, focusing first on what she saw as youthful worldliness and on the pains and trials she endured in her later teens. Her virtues, talents, and strengths are thus insistently hidden here under humility and self-abnegation.

---

she was willing to share, they are not part of this present volume.

[5] Eustelle's original biographers include extensive quotations from Eustelle, apparently drawn from other sources or from persons' memories of conversations with her. Some of these passages are included in this introduction.

[6] Letter 29.

[7] See *Memoir*, ch. 30.

Precisely the opposite issues lay within the two other sources for Eustelle's life, the hagiographic biographies of Claudius Maria Mayet and Edward Healy Thompson. Mayet was a Marianist priest and noted devotional author, Thompson the editor of a series of English lives of more contemporary saints.[8] Both of these men spent time in Saintes in the 1850s and '60s, conducting lengthy interviews with Eustelle's family, friends, and acquaintances, especially her mother, brother Charles, and sister Anastasie. Mayet also drew extensively on conversations with Eustelle's friend and confidante, Sister Anastasia, as well as from written testimony of Cardinal Villecourt (by now deceased) and Father Armand Guérin, whom Eustelle befriended as a young seminarian.

These two works, Mayet in French and Thompson in English, mirror one another very closely, despite Thompson's efforts to complement rather than copy Father Mayet. The results are heartfelt treatments of a deeply admired and holy woman, one both writers openly admit should be destined for sainthood. In this spirit, the works are short on factual details and dates and long on florid language of praise and extended comparisons of elements of Eustelle's with the lives of canonized saints, from Augustine to Agnes of Jesus.

The real Marie-Eustelle Harpain awaits the modern reader neither in her own harsh judgments of herself nor in the charming enthusiasm of her biographers, but rather in her *Memoir* and especially in her letters and poems, shared with only a few, often written and sent on condition that no one but the recipient should ever see them. There she can be heard in her own voice.

Marie-Eustelle Harpain was born on April 19, 1814 to René Harpain and his wife Marie (née Picotin) Harpain. She was baptized five days later at the parish church of Saint-Pallais in Saintes that would become the center of her life. Eustelle was the second of five children to René and Marie; an older sister, also Marie, was born in 1811 but died six months later. Eustelle's younger siblings were Marie Angèle (born in 1818), Charles (1820), and Magdeleine-Anastasie (1824).

By all accounts Eustelle's childhood was happy and unexceptional. Her father René was a *couvrier* or roofer or thatcher, a no-nonsense, practical survivor who provided for his family and

---

[8] Mayet, loc. cit.; Thompson, loc. cit.

played the violin.[9] In later years Eustelle would describe her father as having a shallow faith, content to do the required religious observances and little more. In her memoir she reveals that she offered God her life in exchange for her father's salvation.[10]

Eustelle's *Memoir* gives us a strong sense of her special bond with her mother Marie. A serious health scare with Eustelle soon after her birth,[11] coupled with the death of her first-born daughter at six months, made Marie Harpain deeply devoted to her (now) oldest daughter. Eustelle returned her warm affection; her mother relates several stories to her biographers, including the time Eustelle innocently repeated a dirty song for her mother, who replied, "Never say these words, little one, or people will laugh at you. You are very lucky to have told only your mother."[12]

Eustelle started her brief schooling at age five and was a precocious reader and writer, repeating lessons and readings for her mother after school. At home her reading was from the Bible and *The Imitation of Christ*, but from the beginning her education was an insistently practical one, assuring that she could read, write, and do the arithmetic necessary for a tradeswoman. In any case, Eustelle's mother reported that, by the time she left schooling for good at age ten, she was something of a schoolroom prodigy, impressing Father Maupontet, the parish curé who would visit the classroom. Eustelle herself looks back on these experiences and the doting praises of her parents as feeding a willfulness and pride that made her, at age ten, "intolerable;... accustomed to do whatever I wanted, I became disobedient, rebellious, irritable, and impatient."[13]

These behaviors seemed to disappear abruptly in the summer of 1826, when, at age 12, Eustelle had her first confession, and then her first Communion and Confirmation, the last two on the same day, the Feast of Corpus Christi. The *Memoir* captures the profound emotions Eustelle experienced on receiving reconciliation and the Eucharist, though she observes that didn't fully comprehend the impact of Confirmation. It is not clear why both of these were administered to Eustelle on the same day: Father

---

[9] Mayet 53.

[10] *Memoir*, ch. 1. Mayet reports that, with Bishop Villecourt's counsel, René Harpain was reconciled to the Church before his death; 22.

[11] Thompson 12.

[12] Mayet 24; cf. Thompson 14.

[13] *Memoir*, ch. 3; cf. Thompson 17.

Maupontet might have wanted to take advantage of 94-year-old Bishop Palliou's visit; alternately, Eustelle's precocious mind might have convinced the curé that Confirmation was appropriate. At about the same time Eustelle began spending Sunday afternoons at the convent of the *Filles de la Sagesse* or Daughters of Wisdom, an order of nuns founded by Saint Louis of Montfort, who had established a school for working class girls in Saintes earlier in the century.[14]

Two years later, in 1828, Eustelle's life changed dramatically. While still living with her family, she was apprenticed to a seamstress in the town. She was one of several apprentices to this businesswoman and, according to her biographers, became a favorite in the household. Her interactions with the other girls exposed her to the innocent but exciting obsessions of young teenagers, especially fancy dress and dancing. In the *Memoir*, Eustelle looks back with horror on those days:

> I can say, my Father, that I loved the dance as much as it was possible to love something, and I counted the moments until I could commence this dangerous pleasure, so capable of bringing about the loss of innocent youth. I cannot count the number of thoughts, desires, glances, and words in these evil pastimes that could condemn me in the eyes of God. And I was only fourteen![15]

These adolescent distractions were accompanied, Eustelle says, by a cold and indifferent attention to the liturgy and reception of the sacraments. Looking back on this period, Eustelle sees it as a battle for her will and soul between Jesus and "le lion infernal," "the hellish lion."[16] A shiny trinket in her mistress's house would catch her eye and she would slip it into her pocket, only to put it back before she left for the day.[17] She would confess her infatuation with dance to her confessor and promise to avoid it, only to find herself at a party and join the fun "une seule fois," "just

[14] R. P. Fonteneau, *Histoire de la congrégation de la Sagesse, fondée par le vénérable serviteur de Dieu Louis-Marie Grignon de Montfort* (Paris, 1878), vol. 2. http://catalogue.bnf.fr/ark:/148/cb30448056f, accessed December 12, 2023. On Eustelle's visits see Thompson 23.

[15] *Memoir*, ch. 5; cf. Thompson 25.

[16] *Memoir*, ch. 6; *Recueil* 40.

[17] *Memoir*, ch. 6.

this once."[18] In short, Eustelle says that she "wished somehow to belong both to God and to the world."[19]

Along with an adolescent infatuation with dance and dress, Eustelle confesses that she was impatient and even something of a bully towards her sister and brother, an admission that makes her English biographer noticeably uncomfortable:

> A certain vivacity of nature, with the impatience which is its usual accompaniment, was also one of her characteristics; again, a sensitive temperament like hers, allied to an acute intelligence, is apt at once keenly to feel and vividly to perceive the faults and foibles of others; and without the restraining influences of grace, we know that the lively tongue of thoughtless youth, and of girls especially — and Eustelle was but fifteen — is prone anyhow to give itself a good deal of license in the way of playful censure, the temptation to which is commonly increased by friends, who are amused with sallies from which malice seems altogether absent.[20]

Her hagiographer notwithstanding, according to a relative, Eustelle's "vivacity of nature" sometimes expressed itself to her sister and brother as a slap or two from the would-be servant of God.

These childish behaviors, which seem so typical to us, troubled the teenage Eustelle profoundly; looking back on this period in the *Memoir*, Eustelle recalls her need to exorcise these worldly, all-too-human impulses. She recalls, for example, being at Mass with her eyes fixed on a pious young woman praying a few rows in front of her, admiring her, envying her: "I felt the stab of remorse penetrate my heart. Oh how I wished to imitate her!" she recalls thinking at the time.[21]

For the teenaged Eustelle, this pull of the pious and holy developed from superficial notions into a powerful driving force, manifesting itself in her Lenten confession in 1829. By her own assertion, this confession was the turning point in her young life; her confessor, Father Jossier, reportedly counselled her, "Mon enfant, Dieu a sur vous des desseins particuliers; soyez

---

[18] *Memoir*, ch. 9; *Recueil* 50.
[19] *Memoir*, ch. 6.
[20] Thompson 45.
[21] Thompson 20; *Memoir*, ch. 4.

fidèle" (My child, God has particular plans for you: be faithful).[22]

The confessor's words had a powerful effect on young Eustelle; in the *Memoir* she recalls this as the moment when she chose definitively to

> belong wholly to Jesus! O you people of blessed Sion: celebrate the victory of the God who crowns you! let your joy burst forth! I belong to Jesus completely! And you, my Father, bless him! His love has triumphed; his presence in the Eucharist has given me life, and just as the Redeemer of men overcame the devil and Hell and rose victorious from the grave, now seating himself in my heart like a king on his throne, he triumphed over all the enemies who assaulted my soul and who had for so long prevented him from reigning there.[23]

Confession was followed by Holy Communion, and the result was a transformed young girl. Her mother recalled that it was then that Eustelle cut her long dark hair, emulating the severity of the saints.[24] Staying at home with her family but spending the day at work as an apprentice, Eustelle found more and more time for prayer, penance, pious reading, and especially long visits to the Holy Eucharist in the tabernacle of her parish church, Saint-Pallais. She would arrive at the church as early as 4 a.m. to adore the Blessed Sacrament before heading off to work, a practice that was soon noticed in her tight-knit village. Thompson and Mayet both repeat this anecdote:

> [O]ne day a lady stopped a woman of the peasant class, whom she met in the streets of the town, and said to her, "My good dame, I think you are from Saint-Pallais. There is a young girl belonging to that village, whom I find every morning in the church here; go as early as I may, still she is always there before me. There she remains on her knees, without movement, for an extraordinary length of time. If care is not taken to prevent it, she will injure her chest irreparably. Pray tell her mother." The person addressed was that mother herself. [25]

---

[22] Mayet 69.

[23] *Memoir*, ch. 10.

[24] Thompson 49–50.

[25] Thompson 50–51; cf. Mayet 87–88.

This seems to have been the everyday life of Marie-Eustelle Harpain from about the age of fifteen until her mid-twenties. Except for a brief period as a laundress for a private boarding school,[26] she worked as a seamstress and later as a helper and sacristan at her church.

This period, Eustelle's late teens and early twenties, is not well documented in either the *Memoir* or in the biographies, so only the broadest outlines can be formed. After her conversion in 1829, Eustelle embarked on a varying program of penance and mortification, often tending towards extremes. In the *Memoir* she recalls her initial resolutions:

> I resolved to attend Holy Mass every day, every evening to make a visit to the Blessed Sacrament, to recite the Rosary regularly and not to miss devotional reading on any day. I also resolved to approach the Sacraments often. From then on, I had no more friends; everyday interactions were foreign to me: no get-togethers, no friendly walks. I could, certainly, have stayed close to those people whose company was not harmful to me, but none of them appealed to me and I could see that, with the passage of time, Jesus would take the place of all.[27]

She often denied herself sleep and food — resolving once to eat only dry black bread for six days a week — but her mother and the curé were constantly after her to moderate her behavior. Even with these influences, Eustelle fairly quickly became notorious for her extreme and fervent behavior, and not all of the townsfolk were as charitable as the anonymous lady who approached her mother. Her resolve that "Jésus me tiendrait lieu de tout" (Jesus takes the place of all)[28] naturally resulted in her alienation from her friends and from other villagers, who soon developed a morbid fascination and even an active animus towards the peculiar girl with the strange habits. Thompson recreates the scene:

> [S]he became the object of the most cruel sarcasm and ridicule; and the rancour and virulence, not to say fury, with which she was assailed would be hardly credible

[26] Thompson 84.

[27] *Memoir*, ch. 10.

[28] *Recueil* 55; *Memoir*, ch. 10.

> were it not so well attested. She was pointed at in the streets, and addressed in terms of grossest abuse; she was made the subject of vulgar talk in the public-houses.[29]

Eustelle herself was acutely aware of her alienation, referring to it several times as her "martyrdom," and it seemed that, the greater her ostracism, the greater was her resolve to embrace it.[30] Even family and well-intentioned villagers attempted to moderate her behavior, advising her that not all pleasures were sinful; Eustelle recalls that she responded to this by acknowledging that innocent walks or admiring nature were not evil, but they were diversions and distractions from her defining devotion to Jesus in the Eucharist.

And "Jesus alone" was truly the center of Eustelle's life beginning in these years. Her letters attest to a powerful yearning to receive Jesus in the Holy Eucharist as often as possible. As the notes to certain letters detail, a typical Catholic in the 1830s would have received the Eucharist three or four times a year, typically on the Sunday after receiving the Sacrament of Penance. This practice did not have any institutional basis, but it was likely rooted in a deep acculturated reverence for the Eucharist, such that too frequent Communion would have been viewed as prideful, and reception of the Sacrament weeks or months after Confession would have been presumptuous. In any case the practice was so deeply engrained in the Catholic population that a person like Eustelle had to appeal to her pastor for permission to receive Communion more often. This Eustelle did, enthusiastically and insistently. At about fifteen, she approached Father Jossier to ask that she be permitted to confess and communicate once every two weeks; she returned later to ask for the sacraments once a week. Father agreed to these requests, the first two of several that brought Eustelle closer and closer to the Lord in the Eucharist.

---

[29] Thompson 65.

[30] "A good priest who was a native of her parish, has recorded that nothing was esteemed too horrible to lay to the charge of the maid of Saint-Pallais (il n'est sorte d'horreurs qu'on n'ait dites de la vierge de Saint-Pallais). On one occasion such infamous language was used with regard to her that a sister who was present burst into a flood of tears. She could not help retelling all to Eustelle, who answered with much simplicity, 'Tell them, should they ever talk about me again, that I love them with all my heart and pray for them'" (Thompson 72).

In 1834, the parish got a new curé, Joseph-Alphonse Jouslain, a young and vibrant priest who immediately saw something extraordinary in Eustelle. Moved certainly by both Eustelle's holiness and by her difficult life in the village, the new priest suggested that she enter the convent.[31] Over the very grudging consent of her father, Eustelle traveled the 80 miles to La Rochelle and entered the convent of the Order of Notre Dame de la Charité, an order of teaching and nursing nuns very familiar to Father Jouslain.

Eustelle lasted only about two weeks in the convent, and there were at least two reasons for her quick return home. First was the apparent lack of enthusiasm for her decision by her family and especially the disapproval of her father. René's disapproval stayed with Eustelle for many years; her letters to novices in the same community who suffered from similar family pressures seem tinged with her own memories. Alongside this reason for leaving, however, is another, more intriguing one: by her own admission, Eustelle was uncomfortable with aspects of community life, specially choral and communal prayer. Solitary by nature and deliberate by choice, Eustelle was never able to get comfortable with communal prayer or observance of the hours; her prayer life was an intimate colloquy with *Jésus seule*. But even in failure, Eustelle's experience with consecrated life was transformative, leaving her with friends and correspondents that she would retain for the rest of her short life. Years later she would write to the *sœurs* almost weekly, calling them her sisters and counselling them to treasure the life they had chosen.

After only two years of service at Saint-Pallais, Father Jouslain was suddenly reassigned to a parish at Jonzac, about 25 miles south of Saintes, and a replacement was sent to Eustelle's parish.[32] Presumably because this new curé was still alive at their writing, both the *Recueil* and the biographies insist on withholding his name, calling him only Father A***.[33] By all accounts

---

31 It is not entirely clear when he made this suggestion and when Eustelle spend her fortnight in the convent. The best guess is late 1835, roughly the midpoint of Jouslain's tenure at Saint-Pallais. See Thompson 140; Mayet 278–79.

32 Father Jouslain collapsed at Christmas Midnight Mass in Jonzac in 1836 and was transported to the Sisters of Charity in La Rochelle, the community Eustelle had briefly joined. He died there about a year later, in December 1837.

33 According to Anne Aucher of the Diocese of La Rochelle-Saintes, "Father A***" was the Abbé Bichon (correspondence of August 2024). This confirms

he was pious and well-intentioned but inexperienced in offering direction to a person as extraordinary as Eustelle, alternating between impatience with her and what Eustelle describes as a disconcerting admiration of her holiness. For her part Eustelle's return from the convent seemed only to intensify her desire to devote herself to Jesus alone. In addition to daily Mass, Rosary and Eucharistic adoration, Eustelle approached her curé in 1836, at age 22, to ask permission to take a permanent vow of chastity. Eustelle wanted the vow to be permanently binding but Father A*** refused, apparently agreeing to consider a temporary vow and at the same time requiring Eustelle to wait.

In the end, Father A*** would not be the one administering Eustelle's vow of chastity,[34] as he was reassigned and left Saintes in August 1837, but, unlike Father Jouslain, Father A*** does not leave Eustelle's story. Instead he becomes Eustelle's first important correspondent: beginning in early 1838 and continuing until two weeks before she died, Eustelle wrote 51 (surviving) letters to her former pastor, whom she saw as her first spiritual director. The letters, translated below, sketch a warm and varied relationship between Eustelle and the priest. Her letters give us numerous glimpses into her deepening spiritual life, her extraordinary love of the Eucharist and empathy for Jesus "captive" in the tabernacle. But her letters also treat more mundane matters like the declining health of his former parishioners, Eustelle's sewing altar linens for her friend in his new, poorer parish, (mostly) innocuous gossip about parishioners from Saint-Pallais, and having a gentle laugh at his successor, Father de Laage de Saint-Germain, getting flummoxed after saying Mass for local prison inmates.

Eustelle's biographers are fairly ungenerous in their judgments of Father A***, noting that he was not intellectually or spiritually equipped to serve as Eustelle's director. Eustelle herself realizes this, admitting that Father A*** seemed to hold her in esteem so high that it tempted her pride. While continuing very faithfully to correspond with him, Eustelle recognized that she needed a more seasoned and disciplined director, eventually choosing

---

his identification in *Dictionaire de Spiritualité*, vol. 7.1 (Paris: Beauchesne, 1969), 80. This translation retains his identity as "Father A***."

[34] It was Father de Laage de Saint-Germain who administered the vow on February 2, 1838. For the text of the vow, which Eustelle wrote herself, see *Memoir*, Appendix, document 4.

Father Joseph Briand, a notable author and preacher.[35] She first encountered Briand when he preached at Saintes on Ascension Thursday 1838.[36] After months of prayer and consultation with friends, Eustelle approached Father Briand in Advent of that same year, telling him of her religious practices, her desires and fears, her mortifications and uncertainties. Father Briand agreed to become her director, thereby generating a second regular correspondence with Eustelle, whose letters to him survive.

These three clerics, Father A***, Father de Laage de Saint-Germain, and Father Briand, are among the most important persons in Eustelle's brief life. Father A***, though he was around Eustelle very briefly, from 1836 to 1838, entered her life at precisely the time when she needed to open up to someone sympathetic to her powerful love for Jesus and its everyday expression in her life. And it was Father de Laage de Saint-Germain, her parish priest for the rest of her life, who communicated her and heard her confessions, twice a week or more often towards the end, who ran quiet interference for her with nasty townsfolk, who employed her as sacristan, forbade her to wear a cilice, and who finally consulted Bishop Villecourt about his extraordinary parishioner. And finally it was Father Briand, her spiritual director — though chiefly by mail, due to his daunting schedule of far-flung preaching engagements — who counseled her to be faithful in prayer and not to yield to temptations of *amour propre* or pride, who told her to be respectful and obedient to the bishop, especially when he told her to eat enough and not to hurt herself, who forbade her to read pious books he deemed too immoderate for her, and told her not to rush up to the tabernacle to kiss and embrace it when the church was empty.

It was in roughly this period, around age 23, that Eustelle moved out of her parents' house to rooms in town, literally steps away from the church of Saint Pallais.[37] This was not due to a rift with her family: she continued to take meals at home almost until her death. The move was certainly driven for two reasons: first, the move next

---

[35] The catalogue of printed books in the Bibliothèque nationale lists "l'abbé Joseph Briand" as the author of ten works, mostly short devotional pamphlets centered on Saintes or the diocese of La Rochelle; *Catalogue général des livres imprimés de la Bibliothèque nationale*, auteurs, 19:572–73.

[36] See Letter 6, below.

[37] After leaving her parents' home, Eustelle lived the remainder of her life at 31 Rue Arc de Triomphe (then called Rue de Saint-Pallais), about five hundred feet from the church. For the reasons for the move, see Thompson 159 ff.

door to the church made it easier for her to maintain her devotions to Jesus "captive" in the tabernacle and also facilitated her work as sacristan and helper in the parish. Second, by this time Eustelle was an established businesswoman with clients and apprentices of her own; while her sewing business never thrived — she was especially bad at collecting fees from clients — a place in the town would allow her and her young apprentices to work together comfortably.

It was Eustelle's deepening urge to exterior mortification[38] that drew her to the attention of Bishop Villecourt in La Rochelle. In July of 1839, Father de Laage de Saint-Germain wrote to the bishop to acquaint him with Eustelle, who was on her way to the episcopal see to visit friends in the Sisters of Mercy and to have an interview with the bishop. De Laage's letter, included below, recommends Eustelle to the bishop for her sincere extraordinary holiness, but also asks the bishop to counsel her against damaging acts of mortification such as the cilice (which Eustelle was already using for eight hours a day, six days a week). De Laage describes Eustelle as a poor, frail, hardworking woman of twenty-five, wholly unsuited to bodily mortification.

The bishop first met with Eustelle in July of 1839 and met with her five additional times between March 1840 and March 1842, twice in La Rochelle and three more times during official episcopal visits to Saintes. Eustelle was deeply impressed by Villecourt, whose counsels seemed powerfully to move her, even when they were not what she wanted to hear. In their first brief visit in La Rochelle, he essentially forbade her to do bodily harm to herself; in a subsequent letter to Father A***, she actually complains that Father de Laage misled the bishop about her frailty: "Monsieur le Curé spoke to him before I did and told him I was not well. That was wrong of him, because Monsignor the Bishop believed him."[39]

The most significant and moving encounter between Eustelle and Villecourt was her extended visit to La Rochelle in July 1840, described in detail in Letter 25, to Father A***. Eustelle spent three days in the home of the Bishop, taking meals with his household and participating in daily prayer services and instructions. In and of itself, this experience must have been extraordinary for the simple seamstress from the small town: three days away

---

[38] This is her own phrase, "mortification extérieure," something of a euphemism for inflicting pain on oneself as a penance; *Recueil* 82, 120.

[39] Letter 13.

from home living as part of an episcopal household and attending prayer services and instructions[40] from a learned prelate. Eustelle devotes a paragraph and more to her three private talks with Bishop Villecourt on this occasion. He seemed, tactfully, to broach the subject of physical mortification, stopping short of forbidding Eustelle to use the cilice but cautioning her to use it only in obedience to her spiritual director. He apparently dilated on the subject, citing the experience of Henry Suso (1295–1366), who was chastised by God for indulging in excessive mortification out of vainglory.[41] Villecourt also hinted in these conversations at a topic that would loom larger in later meetings with Eustelle, *amour propre* or self-love. In steering her away from physical mortification, Villecourt, seemingly intentionally, planted seeds in Eustelle's mind that, like Suso, her motives for wishing to cause herself pain needed to be examined carefully. Specifically, Eustelle recalls that the Bishop said that physical

> penances are withheld from all those persons who have the itch to speak about them to others rather than to the repositories of their conscience, or those who are tempted to esteem themselves higher because of these gifts. The persons are in need of severe humiliation.[42]

This topic of self-love recurs both in Eustelle's recollections of later meetings with the Bishop but also occasionally in her correspondence with Father Briand, her "third director." Neither man accused Eustelle of culpable pride, but she nonetheless seemed almost haunted by fear that her special relationship with Jesus made her prideful.[43]

In 1839, at age 25, Eustelle recalls that her Heavenly Spouse lovingly asked a new sacrifice of her, a vow of poverty.[44] As she did not have very many possessions to start with, this new vow brought

---

[40] The term likely refers to expansive, prepared lectures, similar to monastic "conferences," usually based either on daily Mass readings or on a program of biblical or patristic readings.

[41] See *The Exemplar: The Life of the Servant*, ch. 20, in *Henry Suso: The Exemplar, with Two German Sermons*, trans. Frank Tobin (New York: Paulist Press, 1989), 96–97. It is possible that Eustelle was acquainted with Suso's writings, which were available in French as early as 1596.

[42] Letter 25.

[43] See Letters 50, 80, 107.

[44] Mayet 312.

on chiefly a change in attitude in Eustelle. Alongside literal poverty, Eustelle embraced poverty of spirit, calling poverty her "sister." And the letters indicate that her loving embrace of poverty extended to every corner of her life. Never a sharp businesswoman anyway, she now neglected confronting delinquent clients until she was literally out of money. What few possessions she had, books given as gifts, holy pictures, she gave away, along with most of her poor kitchen utensils. Perhaps recalling the teenager who loved pretty clothes, Mayet quotes Eustelle's enthusiasm for poverty in dress:

> One of her joys was to wear well-worn clothes, well-mended; but she did not want them to be torn. "It's disorder," she added, "and not virtue. Saint Bernard had given the same rule to his solitaries at Citeaux: 'Paupertas semper, sordes numquam.' 'Poverty, always; uncleanliness, never.'"[45]

In the summer of 1840 Villecourt and Briand instructed Eustelle to write a memoir of her life. No reason is given for this instruction, but it seems clear that the motive was to capture the details of Eustelle's life against the likelihood that she would eventually be considered for beatification or canonization for her extraordinary virtues, her ascetic lifestyle, and her ardent devotion to the Eucharist. For her part, Eustelle was very unhappy with the request, complaining (not unreasonably) that asking her to do this would constitute a temptation to pride. She agreed in the end and the text is translated below as her *Memoir*. Eustelle seemed intentionally to break off the narrative with events of 1838, when her persecution by townsfolk had begun to abate and when she began to experience extraordinary favors and manifestations of divine love. She indicates that she left off the narrative because she felt that describing her arrival at peace and comfort would seem prideful; it is likely that the pressures of work and declining health were also responsible.

The letters—and not the *Memoir*—contain only a few hints concerning Eustelle's extraordinary experiences at Mass, on receiving the Eucharist, and during her frequent night-watches before the tabernacle. In Letter 160, to Armand Guerin, she says, "It is not possible for me to offer words for the visions, the lights, the sentiments that Jesus intimates to my soul as I partake of

[45] Ibid., 314.

this ineffable mystery," and this is as much as she will say. As Thompson notes, Eustelle mentions these experiences only in letters to her directors and not to her many other correspondents. Her descriptions of the experiences, moreover, are very spare, almost certainly because she was so deeply fearful of pride and self-promotion. In all she briefly describes about twelve extraordinary events, such as a vision of the Child Jesus in the monstrance (Letter 16), a vision of Jesus as the celebrant at Mass (Letter 56), and a vision of a sleeping Jesus at age 6 (Letter 65). The letters to Father Briand also include brief descriptions of extrasensory experiences, such as a sense of her own annihilation at a vision of Heaven (Letter 60) and what she describes as her heart "transubstantiated" into the heart of Jesus (Letter 81). All of these experiences are recorded in letters dated between February 1840 and March 1842, the last two and a half years of her life, and many are accompanied by pleas to her correspondents not to share their details with anyone.

Along with their (apparent) concerns about *amour propre*, Eustelle's director and bishop seemed also to worry about another thread in her conversations and her letters: her leanings towards Quietism.[46] Thompson recounts a memorable moment in one of Eustelle's conversations with the bishop:

> One day, when Eustelle was giving expression to her sentiments respecting conformity to the will of God, she said that she felt her own will so united to that Adorable Will, that she would resign herself to be cast into Hell if she knew that such was God's will; and that, although the whole attraction of her heart was to the love of God, she was ready to consent not to love Him, if it pleased Him to reject her love.[47]

---

[46] Quietism is the name given to a set of ideas initially attributed to Miguel de Molinos (1628-96), a Spanish mystic. Molinos taught that aspiring mystics should seek to discard anything of the senses, including meditation on the life of Christ or other devotions, striving to reach a place of absolute passivity and openness to the divine. In practice these positions led to disregard of prayer and participation in liturgy, indifference to Church rules and other rules, and ultimately to Cathar-like extremes such as the desire for self-annihilation. Quietism was condemned by Pope Innocent XI in the papal bull *Coelestis Pastor* in 1687, though notions that could be seen as quietist endured and continue to endure in Christian mystical writing.

[47] Thompson 252.

Bishop Villecourt was startled by this but had the presence of mind to guide Eustelle to an understanding that, while "my Kingdom is not of this world," it was definitely *in* this world.[48] For her part Eustelle seemed stung by his reaction and expressed deep contrition. Even so, it is not difficult to find moments in the letters that suggest the outlines of Quietism. In Letter 21 (May 1840), for example, Eustelle complains that writing her life story is a worthless exercise and a temptation to *amour propre*:

> There is no need here to tell you about my unworthiness: this you know. You know I am but nothing, even less than nothing; for I sin against him who created me and who, even so, never ceases to pour his graces on my soul in such abundance.[49]

In the end, it seems clear that, despite her fears and scruples, Eustelle held *amour propre* well in check, devoting the last years of her life more and more fully to adoration of Jesus in the Eucharist. Her letters, poems, and *Memoir* all speak to a profound and consuming love for the Eucharist, accompanied more than once by admissions of envy for the priests who are ministers of the Eucharist. Alongside this individual devotion, Eustelle managed to maintain a rich and varied correspondence, especially with women whose personal lives placed them outside the welcome of the Church, including a childhood friend attempting to extricate herself from an extramarital affair.[50] The later letters seemingly include some addressed to these correspondents, always circumspect and gently worded, full of encouragement and hope. Eustelle also spent a good deal of time in her last years with her friend Sister Anastasia, a teaching nun of the *Filles de Sagesse* almost next door to Eustelle's rooms in the town. None of the Letters are specifically addressed to Anastasia although one or two seem almost certainly to have been written to her.[51] To Mayet, Anastasia recalled in vivid detail

---

[48] "For this reason Mgr. Villecourt would not allow her, for instance, to read the works of P. Guillore. She thought that Boudon's writings at least would be permitted her; but even here the bishop hesitated, and clearly evinced his preference that she should abstain, on account (as he said) of some propositions to be met with therein, which, taken literally, wanted for strict exactness" (Thompson 254).

[49] Letter 21.

[50] See Thompson 162 ff.

[51] Letters 99 and 127.

a time when, having heard a sermon on human vices, she became convinced that she was unworthy to receive communion. Eustelle was appalled at the idea, bursting out:

> Promise me, won't you, that you will never deprive yourself of a single one of your communions without a well-founded reason. Oh, believe me, good friend: our Lord loves you.[52]

Eustelle went on in this same vein, chastising her friend for her scrupulousness and ending with a striking phrase borrowed for the epigraph of this introduction, that sums up her spirituality:

> O, my good friend, if only I could place in your heart what Jesus has placed in mine![53]

As the later letters clearly show, Anastasia was only one of many friends and correspondents that Eustelle found herself counselling to receive the Eucharist joyously and frequently.

Near the end, when it was no longer possible for her to walk the couple of blocks from her apartment to Saint-Pallais, the frail village sacristan, once mocked in the streets but now revered for her holiness, spent her days in prayer awaiting Father de Laage with the Eucharist. She died, almost certainly of tuberculosis, on June 29, 1842.

Along with the seemingly immediate veneration of the townsfolk noted above—and the publication of the *Recueil* a scant eight months after her death—Eustelle's life and holiness were well known in France and beyond in the decades following her death. The earliest use in print of her affectionate nickname, "l'Ange de l'Eucharistie," seems to be as Mayet's title (1858), strongly suggesting that the title was already in wide use. Quotations from her letters appear in at least two devotional anthologies in French, Abbé Paul de Terris, *Nouveau Mois du Sacré-Cœur* (Avignon, 1893) and Frére Philippe, *Méditations sur l'Eucharistie* (Paris, 1889). A short biography in English by Sister Mary Bernard, *Angel of the Eucharist: Marie Eustelle*, was published by Talbot Press in Dublin in 1923.

---

52 Mayet 103: "Vous me promettez, n'est-ce pas, de ne jamais vous priver d'une seule de vos communions sans une raison bien fondée? Oh! croyez-moi, bonne amie, Notre-Seigneur vous aime."

53 Ibid., 103–4: "O bonne amie, si je pouvais mettre dans votre cœur ce que Jesus a mis dans le mien!"

EUSTELLE'S READING

In their enthusiasm to capture everything they could of Eustelle's simple life, Father de Laage and Bishop Villecourt neglected to note her favorite books or offer any comment on her reading. The *Memoir* mentions that her earliest readings were the Bible and the *Imitation of Christ* by Thomas Kempis. She quotes the *Imitation* in Letter 3 to Father A***, and Thompson lists it as one of her "very few books of piety," virtually her only personal possessions.[54]

Beyond the *Imitation* the reader can only rely on occasional quotations or references in the writings. Eustelle quotes Augustine's *Confessions* (*Memoir*, Chapter 13), and quotes a line, likely from *The Life of Blessed Mary of the Incarnation*.[55] In Letter 2 she thanks Father A*** for the loan of books by Saint Francis de Sales, though she does not mentions which ones.[56] In Letter 7 she tells Father A*** that she is sending him a "life of Saint Rose,"[57] suggesting what might have been a lively exchange of pious reading matter between them. Beyond this, Eustelle alludes to a wide variety of other works including *L'Échelle du Ciel* (*The Ladder of Heaven*) by the Carthusian Guigo II and *The Practice of the Presence of God* by Lawrence of the Resurrection. More distantly, she evinces a wide familiarity with the lives of the saints, suggesting that she might have had access to an anthology, perhaps a French version of the *Legenda Aurea* but more likely (or in addition) a compilation of the lives and sayings of more modern saints.

There is evidence in the writings and corroborating evidence in the biographies of Eustelle's affection for and veneration of Saint

---

[54] Thompson 183. Thompson goes on to report that she actually gave away her "very pretty" copy of the *Imitation* when she undertook her vow of poverty in 1839.

[55] Jean Baptiste Antoine Boucher, *Vie de la Bienheureuse Sœur Marie de l'Incarnation, dite dans le monde Mademoiselle Acarie, Converse professe et Fondatrice des Carmelites réformées de France: Faite d'après des piéces authentiques; accompagnée de notes historiques, critiques & morales; & suivie 1°. d'une Appendice contenant des écrits & des maximes de la Bienheureuse, 2°. de Pieces justificatives* (Paris, 1800), 28 ("Trop est avare . . . ").

[56] Saint Francis de Sales's (1567-1622) most notable work is *Introduction to the Devout Life* (1609) and *Treatise on the Love of God* (1616) but anthologies of sermons and other occasional writings were widely available in the 1830s in France.

[57] Probably Jean-André Faure, O.P., *La Vie de Sainte Rose, du tiers-ordre de S. Dominic* (Marseilles, 1692).

Louis-Marie Grignon de Montfort (1673–1716), a prodigious and widely read spiritual author and founder of the *Filles de Sagesse*, the Daughters of Wisdom, whose convent in Saintes Eustelle had frequented on Sundays as a girl. In Letter 126 Eustelle recommends that a correspondent pray "a novena to Father de Montfort," recalling the Catholic practice to pray for the intercession of a "servant of God" or person being considered for canonization. Not canonized until 1881, Louis was something of a French "favorite son"; in his introductory letter included in this volume, Cardinal Villecourt himself likely echoes Louis's writings. It is all but inconceivable that Eustelle had not read many of Louis's writings, given his popularity and her several connections with him.[58]

Towards the end of her life, when asked how she endured the privations of self-imposed poverty and mortification, Eustelle answered in Latin, "*Si scires donum Dei!*" (If you but knew the gift of God!), quoting Jesus to the Samaritan woman in John 4:10, the only Latin in her writings.

Far and away the most quoted book in Eustelle's writings is, of course, the Bible. Based on a computer-aided search of the translation, Eustelle quotes or echoes more than fifty separate passages from Scripture, divided almost equally between the Old and New Testaments.[59] Many of these are cited or echoed multiple times, and most of the references are so accurate as to suggest that Eustelle checked a text as she wrote. Most notable among these references are the almost twenty allusions to the Song of Songs, by far Eustelle's favorite book of the Bible, capturing the love of Jesus in visceral, sensual terms. Near the end of his introductory letter to the *Recueil*, Cardinal Villecourt recalls that

> one of her directors had lent her a pious commentary on the Song of Songs applied to the Holy Eucharist. This she read and reread endlessly. Her piety found in it nourishment so sweet that, she said, she would have liked to know the book by heart.[60]

---

[58] See, for example, *The Secret of the Rosary*, *Total Consecration to Jesus through Mary*, and *Letter to the Friends of the Cross*, all still in print in English.

[59] This translation uses a 1744 edition of the *Bible James Martin*, which should have been available to Eustelle, and translates this directly in an attempt to preserve verbal echoes. Notes to occasional passages include references to the King James or Douai-Rheims English versions to illustrate differences between Eustelle's French text and versions familiar to English readers.

[60] See below, p. 57.

Eustelle cites the Song of Songs about 17 times in the *Memoir* and in the Letters, but these citations are to no more than ten separate passages, so it is possible to focus on two or three passages to which she returns.[61] They are not, strikingly, the more sensual passages that regularly appear in the writings of the women mystics, but Eustelle's favorites tell us much about her thinking.

The first revisited passage is Song 5:10: *Mon bien-aimé est blanc et vermeil, un porte-enseigne [choisi] entre dix mille*, "My beloved is white and red, a standard bearer chosen from among ten thousand." In citing the passage Eustelle drops the idea of the "standard-bearer" and simplifies "ten thousand" to "thousand."[62] In two letters, 134 and 152, she uses the phrase as the Canticles-writer does, to refer to the bridegroom (or Jesus). Similarly, in Chapter 27 of the *Memoir*, Eustelle says it was Jesus who was chosen by her "from among a thousand." Eustelle singles out and chooses Jesus just as Jesus singled her out and chose her, the relationship evoked by the image of Eustelle spending the night at watch before the tabernacle where her *bien-aimé porte-enseigne* lay imprisoned.

A second important revisited passage from the Canticles is Song 2:4: *Il m'a menée dans la salle du festin*, "He led me into the banquet hall." Eustelle cites this passage at least three times in the letters (71, 87, and 100), but she never cites the typical French (or English) translation for the room, "banquet hall." In all three instances she refers to the room where the groom leads the bride as the *cellam vinariam* or "wine cellar," clearly echoing the Vulgate's "Introduxit me in cellam vinarium." For Eustelle, it is the "mysterious cellar" (Letter 71), "his cellar" (Letter 100); the haunting "intoxicating cellar of his love" (Letter 87; le cellier enivrant de son amour). Two comments seem appropriate here. First, Eustelle did not read this translation in her Bible; she must have learned it in conversation with someone who knew the Vulgate. We will never know, but it is easy to imagine that Eustelle asked about the image of the Groom leading the Bride into the banquet

[61] I say "about 17 times" here because I am far from convinced that I have identified all of her scriptural references: they are not regularly identified in the text and often adopt phrasing that makes them less than obvious to a twenty first-century English reader.

[62] The word *mille* (thousand) occurs 65 times in Eustelle's writings, usually figuratively for "many": compare in English "a thousand thanks," "a thousand pardons," etc.

hall only to learn that the Latin suggested the more private wine cellar. Second, learning the Latin version in whatever way she did, the image of the newly-weds alone in the darkened wine cellar must have appealed powerfully to the working-class servant girl, uncomfortable at parties but at home with domestic chores, storerooms, and cellars. For Eustelle, there seems to be an almost intoxicating (*enivrant*) quality to the image, perhaps evoking for her the darkened church of Saint-Pallais where she spent so many nights and early mornings alone with her own "Bridegroom."

A third repeated passage is Song 8:4: the reference to the Bride's imagined dialogue between the Groom and the "daughters of Jerusalem," his ordering them, *Je vous adjure, Filles de Jérusalem, que vous ne réveilliez point celle que j'aime, que vous ne la réveilliez point, jusqu'à ce qu'elle le veuille*, "I charge you, Daughters of Jerusalem: do not awaken the one I love; do not wake her until she wants to wake." She uses the phrase twice (Letters 54 and 77) to refer to the angels she sees surrounding the tabernacle adoring Jesus in the Eucharist. As noted above, it was Eustelle's habit to spend long hours at night before the Eucharist in the otherwise empty church, so it is not hard to imagine her thinking of the Bride of the Canticle, imagining her Bridegroom instructing the serving women not to awaken her. The line might even suggest Eustelle imagining Jesus asking the adoring angels not to wake her if she should drift off for a moment in her night watch.

Other passages Eustelle cites from the Song of Songs include:

1:15 "Our bed is covered with flowers" (Letter 71),
2:1 "I am the flower of the field, and the lily of the valley" (Letters 134 and 148),
2:5 "Surround me with flowers and lift me up with fruit" (Letter 142),
4:10 "The throne where he takes his rest, his garden of delights" (Letters 101 and 168),
5:1 "Let my beloved come into his garden, and eat of the fruit of his trees" (Letter 16),
8:6 "Place me like a seal upon your heart, upon your arms" (Letters 119 and 150).

Given the number of letters Eustelle wrote in her short lifetime, her declining health and limited education, access to books, and free time, it is astonishing that her writings are so dense and subtle.

CHARACTER AND THEMES IN THE WRITINGS

In the end, one's own discoveries and judgments about this remarkable person and her writings are well left to individual readers, but some very general comments might be appropriate here. First, Eustelle never intended for any of these writings to be in the public eye. Under instructions from Bishop Villecourt and her spiritual director, she grudgingly wrote the work we are referring to as her *Memoir*, and the result is, in effect, a long narrative addressed to "my Father," presumably Father Briand. Her letters are just that — personal letters — and more than once she interrupts herself to remind the correspondent that she or he is never to share their contents with anyone, anywhere. In some cases, though, Eustelle realized that more than one pair of eyes was looking at her writings: in her letters to the "White Ladies" in La Rochelle, for example, she was clearly aware that several of her friends from the convent were reading her words. And she is aware that her letters to Marie (Letters 165-73; December 1837-July 1840) were read aloud to her correspondent by scribes: she wishes the scribes and readers well in Letter 172.

So a first point to remember in approaching these writings is that they are personal communications, not public pronouncements or teachings. Her *Memoir* is an honest and self-effacing narrative of her life up to about 1838, focusing on her struggles to understand herself and her place in the community. It is a spare, unadorned document, missing emotional flights and rhetorical flourishes. Though unreliable as chronology, the *Memoir* includes some memorable and moving passages. In Chapter 8, for example, Eustelle recalls being at a Mardi Gras party that started to run late: as midnight approached and with it the start of the Lenten fast, an "interior voice" (une voix intérieure[63]) warned her to decline the rich fare, even in the face of her friends' ridicule. Later in her narrative, Eustelle movingly remembers the mockery and cruelty of the townspeople, both the thuggish mockery in the cabarets and the more subtle disapproval of

> seemingly wiser people, [who] were no more favorable to me. In our view, they told me, you have no one but yourself to blame. You invite this contempt by your way of life. It is good to serve God, but you go too far:

[63] *Recueil* 46.

> your devotion is ridiculous. Why do you need to deprive yourself of all these pleasures? Are not some of them merely innocent? Often I would respond that these same pleasures, which the world regards as innocent, are condemned by the Gospel. Say to those people so obsessed with me, that for my part, nothing inspires my devotion like these persecutions directed at me. (*Memoir* xx; p. 22 below in ms.)

This is not soaring theology; it is the raw and even bitter memory of a girl of about twenty, drawn to an extraordinary devotion to Jesus in the Holy Eucharist and who pays the price for her rejection of other loves. She bravely writes that nothing inspires her devotion "like these persecutions directed at me" (comme les persécutions dont je suis l'objet),[64] but the remembered pain is all too evident too: tell them for me, she asks, that I withstood all their assaults.

Another particularly memorable passage in the *Memoir* is Chapter 20, Eustelle's remarkable narrative of her acts of penance and her experience of desolation or spiritual dryness. The chapter contains a very moving account of her descent into a near-despairing sense of complete abandonment. In the depths, she recalls,

> I thought I heard him speak these chilling words to the bottom of my heart: *Go! I reject you. You are nothing to me anymore.*

And the chapter continues with a memorable account of the new pains and temptations that the devil found to assault her.

After about twenty thousand words in French, the *Memoir* ends with a memorable passage that hints at the peace Eustelle found in the final years of her life:

> O Jesus! how good you are! You give me a foretaste of heavenly happiness in this world; so ineffable are the sweetnesses with which you fill my soul!

This notion, "l'avant-goût de la félicité céleste"[65] or "the foretaste of Heavenly happiness," occurs at least six times in the Letters: along with signaling the anticipatory contentment she found in the final years of her life, the phrase is also her signature description of her experience of the Holy Eucharist.

---

[64] *Recueil* 67.
[65] *Recueil* 135.

Eustelle's 179 surviving letters constitute the largest part of her writings, and they are best characterized in large groups: to her "directors," Father A*** (1-52) and Father Briand (53-85), to members of the convent of the Sisters of Mercy, where Eustelle briefly lived as a postulant (roughly 86-111), and nine letters to her friend Marie (167-75). Smaller groups include four letters to seminarian Armand Guerin (160-63), three to Bishop Villecourt (164-66), and three letters added to editions of the *Recueil* with the second (1848) edition. The gap in this list, Letters 112-60, consists of letters whose addressees cannot be confidently identified. The reasons for this fairly chaotic state of the letters are really twofold. First, the *Recueil*, including the letters, was brought to press so quickly after Eustelle's death that there was virtually no time for careful deliberation over editorial policy or even ordering. Second, the quick publication meant that virtually all of Eustelle's correspondents in the collection were still alive at publication, requiring that their names be withheld in the volume to protect their privacy (and to protect the integrity of Eustelle's possible candidacy for sainthood). The result is what sits before the reader in both the original French and in the translation: some confident sequences of letters written to the same addressees, almost always in chronological order, interspersed with what might be parts of other, now lost correspondence threads.

Within these limitations, there are clear stylistic and thematic centers in Eustelle's letters. The first of these is personality: Eustelle always places the correspondent first, asking questions and picking up threads from previous letters. After opening in this way, Eustelle will typically say a few words about herself, and especially about her increasingly fragile health. And then, quite often, would come the beating heart of the letter, a glimpse into her extraordinary love-relationship with the Holy Eucharist: her experiences of receiving the Eucharist or of the long hours spent at the "au pieds du Tabernacle," "at the feet of the tabernacle." This intimation would typically end with an exhortation to the correspondent to join Eustelle in adoration of the Lord, an invitation often expressed as an alternate "communion" or coming together with the correspondent, across the miles but one in adoration. The letter then often ended with either plans or hopes of an in-person get-together in the future.

The letters to her two "directors" follow this general shape with some modifications. The many letters to Father A*** include lots of news and details about the parish and town, along with tidbits about personal friends and affectionate gossip about Father de Laage, Father A***'s successor as pastor. Especially the later of these (from about 45-52) are notably friendly and comfortable in tone, surely reflecting Eustelle's maturation. The 31 letters to Father Briand are more formal in tone and regular in content, reflecting Eustelle's consciousness of the his serious role as her first "real" spiritual director and calling him "father." These letters contain many personal reflections and reminiscences, showing Eustelle trying to maintain a constructive relationship with this man devoted to her spiritual well-being but constantly traveling from town to town preaching and giving missions. The letters often include questions about when he might next come to Saintes for a sermon series and with it the chance for a brief talk in person.

In many ways, the loose central group of letters, roughly 90-140 and mostly (it seems) addressed to the community of Sisters of Mercy in La Rochelle, is the richest of the collection. Eustelle was deeply ambivalent about the life of convent, at once yearning for it but uncomfortable with important elements such as communal prayer. Though she dropped out as a postulant after only a couple of weeks, one can readily see that Eustelle tried to replicate the life of the nun back home in Saintes, both at her parents' home and later in her own rooms. The description of her rooms and belongings (*Memoir*, Chapter 27) and her dress clearly evoke the nun, a resemblance she tried to formalize by taking vows of chastity and, later, poverty.

Given this unfulfilled yearning, it is easy to read Eustelle's letters to the sisters as deeply felt, full of admiration and encouragement. Many of these letters to the sisters treat of the very issues that, in the end, resulted in Eustelle's own decision to leave the convent: conflicts with family members, discomfort with the regimentation and other aspects of convent life, uncertainty about one's vocation. More than simply cheering her "sisters" on, Eustelle in these letters almost takes the role of an unofficial novice mistress, unselfconsciously offering advice and encouragement to uncertain young members of the house, all of whom she apparently knew by name. Nestled in this sequence of letters are three apparently addressed to the Mother Superior of the community, letters that are notably stiff and uncomfortable in the original, effects I attempted to replicate in the translation. We cannot know, of course, but it is possible that, even years later, Eustelle felt or imagined the disapproval of the woman who would have been her superior in the convent.

It is in these letters that readers can find Eustelle's most poignant and powerful moments of self-reflection. Though wary of showing any pride about her "favors" from her Lord, Eustelle feels real freedom in these letters to describe her most intimate and extraordinary experiences with Jesus in the Eucharist, no doubt because she is confident that her "sisters" in La Rochelle can soon experience the same.

From among many themes or topoi in the letters, two stand out and invite attention, one figurative and one rhetorical. The signature metaphor in Eustelle's letters is certainly her repeated reference to Jesus as willingly imprisoned in the tabernacle, her *captif d'amour* or prisoner for love. Variations on the idea occur throughout the Letters, notably in 45, 48, 89, and 138, where she exclaims "O Jesus, adorable captive in the Eucharist." Though technically a metaphor, the notion of Jesus as imprisoned in the tabernacle is not a figure of speech for Eustelle: for her and for every Catholic, it is a literal—if uncomfortable or unremembered—truth that Jesus is physically present in the consecrated bread enclosed in the tabernacle. And for Eustelle, this truth accompanied by her powerful love for Jesus and His for her, drawing her daily and nightly "au pieds du Tabernacle," "to the feet of the tabernacle," to abide with her beloved. Her insistent return to this haunting image gives many of the letters an especially powerful, almost romantic, undercurrent.

A second signature element in Eustelle's letters is her powerful exploitation of *Je vous laisse*, "I leave you now...," a conventional closing phrase in letters of this period and beyond. In everyday use, the phrase is nondescript enough: "I leave you now with my warmest wishes" or "...with my hopes for your safe journey home," etc. Eustelle clearly learned the formula along the way, and heard in the conventional phrase the seeds of something more rich and rare. More than sixty times in the letters Eustelle concludes with a close variation of Letter 18, "Je vous laisse dans le cœur de Jésus, où je demeure avec vous," "I leave you in the heart of Jesus, where I abide with you." The effect of this adapted formula is multiform and powerful. First, it is something of an epistolary flourish, an affectionate and even flattering gesture of respect to the correspondent. Second, the notion of leaving one's correspondent not weakly with warm wishes but actually *somewhere* and specifically *dans le cœur de Jésus*, transforms the commonplace formula into a deeply personal, prayerful wish. Eustelle was well aware that it might come as a surprise to many of her correspondents that she "leaves them in the heart of Jesus," all but entailing that it was she herself who brought them there. Finally, the last phrase of the Eustelle's version of the convention focuses precisely on this spiritual locus, the heart of Jesus, where the correspondent will not only find himself or herself, but also Eustelle, for this is the place "où je demeure avec vous," "where I abide [or stay] with you." Especially in her final years in dire financial straits and (especially) in deteriorating health, Eustelle was typically writing to distant friends that she feared she would not see again, so, with the most ordinary of phrases, she placed herself spiritually alongside her loved ones in her one and only refuge *ici-bas*, "here below": the heart of Jesus.

Like the *Recueil*, this volume concludes with a mini-anthology of Eustelle's *cantiques* or songs. They are not grand lyric poetry, but they are nonetheless remarkable products of a frail, simple seamstress with no time and five years of education. Like more than a millennium of Catholic masses the world over, Eustelle's liturgies were conducted in a language she did not know, but the phrases and rhythms of the Mass were as ingrained as her mother tongue. Still, as haunting as the Latin text of the Mass was (and still is, for many), it would have been the hymns in the vernacular—lyrics and music—that would most deeply impact the regular churchgoer. Like so many other worshipers down the years, Eustelle carried these tunes around in her head and found herself composing new lyrics to these melodies that had such a hold on her. And so several of Eustelle's *cantiques* are "sung to the tune of" hymns that the whole parish would know immediately. As for other *cantiques*, all employ the simple rhythms and rhyme schemes that evoke lyrics set to music. Specifically to avoid a distracting musicality, I consciously chose not to attempt to translate the poems in verse, and have been attentive to avoid occasional rhymes. The translations do attempt to capture something of the tone and figurative language of the originals.

NOTES

In preparing the translation I consulted five editions or printings of the *Recueil*: 1843, 1848, 1850, 1860, and 1883, each of which orders the letters slightly differently. The translation is based on the latest 1883 edition, meaning in practice that the translation adopts the numbering of this edition. To the 178 letters of this edition I have returned a third letter from Eustelle to Bishop Villecourt of October 25, 1841, which appeared only in the 1848 and 1850 editions. I have numbered this letter 165 and placed it chronologically between the other two letters to the Bishop.

The final three letters, undated Letters 177–79, do not appear in the first edition of the *Recueil* but were included without editorial comment in the later editions. They are subtly different in tone, pace, and texture from the others, and the two letters end with strikingly identical final paragraphs. The later editions of the *Recueil* were still under the auspices of Cardinal Villecourt, so there is no reason to question the letters' provenance.

It was noted above that the original French editors removed almost all of the proper names in the letters. This was done, in all likelihood, to protect the identities and privacy of Eustelle's friends and correspondents that were still alive in 1843. The editors replaced the names with initials followed by three asterisks or used common nouns or titles. In cases where a particular abbreviation occurs only once or twice, it is not possible even to guess the person being referred to, but there are three prominent exceptions:

1) In letters to Father A***, "Monsieur the Curé" always refers to this man's successor as pastor of Saint-Pallais, Father de Laage de Saint-Germain;

2) "Monsignor the Bishop" always refers to Bishop Clément Villecourt;

3) In letters to Father A*** (i.e., Father Bichon), "Monsieur N***" always refers to Father Joseph Briand, Eustelle's spiritual director.

A FINAL NOTE

It is the job of the translator to disappear noisily; to transplant an individual voice — consciousness, personality, milieu — from one language and culture into another while making just enough noise that readers will not forget the transplanting process. For every sentence, phrase, and word that migrates from Eustelle's nineteenth-century French into our twenty-first-century English is the result of many conscious decisions. What did Eustelle sound like? How did she think? What made this sentence come after that sentence in this letter, to this correspondent? How can we make her sound both like herself and also like someone we can understand and embrace? These and others are messy questions, which require that an honest translation be a little noisy, lest readers forget the process and lose themselves in a hollow, artificial "voice" that is nothing more than a translator's fantasy.

In this spirit I offer a couple of thoughts on my conscious process. In attempting to bring Eustelle's voice to English, I was guided principally by her tone in French and, to very large degree, by the remarkable little description of her in Bishop Villecourt's letter below. He says she is tall and pretty, reserved and dignified, respectful and deliberate. Her language and idiom, he says, are remarkable for a young woman with only the most rudimentary education, and her words have an ardent, almost otherworldly quality.

To try and capture this I avoided both informality and artificiality and stayed away from contractions and most conversational conventions. As much as possible, I reproduced the length and complexity of Eustelle's sentences and tried wherever possible simply to reproduce her most fervent expressions. In this spirit, the reader will encounter bland, fallen English words such as "sweet" and "adorable," words that have lost the reach and intensity of Eustelle's *doux* and *adorable*. A culture that might call a greeting card "sweet" or a picture of a kitten "adorable" will need to work a little to understand how differently and powerfully Eustelle is using these words.

In the end, as we try to draw close to this remarkable woman who lived in France two hundred years ago, we should recognize that if our words fail us, hers failed her as well, especially as she tried and failed to articulate her miraculous relationship with Jesus, her beloved *captif* in the tabernacle. Her wish to her friend Sister Anastasia, reproduced above as the epigraph, is to "place in your heart what Jesus has placed in mine," to place in her a presence, an intimacy, and a peace beyond words.

+CLÉMENT VILLECOURT

by divine mercy and the grace of the Holy Apostolic See
Bishop of La Rochelle

TO ALL OF THE FAITHFUL WHO READ THIS work, greetings and blessings in our Lord Jesus Christ.

A few years after God's providence called us to be governor of the Diocese of La Rochelle — in mid-July of 1839 to be exact — we met a twenty-five-year-old person, who, until then, was unknown to us. She was recommended to us by the estimable curé of Saint-Pallais de Saintes, who employed her to take care of the linens and ornaments at the parish church. He asked us to give a favorable hearing to his parishioner, who, he assured us, was a model of virtue and piety. And Marie-Eustelle Harpain — this was the young person's name — appeared before us with all the marks of the most profound respect, alongside a most daughterly confidence. Her dress was that of a modest, unpretentious worker, showing neither affectation nor negligence. After asking for and receiving our blessing, she replied, with simplicity and candor, to the questions we put to her. Her language was pure, clear, and precise. She actually projected a certain dignity and carriage that would have led one to believe that she had received a proper education, although in fact she had only received the simplest of schooling in reading and writing. All the words from her lips declared, in fact, that her soul had been tutored in the school of Jesus Christ, faithful to the marks of his grace, and alive to the ways of highest perfection.

When she left us, there remained as if perfumed an indefinable odor of holiness, and we admired the perspective of divine Providence, which chooses for itself the most feeble vessel into which to pour its divine power, the most humble of the human condition to serve as the instrument of its glory.

We have seen this pious virgin many times since, and all of our times with her have confirmed and strengthened the sentiments inspired in us from the first.

She seemed to us of a tender, even weak complexion, as her pastor had described her to us; and we decided then to employ the authority with which Heaven had clothed us and order her to limit the holy rigors which she wished to impose on her body. Fasts, vigils, instruments of penance, mortifications of all kinds: she would have been willing to use anything in the work of subjecting her flesh to spirit.

Already some time had passed since she had obtained, after years of trial, requests and prayers, permission to consecrate herself in a perpetual vow of chastity. She had equally bound herself to a vow of poverty, and each day she renewed that of humility; this was because we did not deem it proper to permit her to take lifelong vows.

The enemy of the world, she would have been happy to quit it altogether and to care only for her God, in a desert or in a monastery. But Heaven had other plans for her: Heaven wanted to show in her that there is no station of life in which one cannot attain the most sublime perfection. For her, it was the sacristan's work that gave her every opportunity to express her fervent love at the foot of the altar. A reading of her letters will show how deep was her attraction to the adorable Eucharist.

At the same time, Eustelle was animated by an immense desire for the salvation of souls. What would she not have undertaken to save just one soul! Had our Lord wished for her to serve him in this way, she would have joyfully traveled to the ends of the earth and shed the last drop of her blood.

Sooner or later, the Lord bestows signal graces on those who cleave to the earth only with their bodies, *and whose conversation*, as the Apostle says, *is of Heaven.*[1]

As soon as God made known to us the treasures and graces with which he had enriched his pious servant, we thought to urge her to reveal to us, as far as she was able, something of her inner life: her earliest steps in the spiritual life, the various battles she had

---

[1] Echoing Philippians 3:20, "Mais pour nous, notre bourgeoisie est dans les Cieux," "But for us, our community is in Heaven," but more closely resembling Saint Louis de Montfort's *Les Amis de la Croix* (1714): "Un Ami de la Croix est un homme saint et séparé de tout le visible, dont le cœur est élevé au-dessus de tout ce qui est caduc et périssable, et *dont la conversation est dans les cieux*, qui passe sur la terre comme un étranger et un pèlerin," "A Friend of the Cross is a holy person separated from all that is visible, whose heart is elevated above all that is shabby and perishable, and whose conversation is in Heaven, who passes upon the earth as a stranger or pilgrim" (1A). Eustelle had a special devotion to Saint Louis; see Thompson 353.

must have fought, the victories which God had accorded her, and the divine favors which she had been given. We hesitated asking this for three years, and we will explain here why we feared to do this: we waited because it seems to us that there is nothing more dangerous to suggest to a soul, especially at a certain age, that it may be on an extraordinary path. However humble she may have been until this time, we feared to expose her to a great temptation: this high regard that people would show her — and there are several examples of this in ancient times — would have disastrous results for her because her confidence would not have come from the Holy Spirit. It also concerned us that, learning of our determination to record her story, pious but inexperienced directors might set out to do the same thing, believing that they were doing what we would have done.[2]

We must say, however, to the glory of our clergy, that by the daily proofs we received of their deference and the eagerness they show to receive our advice in all serious and important cases, we are thoroughly convinced that there would not be a single one of our clerics who did not make it their sacred obligation to refer themselves to us before taking any action of this sort.

Thus, on February 23, 1842, finding ourselves in Saintes where we had come to preach the Lenten station, we had an interview with Eustelle where we informed her of our judgments. A thoughtful and pious cleric had already suggested the same thing to her, seeing to it that we were aware of what he had already done. The virgin of Saint-Pallais responded to this that she would conform herself to our decisions with every enthusiasm; that she had always dreaded the illusions of the lying spirit; that she would be at ease when we had decided on a path for her; that, moreover, she should be more concerned to humble herself for the temptations with which she had been tried than to bless Heaven for the graces which it had showered on her; that she felt how unworthy it would be for a little creature to pretend to attribute to herself something from the Holy Spirit; that she had been very

[2] This somewhat simplifies Bishop Villecourt's original: "Nous tremblions aussi qu'en apprenant notre détermination, des Directeurs pieux, à la vérité, mais manquant encore d'expérience, ne se crussent autorisés à marcher sur nos traces, en des circonstances qu'une certaine préoccupation pouvait leur représenter comme ne différant point de celle que nous avions crue sortir de l'ordre commun." His particular concern seems to be that well-meaning spiritual directors might be moved to see extraordinary supernatural marks in Eustelle's case.

reserved until now to reveal her inner life to anyone, as far as supernatural things were concerned; and that, nevertheless, she thought it necessary to speak about this to a grave cleric, someone with whom she had been communicating for some time.

We approved of her reserve and her openness: of her reserve, because the Holy Spirit does not reveal his heart indifferently to a newcomer; of her openness, because the Holy Spirit invites us to take spiritual advice from prudent people. And moreover she understood that, since the Lord had established bishops to govern the Church of God, she owed us pre-eminently any communication which we deemed useful.

In any case, the number of our obligations not permitting us long conversations, we made her understand that it would be most advantageous for her to commit all her memories to paper; doing this would obviate any confusions arising from repetitions or imperfect memories. She accepted our proposition with simplicity.

There was no time to waste, for Eustelle had only a few months to live. She was feeble, languishing, and sorrowful, announcing each day her approaching end. At the same time she had very few moments of rest after having satisfied the diverse duties of her station in life: this is why the notebook she had to complete is so foreshortened. In fact it is surprising that she could get so far in her narrative, and that, with the final lines she wrote only a short while before her death, in an already failing hand, she expressed thoughts that were always beautiful, in a language that was unfailingly lucid and always imprinted with the sacred flame that fired her soul. We can scarcely believe our eyes when we see the astonishing and beautiful style of this poor girl who provided for herself—with great difficulty—by the work of her hands. Where had she learned to speak and write with such regularity and precision? A strange or displaced reflection or thought never appears in her writing; she says everything she means to say in the most proper, natural, agreeable language. Once more, there is no better school than the school of the Holy Spirit.

We soon learned that her condition was desperate; her faithful friends then multiplied their visits to her. She saw persons distinguished by rank mingled with those of simple condition: virtue makes up for whatever birth does not give. Until her last moments by her side, we found ourselves buoyed by her unwavering angelic sweetness; by her unshakeable patience that never so much as hinted at her most cruel pains; by her words of fire, which elevated the soul to Heaven; by the divine love which relentlessly consumed its docile victim; and by her faith so lively that it contemplated the Invisible as though it were sensibly present before her eyes.[3]

She frequently received our Savior in the course of her final sickness. What holy transports were there in these happy moments! What delicious tears flooded her enflamed face![4] She peacefully fell asleep in the Lord at about 6:30 in the morning on Wednesday, June 29, 1842, the Feast of Saints Peter and Paul.

She lived for twenty-eight years, two months, and twelve days, having been born on April 19, 1814.

No sooner had she breathed her last breath than the news spread throughout the village of Saintes, like an event of which all the world should be aware. The story of the virtues of the deceased was on everyone's lips, and the memory of her left a vivid impression of respect on everyone's heart. They said prayers for her — it is the way of the Church — but they were more tempted to ask her intercession for them before God. We will not detail the many touching examples of the general veneration of her; suffice it for us to have mentioned it in passing.

We have already spoken of the worthy cleric[5] to whom Eustelle uncovered her soul. She had come to appreciate his enlightenment, his zeal, and his piety. We find, in the large number of letters addressed to him in the last two years of her life, her thoughtful testimony of her confidence in and gratitude to him. He was well aware how anxious we were to be informed of the particulars concerning her. When she had completed her earthly journey, he hastened to send us news of it through a letter from which we quote the following extract:

> I bless and will bless for all the days of my life the divine master who opened the heart of the saintly girl Eustelle to me, to make me understand the treasures of graces and the wonderful gifts which the Holy Spirit deigned to enrich

---

[3] The final phrase, beginning with "and by her faith," is italicized in the original, indicating a citation. The phrasing loosely echoes Bernard of Clairvaux's Fourth Sermon for the Feast of Saint Benedict.

[4] French: "Quelles délicieuses larmes inondaient son visage enflammé!"

[5] French: *Ecclésiastique*. Villecourt is referring to Father Joseph Briand, whom Eustelle chose to be her spiritual director and to whom Letters 53–85 are addressed.

> her. I have thirty or forty folio sheets written by this angel: the spirit of God is alive in them. You will learn for yourself, Monsignor, when I am at La Rochelle: the love of this predestined soul has broken free of the bonds of the body. I am filled with the memory of so many virtues, but unfortunately Eustelle's work remains unfinished. Her illness forced her to abandon the project, but I rejoice that I have what she was able to put on paper. Not all of our Lord's communications with her are to be found in the volume. Happily Jesus inspired her to consign, on several small pages, the intellectual visions[6] which he had the goodness to give to her. Moreover, having had the pleasure of conversing with her, since she had made known to me her inner life, I find in her letters revelations of her gifts from Heaven. So, in truth, the narrative is complete: she had manifested to her many friends her pious desire that they receive Holy Communion at her funeral Mass, and this happened in a most touching way.

Soon after and following his promise, that same cleric sent me all of Eustelle's writings that he could obtain. As we have seen, these consist of the unfinished narrative of her life and about two hundred letters, in which the beautiful soul of the pious virgin reveals the inner sentiments that fill her. These letters are written to different people, whose names have been deleted; other details were suppressed that would have exposed private family matters. And there follow other important pieces which were to appear in the work, so as to include all of the available knowledge about the pious Eustelle which the faithful could desire.

This is the work whose publication we have authorized; we know most certainly the good it is being called to do. All that we have been able to gather of the writings written in Eustelle's hand have been deposited in the episcopal archive, to serve as testimony to the precision of the transcription of all the writings that have surfaced and to support the title of veneration of her who wrote them.

Souls who know the indwelling of the Holy Spirit have a language all their own, a language that strangers to these sentiments, even the most learned, cannot imitate. They speak from the abundance of their hearts;[7] and although they are incapable of

[6] French: *vues intellectuelles*.

[7] Luke 6:45.

expressing all they experience in human words, they will say and write the most ravishing things, under the dictation of a Master who can make eloquent even the tongues of infants at the breast.[8]

One immediately finds in Eustelle's writings the imprint of her adoration of the Eucharist. How lively is her faith in this divine mystery! How ardent her love! How boundless her gratitude for this, the masterpiece of God's wisdom! She is driven to speak of it ceaselessly; on this subject she is instantly aflame; it is as though her heart is in an ocean of fire, both intoxicated and consumed. She then experiences a holy and delicious transport, we might almost say, a divine madness. Even daily reception of Communion was seemingly not enough to quench the vehemence of her desires; she wished herself to be a living, perpetual tabernacle. Why is it not possible for her to open her heart and there deposit this treasure in a place of safety not subject to any alteration or diminishment? She calls the God of the Eucharist her brother, her beloved, her all. She is so intimate with the divine object of her love that one is tempted to see a sort of excess in it. But she is not the first to say such things: she is preceded by a crowd of saintly souls, even those whose names Eustelle would not have known.

The Holy Spirit always has a purpose — to glorify God and for the good of the Church — in inspiring the sentiments of his servingmen and servingwomen.[9] What aim did the Spirit have in the dispositions on the adorable Eucharist he placed in the soul of Eustelle? We would not be surprised if the Spirit did this to renew the faith in this divine mystery and to revive reception of Holy Communion in our people which have become such strangers to the bread of life.

Modest servant of Jesus Christ! May the power of the pure and persuasive words that come from your heart awaken the languor of our dear diocese! Alas! So many approach the holy table no more than two or three times in their lives! You yourself moaned about this, O fervent Virgin; it astonished you that anyone could claim to belong to the Holy Church and pay no attention to the touching invitations of her divine Spouse. Ah! if you possess in your glory the one whom you so often received in your exile, pray for your

---

[8] Echoing Psalm 8:2.

[9] French: "dans les sentiments qu'il inspire à ses serviteurs et à ses servantes." The awkward phrase seems intended to place the devotion of men and women on an equal footing.

compatriots, that it may be given to them to feel the force of the language of the Savior: *For my flesh is true food, and my blood is true drink, and unless you eat my flesh and drink my blood, you shall not have life within you.*[10]

Ah Lord! All instruments are good in your hands for the accomplishment of your mission of mercy. Great God! We will no longer bemoan to you the sterility of our zeal or the uselessness of our efforts if, by the prayers of this humble girl, you restore frequent reception of the sacraments to the faithful whom you have placed to our care.

It would not be the first time that the prayers of one young virgin resulted in the calling of poor sinners to the love and practice of their obligations. Saints Blandina and Potamioena, for example, inspired others by their own martyrdom.[11] The young Catherine of Siena, the daughter of a simple dyer, made sinners return to themselves by her mere presence, and her pious writings have not ceased to bring about conversions in which the Church rejoices.

It should not necessary that we should warn readers here that, despite our own beliefs about Eustelle, we make no pretense of determining the place she occupies in the afterlife. No one more than ourselves is subject to the decree of Pope Urban VIII.[12] We understand that only the Holy See has the authority to pass judgment of the faithful on the past or present state of the servants and handmaids of God when they have ended their earthly journey. The conclusions of Christians, concerning either what we have said here or on the writings which follow, must be understood as based on human authority alone.

May it please Heaven that this publication contribute to the edification of souls and to the return of some lost sheep!

Given at La Rochelle and written in February 1843.
✠ Clément, Bishop of La Rochelle.
By mandate of Monsignor Ricolage, Secretary General.

---

[10] John 6:53.

[11] Young women martyrs of the early Church, both burned to death, Blandina during the reign of Marcus Aurelius (c. 150), Potamioena in the reign of Septimus Severus (c. 202).

[12] The reference here is to the decree of Pope Urban VIII, who held office from 1623 to 1644, prohibiting the public veneration of servants of God without approval of the Holy See.

Memoir of her Life

BY MARIE-EUSTELLE HARPAIN

ALL IN JESUS AND FOR JESUS. INVOCATION TO JESUS AND MARY.

O my only love! Jesus, the joy of my soul, my life — the soul of my life, my true beatitude! You are all that I want, all that I see, all that I know. Oh! after such a love of which I have been the object, my lips are without words before you; my heart, which you quicken with sweet sentiments, grasps these in the very inability to put them into words. YOU ARE, and before you I am nothing.[1] However, O love beyond understanding, you consume my nothingness with the energy of your glory. Jesus! the only fount that can quench the thirst that devours me — end my thirst soon! let me see you, or let me love you. Be with me, O ineffable Master, in what I undertake by the will of him whose word and life you are, and who burns only with the desire to see you glorified. O my well-beloved Savior! You know the love that drives me — or rather the love that animates yourself.

O that I might comprehend the breadth of mercy and love you have had for me for all eternity! Let it be in my memory, my spirit, my heart. Oh! embrace the heart that wants only to burn with the fire of your pure love, for it is your goodness beyond price that I am going to talk about.

---

[1] French: "Vous êtes, et, devant vous, je ne suis que néant." The use of *être* certainly echoes references to God beginning at Exodus 3:14, the dialogue between Moses and the Lord at the burning bush: "Et Dieu dit à Moïse: Je suis celui qui suis," "and God said to Moses, I AM WHO AM"; and John 8:58 "Et Jésus leur dit: en vérité, en vérité je vous dis, avant qu'Abraham fût, je suis," "And Jesus said to them, 'Truly, truly I tell you, before Abraham was, I AM.'" Scripture quotations from *Bible James Martin* (1744); translations are mine.

O august queen of Heaven and earth, dispenser of celestial graces; O protector of virgins, queen of virginity, powerful advocate: it is through you, O Mary, that I owe before God the unimaginable blessing of my conversion. It is through your protection that the bonds were broken that held my soul so far apart from its true freedom. Yes, it is to you that I am indebted for bringing me to know how sweet and easy is the yoke of the Lord. O holy Virgin, please continue your powerful help to me; under your unfailing guidance may I begin and fulfill that which the will of Jesus, your Son, inspires in me. O my sweet Mother, you glorify his glory, and I rejoice to testify to the feelings of gratitude and love for you with which my heart is filled. O harbor of my salvation, you are, before Jesus, all my trust. O my beneficent star, may you ever be the guide of my frail little boat upon the stormy sea of the world. But I fear nothing, for you are with me, O Mary;[2] you are my light, my guide and my hope, especially in my final hour.

CHAPTER 1

Eustelle joyfully accedes to the will of her Director to undertake the story of the favors granted to her; Portrait of her parents; The generosity of her sacrifice for the salvation of her father.[3]

In acceding humbly and simply to your desire, my Father — because I believe it conforms to the will of our Divine Master — my soul no longer feels that almost invincible revulsion that it felt for more than a year thinking that I would have to tell you, in writing, about myself, or the fear that people other than you or others privy to the secrets of the heart might come to know the secrets of my heart. Oh! I am so small that I want to talk about myself only to learn how better to channel the dispositions of my heart and never to wander in the paths of pure love.

Now my revulsions are no longer the same. What have I to fear by yielding to your lights, your discretion, your wisdom?

[2] Echoing Psalm 23:4 "Même quand je marcherais par la vallée de l'ombre de la mort, je ne craindrais aucun mal; car tu es avec moi," "Yea, though I walk in the valley of the shadow of death, I will fear no evil for you are with me."

[3] The original italicized headnotes to chapters of the *Recueil* and to the letters are not Eustelle's. They are the work of the unnamed editor of the original French edition (1843). Additions to them for this translation are indicated by square brackets.

You are the guide to my soul: I accede to your direction, and, from the depths of my heart, I am going to share with you what excited my regrets, what awakened my thanksgiving.[4] My soul knows a special joy in thinking that I may lay open my heart to a man whose soul is animated by the purest zeal in divine glory. Oh how consoling for me it is, in this vale of tears, to find a true friend of Jesus! What you ask of me, Father necessarily recalls to my memory those fabulous workings of grace from our good Savior, bestowed upon an unworthy creature. O Jesus, my love and my life, my sweet honey—my dear Redeemer—give me your spirit, give me your love—it is so sweet to be in your domain.

Heaven gave birth to me of Christian parents.[5] My mother, above all, was a woman of abounding sweetness and patience, while my father exemplified in himself the essential duties that religion prescribes. Oh how have I desired his perseverance![6] How many prayers have I lifted to Heaven, that the bad examples and disastrous counsels of this perverse century not move him entirely to abandon the Lord's commandments! Nothing is more bitter for a Christian family than to see some of its members forget the holy laws of the Gospel. O my God! You know all the inmost thoughts of my heart on this point, and you know the boundless devotion with which I begged you to accept the sacrifice of my life to obtain with the offering of my death, that my father not become the unfortunate victim of eternal damnation.

CHAPTER 2

The infancy of Eustelle; Her earliest education; Her dispositions; Her character.

I was born on the nineteenth of April 1814 and received baptism on the twenty-fourth of the same month.[7] I do not know

[4] Eustelle here is addressing her *Memoir* explicitly to Father Briand, who, with Bishop Villecourt, had instructed her to undertake it.

[5] See Appendix, document 1.

[6] French: "Oh! que j'ai désiré sa persévérance!" It is possible that Eustelle is thinking of Romans 3:5: "Bien plus, nous nous glorifions même des afflictions, sachant que l'affliction produit la persévérance, la persévérance la victoire dans l'épreuve, et cette victoire l'espérance," "and more, we glory even over our afflictions, knowing well that affliction gives rise to endurance [*persévérance*], and endurance brings victory in the struggle, and that victory brings hope."

[7] See Appendix, document 2.

the reason for this delay, which could have been so fatal to me for, had I ceased to live before receiving the sacrament of rebirth, I would have been deprived for eternity of the sight of my God. The very thought of this is enough to make me shudder, but at the same time that same thought fills me with gratitude for the divine favor that preserved my frail life,[8] and so adding this benefit to the many others which fill me with love for the Lord.

From my earliest infancy, my parents took pains to procure instruction for me as far as their means allowed: they had only their work to live on.[9] So I began school at five and left at ten. I will say, simply, that our Lord blessed me with a good memory and a facility for learning. I had a lively personality, a susceptible, passionate, and impressionable imagination, a tender and compassionate heart, inclined to pleasures and attachments to creatures. This passion for pleasure, joined to the dissipation which gives rise to it, increased greatly as I began to grow up, and prevented me from hearing the voice of our Redeemer God, a voice full of love. In those times, pride was my dominant impulse, and with it how many other evils did it invite into my soul! O Jesus, my Savior, my Love! I was so young and yet I offended you so much! I saddened your heart, so tender and so paternal! O my dear Master, forgive me. I have loved you since those sinful days, and the love you yourself deposited in my heart quiets my fear of your merited severity towards me.

CHAPTER 3

Examples of Eustelle's pride and vanity; Her parents' excessive tenderness towards her; The cries of her heart in her first infidelities.

Outside of school and more free to enjoy my freedom, I received the fatal imprints of the spirit of lies, which worked their way more and more into my young heart. The world and its vanities already captivated my soul, but more, in my age of innocence and openness, I let the dangerous roots of corruption penetrate into my soul. The feeble gifts that God had given me and the self-love

---

[8] This may be a reference to the "dangerous illness" Eustelle suffered from as an infant: see Thompson 12.

[9] The phrase "only their work to live on" is Eustelle's gentle way of acknowledging that her parents were not landed gentry or property owners.

that made me believe myself so superior, far from leading me to give glory to the Giftgiver, awakened in me an intolerable pride. I had the presumption to believe that I was better than others. The Demon, who had studied my inclinations, placed flattering compliments on the lips of persons I knew; these sank into my heart, puffing it up more and more with the fatal love I had for myself. My parents' doting on me was excessive; they never dared deny me something that would satisfy me or bring me happiness. And so, accustomed to do whatever I wanted, I became disobedient, rebellious, irritable, and impatient; in a word, I came to feel all the passions that had festered in my heart. How long did my heart stay innocent and pure? You alone saved my heart, O my God. Alas! I did not long preserve the whiteness of the mystical garment with which you vested me on the day of my baptism. I was not slow to join those who pierced your Sacred Heart, to give away the rights to the heavenly homeland which the waters of regeneration had given me. O divine Liberator! Was this the recompense you should have expected after giving me so many benefits? And where were the gratitude and love that you deserved? O Jesus! Why did my eyes close so soon to your light? Why did they prefer for themselves the false glimmer of an enchanting world? But your great mercy was not exhausted towards me, O my Savior. I was moving away from you, O my Beatitude, but your fatherly heart called after me, came after me. Blessed be you, merciful Jesus: my heart, then deaf to your loving solicitations, would not always stay closed to your voice. Even if my heart strays from faithfulness to you again, the time will come when, overcome by your love, it will have life and breath only to sacrifice it to you.

CHAPTER 4

Eustelle thinks about her First Communion; The spectacle of its piety and modesty delights her soul; She denies herself certain amusements; The Way of the Cross exercise; The happiness of her First Communion; Jubilee.

In my eleventh year, I had to prepare for my First Communion. The power of divine grace began from this time to make itself felt in my soul. Through the power of that same grace, I began to realize how happy I would be if I were more thoughtful, more obedient, and if I attended better to my religious duties. And it was my First Communion, for which I wanted to prepare myself, that committed me to amend my young life. I had always loved people who lived in piety. I remember one day seeing a pious young woman in church, but I found myself thinking about her and not about the awesome sacrifice being offered at the altar; this happened many times. And even as I was focused on that young woman, I felt the stab of remorse penetrate my heart. Oh how I wished to imitate her! It was above all her modesty that enchanted me and made her seem almost an angel. So I resolved to avoid the little gatherings of children who made the rounds of the village. This in itself is simple foolishness, but pastimes that are essentially innocent often have mortal consequences, especially when children of both sexes are gathered together.

The grace of Jesus pressing me more and more, I resolved to remove anything that could be an obstacle to the results of the precious favor that was soon to be granted to me. There was no devotion that was more pleasing to me than that of the Way of the Cross.[10] I began to perform this exercise of piety four times a week to obtain the grace worthily to make my first communion. And at last, the desired day arrived. Jesus, Love eternal, God with us, after having for the first time purified my soul in the healing bath of penitence, admitted me to communion in his blessed body. Ah! I was fed with the living bread descended from Heaven; I received this pledge of the mercy and love of the one God; Jesus entered my soul, a soul which could not yet comprehend him. Even so, how filled with joy I was then! And how holy, how selfless were my resolutions then! Alas, in only a short time my cowardly heart had forgotten them.

Our Lord did not limit his favors that day, for the day of my First Communion was also the day of my Confirmation. I confess, my Father, that I received this last sacrament without fully understanding it and so without receiving its precious gifts. The year was 1826, the time when the Holy Father declared a Jubilee

---

[10] French: "chemin de la croix." Eustelle is referring to the "Stations of the Cross," the Catholic devotion that reenacts Jesus's final journey from judgment by Pilate to his burial. The sequence is typically represented in fourteen small paintings or bas-reliefs along the walls of Catholic churches. Praying the "Way of the Cross" or the Stations, worshippers walk alongside the fourteen stations reciting prayers associated with each station.

for six months. How easy it would have been for me to pay off the debts to God I had contracted for my many sins![11] But I fear now that in those days I abused these means of salvation and pardon offered to me to purify completely my soul. Oh! if I had been better disposed, I would have found new strength to defend myself and to secure myself from the pitfalls which kept me far from port and caused me to shipwreck.

CHAPTER 5

Her self-love harms Eustelle's piety; it inspires in her the love of pleasures and of ornaments; The dangers of dance; She keeps the laws of God and the Church, but with coldness and indifference.

At the time of my First Communion, I was but little changed: I had something of piety, but self-love wholly reigned in me. When I assisted in the catechism and instructions of the other children of my age, I always flattered myself that I was better educated, wiser, and more devout than the others. How mindless! To believe that I could construct an edifice of holiness on the ruinous foundations of pride and self-love! Alas! In the first storm, everything collapsed, a just chastisement for my foolish pretension.

One of the children in the First Communion class told me that my devotion would not last very long, that I was just like all the others, a prediction that was only too faithfully fulfilled.[12] I persevered for a time, but after a short time I was placed in apprenticeship. There I made new acquaintances and was drawn into a place where the attraction of pleasures made the soul sense dangerous assaults. In no time I developed an excessive taste for finery.[13] It is true that my situation did not permit me to satisfy this taste, but my poverty made me no less reprehensible for the disposition that took root in me. I can say, my Father, that I loved the dance as much as it was possible to love something, and

---

[11] Eustelle is referring to the Jubilee year of 1825–26 proclaimed by Pope Leo XII. A plenary indulgence was offered to those who participated in the Jubilee.

[12] Note the sarcasm in the self-reproach; French, "trop fidèlement accomplice." The passage compresses some biographical details: Eustelle is saying that her pious resolutions were compromised when she entered into her apprenticeship as a seamstress and was exposed to new people and new distractions.

[13] The irony in the French is "Je ne tardai pas," "I was no laggard in developing"; "finery," translating "parure."

I counted the moments until I could commence this dangerous pleasure, so capable of bringing about the loss of innocent youth. I cannot count the number of thoughts, desires, glances and words in these evil pastimes that could condemn me in the eyes of God. And I was only fourteen! Even then, I sought only to please and to make myself loved. This is to say to you that my soul could no longer be called innocent.[14]

So wholly occupied with the world and with myself, I forgot the gifts of the Creator God. His love watched over me, but my heart did not recognize him and offended against him. I contented myself in those times to approach the sacraments only twice a year. I attended Mass[15] on Sundays and holy days and said my prayers, morning and night, and I scrupulously observed abstinence on the prescribed days, but all this I did with coldness, indifference. And what is worse: I often went to church only to see and be seen. O my Savior! O Jesus! your love for me imprisoned you in the holy tabernacle or upon the altar,[16] but the time I spent near you seemed to me so long! The celestial intelligences surround you, prostrate, seized with awe and devotion while I, a vile nothing, dared to stand in your presence in a posture so disrespectful, so unworthy of your greatness. Your adorable heart consumed itself for me while mine, in response, only smoldered in a foreign, profane fire. Your infinite love brings you to renew, upon the altar, the sacrifice of Calvary; but I attended only to renew your sorrows and steal away hearts created to love you, hearts for which in every Eucharist you offer your blood and your infinite merits.

O lovable Jesus, even after so many ingratitudes, your heart did not close itself to me; it sighed ardently for the day when I open my eyes to your light, break my miserable shackles, and return to the liberty of your children. Undying graces be returned to you forever, O my powerful Liberator! I was soon to feel the marvelous effects of your regenerative grace.

---

[14] The specifics of the passage — the reference to thoughts, desires, and actions, to misdirected love and to Eustelle's age — seem to be evoking catechism definitions of sin and of culpability after the age of reason.

[15] Attendance at Mass was mandatory but frequent confession and weekly Communion were not the norm in the nineteenth century.

[16] The motif of the tabernacle as the Eucharist's prison is common in Eustelle's writing. The French is "votre amour vous enchaînait pour moi," "your love for me enchained you."

CHAPTER 6

Battles between nature and grace in Eustelle's heart.

In the middle of the storm that raged in my soul, a voice from Heaven made itself heard from time to time, the voice of God the Redeemer calling me to him. Oh, I felt the weight of my chains often enough but I loved them still; I wished somehow to belong both to God and to the world. On the one hand, I felt the vivacity of my remorse, the longing for my salvation; on the other hand, the world, its pleasures, and my own heat tightened their grip, and I could not bring myself to renounce my affections and inclinations. The Demon made me envisage what seemed to me the impossibility of ever correcting myself, and this lie became the pretext for my continuing in that unhappy state, continuing in my infidelities. In the time that passed between these days and my conversion, I was urgently pressed, on three different occasions, to return to God; grace spoke to my heart with more force than usual. Sometimes I felt movements of uncommon fervor, when it seemed as though I could change all at once. But then, with nothing more than an invitation to a party, my pretend conversion vanished like smoke and I stilled the voice of my divine Master urging me to return entirely to him.

O my Father! How much must I have saddened the heart of Jesus with these continual rebuffs to his tender solicitations! How much I would have deserved to be abandoned to my exile!

Back then, if only I had reproached and accused myself, for even one of these rejections! But how many times did I find the same feebleness in my heart. The hellish lion held me subject. He played on my feeble resolutions; what has he not done to prevent his prey from escaping him! One day I was alone in a house when the temptation struck me to take for myself a pretty little thing[17] that found itself before my eyes, something so little and trifling that it is not worth describing here. I gave in and took it, but immediately reflected on what I had done and put it back in its place. I was happy to have undone this little fault that could have had disastrous consequences, but I did not reflect that the whole incident was a result of my not taking care to watch over my affections. Some months passed, and then there arose numberless anxieties and perplexities in my heart, divine mercy always pursuing me.

---

[17] French "bagatelle."

CHAPTER 7

Effects of examples of piety upon Eustelle's heart; New battles between nature and grace.

I have already spoken, my Father, of the effect on me of the example of persons of piety. Once more they were the means employed by our merciful Savior for my salvation. Oh, how that love pursued me! Only now do I comprehend all the tenderness of his designs for me, but my battles were not yet won.

Having many times observed, at the foot of the altar, a young person whose piety was angelic, I felt a strong desire to imitate her. My mind so fastened on her piety that she became a continual distraction for me in church. Returning home, I asked myself inwardly why I did not do what she herself had done, and what so many others had done. Look here,[18] I asked myself, have I not the same graces, the same helps? It seems to me that the service of God is so sweet! So why am I distancing myself from his divine law? Why not break with the world? Break with my passions? O my Father, I cannot tell you what was happening in my soul in those times. I listened at the bottom of my heart to the voice of my conscience — or rather to that of Jesus — who reproached me for my continual resistance. Oh! how he desired me! How I was drawn, despite the opposition of my heart, towards this unique center! I thought I could find peace and happiness far from him, but my remorse proved me wrong. And once more Hell opened up before me: the Demon, furious at these new touches of grace,[19] made every effort to keep me snared in his nets. He showed me all the discomforts this change would bring in me: the friends I would push away, the pleasures I would renounce. What would my world say about me now, when it had showered me with such esteem? In giving myself to divine devotion, I was condemning myself to a life that was sad, serious, melancholy. I was young; did I not have the right to allow myself the joys of youth?

Despite all of Hell's efforts, I felt the necessity to break my chains, but I would have need of the eloquence of Saint Augustine to depict the battles that agitated my soul. Alas! Jesus was not yet victorious; it was my cowardice that delayed his victory. What, I said to myself, shall it never be possible for me to arrive at a perfect conversion? I have not the strength to conquer myself; my passions hold firm.

---

[18] French: "Et quoi!"

[19] French: "touches de grâces."

So shall I never love my God? Shall my conscience never be at peace? Shall my soul never taste peace? Shall it never come to know God, search only for him? What? Shall this God of goodness never satisfy my desires? It seems to me, however, that I would like to save myself. This is the end, I cried sometimes; God does not want me to be saved, his mercy is not for me. It was not for me that he suffered death on Calvary; I am not to partake of the blessing of redemption. Sometimes I went so far as to say — with doubt and uncertainty — that God is unjust; he wants me to be his own but he denies me his help.

I cannot, my Father, describe this state of mind to you as it was, but you know it, you understand it. I was in unbelievable anxiety as to what way to follow,[20] and I sought to make God himself somehow responsible for my irresolution.

O Jesus my Savior, my adorable Master! Did you have to so twist and pivot to win me to your service? Is there anything sweeter than to belong to you? Is it not in observing your precepts that one finds peace of heart and a happiness that the world cannot offer? Ah! Peace is in you alone, the promise of the everlasting feast assured to the virtuous.

CHAPTER 8

Prevenient grace;[21] *A transgression commenced, albeit involuntarily, in regard to abstinence; Sincere confession; God's plan for Eustelle; Good resolutions; Trust in and dedication to the Virgin Mary.*

I can say only with much sadness and bitterness that once more I resisted the voice of the Savior, answering him this time: God does not want me to save myself.

But the fatherly eye of this God of love and mercy watched over me. I slept in the night of sin and his divine heart labored for my salvation; I embraced the sinful project of remaining disgraceful to him, and his only revenge on me was to prepare new helps for my conversion. O goodness! O charity! O boundless mercy! But more, O Jesus! I only increased the excessive thirst that you suffered on Calvary for my salvation. You urged me to restore my

[20] French: "sur le parti que je devais prendre."

[21] Prevenient grace is grace (strength from God) sent unasked-for in advance of a temptation or period of trial.

soul, but my cold heart only multiplied its offences and ingratitude towards you. O Godly Redeemer! Will you triumph soon? Will your glory endure my resistance forever? I long, O Jesus, to proclaim your victory over the tyrant that enslaved my heart!

One day I found myself at a pleasant gathering; it was the day before Ash Wednesday.[22] At midnight, the partiers talked about eating something, and a fatty treat was served. All the partying I had experienced that night prevented my noticing that the time of abstinence had begun.[23] Soon I was warned by an interior voice and I stopped eating the proscribed foods. And I said to the people near me, it is midnight and we are eating meat: I do not want to continue. They thought I was being scrupulous, but our Lord gave me the strength to dismiss the need to conform[24] by taking care of me when I so little deserved it! Why? Why did I not in that moment turn my back completely on Satan's empire? In that moment I could not imagine the work that Jesus would perform in me in only a short while. Surely foreseeing the happy moment of my emancipation from him, the Demon did everything he could to keep me in bondage to him.

In that year [1829], there was a jubilee of two weeks. I desired to participate in the spiritual gifts which our mother the Church offered to her children in these days. So I sought out for confession an admired, holy cleric who had served as the curè of our parish.[25] It was through this man's ministry that our Lord wished to complete the work of my conversion. Oh! how my heart is struck with gratitude for him! Never, with God as my witness, will I forget the important service he rendered to me.

I made my confession with great clarity and simplicity. It was required of me that I renounce pleasures, and this I did. My confessor seemed satisfied with the dispositions I seemed to have, and he immediately realized God's vision for me,[26] and he said these

---

[22] Shrove Tuesday or Mardi Gras, a traditional day of celebration in France and elsewhere.

[23] Eustelle's tortuous original emphasizes her discomfort with the memory: "At midnight, the talk was to take something [*prendre quelque chose*]; something fatty was served [*on servit du gras*], and the dissipation with which I had passed that night [*la dissipation dans laquelle j'avais passé la soirée*] did not permit me to notice. . . . "

[24] French: "le respect humain," literally, human respect.

[25] Abbé Jossier, curé of Saint-Pallais de Saintes parish.

[26] French: "il connut de suite les vues que Dieu avait sur moi."

words to me, words I shall never forget: "My child, the Lord has special plans for you; I implore you, respond to him." The words penetrated and took forcible hold of my spirit; the Lord, I said to myself, has particular plans for me? What? Shall I not attach myself to this God of goodness? Shall I continue to offend him? When my confessor laid out the penance I was to perform, I asked his permission to add to it, imposing on myself the obligation to eat only dry bread in the morning, six days a week. My confessor agreed to this, saying "see the confidence I have in you: I allow you to observe this for the week, and then I will admit you to Holy Communion." And it was so: I was resolved never to turn back. I had a firm intention to avoid sin and the occasions that lead to it. I placed myself under the protection of the holy Virgin; I recited the chaplet[27] every day, calling on my good Mother to obtain the grace for me for a true return to virtue.

Yes, holy Virgin, I understand, before the heavens and the earth of which you are the sovereign queen, that it is through your powerful intercession, your more than maternal goodness, that I have come to arrive before the adorable heart of your divine Son, who is the way, the truth and the life. O tender Mary! How can one respond to such love that you have? How to express my lively, deserved gratitude to you? I am incapable of these: all I can do, you well know, is ardently yearn to make myself agreeable in your eyes, strive to imitate you, and, if the Lord gives me the means, make you loved and revered.[28]

CHAPTER 9

The last vestiges of weakness; Prelude to a perpetual divorce from the dangerous pleasures of the world.

For all this, my conversion was only roughly sketched, and I had reason to be afraid because I was still very weak. I was quite faithful for two months, because I recalled from time to time

---

[27] I.e., the Rosary.

[28] The sense is somewhat tortured. With the passive voice of the final verbs, "c'est de vous faire aimer et révérer," Eustelle seems to be saying that she hopes that her efforts to be pleasing to Mary and to imitate her will be recognized as love and reverence. Thus the sense completes the thought of "Je m'en sens incapable," that it is foolishness and pride to believe that one's mere human actions are capable of offering adequate or commensurate love or reverence to God.

the resolution I had made to separate myself from the pleasures of the world. It was Lent and in these days of penitence it was not difficult for me to distance myself from the follies of the age, since people abstain from them then. But these days passed and an unforeseen circumstance arose — unforeseen to me but well prepared-for by the Demon. I was asked, along with a parent, to attend a supper, and I consented. The party wound on into the evening and it was decided that it should end with dancing. There were a few young men and young ladies, and one of these was, unfortunately, a musician. The memory of my promise to refrain from the dance welled up in my memory, but the pull of pleasure spoke louder than the voice of conscience. One of my friends whispered softly to me, "What would your confessor say, who thinks you so devout?" I answered that it would be just this once, but I gave in two times more. But I no longer felt the same pleasure, for the finger of God was there.[29] That final time, the parent who had accompanied me got into some sort of dispute with some people at the gathering. After that, he did not go there anymore and I dared not go alone for fear of being treated badly; so when they asked me why I would go back, my pride made me answer that someone in the company displeased me. This was not true, and what I could have said was that I felt a great distaste for that amusement. For our Lord had set me apart. Since this moment I am speaking of, I have never again felt a single desire or a single temptation for the pleasures of the world. My will, by the grace of God, was so firm and unmoving that it destroyed all the affection I had had for these sorts of amusements. In the whole of my being, I felt a sudden and extraordinary change, though I declare it is impossible for me to express the sensation. I tell the world sincerely that it is no longer anything to me; I am resolved to shun anything that might bring me closer to it.

When I presented myself for the Sacrament of penance[30] to fulfill the Easter duty, my confessor seemed surprised that I had not kept my word to him, given the firm disposition that I had manifested at my last confession. He expressed the pain he felt at

---

[29] French: "le doigt de Dieu était là."

[30] French: "je me présentai au tribunal de la pénitence," literally, "I presented myself at the tribunal of penitence." The "Easter duty" (le devoir pascal) is the requirement of Catholics in good standing to make a confession at least once a year, between Ash Wednesday and Trinity Sunday.

my unfaithfulness to grace and pressed me urgently not to delay my sincere conversion any longer. So then I told him everything that had happened, assuring him that, in the future, with God's grace, the world would be nothing for me.

I observed, in these days, that some pious people approach the blessed table very often and nothing surprised me more than such frequent communion. But I envied their happiness, and it was then that there commenced in my heart the most ardent desire to unite myself more and more deeply with the God of the Eucharist.

CHAPTER 10

Eustelle belongs completely to God; Victory is signaled over human respect; Daily exercises of piety; More human satisfactions; Vigilance; Holy precautions.

I completed my confession and had the happiness of satisfying the precept of the Church. Holy angels rejoice! For I belong wholly to Jesus! O you people of blessed Sion, celebrate the victory of the God who crowns you! Let your joy burst forth! I belong to Jesus completely! And you, my Father, bless him! His love has triumphed; his presence in the Eucharist has given me life, and just as the Redeemer of men overcame the devil and Hell and rose victorious from the grave, now, seating himself in my heart like a king on his throne, he triumphed over all the enemies who assaulted my soul and who had for so long prevented him from reigning there.

One of the principal effects that I felt from my Easter communion was manifested in a power that our Lord had communicated to me in an extraordinary way: for, from the moment of my conversion, despite the sarcasm and ridicule of the world, I never again felt the shameful and degrading tyranny of "people's respect." In fact, nothing was more agreeable to me than to say out loud and in public, whenever the occasion arose, how I repented having a love of the world and its principles, how disposed I am now to condemn them by my conduct.

In all of the encounters, I sought for the means to make known the new feelings that now moved me. In fact, sometimes I sought out the very people from whom I knew I would receive the most mortifying mockery. I endured this to the end and then left them, happy to have won a victory over "people's respect," and enduring something for our Lord. I even told these people that I would be all the more eager to serve the Lord if I had to suffer more persecutions in the path to which the Lord had called me.

I resolved to attend Holy Mass every day, every evening to make a visit to the Blessed Sacrament, to recite the Rosary regularly and not to miss devotional reading on any day. I also resolved to approach the Sacraments often.[31] From then on, I had no more friends; everyday interactions were foreign to me: no get-togethers, no friendly walks. I could, certainly, have stayed close to those people whose company was not harmful to me, but none of them appealed to me and I could see that, with the passage of time, Jesus would take the place of all.

O my Father! My spirit is amazed, even erased in the bottomless well of the good Savior's mercy, of Jesus. O Jesus! a name a thousand times more dear than life itself! A name for whose glory I would count myself happy to shed my blood! But I digress.

Early on, our Lord made me understand that religious exercise alone did not constitute true piety. Indeed, from the moment of my conversion, my principal study was to avoid any gatherings, quit any activities, guard my senses, renounce all my inclinations, enjoyments, and desires[32] of self-love, and finally to renounce all the various attachments that remained in my heart.

CHAPTER 11

The happy metamorphosis in Eustelle's dispositions; The gifts of the adorable Eucharist; More frequent Communion.

I will say, to the glory of Jesus our God, that three or four months after my conversion, I no longer felt within myself either the desire or the habits or even the inclinations to sin, not even the slightest affection for any sin. I was formerly so high-strung, but now I felt no impatience; I was formerly so slanderous, but now I had not the slightest inclination to accuse another in confession; I was formerly so ardent and scrupulous, but now I no longer had to accuse myself for every thought, desire or word — or anything — that might detract from an angelic purity; I was formerly

---

31 "Sacraments" here refers to the Eucharist and to the sacrament of penance. As noted above, the faithful in this period regularly attended Mass but did not always (or even usually) receive the Eucharist.

32 French: "renoncer à mes inclinations, à mes vivacités, à mes sensibilités."

so disobedient, so disrespectful to my parents, but now it was my joy to be docile, respectful and obedient to them, because I recognized God's authority manifest in them. I was once so dissipated, so distracted in that holy place, but now I had eyes to see Jesus alone. These virtues came to dwell in my soul without pains or violence or struggle: one would have said they were natural in me. Behold the work of grace; behold the fruit of the love of Jesus. But "my tender Master" did not limit himself to these gifts.[33]

I owe it to the divine Eucharist to have been freed so soon from the bonds of sin; it is the divine sacrament, the very thought of which made my soul expand with hope and which made me understand, with such suddenness, the distance I needed to traverse from the world to God. I beg your pardon, my Father, for such an unworthy analogy.

O pledge of the tenderness and charity of the Savior God! Precious memorial of Calvary! O ineffable sweetness to the soul that knows you! How my heart is drawn to you,[34] O Jesus, my love! You are my all in all, especially in the Eucharist.

Jesus knows my feebleness and so also knows the need I have to nourish myself often with the bread of power, and he inspired my confessor to permit me to receive Holy Communion more frequently. And this desire of Jesus's Sacred Heart only mirrored the desire in my heart to receive his blessed nourishment.

And so I began to receive Holy Communion once every two weeks. Such joy for me! How happy I was! And oh! how deeply I felt the difference between serving God and serving the world!

I continued for a time to receive Holy Communion in this way, but, as my soul was sated with this heavenly manna, Jesus who is all good, was pleased to awaken in my soul the ardent desire to approach him in the Eucharist even more often. I counted equally the greatest and the smallest sacrifices as nothing, in the thought that they disposed me to that important action, and I believe I can say that the acts of renunciation I have made since my conversion were universally done out of my love for Jesus, and particularly that I dispose myself to approach my great and most lovable Master more and more often.

---

[33] French: "Et pourtant il était bien loin 'ce tendre maître' de s'en tenir à toutes ces faveurs."

[34] French: "Que tu as d'attraits pour mon cœur!" Literally, "How attractive you are to my heart!"

CHAPTER 12

Eustelle's more ardent thirst for Holy Communion, subordinated to obedience; Spiritual delights; Generosity; Holy desires.

To wait for two weeks before a new Communion seemed to me too long, and yet I did not dare express the desire for a shorter delay. I said to myself, if I could receive my God every Sunday, what joy it would be for me! Even so, I followed the will of my confessor, and after a short time, a grace was granted to me. I divided the times between communions between preparation and thanksgiving. And the more frequent my Communions became, the greater the desire to see them multiply took hold of my heart; I envied the happiness of those whom Jesus received more frequently to his divine banquet; but despite these desires, I never went against the will of my confessor in this matter. When he decided at length to add to the number of my communions, I obeyed with joy and simplicity; and if he saw fit to deprive me of Communion I immediately submitted, thinking that this was the will of our divine Master. The good Savior had made me to understand that this renunciation of my own will was agreeable to him, that he would want me to apply myself to it with all my might. And the more I labored to detach myself from everything that could displease him, the more he favored me with the abundance of his consolation. Jesus willed, in these days, to intoxicate my soul with his chaste delights, and so is it any surprise that I made progress in piety? Ever soaring on the wings of divine grace and led as though by hand by Jesus himself to the blessed calling[35] into which he was leading me, oh! how happy I was! How full of confidence I was in the God who so loved me! It seemed to me that I should never again have any fear of turning back.

One day someone asked me, since I did not attend the dances any more, would I not at least consent to go with her on a walk in public. Even the most fearful conscience, she argued, could not find this recreation condemnable. Oh, you are right, I said to her, but I am weak and I do not want to expose myself to temptation to go further; do not think it wrong if I abstain. My words displeased her and she left me. As for me, for whom nothing was a sacrifice, as soon as I acted for Jesus at the impulse of his grace,

---

[35] French: "la sainte carrière," "the holy career."

I judged myself happy to occupy myself only with the one who drew me so powerfully to his love.

I believe I can say now, my Father—to the Lord be glory—that the labor of my conversion, insofar as it could be, was sincere and complete. The confidence that I had in God led me often to tell him with filial abandon, Lord, what more could I do that I have not done? What more do you demand of me? You know the disposition of my soul: show me your ways and I will fulfill your holy will. Your holy law is infinitely dear to me; I burn with desire to be faithful to it, and I want to engrave it forever at the bottom of my heart.

You can readily see, O my Father, the mercies of the Savior God towards me. The Lord has bestowed on you more light to recognize these mercies and more discernment to appreciate their innumerable benefits showered on me. Help me, I beg you, to thank and bless my supreme benefactor. For my part, I offer him, out of gratitude, my blood, my life. May he accept my sacrifice and the loving motive that inspires me!

CHAPTER 13

Transports of gratitude alongside groans of repentance; A furious Hell rises.

O good and merciful Jesus! Beloved Savior of my soul! At last he has achieved the work of my conversion! At last he has completed the joyous change against which my rebellious nature sometimes revolted! My repugnances are at last completely overcome! They are at last driven off, these passions I so often preferred to you: may they never return! The deadly chains that bound my heart to created things are broken! Your grace is victorious; your love has triumphed, O Jesus my Redeemer! I am, now and forever, your conquest. Oh! a thousand blessings be on the flood of your ineffable mercy![36] Oh that I might have a million hearts to consecrate to you, a million voices to proclaim your prodigious works for me!

Holy Redeemer! Oh, when I recall to mind the evil days when I offended you with such pleasure and blindness, my heart feels broken with sorrow and filled with a remorse I would wish to be everlasting. Why can I not erase these days so full of sin from my life!

[36] French: "l'excès de votre miséricorde ineffable!" Literally, "the excess of your ineffable mercy"; "excess" seemed too negative in the context.

Your fatherly voice, which so often called out to the depths of my heart, had always found it closed to your loving invitations; that heart so wrapped up in guilty projects while you, its peaceful friend, prepared for it the kiss of peace and reconciliation! I was your enemy, the slave of Satan, while you, boundless Love, looked forward with happy patience to the days when by your grace, I would so often become your tabernacle, the days when you would wrap me in your dear delights!

You have deigned to tell me yourself, O Truth eternal! You have told me you have no more secrets for me. Goodness! Love! Mercy! Now, in the language of the prophet-king I cry out with him, You have broken my bonds, O Lord! I offer you a sacrifice of praise; I invoke your adorable name.[37]

So late have I begun to love you; help me as you did Saint Augustine, yes! So late have I begun to love you, O beauty always ancient, ever new![38] At least, oh at least, O lovable Jesus, receive the rest of my life, the rest of my youth, which I should have devoted entirely to you. Was it necessary to wait for the fifteenth year of my life for me to make you the absolute offering of my heart? Can I bear the thought of even a single instant of my life that was not yours? But praise and blessings to you, O divine spouse of my soul, who stopped me in the middle of my fatal career, who did not permit me to sacrifice it wholly to the world and to the Demon. A thousand thanks to you, O good Savior! I am yours; accomplish the work of your grace.

You know, O Father, how the lion of Hell grew furious towards me. What tricks he employed in his effort to keep me from breaking my bonds! What vain pretexts, what seeming impossibilities did he offer me when he found himself being driven from his dwelling that was my heart! So he sought to avenge himself by stirring up against me the fury of Hell and all the persecutions of the world.

---

[37] Echoing Ps. 116:16–17: "Ouï, ô Eternel! car je suis ton serviteur, je suis ton serviteur, fils de ta servante, tu as délié mes liens. Je te sacrifierai des sacrifices d'actions de grâces, et j'invoquerai le Nom de l'Eternel"; "O Eternal, lo! I am your servant; I am your servant and the son of your handmaid. You have broken my bonds: to you I will offer a sacrifice of praise, and invoke the name of the Eternal."

[38] Echoing *Confessions* 10.27.

CHAPTER 14

The world persecutes Eustelle; She is the object of accusations of false piety; Some in her family blame her.

Such a sudden change — and one so contrary to the maxims of the age — became the preoccupation of some people in the world. I cannot say how much their fury stirred itself up against me, and it was then that I truly understood this twisted world. That world loved me, caressed me when I seemed to give myself to it; how had I suddenly become so culpable in its eyes, by embracing the company of piety?[39] Surely the world would not have treated me so harshly if I had abandoned myself to its greatest excesses. How I suffered sneering, persecutions, and mockeries without number! People were obsessed with me: they would single me out as I passed on the street; I was the object of the grossest injuries.

When I found myself in somebody's home, people would assemble there to blame me and make a mockery of me, and invent the most unbelievable things against me. And there were people who made me appear crazy; they imputed actions to me that could only come from madness. When my parents reproached them, a thousand arguments were hurled at them to prove the harm they had done in letting me act as I did. Do you not see, they told them, that your daughter should not withdraw herself in this way from every pleasure? It is your job to prevent such bizarre conduct. I was the topic of conversation even in the cabarets. What foolish, absurd things they said about me there! And they did not spare the one who directed me there, who was said to be the cause of my transformation. And me? On the one hand I felt the most uncomfortable pains; on the other, I could not help feeling joy in these instances, convinced that these same unjust attacks will earn him a distinguished place in Heaven.[40] Once again, all of this made me perfectly understand the justice of my perception of the world. If I had actually become so despicable to the world, why did the world still bother to care about me? If I were a criminal,

---

[39] French: "le parti de piéte," "the party [i.e., association, faction] of piety."

[40] French: "dans la persuasion que d'aussi injustes attaques lui mériteraient dans le ciel une place distinguée." The "him" of this passage is Father Jossier, Eustelle's parish priest in this period and (unofficial) spiritual director. Accordingly in the preceding sentence, Jossier is "celui qui me dirigeait alors," "the one who directed me" in her pursuit of holiness.

why would the world not cry out its complaints to reproach me and prove that my conduct was against the Gospel? But if I was innocent, how could the world not find condemnation in conduct which was the object of its most bitter censure?

Certain other, seemingly wiser people, were no more favorable to me. In our view, they told me, you have no one but yourself to blame.[41] You invite this contempt by your way of life. It is good to serve God, but you go too far: your devotion is ridiculous. Why do you need to deprive yourself of all these pleasures? Are not some of them merely innocent? Often I would respond that these same pleasures, which the world regards as innocent, are condemned by the Gospel. I would say to those people so obsessed with me, that for my part, nothing inspires my devotion like these persecutions directed at me.

The worldly people were not the only ones who criticized my conduct; some people who wished to be recognized for their piety censured me bitterly and made fun of me to the extreme. It is hard to get a fair idea of all their accusations and inventions against me; it would be a waste of time to go into such detail. Though it is unclear to me, I sense that their piety did not conform to the inspirations given to me by our Lord, so I thought it proper that I should have no connection with them unless it was required. So I always spoke to them sweetly, cordially, and hastened to do them a service when the occasion arose, but when they pronounced that their form of piety did not resemble mine, that I did not like to tell tales and concern myself with others, they caused a thousand troubles for me and judged me very unfairly, ascribing an evil motive to my devotions, alleging that I acted so only to give my confessor a good opinion of me. To them, my confessions and communions were nothing more than false faces made from a desire to be noticed. It was said that I did nothing with my parents, that I spent all day in the church, and that I did more than the nuns; and I should note that among these people who railed against me was a former nun.[42] To all these reproaches I

[41] French: "On débite, me disaient-elles, telle et telle chose sur votre compte," "we deduct, they said to me, such and so from your account."

[42] Thompson (67–68) identifies this woman as a former lay-sister of the Benedictine convent at Saintes, closed in the French Revolution. She saw Eustelle's extraordinary piety and desire for frequent communion as "an affront to herself as a nun."

said nothing, and my silence only enflamed them the more. But what pained me the most was that they hurled a thousand gossips towards my parents, persuading them that I could not continue on the road I had taken. They quoted one of those people who was certainly pious but who did not carry things as far as I did, that I should be content to behave in the same manner. All of this wore down and broke the spirit of my parents, who, poorly educated, railed at me continually and told me that those people were right. They wanted absolutely for me to change my way of life; it was a continual annoyance. They hoped to win, but I resisted them, I believe, not out of stubbornness, but because I was following a path from which I could not waver, a path traced by God himself, whose will I recognized in that of my director. My parents could never understand the force that the divine will exerted on my soul.

CHAPTER 15

Eustelle's frequent communion is perceived as a crime; She is accused of stubbornness and pride; Her perfect calm; Jesus is sufficient to console her; More vital attractions of the Holy Eucharist.

It was my frequent communion that was on everyone's mind. One day my father told me that he did not want me to go to Communion every Sunday and I would regret it if I rejected his standing by me.[43] I answered him firmly that it pained me to hear him use the language of the faithless ones, that the true spirit of religion did not permit that kind of talk, that it was perfectly useless to keep harping on that point, and that nothing would make me change my resolution. I will say here, in passing, that pious people sometimes need a certain measure of forcefulness, and that God grants graces to the faithful that they can follow the path that he lays out for them.

It was at this time that people brought complaints about my piety to my confessor, which he said were misunderstood. They suggested that I be prevented from performing what they called bizarre, odd practices. They accused me of excessive modesty and they wanted me to give a thought to the other people who were in

[43] French: "si je méprisais sa défense, je m'en repentirais," "if I scorned his defense I would repent of it."

the church. It was a crime, in their judgment, that I never raised my eyes; they blamed me because, they said, I was always in prayer. If everyone behaved like this young girl, they said, always so absorbed, always so deep in contemplation, there would be no need of booksellers. I became the center of an actual scandal in the parish, and my confessor, people said, should put an end to this for the sake of the church. In a word, my every step, action, and movement was examined, critiqued, blamed, and exaggerated to infinity. Truly, they made so much noise over the behavior of one young girl whom they would have left alone had she been worldly, dissipated, and fickle.

My response to all of this was silence, but then they called me stubborn, saying that I acted like this only out of pride. How could I calm these turbulent spirits? I focused myself, so far as I was able, to be considerate and to perform all the duties that were expected of me; I prayed most sincerely for my detractors, and I do not remember ever showing them the slightest displeasure for all the sorrows they brought on me.

I went to confession every week and I received my God in the Eucharist, as I have said, every Sunday. But the desire for even more frequent reception of the bread of Heaven make me implore our Lord for the dispositions which would merit such a precious grace; I ever aspired to a great purity of heart, and the Master so good, ah! was pleased to fulfill the wishes of his poor servant. His help made everything easy for me; every day he led me, as though by hand, on the most slippery and difficult paths; and he led me so kindly, so tenderly that to pull away from him was unthinkable.[44] And I did not pull away, and this attachment, which was his work, greatly pleased his divine heart; and it was not long before he bestowed on my heart an even more ardent love, and with it a new and most particular longing for the Holy Eucharist.[45] Oh how I loved him, from that very time, in the adorable sacrament! O my Father! How happy I am to have spoken to you so often of that ineffable memory of his charity! Ah! If it is not given to me to be heard by the whole world, I am at least satisfied — imperfectly, to be sure — in implanting in your fatherly heart my feelings and most tender memories of this so precious pledge, of the love of Jesus.

---

[44] French: "qu'il m'aurait été impossible de ne pas m'attacher à lui," "that it would have been impossible for me not to attach myself to him."

[45] French: "un attrait nouveau et tout particulier pour la sainte Eucharistie."

CHAPTER 16

More frequent communion and its blessed effects; Her family considers placing Eustelle in service; Heaven exempts Eustelle from an obstacle to the progress of her fervor.

Six days without uniting myself to Jesus seemed too long a time, and yet I did not dare ask permission for more frequent reception of the sacrament. And it only followed, of course, that new persecutions fell to me from those persons who made a confused profession of piety: nothing set them off against me like my desire for more frequent communion. These considerations could not stop me; they only ignited my desire to be more often the very tabernacle of my God. And here is the way I went about obtaining this favor.

In this period the curé of our parish received a new assignment. It occurred to me that, if he would permit me to go to confession on Wednesday instead of Saturday, this would permit me the second Communion I wished during the week. This plan succeeded tremendously: my confessor accorded perfectly with my thoughts. Sometime later, he asked me why I did not go to confession on Saturdays; I responded that Wednesday was more convenient for me but if he wished I would willingly follow his decision. This changed, in effect, the day of my confession and this permitted me to receive two Communions a week.

Oh! how happy I was then to participate in the divine banquet! Oh how I set to work with all my power to adorn my soul with more and more perfect dispositions, to please the divine host who would come to stay there! All my thoughts, my words, and my actions were directed to this one purpose. Thoughts of our Lord occupied me ceaselessly. I continually sought out new ways to show him my gratitude. Just as the things of earth once captivated my heart, now thoughts of the divine Eucharist overcame all those disgusting things, vanquished all those barriers, that I might offer all the sacrifices that arise each day, when the beloved Master wished to subject my soul to new tests.

As it had been but a short time since I was out of my apprenticeship,[46] I had only a little work in the beginning. My parents attributed my lack of customers to my devotions; they said my way of life kept me apart from people who might bring me business,

[46] Probably about 1832, when Eustelle was about 18 years old.

that it made me so solitary and strange. They said as a result that I could not stay in this situation, that I had to think about putting myself in service. Nothing about the idea of service bothered me in the least, but an interior voice seemed to pull me back from it: it seemed, I thought, to offer inconveniences and obstacles to my numberless plans. Even so, I was preparing to obey my parents when our divine Savior, who had other plans for me, allowed things to change. Soon I had enough seamstress work to keep me busy, and my parents stopped talking to me about executing the plan they had been considering. This left me free to pursue completely the plan of devotional practices I had sketched out, a plan whose only aim was to please the God of my soul. Oh with what joy did I taste this beloved burden! How easy it was, sustained as I was by the grace of the divine Redeemer! My days passed in the most perfect peace. I could not adequately admire the merciful love which had led this beloved Master to fill my soul with such favors; I could only wish to return his love with love. I begged him to cure my weakness and to offer himself my gratitude.[47]

CHAPTER 17

The attraction of prayer for Eustelle; Jesus the center of all of her affections and pleasures; Interior mortifications; Jesus is everything to her.

Early on, our divine Master inspired in me a particular attraction to contemplation in prayer: it pleased me to be in his presence, especially at the foot of the tabernacle. There, every day, first thing in the morning, at the school of the Savior, I went to learn the practice of meditation. He was truly my master, for no one other than my Master instructed me on the subject. When I first started, I would give only a quarter-hour to meditation, then I devoted a half-hour to it. Soon our Lord permitted me great difficulties there; and I was as yet so weak that I abandoned this practice for a time. But I recognized my fault in abandoning my daily meditation and the harm the interruption was doing to my soul and so did not hesitate to make a new resolution not to miss a single day of prayer, and to devote to it as much time as I could. Since that time, I do not remember missing another day.

[47] French: "et de se remercier lui-même par lui-même," "and to thank himself by himself."

This desire to talk with God caused me to renounce walks, recreations, and even the most innocent conversations; I desired but one thing and this was Jesus; my heart went wholly to this most dear object of love. For too long I had denied my heart her single need, her daily nourishment; I had instead preferred to drink from the deadly cup of dangerous pleasures. When at last my heart felt the happiness of knowing Jesus better and better, how quickly did she move closer and closer to him; when, after resisting him so much, how readily did she finally accept the invitations of the God of love![48]

O God, a thousand times good, or rather infinitely good! How limitless is your charity![49] Your great mercies are incomprehensible to me! What could bring you, from the throne of your grace, to lower your gaze to my baseness, to rescue me from the abyss into which I had chosen to plunge myself? This I think, Lord, as I trace out the line from where I was before to where I am now by your grace. Glory, praise, and thanksgiving be to you, O my God!

Oh! For so long have I saddened your fatherly heart; it is now my wish to glorify you by consuming myself entirely in your love and, as much as I can, to make you love me.

It was to the practice of interior mortification that our good and most lovable Savior led me, as much in the little things as in the greatest ones. Let me tell you, O my Father, the different circumstances by which the sweet inspiration of Jesus led me to this practice of mortification.

Not only did our lovable Master wish that I apply myself to die to every sin, every inclination, and every sentiment which was not for him; more than this, I often heard these tender, loving words in the depths of my heart: *I am all that you need.*[50] And with such tenderness did he address these words to me! Oh! it seems to me I can hear and see him now, kindly affirming his

---

[48] The French is somewhat tortuous: "Aussi, avec quelle rapidité ne se porta-t-elle pas vers son centre, quand elle eut le bonheur de le mieux connaître, et qu'après tant de résistances, elle se rendit enfin aux invitations de ce Dieu d'amour?" "Also, how rapidly did she transport herself to his center when she had the happiness of knowing him better, and when, after so much resistance, she finally yielded to the invitations of the God of love?" Like the French, the translation uses the feminine pronoun for *cœur*, a grammatical masculine.

[49] French: "Qu'elle est excessive votre charité!"

[50] French: "Je dois te suffire en tout."

desire to bestow on me all his delights. It is absolutely impossible, in human language, for me to express adequately the tender and merciful conduct of our Savior towards me during the period of which I speak.

When on Sunday, after the offices, the thought came to me to take a walk, I heard the voice of my Heavenly friend say to me: "Can I not take the place of everything to you? Can I not renew you and untense your spirit? O my daughter, what joys will be given to you if you deprive yourself of every created thing for my sake! My joys will surpass all of the satisfactions here below and all that your own mind could imagine for itself. I am infinite," said the good Master, "and all that I am is for those who love me. However," continued the divine Savior, "I do not want to force your will: I leave you free to accept or resist my tender invitations. Your openness, your generosity toward me will be the measure of my love towards you. O my daughter! My heart burns with desire to communicate itself to you. You fulfill my wish for you when you place no obstacle to the effusion of my love."

My Father, this is the tenderness with which the God of goodness urged me to be completely his. This is how he came to attach me to everything that could please him, an attachment which, I hope, not even the bonds of death will ever break. Oh, was it even possible for me to escape these ravishing attachments of the love of the angels? O Jesus, so good! Could I refuse to quench the thirst which my own soul made him suffer on Calvary, and that I knew still afflicted him in those moments when he invited me to love him, to give myself entirely to him?

CHAPTER 18

Privations; Instruments of penitence; Mortification of the senses; Advantages of this practice.

I did not devote myself exclusively to the practice of exterior mortification, for I understood that this is only the bark on the tree of the interior life,[51] but I desired nonetheless to observe some of these practices. So I began by imposing on myself certain

[51] French: "l'écorce de l'arbre de la vie intérieure"; the phrase occurs again in *Memoir* 17 and Letter 174. I have not found a source for the metaphor; Thompson (100) refers to it as "her own expression."

privations during my meals. On Fridays I limited myself to eating dry bread in the morning and denied myself an afternoon collation. I was not old enough to fast but, a bit later, our Lord inspired me to eat only black bread and to limit myself only to pure water as my drink. It is true that I did not eat bread alone, and this lessened the privation. I did this for several years for two reasons: first, for the mortification I wished to practice and, second, for the love I had for the holy poverty which I wanted to embrace in my eating. My parents, however, when they noticed that my health had deteriorated, forbade my continuing in this way of life. My mother spoke of this to my confessor and I was obliged by obedience to discontinue these things I practiced. It is not certain that the weakening of my health was caused by these mortifications which I have described, for I suffered even more from the interior pains which troubled me, and which I will describe later.

Even with this, the prohibition placed on me did not extinguish the love of mortification in me. I thought of subduing my body with some instrument of penance and I had a cilice[52] made for this purpose which I asked permission to wear. At first this was refused me but later they gave in to my wishes and I was permitted to wear it four days a week for eight hours a day. My confessor placed a condition on his permission, to which I agreed, that I speak with his Excellency the Bishop[53] about it when I had the chance to speak with him. That occasion soon presented itself. My lord the bishop was not as agreeable as I would have wished, for he forbade me absolutely the use of any sort of instrument of penance. Somehow, though, I believed that he might be more disposed in time to allow me the use of a discipline, so I had one made, but my lord the bishop still prohibited my using it.[54] So I had to obey and confine myself to the practice of interior mortification: I was not prevented from doing this.

---

[52] French: "haire." This seemingly refers to a hair shirt; but the word used by Father de Laage in his letter to Bishop Villecourt is "cilice"; see Explanatory note 3, pp. 60-61. The biographers' descriptions of the device suggest an iron fabric belt, perhaps akin to chain mail. Thompson (102) reports that Eustelle's family kept her penitential device as a memorial, "iron, armed with points"; Mayet (210) has a similar description.

[53] This person is Clément Villecourt (1787-1867), Bishop of La Rochelle from 1836 to 1856, and later Cardinal.

[54] See Explanatory note 3, pp. 60-61.

It was with the mortification of the senses, my Father, that I always especially occupied myself. I made a pact with my eyes, my ears, and my mouth, to see or hear or say only those things which conformed to the will of our divine Master. I acted in this way, not only in whatever might wound the heart of Jesus, but also in the most permissible and innocent things. Never, either in church or on the street, would I lift my eyes for no reason. Whenever I entered a place where there were objects that would pique my curiosity, the voice of Jesus immediately made itself heard in my soul, to urge me, out of love, to deprive myself of them. If I entered a garden where beautiful flowers could attract my attention, I immediately averted my look, thinking that our Lord meant more to me than these things, and that he alone should occupy my spirit. When I found myself with something delightful to smell, I deprived myself of that satisfaction, but I did this in a way that no one would notice. If there was something going on in the world which, without being harmful to my soul, did not contribute to my soul's spiritual advancement, I would refrain from attending to it, to avoid either distractions or simple idleness. The things of religion had great appeal to my senses; however, when I could do my piety while exposing myself as little as possible to these attractions, I gladly offered this as a sacrifice to God.[55] Thus, if a funeral procession passed me on the street, I limited myself to prayers for the deceased without lifting my eyes to watch the spectacle. It is certainly unimportant, my Father, to record such insignificant details, but I include them here for you as proof of my obedience to you. I add that, for the same reason, I prevented as much as possible those who cared for and loved me, in a spirit of innocent piety, giving me hugs and kisses as tangible signs of their affection for me. Monsignor the Bishop came one day to the parish of Saint-Pallais; it was the first time he had come here. On that day he preached, on the occasion of our patronal feast day. The clergy who accompanied him were numerous, and I confess that my heart thrilled at the advantage

[55] French: "Les choses de la religion," presumably candles, golden chalices, statues, stained glass, incense, and the like. I render the second half of the sentence somewhat loosely; French: "quand je pouvais satisfaire la piété, tout en m'imposant, à cet égard, de petits sacrifices, je m'empressais de les offrir à Dieu," "when I could satisfy piety, while imposing on myself small sacrifices in this respect, I hastened to offer them to God."

that came to religion from the event.[56] However, our Lord inspired me to deny myself the chance to look upon the bishop, to whom I owed so much gratitude for the interest he had shown in my soul. I was, however, amply compensated for this little self-denial for, Monsignor the Bishop having come into the sacristy, where I was occupying myself with arranging the little altar boys, the parish priest took me to his Excellency to receive his blessing.

Another time, I received a letter which I knew would be of great interest to me, I was inwardly urged not to read it immediately, and so I waited for over a month to open it. In short, my Father, these sorts of mortifications constantly attracted me without cessation. It was Jesus who subjected me to this mysterious death, to give me a larger share in a true life.

Oh! how useful this interior death is for the soul, my Father! How it brings security to the spirit and peace to the heart! How free one becomes then! How the soul can soar when it is freed from created things! Oh if we only knew the reward for this interior emptying! And I, who speak of it—do I dare think that I practice it as I understand it?

CHAPTER 19

The cruel trials of Eustelle; Distractions; Assaults of an impure spirit.

Jesus made me understand that the peace and security which my soul then enjoyed would soon be troubled, at least in the "lower part," to use the language of the masters of the spiritual life.[57] So I disposed myself to receive these trials with submission and joy and love, by which it would please the Supreme Goodness to purify me. And these turbulent days soon arrived.

Jesus permitted my soul to be carried to a deluge of interior pains. They were so horrible that their very memory makes me

[56] French: "J'avoue que mon cœur était bien joyeux de l'avantage qui revenait à la religion de ce concours."

[57] A familiar trope, distinguishing "lower" corporeal or sense-based urges (gluttony, lechery, and sloth) from ones thought to be more of mind (pride anger, avarice, envy). See, e.g., Saint John of the Cross, *Dark Night of the Soul*, trans. E. Allison Peers, 4.2: "For then the spirit, which is the higher part, is moved to pleasure and delight in God; and the sensual nature, which is the lower part, is moved to pleasure and delight of the senses, because it cannot possess and lay hold upon aught else, and it therefore lays hold upon that which comes nearest to itself, which is the impure and sensual."

shudder. Far from exaggerating their number and their intensity, it would be impossible for me adequately to describe them. Some of the trials that I suffered I do not even now understand; I will talk about the other, lesser ones.

First, I was assailed by a host of distractions during my prayers, distractions which I do not believe had their origin in my mind. I suffered strangely from this chaos of imagination.

Then came the temptations against chastity. At first I was a little afraid of these trials, since it had been two years since I had last experienced them. I did not know then how many holy souls had had to endure these blows from Satan's angel. However, when a ray of divine light illumined my understanding and I came to understand that the crown of the elect is never more beautiful or dazzling than when it comes as the result of victories over all sorts of adversaries, I resigned myself to the struggle, persuaded that I would receive the help of him who permitted my enemies to attack me. For I had already received so many proofs of his care for me that my slightest distrust of him would have been an affront to his mercy.

How can I describe how much I was tormented by these temptations to angelic virtue? I would not dare give details; in any case, I would not have the strength. They overwhelmed me night and day; I had not a moment, not a day of calm and tranquility. I seemed relentlessly to see around me a legion of evil spirits, offering me the most horrible images. Others sought to becloud my understanding, my memory, and my will, and then they sought to convince me that I had consented to their infernal ideas. Jesus seemed to abandon me to myself in these painful moments; I could not recognize how he was upholding me in my weakness. Even so, my heart never separated itself from him during this storm so long and terrible. He was then in my heart unnoticed,[58] this God so good, for how else could I have stayed so inviolably attached to him? How could this filth, which seemed to accompany me everywhere, not eventually stain my soul? For my soul, this was then a triple temptation, rolled up into one: first, in the awful images which the devil sought to make me embrace; second, in the belief that he was pressing on me that I had consented to these horrors; and third, in that I could see my very soul appear

[58] French: "invisiblement"; "unnoticed" seems less figurative in context.

to have given itself to the second.[59] The latter was both a despite and a discouragement; a despite in that God left me so long to struggle with the lowest of the demons; a discouragement that would infallibly have caused me to abandon the fight, as I was too weak to resist all of these assaults. It seemed as though the devil was saying to me: there is no need for you to struggle so hard to beat me, for it is I who will beat you: you cannot escape my hands. He used the shadows of night to add to his subterfuges and to my terrors. O my Father! What a martyrdom! Only those who have experienced it could understand.

CHAPTER 20

Abandonment; Interior shadows; Temptations; Scruples overcome by obedience; Desolations and snares of the devil, with regard to mental and spoken prayers.

These temptations were soon accompanied by a state of internal abandonment. Deep darkness enveloped my spirit. The very sky seemed like bronze to me. Jesus, who once treated me so kindly, had seemed to have abandoned me. In the midst of these anxieties, my cold and dejected heart wanted to turn towards its unique center, to seek there not consolation but the strength I needed, to seek that God, so good, so full of mercy, but who now seemed deaf to the groanings of my soul. Wishing nothing from creatures and rejected now, it seemed, by the only one I loved, I took refuge in the very wound of his heart, abandoning myself wholly to his mercy. So imagine my pain when, after this act of surrender and testimony of my steadfast and inviolable love, I heard him push me away with more contempt than the poor Canaanite woman felt from him? I thought I heard him speak these chilling words to the bottom of my heart: *Go! I reject you. You are nothing to me anymore.* O my Father! What a terrible sentence to lay on me, who had rejected everything that I thought would displease Jesus! What a judgment to render on me, who desired only him, who until now had felt myself consumed with love for him, who

[59] French: "la troisième, je l'entrevoyais, et elle semblait attendre, pour se présenter, que la seconde eût produit son effet." The sense, I believe, is that the third temptation is to despair that the soul had appeared to have been tricked into culpability by the devil.

loves him alone, loves nothing other than him! Oh this dear and tender Master — if I may be permitted to say this — wanted me to love him only for him and not for my own satisfaction. Oh how I bless him for this conduct towards my soul! I bless him in the moments of these terrible trials.

To these temptations were joined others: temptations to vanity, to blasphemy against God, and to despair. O my Father, you cannot imagine how these last temptations made me suffer. And worse yet, I fell into a state of frightful scruples. Burning with desire to unite myself to Jesus in the adorable Eucharist, I was at the same time seized with fear by the thought of the sacrilege I might commit.[60] My confessor, recognizing my painful situation, applied a prompt remedy: he imposed on me the strict obligation to go to confession no more frequently than every two weeks and never to miss a single Holy Communion that was permitted to me. I immediately and joyfully obeyed, and I was soon delivered from this disease of the soul. Even in the battle with scruples, not once did I fail to take a Holy Communion that was permitted to me, and it would have been infinitely more painful for me to deprive myself of this food of life[61] than were the pains of all the trials that overwhelmed me.

Our Lord, having delivered me from this pain, wished then to replace it with another, and so came desolation, spiritual drought and continual dryness in prayer. So the devil redoubled his efforts to bring me to discouragement and to have me abandon the important habit of prayer, making me believe that I could no longer pray. But I was never unfaithful to prayer. The sovereign guide of my soul was always there to sustain me, make me triumph. The divine Master made me understand the power of mental prayer so well that I could withstand the solicitations of that enemy of my salvation.

A little later, I witnessed a completely different kind of attack. The devil sent me the idea that my spoken prayers were badly done, that they lacked any sort of merit, and, worse, that in praying thus, I only caused the Lord to be annoyed with me. And he tormented me concerning these spoken prayers in another way, a rather

---

[60] The sacrilege Eustelle feared was that she might receive Holy Communion in a state of mortal sin.

[61] French: "aliment de vie."

singular way. When, morning and evening, I had made my prayers, the enemy of my salvation placed the worry in my mind that I had not in fact fulfilled this duty. He darkened my soul and my memory with shadows so deep that it was not possible for me to recall if I had completed this obligation. This worry tormented me and I believed I was obligated to recommence my prayers. But this idea was inconceivable because I had so pained myself to complete my prayers the first that I could not imagine how, after such a struggle to attend to them,[62] I could be brought to forget them. I was advised on this matter by my confessor, who told me that in such circumstances I should omit my prayers and replace the omission with other prayers. I did this, but I was always obsessed with the same anxiety, until I had recourse to another remedy. When I had completed my prayers, I made myself write down the month, the day and the hour when I had said them. I have to admit, I found something pleasant in doing this, but it worked, and the Demon left me alone on that side. He did this, it is true, only to redouble his malice by other temptations he had prepared for my soul.

CHAPTER 21

Other shocks to the angelic virtue.

I have already told you, my Father, of the temptations I experienced against chastity, but these were only the prelude to the assaults of this kind which I had later to undergo. They came on me ceaselessly and they were so disgusting that the smallest remembrance of them still causes me to tremble. I will not go into the details of these horrors, but I will say that the Demon took that which was most holy and adorable in religion to make it the subject of his infamies to shake my constancy. When we think about these matters dispassionately, with a soul that wants to be entirely of God, we cannot deceive ourselves that these images clearly announce themselves to have come from Hell and that, in reality, we should not bother ourselves with them; for is it not

[62] French: "ennui." Thompson's paraphrase is "difficulty and lassitude" (118). The sense is that she was bored and had trouble attending to the words so that she could get through them. Later, during her brief experiment with cloistered life, Thompson (140) reports that Eustelle decided she was unfit for the cloister due to her "invincible repugnance to the repetition of long vocal prayers."

obvious that a religious heart would not hold onto thoughts that even a criminal soul would reject? Even so, there was no longer any way for me to pray in any manner, for I was continually in battle: it required my perpetual efforts of endurance to succeed in holding on to my soul. Legions of impure spirits obsessed me, encircled me to force me to witness the frightful spectacle which they produced to my alarmed imagination. I dreaded the end of the day and the onset of night's shadows, for it was then that the infernal troop became more daring and impudent. More than once I found myself at Death's door: I was in a state of agony due to the violence of the combats which I had sustained, and I trembled out of fear that I had somehow given consent to witness these odious scenes which the devil had presented to my imagination. And yet through it all, something inside me told me that I remained innocent and that the devil was responsible. The Lord permitted me these attacks and alarms for his enjoyment and to reward me for the fear I had of having displeased him or to have wounded his fatherly heart, even slightly. His love, of which I had received so many testimonies, increased my pain excessively. I wanted to give myself over to reflection but I had only time to defend myself and to repel the darts that rained down on me from all directions. I had not a moment to breathe: one shock succeeded the other; as I said before, sometimes it seemed as though my soul was going to separate itself from my body. I felt in my whole being such a violent shock, and sometimes an exhaustion so profound that I felt beside myself. Others have sometimes told me, when I retrace the feeble sketch of this unnatural state, that they were surprised that something was not damaged in my chest, that the rupture of some vessels did not cause my sudden death. I replied to them that death did not frighten me; as long as I did not offend my God, I was absolutely indifferent to the loss of my life.

I cannot, however, pass over in silence the infinite precious favors accorded to me by our good Savior in these terrible moments; in that moment when the assault of the devil became strongest and I not knowing from which side the blows would come, fearing myself already defeated (but not defeated), afraid, and alarmed, I raised my hands, my heart, and my whole being to Jesus the beloved, and in his humanity he presented himself to my soul with unequaled majesty and goodness and caused me to hear these words: *Here I am; fear nothing.* With the dawning of the sun of justice the tempest immediately subsided and calm was reborn: peace embraced my soul. So, blessing my Liberator, I surrendered myself to sleep; I needed it, I assure you, for I was wasted by lassitude and fatigue. Looking back, it was for Jesus, uniquely for Jesus, that I sustained these furious battles; how could I complain?

Unaccustomed to the intellectual visions[63] I have been describing, my Father, I admit that they frightened me a little the first times, especially when I reflected on how unworthy I was; but the confidence which the goodness of our Lord gave me reassured me and made me humbly and simply accept the favors which he accorded me then. I asked him for the grace to respond with a profound humility, with an ardent love.

CHAPTER 22

Vicissitudes of fear and love; All for the love of Jesus.

I was subjected to another test, a test I did not understand. I can give you, my Father, only an imperfect idea of it. It happened during prayer, or when I heard the holy word, or even when I was talking to someone. I will try somehow to describe it, using the following comparison: when someone finds himself at sea for the first time, he often finds himself preyed upon by fear and dread because he is not accustomed to that element. A rising wave deepens his fear and the fear becomes more terrible, when wave after wave, gathering above the vessel, seem ready at any moment to swallow it down into the bosom of the abyss; such a person, I say, in that moment believes that his final hour has come; but as the waves begin to calm, hope of life brings peace and tranquility. Well, when during prayer or in any other situation I perceived the moment of combat approaching, I would initially find myself drawn to meditation. My soul was calm and peaceful; but then, without my having in my mind any image or representation, I felt my soul oppressed, ashamed, and overwhelmed, as if it had been brought to nothing. I cannot tell you why, but this despondency, this annihilation, lasted for only a second. I cannot describe how I suffered in this instant; it was as if I were being strangled. Then,

[63] French: "visions intellectuelles," "intellectual vision," a term borrowed ultimately from Augustine (e.g., *De Genesi ad litteram*, bk. 12), an intuition of divine things not relying on sensory images. See also Teresa of Avila, *Interior Castle*, Sixth Mansion, 4.5.

all at once, all my anxieties evaporated and I was calmed. A bright light spread in my soul; I seemed pure, transparent as crystal: I was happy. In that moment I was the criminal freed from his shackles. And then, after hardly tasting this new, sweet situation, I found myself once more in that earlier wretched condition. This alteration, this flickering, typically lasted for about a quarter of an hour. What I have just told you, my Father, is very poorly done, but it is the best I can do to describe these sorts of things. But I can say this: these experiences bore no resemblance to my other inner sorrows.

What you do know, my Father, of the trials which it pleased our good Savior to pass on to me cannot be revealed except in a very imperfect way. I have only barely touched on the tribulations to which I have been subjected over six years, not to mention the persecutions I have suffered from the world. So I will describe in total simplicity — in obedience to you, my Father — my sentiments, or rather the sentiments which Jesus gave me, during this long chain of inner anguishes.

You are aware of how indebted I am to divine justice for its indifference to all of the missteps of my early youth. It is perhaps only natural that I might daydream that I was acquitting myself before God in offering him the trials that I had to suffer for the expiation of so many faults; and yet our Lord seemed to demand that I be made to suffer everything for my love for him: it is this disposition that I believed I had inspired from the moment of my conversion. *All for love*: this was the cry that my Master, so full of mercy, caused me perpetually to hear. I resolved then and there to devote the rest of my life to gratitude, to make every moment a continual act of thanksgiving. I cannot say, however, that I was newly indifferent to sorrow for sin, to repentance, and to acquitting myself fully before God, but it seemed to me that the divine love reigning in my soul had paid my debt with superabundance, for it seemed that Jesus himself demanded that I accept this. I entered into his adorable sight, just as he was in me. I accepted in love and gratitude all the rigors that I formerly had to endure, rigors which I recognized now as true kindnesses. I yearned to render myself in total conformity to my divine model. This is why I embraced, for his glory, this state so crucifying and so painful. O how well my soul is now! I would now not wish, for all the world, to have been a stranger to all the tribulations which

I had endured. Already then, in times of violent tempests, I was inwardly happy to be able to testify to our Lord to my devotion to his divine service in suffering for his love.

CHAPTER 23

Unshakeable confidence; Eustelle fears only sin; She does not wish to ask God for the cessation of her pains.

I have never felt my confidence in God waver or diminish; the more struggles I had to sustain, the more my faith redoubled. Jesus, yes, Jesus! was my sweet and unshakeable hope. I told him that, even if I were assured of my own eternal damnation, I would still hope in him.[64]

Nevertheless the violences visited upon me were continual, resulting in a noticeable alteration in my health, which was naturally fragile. You can see something of the deterioration even in my outer self, brought on by the torments which I had ceaselessly to endure, such that people came to tell me that, if I did not take care, I would go mad; but, persuaded in all of this that God's will would be infallibly accomplished, I did not trouble myself because I was in no way the cause of the troubles I was experiencing. As regards my health, I cared more for the life of my soul than for the state of my body. My thought, my only desire, was to avoid, for the love of Jesus, everything that had even the shadow of sin. O my Father, I believe I can say, in all the simplicity of my heart, that I have feared — no, hated — sin; I would prefer to die a thousand times than deliberately to commit a sin, even in a very light matter. Oh! the very idea of bringing sadness to the heart of that most tender of fathers, of the greatest of friends, of Jesus, Love eternal, makes me endure a sort of death, so great is the fear I have to commit a sin.

O sweet and merciful Jesus! Was I worthy, after having loved iniquity so much, to experience now, by your grace, such a lively dread of it? Am I worthy, who have formerly offended you so much, of the search you undertook for my soul, for that heart on whose door you have stood for so long, knocking ceaselessly until it opened to your love? You know, my most adorable Master, that I would rather consent to the destruction of my very

[64] This is one of several places where original readers fretted that Eustelle was leaning toward Quietism; see the Introduction, page xxvii and note 46, above.

being than, against you, to give it into the hands of that enemy of my salvation. I withstood all his efforts, feeling buttressed by your powerful aid. It is true that I was saddened to see myself ever on the brink of the abyss, because I feared the result of the violent temptations which harassed me; I trembled to find myself suddenly in the claws of the Demon; but the chief reason for my dread was, O my God, because I dreaded above all to offend you. In the midst of my frights, it was you who gave me boundless confidence, and this confidence gave me endless access to your inexhaustible kindness; this strengthened my soul to overcome all my neglect. Oh, when I remember the extraordinary power that you sent me a hundred times in my battles: what consolation, what love, and what gratitude I feel!

It never occurred to me to ask the Lord for the cessation of my sorrows: I even told myself, when the battles were most tumultuous, that my soul was itself eager for new tribulations. And Heaven did not let me down: tribulation was my daily bread, night and day, leaving me not one moment of repose. I was tormented equally, both in times of solitude and in moments when I was obliged to interact with creatures.[65] There were many times that I had to leave the company I found myself in, because I could not conceal from my outward self the upheavals that agitated my soul. Truly, if, in those moments of the most powerful interior upheavals, in those moments when I was obsessed by legions of infernal spirits, if, I say, our Lord had asked me if I wished to be delivered of them, I would have protested that I demanded nothing other than his good pleasure. And I further declare, within these cruel tempests, I understood better than ever how these trials are gifts;[66] I went so far as to wish the trials would increase, because my soul, holding itself fastened to the cross of the Savior, felt its dedication and energy redoubled. I would often say to myself, cry out to myself, Yes, my Savior! I will be faithful to you. Nothing on this earth or in Hell shall be able to separate myself from you. Let it be either victory or death — or death for victory, if that should be necessary.

---

[65] French: "comme dans les rapports que j'étais obligée d'avoir avec les créatures," "just as during the interactions I was obliged to have with creatures." The term here, "les créatures," is not necessarily derogatory but merely the logical opposite of God, the Creator.

[66] French: "je comprenais mieux que jamais le prix des épreuves," "I understood better than ever the reward of the trials."

CHAPTER 24

Eustelle is enlightened as to the rewards of suffering; The habit of the presence of God; Externally she is composed and calm; Aspirations to Jesus and to Mary.

I remember that on the feast day of Saint John the Evangelist, I was suddenly delivered of my anguishes and temptations. This suspension in my struggles lasted for a week, and it was during this interval that Jesus made me understand, by a special light that endured throughout that whole time, the reward of my suffering and the good my soul received from it. I confess to you, my Father, that it was the divine will alone which I perceived in this that permitted me to accept the loss of those lovable crosses which God's will had seemed to have removed from me during those days. I was troubled by all of this — and a little surprised. I had lost but one thing; I had lost the cross, and in truth I had it precisely because I did not have it.[67] And when the trials commenced once again, I welcomed them with joy and gratitude, like a person who had a treasure that had been lost returned to him.

This continual martyrdom caused me to acquire, in a very short time, the habit of the presence of God.[68] It was as though it was impossible for me to quit myself of this presence, for the sorrows to which I have been brought reminded me constantly of this presence. I found I could say with the saintly King David, *My life is but a constant groan.*[69] And this groan is directed to the one who prays in those who love him. *My eyes tire from looking to the sky from which alone comes my help.*[70]

---

[67] French: "il me manquait une chose, c'était la croix, et vraiment, je l'avais précisément, parce que je ne l'avais pas," "I had lost one thing; that thing was the cross, and truly I had it precisely in that I did not have it."

[68] French: "Ce martyre continuel me fit acquérir, en très-peu de temps, l'habitude de la présence de Dieu." The wording and especially the choice of the verb "acquérir" suggest the French title of the work known to English readers as *The Practice of the Presence of God* by Brother Lawrence of the Resurrection, originally written in and first published in French in 1692. The following sentence, "[c]e gémissement avait toujours pour objet celui qui prie dans ceux qui l'aiment," may be saying that, while these faithful petitioners' prayers are directed to Jesus, their "groans" are self-directed.

[69] Possibly echoing Psalm 38:10: "Seigneur, tout mon désir est devant toi, et mon gémissement ne t'est point caché," "Lord, all my desire is before you, and my groaning is not hidden from you."

[70] Echoing Psalm 119:82: "Mes yeux se fatiguent à attendre ce que tu as promis," "My eyes grow tired awaiting what you have promised." Also Psalm

I wrote earlier there were many times when people perceived in my exterior the troubles that agitated my soul, but in fact this was nothing other than an effect of the weakening of my health that was visible to the eyes of all. Nothing could be seen to be disordered on my face, for I forced myself to preserve a calm and tranquil air and to put forth a level, peaceful character. When people would speak of me, sometimes I would hear them say: "Ah, how happy this person is! Nothing troubles her: you can see it on her face. How, with the life she leads, can she enjoy so profound a peace?" A person who lived with me once remarked: "Really, Eustelle, I do not know how you compose yourself as you do. I often see you overwhelmed with sorrow, but when anyone comes to see you or conducts business with you, you seem to me not to be troubled at all. How do you constrain yourself in this way?"

Ah, I do this because putting on some other face does not lead to virtue. And anyway, it is enough for me that Jesus is the repository of everything that happens in my heart.

I regarded these various crosses as testimonials of the love of our divine Master, as the prelude to the special favors with which he has filled me since then, and as a way to acquire some traits in conformity to his divine model.[71] My heart overflowed with joy; I was happy in my suffering, in remembrance of that which Jesus suffered for me. Oh, for all the heavens, I would not refuse to drink the smallest drop from the chalice which he offered me. I continually blessed him for this and even asked him to add to my trials, and sometimes saying to him: Even more, Lord; even more!

Often on my lips and more often in my soul I had the words of David: *O God! I belong to you; preserve me pure in the love of your holy law.*[72] Sometimes I would say to him: Jesus, be with me; Jesus, be with me! *Lord, you can see where all my desires lean; none of the groans of my heart are hidden from you.*[73] In abandonment, in desolation, in times of dryness I would say: Lord, do not expel me from your presence; do not take your Spirit away from me. Return to me the joy of your saving assistance. Send me but one word of consolation

---

121:1: "J'élève mes yeux vers les montagnes, d'où me viendra le secours," "I lift my eyes to the mountains, whence comes my help."

[71] French: "et d'acquérir avec ce divin modèle quelques traits de conformité," "and to acquire with the divine model some traits of conformity."

[72] Psalm 118:80.

[73] Psalm 38:10.

and joy, and these bones broken for you will tremble with bliss.[74]

And I invoked the sweet and powerful name of Mary. Oh! what help she brought me, the good and tender Mother. How conscious I was of her protection during those years of battle! How many times did she save me from shipwreck! I surely love the love she has for me, after so many proofs of her goodness towards me. I know well that I am not worthy of her tenderness, but I know even better how much I love her and how much Mary cherishes those who have love for her.

CHAPTER 25

Eustelle's inviolable love of purity; She obtains, after two years of prayer, pleading, and tears, permission to make a vow of perpetual virginity; She is intoxicated with happiness; Thanksgiving; Increase of graces.

It was in this time of sorrows of my spirit that the Lord gave me the idea to consecrate myself to him by a vow of perpetual chastity. From the instant of my conversion, the good Master inspired in me a particular love for this beautiful virtue. As much as I was formerly given myself to levity, vanity, and impudence;[75] this much, since my conversion, I felt affection and respect for that flower, so beautiful, so angelic. Even in the grip of so many battles that made me fear for her,[76] I do not remember, since my return to God, any accusation I could make against myself on this subject. Indeed, I never had an accusation to make against myself on this when I came to the tribunal of penitence.[77] I would have preferred to die a thousand times rather than consenting to even the slightest disgusting feeling in this delicate area.

The desire I had to offer my virginity to God could not have come from anyone other than him. I wanted to belong to him entirely, so that he alone would have absolute dominion over my heart and my affections, of my mind and its thoughts, of my soul and its movements, of my body and all my senses. In a word, I wanted nothing of me withheld from this holocaust that I burned to offer him.[78]

---

[74] French (for "bliss"): "allégresse."
[75] French (for "impudence"): "témerité."
[76] The feminine pronoun is referring to *vertu*, grammatically feminine.
[77] French: "quand je me suis présentée au tribunal de la pénitence."
[78] French: "l'holocauste que je brûlais de lui offrir"; note the subtlety in grammar: "que je brûlais."

My lovable Savior made me hear these words many times: *I am a jealous God;*[79] *I want to possess your heart entirely because I want to bestow on you my grace and love without measure*. It was then, by the inspiration of this same grace, that I was shown with extraordinary clarity of this, *the better part*;[80] and who showed me this? The one who makes the virgins fruitful in virtue, who delights in the lilies, he who cherishes, he who guards virginity. I asked my director for permission quickly to carry out this wish that came from the heart of Jesus; I wished to attach myself irrevocably to him with a vow. At this time I was totally unaware of the wise rules of prudence laid down by the Church, rules under which directors were not permitted to deviate, when persons under a certain age[81] express the desire to bind themselves to virginity by a perpetual vow. Candidates must be tested and exercised for a long time before consent is given to their wish, out of the concern that, in an indiscrete or impulsive fervor, one would take upon herself so serious an obligation, one which is irrevocable. This is why confessors, as a general rule, only allow temporary vows. So for example, from one feast of the Blessed Virgin to another, for six months or a year: this is a period long and serious enough to reassure them of a bond that will last a lifetime.

I was twenty-two years old when I made known to my confessor my thoughts in this matter. It is likely that, had I made my desires known to him, he would have agreed sooner, after the trials required by the holy regulations of the Church; but despite all my pleadings, my prayers, and my tears, I had to wait two whole years for what I desired with such intensity, so many sighs and groans. Oh! I would have overcome any obstacle to enjoy the favor of fulfilling all my wishes. For I loved nothing as I loved chastity; I thought only of possessing it in all its perfection; I

---

[79] Echoing Deuteronomy 6:15.

[80] Echoing Luke 10:42, Jesus's observation that Mary, over Martha, "has chosen the better part," a notion traditionally associated with the choice of the contemplative over the active life.

[81] French: "au milieu du siècle." There was not and is not now an official minimum age at which a person can take a vow of perpetual chastity, but both Codes of Canon Law (1917 and 1983) prescribe deliberate discretion on the part of the bishop approving the vow and the assurance that the vow-taker has reached an age and level of maturity at which she or he understands the nature of what is being sacrificed. The context here shows that these principles were followed in Eustelle's age.

had no thought or desire for anything else; not only because this virtue ravished me with her beauty, but also because I knew Jesus's love for her. So I would testify to my love for Jesus in attaching myself more and more to that which he loved.[82]

At last, after a delay of two years, our Lord permitted my confessor to comply with my wishes. The happy day finally arrived when I would be admitted to the rank of the spouses of Jesus. I cannot find words that could capture my heart's sentiments in this circumstance. I was beside myself; this was a veritable intoxication of happiness and joy. It was on the feast of the Purification of Mary[83] that I took the vow of perpetual virginity. At the same time I consecrated myself to the Queen of Virgins. Following the sentiments to which Jesus inspired me, I drafted two formulae of consecration which I have since carried in my heart and withdrawn into the cross of Jesus my spouse. O signal favor, of which I am so unworthy.[84]

Yes! My tender Master, Jesus, my God and my all! I am unworthy of a benefit so grand, having separated myself from you for so long by my iniquities. I deserve instead to be banished from your fatherly heart, from that heart I so often saddened, whose wounds I reopened so often by my attachment to the earth, to vanity, to nothingness. I am too poor, to feeble, too denuded of virtue to see myself raised to the dignity of being your spouse. O my Savior, to show you my gratitude for so great a favor, I will follow you, I do not say to Tabor, but to Calvary.[85] For it is on your cross that your true spouses are born, and it is there that,

---

[82] This passage is rendered to suggest that Eustelle is personifying chastity, though this impression might be an artifact of French gendered nouns and pronouns.

[83] February 2, 1826.

[84] At this point the French original adds a long footnote that seems to contradict the text. The French note asserts that Eustelle had the texts of these two vows translated into Latin and that she wore them next to her heart for the remainder of her life. She had intended to be buried wearing them but was not, for unknown reasons. The French note inexplicably then asserts that these two Latin texts were not available because the translation was so "lourdement inexact" or grossly inaccurate. Finally the note asserts that, the testimony here notwithstanding, Eustelle only took a vow of virginity for six months, citing the undated document reproduced below as Appendix 4.

[85] Mount Tabor is the site of Jesus's transfiguration; see Matthew 17:1-8; Mark 9:2-8; Luke 9:28-36. The reference suggests that Eustelle sees herself as following the suffering Jesus, not the triumphant Jesus.

from this moment on, I wish to be attached to you, to live and die with you. Creatures mean nothing to me; I myself mean nothing to me. Jesus alone: my only good; Jesus in all, my every wish. Jesus everywhere, my every ambition. Jesus crucified, my every love, everything I know.

Oh how abundant is the grace of my Savior God in my soul from this irrevocable commitment. How abundantly has Jesus repaid this little sacrifice I have made of myself, which he has inspired and consumed by his grace! One might be tempted to say that this little step has added somehow to his glory. But no, O divine Jesus! when you seem to yearn for our love it is only out of your own love for us, out of your searching for what is best for us. O infinite goodness! O Love! O Jesus!

CHAPTER 26

Her love of silence, withdrawal, and prayer; She is dead to sin; Her dedication to all virtues; Her universal detachment.

Our Lord increased contemplation, the love of silence, and withdrawal from the world, in my soul, increased them to such a degree that it became painful for me to interact with creatures.[86] I found myself only rarely with them and I would retire from their company as soon as I had satisfied the obligations of charity, for I knew of no consolation sweeter than to converse with the divine Savior. The good Master had bestowed on me such a love for mental prayer that it was almost impossible for me to apply myself to vocal prayer. From this time, prayer became my most cherished delight: I reduced all my practices of piety to this one exercise. Oh! what good things came to my soul through this sacred channel! O my Father, it was through this, I can now say, that I learned to know myself, and it was through this that I recognized the precious advantage of renunciation and of the inner life, and it was through this that I was taught the paths that lead to perfection.

Our good and most lovable Savior was my only director in this blessed exercise of prayer. I would have thought I was committing an indiscretion by asking my ordinary confessor to tell me the rules; his many daily tasks made me feel the necessity to respect the moments when he was so zealously employed in the conversion

[86] See note 65, above.

of sinners. But I also understood the care which directors needed to bring, as much as they could, to forming consciences for prayer in the souls to which they had been entrusted. In doing this work, spiritual directors must abridge their own sorrows in some respect, for a soul well given over to prayer easily avoids a multitude of moral pitfalls which, without prayer, all the advice of directors could not prevent. For myself, taught in the school of Jesus Christ himself, my profound unworthiness notwithstanding, I tried to be attentive to all his lessons and to engrave them at the base of my heart. In my ignorance, I implored him to bestow his light on me; often I would say to him: *Lord, show me your ways and teach me to follow your will; for you are my God; lead me on the way of your commandments, on the paths of virtue.*[87]

So I spent three hours in prayer every day, and it was with this that I prepared myself for confession, for Mass and for communion. Besides this, since I sought to keep myself continually in the presence of God, I could say that my prayer was almost continual. Called, as I believe I was, to the contemplative life, I understood by the spiritual light that was within me, that Jesus desired my whole heart, without sharing it, without other attachments. He seemed then to show great severity towards me, demanding so much renunciation and so much perfection of me. But O my good Master! I understand you; blessed be you in all your bounty. Your demands were accompanied by such love that it was impossible to refuse you anything. You know, my good Savior, with what sincerity I desire to conform myself to your purposes and that, not for the whole world, would I wish to turn back from you.[88]

I have told you, my Father, that, since my conversion, I have never felt any attraction to any sin whatsoever; I can add that I felt myself drawn to virtue as though by a natural inclination. I loved all the virtues, one as much as the other, with a whole and perfect love. I cannot really say which virtues I favored more, which one to which I was more attracted. I very much love humility and charity, but just as much do I love patience and sweetness.[89]

---

[87] Psalm 25:4.

[88] French: "je n'aurais pas voulu revenir sur mes pas," "I would not wish to retrace my steps."

[89] French: *douceur*; Latin: *dulcedo*. Sweetness is one of the ten virtues of Mary; cf. "Salve, Regína, Máter misericórdiae, víta, dulcédo, et spes nóstra, salve," "Hail holy Queen, Mother of mercy, our life, our sweetness and our hope, hail."

Obedience delighted me, then charity for my neighbor charmed me; prudence, justice, fortitude, and temperance were infinitely dear to me. I call poverty *my sister*; I am drawn to mortification of the body, and I know the great gift of inner mortification, the guardian of heavenly purity. Faith gathered no clouds for me; hope was so firmly dwelling in my soul that it made me taste, in advance, the first fruits of Heaven; and love divine, this ravishing love, this enthralling love, this intoxicating love..., you know, Father, that this love is on my heart.

Nevertheless, the virtues most necessary for the interior life became the principal object of my labors. Confidence and love were for me like two guides which directed me, led me to the other virtues. It was never fear that moved me, for there was only one fear within me: I feared sin, and at certain times, this fear was excessive, especially in those times of my spiritual sorrows. Detachment caused me no grief, for I held on to nothing, absolutely nothing — not even holding on to a drawing on paper. Jesus was my only need, my only love. Every created object disappeared for me with the singular thought of Jesus. But all that I sacrificed for him was, for me, no real sacrifice at all. In all my actions, my sorrows, exertions, battles, privations, I often repeated these words: This is for you, my Savior! For you. Everything to please you; everything for your love.

CHAPTER 27

A redoubling of her love for the adorable Eucharist; Vow of absolute poverty.

My Lord had already bestowed on me a great love for the mystery of the adorable Eucharist. But now, my divine Savior, to whom I belonged through the consecration of my whole being, caused this love only to expand. I am always, O my Father, transported — feeling almost outside myself — when I speak of this divine sacrament, for I cannot express all that is in my heart: how it is filled, overwhelmed, and consumed by this subject. I communed with Jesus three times a week in these days, and I burned with the desire to do so every day; but always subject to the will of this same Jesus, made manifest to me in that of my director, I contented myself with obeying what he ordered me in Jesus's name, while hoping that, later—if it pleased him—I might receive Communion more often.[90]

I could not bear, without the bitterest pains, to see our Lord abandoned in his tabernacle; I wish I could stay there forever; I stayed there as long as I could. On Sundays and feast days, I left the church only after the Angelus, and I would have stayed longer if could have. It was some sort of magnet that kept me in this place full of enchantment. How could it be otherwise? Could a wife leave her husband? Could she see or love something other than him? Jesus was for me, like the bride of the canticle, *the beloved one chosen from among a thousand.*[91] Oh how holy are the conversations we have with Jesus! How quickly the hours pass! How delightful are his sayings! How tender they are; how peaceful. How gentle his caresses! *My soul melted in the divine fire of his word.*[92] And when my heavenly Spouse has placed my soul in this disposition, he asks another sacrifice of me, though it is no sacrifice for me, I am already poor by his holy will; owing to my place in life I have no share in the perishable goods of the world, but one day he asked me, out of love, to vow to him an even more perfect poverty: he demanded of me poverty of spirit, of judgment, and of will. And immediately the ardent desire fired my soul to follow faithfully this new inspiration. For I had received from my dear Master a special yearning for holy poverty: it was my sister, my inseparable companion: I love nothing in the world except poverty.

Pressed now to embrace this new movement, I hastened to ask permission. I did not take this new step without reflection; Jesus himself had shown me its value. So I aspired to strip myself more and more of everything, both internally and externally, always out of love for my adorable Master. Permission was granted to me and I made a vow of poverty; I was delighted to practice as an obligation what I had hitherto observed only

---

[90] French: "il me serait donné de le posséder plus souvent," "he might permit me to have it more often." The masculine pronouns here seem intentionally to blur just who it is that Eustelle is obeying.

[91] Echoing Song of Songs 5:10: "Mon bien-aimé est blanc et vermeil, un porte-enseigne *choisi* entre dix mille," "My beloved is white and ruddy, a standard-bearer chosen from among ten thousand."

[92] I was unable to find an exact source for this italicized expression; "mon âme se fondait," "my soul melts," echoes Psalm 119:7 in a different context.

out of preference.[93] Although I already possessed nothing, so to speak, before making my vow, I now renounced all the other little things that I could have kept. And I will even go into detail, my Father, about what I had and what I did not have, that you might understand that Jesus took the place of every thing, that I gave up everything for him.

I only possessed one spare set of clothes: one dress, one handkerchief, one apron, one bonnet, and one pair of stockings; only one pair of shoes and about the same for underwear. I had no sheets or towels or hand towels: my parents lent me all of that. I had no kitchen utensils either, or else I had only what was strictly necessary. No money either, such that I often was without what I actually needed. And this was the time I was happy, that I sent blessings to Heaven—when I had nothing and that nothing sufficed for my needs.

You know my furniture: a poor cot, a chest of drawers, a little table, and four chairs; a few humble objects of devotion, a very small number of pious books; a few simple pictures hung on the wall, a crucifix that I did not think of as belonging to me, some wooden crosses which I liked for their simplicity, but I gave them away nonetheless. I was even going to give away some pictures that were in my room to reduce myself to greater poverty, but I did not do this out of fear of hurting my parents. My rosary was strung with cord, with a copper crucifix attached. I also had a silver one, worth about a franc; I gave it away under my vow. I had a medal of the Blessed Virgin and of Saint Philomena, in copper. It would have been very easy for me to have many more pleasant and agreeable objects of devotion, but I renounced them all out of love for holy poverty, wanting to keep nothing that could occupy or attach itself to my heart. I had been given very pretty little reproductions of these images: this happens often, and I always gave away these objects and lots of others of the same sort, some of them quite valuable, wishing to detach myself from everything. Another part of holy poverty that I observed was in my food, in only the simplest and least expensive, the only things appropriate to a poor person. For three years I ate only black bread and drank only water, always for the same reason. And I would have continued longer if my parents had not opposed it.

[93] French (for "preference"): "goût," "taste."

CHAPTER 28

Poverty of spirit; Total abandonment to the providence of Jesus.

I understood, however, that I should not attach myself only to these exterior practices; and so, by the grace of Jesus, I applied myself much more to the acquisition of spiritual poverty,[94] which alone brings true liberty to the soul.

Our good and most lovable Savior once more became my sole director in regard to this poverty of spirit. With such love did he lead me to the perfection of this virtue! How he made me understand the satisfaction I rendered to his heart if I became faithful in this area! Even now I seem to see him lovingly urging me to respond to his tender entreaties. He never exacted anything of me by force: *All for love of me*, my dear Master said to me, *because I myself am all love for you.* The good Jesus accompanied these solicitations with a light so lively, so penetrating that it would have been difficult for me to resist it. I then comprehended quite perfectly the beauty and value of this superhuman virtue; I understood this through the affection which he himself had for it, he who is all virtues. I discovered that all my exterior acts were nothing other than the bark of the tree of interior life, but nevertheless there was nothing I might neglect in these external practices. Saint Paul says: "Let your modesty be known to all men. Let all that is just, all that is holy, all that edifies, all that exudes the divine odor manifest themselves in your words and in your deeds."[95]

Out of love for spiritual poverty, I renounced the idea I had to embroider a monstrance to put in my chamber. It was out of love for the Holy Eucharist that I had wanted to undertake this, but the God of the Eucharist inspired me to deny myself this. Our Lord even wanted me to set aside the desire to be paid what was owed to me by people I had worked for. Many times I had not even a sou, and I lacked, as I have said, even the most necessary things

[94] Spiritual poverty begins in the beatitude "Bienheureux sont les pauvres en esprit; car le Royaume des cieux est à eux," "Blessed are the poor in spirit; the kingdom of Heaven is theirs" (Matthew 5:3). As developed by Ignatius Loyola and others, the virtue refers to the inner state of detachment from possessions striving to indifference to possessions inspired by singular devotion to God.

[95] Echoing Philippians 4:5-8. The final phrase, the exhortation to let the virtues shine forth in words and deeds, is original to Eustelle.

for life; but, I said to myself, Jesus well knows what is owed to me and what I need. So, when he deems it appropriate to cease my state of need, he will bestow on those persons the will to pay me. I did not renounce what was due to me, but I submitted to the deprivation that resulted from the long delay during which they thought they were free of me. I did this because I thought that our good Savior wished it. Let me relate in passing one example of this disposition.

There was this one person who owed me thirty sous and, one evening as I passed by her house and I was absolutely without a single obole,[96] this thought entered my mind: this decent person ought to pay me; it would well address the need in which I find myself. At that same instant, I had another, very different thought: Jesus, my Father, my Spouse, knows this: he sees my need. O my Jesus! I said to him at once, I renounce this desire and I give everything into your hands; you will send me this money when you judge it to be appropriate, and I will take it from your hand.

This happened on a day in Lent; I went on to prayer and had just returned to my room when this person came to give me what she owed me. And this is what our Lord did for me in many circumstances. Was I not right to credit our Lord for the attraction I felt for this virtue of poverty! Surely with the special aid of his grace, I could not have endured the privation of these most essential things. Yes! It was to his grace, his powerful virtue, and to his love that I myself am debtor, knowing that of myself I am only weakness, misery, and frailty.

Good Jesus, my love, have I not always been faithful in this, as much as you wanted? Have I ever sought to reject even one of your inspirations? Can I declare that my will has always been in conformity with your own? Oh Jesus, my most lovable all, though my conscience does not reproach me with any failings in this regard, it would be with great temerity that I would pretend to be without any reproach. Pardon me for my failings, Lord, and deign to enlighten me in the future. Oh that I may die rather than wound ever again your heart so infinitely good. I am unworthy to imitate you, to follow you; but you desire it, you command

---

[96] A medieval French coin worth half a denier or a quarter sou or minimal value; in Eustelle's time the word had become roughly the English equivalent of "pittance" or "mite."

it, O my adorable Master; I see how you are urging me, through the love that you have for my soul, to surrender without reserve to the pull of your loving grace;[97] oh! it is only through you, my love, that I will respond faithfully.

CHAPTER 29

Conformity to the will of God.

Even now my soul expands with the memory of the lovable virtue which I will now describe to you: conformity to the will of God. Oh, how I love it! O, my Father, how can I express the love, the attraction, that Jesus sends me for this total surrender of my will to his? It is my paradise, my vocation, my delight; it softens all things, makes me endure all things, see God in all things; it allows me to accept all things, and to rejoice, wholly, in all things.[98] When dear Jesus wants something from me, he shows me how to discover his merciful heart and, with an air of tender majesty, he says these words with affection: *This well pleases me.* This union of my will with the will of God is an unceasing union, both in great things and in small. As Jesus still directed me in the practice of this virtue, it became impossible for me not to see everything in the order of that same will. Every event that takes place in the universe — the sorrows, the sicknesses, the reversals of fortune or greatness or dignity; everything that our heavenly Father permits for his creatures; in the spiritual realm, all the trials, temptations, all the times of dryness and desolation and even of interior abandonment, in short, all the tribulations of the spiritual realm; and equally all the persecutions, calumnies, mockeries, and humiliations of poverty — all the miseries of human life were revealed to me with such clarity and such divine approbation that it was impossible to turn my will, even for an instant, from its habitual union that God had granted me with his. Oh, how this revelation intoxicated me! I had grave sorrows

[97] French: "je vous vois me supplier, par l'amour que vous portez à mon âme, de me livrer sans réserve à l'impulsion de votre grâce amoureuse," literally, "I see you begging me, through the love you have for my soul, to deliver me to the impulse of your loving grace."

[98] Possibly echoing the litany of love in 1 Corinthians 13:7: "Elle endure tout, elle croit tout, elle espère tout, elle supporte tout," "Love endures all, believes all, hopes for all, supports all."

in my family; among them was someone to whom I owed respect and admiration but whose attitude towards eternity was something I despised, along with my tears and the bitter grief of all those around him; there I was witness to the persecutions that repay virtue, consideration, and patience. But I will say no more on this; I have gone on too long. But it was during this time, full of the subjects of sorrow and bitterness, that, in complete and unfaltering submission, I surrendered to everything that God allowed to happen to me, and everything that happened to those who were most dear to me. I urged my family humbly to submit to God's plan, telling them that their pains can hasten the day of conversion of those who cause the pain, even if that day were their death day.

In all these painful and difficult circumstances, I had on my lips and even more in my heart these words: *What you desire, my beloved Savior, this I desire too: blessed be God. I thank you for showing me your will and for the mercy you have shown towards me.* Jesus had taught me to see all that he had made me suffer as coming from his purest love for me. And then, my good Master accorded me a very special grace, not once but frequently. It was this: whenever Jesus demanded of me some sacrifice of whatever kind, he presented himself to my soul in his sacred humanity, with goodness without equal. Opening his tunic, he would show me his heart saying to me: *It is from here that all my desires for you come, and it is from here that all my invitations for you to sacrifice come.* I was so suffused[99] by gratitude for the love which he witnessed to me that my heart seemed to take wing to respond to whatever he asked of me.

When by God's will persecutions, calumnies, humiliations, and inner sorrows burst upon me, I never had a thought of complaining about them because I received them only as expressions of the love coming from the heart of him whom I loved exclusively. Indeed, I overflowed with joy when I had something to suffer; I had not the words to express the gratitude that flooded my soul, coming always from my conforming myself to the supreme will. This good, Godly pleasure was such in my heart that I would have accepted, out of love for him, the most cruel and ignominious death, after a life full of suffering and sacrifice.

---

[99] French: *pénétrée.*

O my Jesus, my heavenly, my peaceful friend, my Father, my all! I know you are faithful to your promises, and that you command your creatures to love you only out of the love you have for them. It is only our own interests that you have in view as you invite us, so tenderly, to attach ourselves to you. To hold us in your love, you promise us indescribable goodness which the human spirit cannot comprehend. O Jesus! how good you are! You give me a foretaste of heavenly happiness in this world; so ineffable are the sweetnesses with which you fill my soul! [Here ends the manuscript which Eustelle left concerning her life.]

CHAPTER 30

Reflections on the preceding unfinished text.

[Unattributed; probably written by Father Briand or Bishop Villecourt.] The pious Eustelle, arrested by the sickness that took her from the earth, could not press further in the story of her life. It was hardly possible for her to occupy herself with it for a long time, either because of her great weakness or because she devoted the few moments that she had at her disposal either to receiving people who came to visit her, or to work with her hands, or to keep up with correspondence that took up a great part of her time, especially for the two years that preceded her death. She therefore broke off her narration at the moment when it was about to become more interesting.

She recounted her conversion from a life which, despite what she said in her humility, was already a Christian life, to a truly admirable life of perfection and virtue. After a thousand battles between nature and grace, we can see a child of fourteen or fifteen trampling human respect underfoot, renouncing all pleasures, even the most innocent, submitting daily to acts of piety, guarding herself with a vigilance that bespoke a soul consumed in the ways of God. As her journey progresses, her communions become more frequent, and she arrives, by degrees, at the most sublime prayer: it is at the school of Jesus Christ that she was formed. All of Hell rises up against her: a simple working-class girl[100] occupied almost all the demons' minds, not exciting admiration for her conduct, one of an age so tender, but exciting a fury born

[100] French: "ouvrière."

of the sight of a life entirely opposed to that of the world. Her enemies and persecutors were sometimes the very people who should have encouraged or consoled her. But her fervor never wavered amidst all the contradictions she experienced. And at the very time when she was the object of so many external attacks, she was herself her most severe adversary. She imposes on herself every sort of privation, mortification, and penance: and what more would she have added to these pious rigors if obedience had not stopped these movements of her ardor and her courage! For her, it is true, interior consolations amply compensated for the pains she had to suffer from the world or which she imposed on herself for the love of God, until the moment comes when she is deprived of the comforts and mercies which usually accompany pious acts. Jesus allows her to be given over to all kinds of inner torments. Abandonments, inner darkness, dreadful temptations, devouring scruples, desolations, rebukes, anxieties, fears, perplexities, anguishes—there was not a single kind of suffering to which she was a stranger. But this courageous virgin, far from complaining about the evils that overwhelm her, or to ask for some respite from this continual martyrdom, seems not satiated by trials and pains; she desires an increase in her cross; and the heaviest cross she would seem to bear would be to be free of pains altogether. She held an inalterable calm in the midst of these horrible storms, and the serenity on her face would make one believe that she was continually plunged into a torrent—of delights. Witnessing her power one wonders if it is possible on this earth to advance so in perfection, to follow more closely our divine exemplar, Jesus Christ. To this add humility that never falters, purity that evokes the admiration of the angels themselves, detachment from the world carried to the heroic, a faith ever lively, a hope ever unshakeable, a fiery charity, conformity to the will of God that all but effaces her in her beloved himself: what then is lacking in Eustelle's perfections?

She had still to sketch out the last four years of her life; how edifying would that narrative have been for us! Her combats were over, and her divine Spouse introduced her to the intimate sanctuary of his love, *into the intoxicating cellar of his favors*; her winter of tribulation has passed; now every day she unites herself in communion to the object of her love. The God of goodness deigned to communicate frequently with his humble servant, in some of those intellectual visions which, according to the theologians, are not subject to illusion. She was at rest, but her rest is that of the holy love bestowed on her soul as a foretaste of eternal happiness. Her adversaries have dissipated, and those who once persecuted her now show her only veneration and respect. Now people come to her poor home, people of every rank and situation, pressing to ask her advice or begging her for help in their fervent prayers. We read no trace of these beautiful days of peace in this narrative of her life, but we can find them depicted elsewhere. Perhaps this is because, having written here of what she called her wanderings and recounting in detail her hardships, the pious virgin shrank from presenting a picture of the most special favors which had been bestowed on her.

For the last three months of her life, Eustelle, more intoxicated than ever in the love of Jesus, could not unite herself to him every day as she had done; when her weak health presented an obstacle, she tried at least to feed the celestial flame that burned for him. One of her directors had lent her a pious commentary on the Song of Songs applied to the Holy Eucharist. This she read and reread endlessly. Her piety found in it nourishment so sweet that, she said, she would have liked to know the book by heart.

Inevitably, divine love was consuming its languishing victim. Eustelle had nothing left to offer in sacrifice, for she had unreservedly immolated herself to the God of her soul. Her heart had already been consecrated to him by her love most generous and pure; her mind, by the firmness and simplicity of her faith; her thoughts, by her constant meditation on eternal truths; her memory, by her boundless gratitude; her temporal hopes, by her most absolute poverty; her body and senses, by the most inviolable purity; every pretense of vanity and self-love, by her humility most profound; all the joys of the world, by her unshakeable choice of the cross, which she had made her singular choice. Beautiful youth, which is for so many others the springtime of life and the age of pleasures, was for her the term of her exile and the epoch of her journey to her immortal home, for which she sighed and yearned so much. In the moment before she took her last breath, she seemed in a state of ecstasy, her eyes aflame and fixed on Heaven. Suddenly she said to her sister, *Pray, pray to the Lord for me!* As she said these words, she expired. It was on the feast of Saints Peter and Paul that this shining lily was lifted from the field of the Church Militant, to be transplanted in the garden of the Church Triumphant. While the earth was still sweetened by the perfume of her life so short but so full of virtues, we like to believe that Heaven celebrated its happiness; Jesus crowned his spouse so pure, so courageous, so faithful; Mary welcomed her as her dear daughter and imitator of her piety and her love.

Eustelle's letters, especially those that follow in the second and third books,[101] supplement in large part what she did not say in the narrative of her life. She recounts in these letters, with great effusion of her heart, some of the heavenly graces with which she was favored. We note especially 16, 20, 54, 55, 56, 61, 71, and 81. And we observe that all of the letters included in the second and third books were addressed to one of two clerics in whom Eustelle had confided. It is only to these two that she speaks of the favors she received, never mentioning them in letters she writes to other people, no matter how pious they may have been.

We end these reflections with a verbal portrait of Eustelle's outward appearance.

She was tall and held herself with dignity; her facial features had a perfect regularity; her speech gentle and sweet, her language pure, her manners simple but full of propriety and, I would say, dignity. Towards the end of her life, the diminishment of her strength usually resulted in a slight bending of her head, especially when she was seated. Her whole person breathed an air of sanctity which struck all those who had never before seen her.

---

[101] The French editions of Eustelle's writings were published in separate volumes.

APPENDIX
Supporting notes to the 1843 Edition

1. ON THE MARRIAGE OF EUSTELLE'S PARENTS.

From the Catholic Register of the Parish of Saint-Pallais de Saintes.

ON JANUARY 30, 1810 AFTER THE PUBLICATION OF banns announced three times, without any impediment emerging, and after an engagement ceremony between, on one side, René Harpain, harrower and elder son of Michel Harpain, carpenter, and of Marie Bergier, both residents of this parish and, on the other side Marie Picotin, legitimate and minor daughter of Jean Picotin and Madame Garreaud, both residents of the village of La Groin, parish of Marsillac; we, the undersigned vicar, certain that the parties have fulfilled their duty as good Catholics, conferred upon them my nuptial blessing in the presence of Michel Harpain, Louis Picotin, Joseph Picotin, Jean Plurchon, Eutrope Guillot, and Simon Rembert, witnesses known to me who sign with us.

Signed: L. Picotin, J. Picotin, Eutrope Guillot, Rembert, J.-J. Menpontet, Vicar. Verified in the Catholic register of the parish of Saint-Pallais de Saintes, preserved in the archives of the Diocese of La Rochelle, certified compliant.

La Rochelle, January 30, 1843.
+CLÉMENT, Bishop of La Rochelle.

2. ON THE (BIRTH AND) BAPTISM OF MARIE-EUSTELLE HARPAIN.

Extract from the Catholic Registers of the Parish of Saint-Pallais de Saintes.

ON APRIL 24, 1814, MARIE-EUSTELLE WAS BAPTIZED, who was born on the 19th of the same month, legitimate daughter of René Harpain, *couvreur*, and of Marie Picotin, his wife.

Godfather was Étienne Morisson and godmother Marie-Eustelle Bergier, wife of Michel Harpain: in the presence of father and daughter.

Signed: Harpain.—J.-J. Menpontet, vicar.

Verified in the Catholic Register of the parish of Saint-Pallais de Saintes, preserved in the archives of the Diocese of La Rochelle, certified compliant.

La Rochelle, January 30, 1843.
+CLÉMENT, Bishop of La Rochelle.

Nota. Réné Harpain and Marie Picotin had five children: Marie-Anne, born September 8, 1811 (who died six weeks later); Marie-Eustelle, born April 19, 1814; Marie, called Angèle, born March 27, 1817; Charles, born June 17, 1820, and Magdeleine-Anastasie, born February 12, 1824.

3. LETTER FROM EUSTELLE'S PARISH PRIEST TO BISHOP VILLECOURT ON EUSTELLE'S WISH TO WEAR A HAIRSHIRT.

Letter from M. de Laage de Saint-Germain, Curé of Saint-Pallais de Saintes, to his Excellency, Bishop of La Rochelle.

Saint-Pallais, July 18, 1839.

My Lord,

This letter will be given to you by a young person of my parish who is going to La Rochelle to see two of her friends, postulants in the convent of Providence. She seeks your permission, your Grace, to enter the cloister of the monastery. This young woman, my Lord, is a model of my parish, one of those privileged souls whose virtues are rare and sublime. Last year, she expressed to me her desire to take the cilice. But, since I do not wish to decide such matters on my own, I postponed acting on her request until your first visit to Saintes, promising her I would consult with you and arrange a conversation with your Excellency. But coming herself to La Rochelle, she asked me to write to you on her behalf, but, if you were good enough to hear her confession only once, she would be at ease and her soul would better known to you. And

I myself would be more at ease with the decisions I have taken with regard to certain articles which she will explain to you. I have permitted her to receive Communion every day. She lives by the work of her hands, and she is in poor health: two reasons why I am not inclined to accede to her desire to wear the cilice.

Please accept...

de Laage de Saint-Germain,
Curé of Saint-Pallais.

4. TEXT OF THE TEMPORARY VOW OF CHASTITY WRITTEN BY EUSTELLE.

In the name of the most holy Trinity, Father, Son, and Holy Spirit. Prostrate in your holy presence, my lovable Savior, and under the protection of the Holy Virgin, my good mother, of my holy Guardian Angel, my holy Patron and all the Heavenly host, I, Marie-Eustelle, in conformance to the judgment of my Director, vow, for six months, to your divine Majesty, a commitment to chastity, wishing not to live other than for you alone; striving for no glory other than to serve you, and becoming a perpetual victim of your holy love.

Here I am, Lord: all yours. Here I am, totally in your heart, bound by new oaths. Do not permit me ever to break the union that must exist between you and me. It is true I am fallible, but in stripping me of all that is myself and clothing me completely in your merits beyond all value, I have confidence that you will sustain me in my resolution until the day when, disengaged from the ties that bind me to the earth, my soul will rise to you to chant forever your infinite mercies.

[*EUSTELLE'S MEMOIR DATES THIS EVENT ON FEBRUARY 2, 1838, the feast of the Purification of Mary. The most cursory reading shows that this is a temporary vow, to last for six months, but the language of the text, especially that of the second paragraph, "vous me soutiendrez dans ma résolution, jusqu'au jour où, dégagée des liens qui m'attachent à la terre, mon âme s'élèvera librement vers vous," "you will sustain me in my resolution until the day when, disengaged from the ties that bind me to the earth, my soul will rise to you," asks the Lord to recognize her bond until her death.*]

Spiritual Letters of Eustelle

[LETTERS 1–52 ARE WRITTEN TO THE SAME PERSON, THE curé of the parish of Saint-Pallais, Eustelle's home parish, from August 1835 to August 1837, between the tenures of Father Jouslain and Father de Laage de Saint-Germain. His name is not given in the French original, but he has been identified as the Abbé Bichon. Thanks to Anne Auger of the Diocese of La Rochelle for providing his name. The headnotes in the French edition were, of course, not written by Eustelle; they are likely the work either of Father de Laage or Bishop Villecourt.]

LETTER 1

Expression of thanks; Gratitude to God does not dispense one from the gratitude for the instruments of his grace; The cross is the way of holiness; Eustelle's submission to the decisions of her Director; Her sorrows in prayer; Her holy confidence; Her desire for divine love; An anecdote.

N.d., 1838.

To Father A***.

May the grace of the Holy Spirit be with you.

Monsieur,

My sister Angela asked me to thank you for the interest and care you took of her soul, during the very short time that you directed her. Pray to the Lord that he deign continue, augment, and perfect the good begun in her through your ministry. I believe I know what you would say to this:[1] Glory be to God alone. Yes, certainly; but blessed is he whom the Lord uses to do these things, and in my gratefulness to you is my wish that the Lord continue

[1] French: "Je préviens votre pensée; et vous dites," "I anticipate your thought and you say."

and increase what in you serves the glory and salvation of souls.

Let me talk a little about myself, although it is uncomfortable for me to do so.

To tell you the state in which I found myself this past week will be somewhat difficult for me. I have never had such a need for patience. Do not think that I wish to complain; far be it for me to desire an end to my sorrows. How can one see Jesus hung on the Cross and not wish to be with him there? The Cross! This is our way. It is the way of all the saints. And it must be our way, since we are the children of the saints.

As I write to you this moment, I find myself a bit more calm. I talked to my director[2] about the state of my soul, and I told him what I have told you. He told me it was best that I place all of this at the foot of the Cross and not concern my conscience with it. I want, I assure you, to follow in all things the directions of those whom God has given to lead me, but to me this does not seem right. It is ordinarily in prayer, as you know, that I find the consolation I need. But now, it is just when I want to set myself to this exercise that I feel more pain. Blessed be God! Join me in giving thanks to him. I abandoned myself to his good pleasure and, as he delivers my death blow, I hope ever in him, as the blessed man Job said, whose thoughts I am not worthy to borrow. Pray then for me; I never cease to pray for you and to beg for all the graces you need in that sublime state in which the Lord has placed you. May his love be your life. It is at the foot of the altar that the divine Savior delights in spreading the divine fire on the ardent souls of his heavenly community.[3] Ask the good Savior to augment in my heart the desire to be more and more faithful to him, until the day when, reunited in Heaven, we can bless him, praise him, and love him without any fear of ever being separated from him.

Mademoiselle N*** told me a little story that I will pass on to you: it happened on the first Sunday that the abbé said Mass in the prison. After the celebration, the prisoners went up to the sacristy to speak with him and ask him for books, as was their

---

[2] Probably Father Joseph Briand, who agreed to be Eustelle's spiritual director late in 1838, during a short stay in Saintes to preach Advent sermons.

[3] French: "conversation," sometimes found in Philippians 3:20, more typically "Mais pour nous, notre bourgeoisie est dans les Cieux," "As for us, our citizenship is in Heaven."

habit with you. He did not know this and was so afraid that he closed and locked the door, so the poor prisoners turned around and went away. I cannot think they were very happy about that, especially since it was their interest in reading that brought many of them to him. So, do not you lock me out, refuse to give me your counsel: I need it. Tell me if you have a lot of work or if you are comfortable.[4]

I leave you in the divine hearts of Jesus and Mary.

Your obedient and respectful sister in our Lord,
Eustelle.

LETTER 2

Sorrows mixed with confidence; A thousand reasons to love God; His presence; Her desire never to sin and to achieve humility; Visit to the prison; Sacred ministry, images of the labors of the Savior; Promises and sentiments for the new year.

December 28, 1838.

May the Cross of Jesus ever live in your heart.

My soul is presently in a sad place,[5] though it is a little better now than it was. God alone, I tell you from the bottom of my heart, was the repository of innumerable sorrows which have overwhelmed me, for four weeks now. Oh, what a terrible test of my frailty! And who can assure me that I have done nothing wrong?[6] I will not give you the details of my sorrows, because I cannot imagine that you would believe them. I give thanks to the Lord, and I ask you to join with me in thanking him for the very special strength he has given me during this time. If you wish to know more, I will send you another letter. However, far be it from me ever to lose my trust in God. As I write you these lines, I sense a rebirth in my soul, and the memory of Jesus's love for me animates me and presses me to attach myself to him more and more by the sweet cords of his love.

---

[4] French: "si vous vous accoutumez," "if you are accustomed."

[5] French: "dans une triste assiette," literally, "on a sad plate." The same idiom occurs in the next letter. The phrase is used today to refer to a small plate for hors d'œuvres or samples.

[6] French: "Et qui peut me répondre de n'avoir point fait de faute?"

Try then, Sir, through your prayers, to obtain for me a spark of the divine fire, for to live without the love of God is the worst of all miseries. How many reasons have I to love him; I, who perhaps more than another, have been showered with his benefits, on whom his mercy has been showered with such abundance! Let us love a God so good and so liberal; let us love that tender Father whose hand is led by his heart, who chastises only to reward. In desiring his love for me, I desire it for you too. Let us love this good and lovable Master; love him and work with all your might to make him loved. May his love be the sweet rest of your soul, your consolation in the hardships that are an inseparable part of your vocation. Pardon me if I take the liberty to speak thus: it is not my manner, but God knows the reason. I want to love him but I am unequal to the degree of love to which I aspire. I desire it in others; I desire it for you, who already feel its charms and sweetness. I desire it not only for those who, like us, have the happiness to belong to the Church of Jesus Christ, but also for our brothers who, distant from the ark of salvation, live in the shadows, strangers to the truth. Happy are those whom God has placed in this Church, to labor to return to the celestial fold the lost sheep, who, by their sincere return, become the joy of the good shepherd. For me, the least in the house of the Lord, I will not cease to pray that he pour out his most abundant blessings on those whose salvation he so ardently desires, and on those to whom he has entrusted the ministry so important to the sanctification of souls.

I was telling you about the state of my soul, and I strayed from this, as you see. I return to it. For the past few days I have been a little calmer. Certain of my pains have diminished. The holy presence of God, which had seemed then so utterly eclipsed, has begun to rekindle in my heart the fire of charity that had seemed extinguished. Prayer comes a little more easily to me now, but you know that our good Lord has not released me from my cross: he loves me too much to do that. I accept this with joy from his beneficent hand, and I wish for nothing other than the fulfillment of his adorable plans for me. Pray that the divine Spouse of our souls never permit me to offend him, and let us pray that he bestow on me the holy virtue of humility. I fear I am often lacking in this virtue, perhaps even in what I am saying to you. But if I knew there was some good in me—which I do not believe—and you had been tempted to attribute this good to me, I would speak to you no more.[7] I only make these overtures to you because I know your feelings conform to mine. So if you notice any fault in me, tell me and I will correct it.

I went to the prison to visit with the prisoners; they did not seem unhappy to see me. I have permission to go there whenever I wish. Mademoiselle N*** said she will give me the key.

From what you said in your letter, I thought I understood that you had a lot of work to do, even more than when you were at N***. Be of good courage: in this I see you, conforming more and more to your divine Master, who, during his mortal life, was consumed with zeal for the glory of his Father, and who never sought repose from the continual works through which he sought the salvation of the peoples. You do business with a good Master, who pays you, down to the last sou, whatever you have earned in his vineyard. But you know that the reward should not be the only thing that moves us. Are we not already overpaid because he finds us worthy of performing some task for him? Let us always move towards the more perfect. Let his glorification be the motive for our thoughts, our words, our actions, our intentions; and never let a cowardice that should be beneath us make us shrink from the sacrifices which he has the right to demand from us.

I have finished the books of Saint Francis de Sales. I greatly desire your coming. I have many things to tell you that would take too long to explain here.

It is year's end; how rapidly has the year gone! Such graces have I received, and how little to show for them! A new year soon begins, and the Lord makes ready to shower us with new blessings. Allow me, for the new year, to send new wishes for you to the Lord, for your advancement in the ways of holiness, for the conservation of your days, that you may the longer bring about his glory. For you I do not ask for the good things of the world: you know these are both fragile and costly. I thank the Lord for the holy simplicity and the disinterestedness I find in

---

[7] French: "Mais si je savais qu'il y eût en moi quelque bien, ce que je ne crois pas, et que ce bien, vous fussiez tenté de me l'attribuer, je ne vous le dirais pas"; "but if I knew there was some good in me, which I do not believe, and this good you were tempted to attribute to me, I would not tell you." Reworking the final clause seemed to be in keeping with the paragraph's focus on Eustelle's acquiring humility.

you. Both of us love and practice the dear virtue of poverty. Oh! the riches of that virtue! Let us hold to it until our last breath, that we might die in his arms! And, empty of earthly things in our celestial homeland, we can fill ourselves with the sovereign good which is God himself.

Pass along my best wishes to Marie; I wish for her a better year than this last one, and I hope God will grant her this. As for me, I will ask for her everything that can help bring her to holiness. Let her therefore have more confidence in God, more love, and more gratitude for his benefits. Finally, I wish for her what I wish for myself: that God live in my spirit and reign in my heart.

For you, sir, always abide in the heart of Jesus: I find you there often. Such goodness there is in this blessed dwelling place! It is this tabernacle that the plagues of God cannot approach.

Accept, sir, the submission with which I am, in our Lord,

Your respectful sister,
Eustelle.

LETTER 3

Act only for God, in union with our Lord Jesus Christ; Eternal rewards; Confidence in God; Eustelle's shyness prevents her from disclosing her sorrows; The Holy Thursday altar compared to the altar of her heart; The wounds of Jesus: the source of life and consolations; His delay saying the breviary; Discretion; Fruits; Sighs for holy love; Couplets.

April 4, 1839.

God alone! God alone! All for God alone!

How I desire, for the glory of our Lord, that the meaning of these words be fulfilled in you, just as you desire, I believe, that they be fulfilled in me! How can I, by my poor and feeble prayers, establish in you the Lord's divine reign, just as you, through your ministry, establish it in the souls entrusted to your care? Oh! how delightful[8] it is to act solely in the interests of God alone! But is this really always the principle of our thoughts, our words, our

---

[8] French: "Oh! qu'il est doux," "Oh how sweet it is." A literal rendering seemed inapt for the context. Given the narrower, taste-related range of *sweet* in English, this translation will often render *douceur* as "delight" and *doux* as "delightful."

actions, and especially our intentions? So let us apply ourselves, as far as we are able, through the practice of this pure and perfect devotion to God alone, to remain united to Jesus Christ, our divine Head. Through this devotion alone, our actions take on a supernatural and divine merit, worthy of the God who rewards so magnificently those who, out of love for him, keep themselves faithful to the evangelical counsels. This reward awaits us: the crowns are prepared that are destined to encircle the foreheads of the elect for all eternity. Oh! how small are all the sorrows here below compared to the immense weight of glory which God has reserved for his friends! You also have sorrows: accept them from the hand of him who honors you now with a share of his cross. Ask him that I may accept the one he gave to me, just as I desire that you accept yours, that he may be glorified for ages of ages.

How my poor soul has been in a sad place,[9] it seems to me, for some time! But if God permits it, bless him. How often would I need to empty my heart to you, if you were nearby. What unrest, what perplexity, what battles and sorrows of every kind come to assail me on every side! Oh how I fear in all of this to offend God! It seems to me that I am often in need of counsel; and you know my natural timidity when I have to ask for help from someone other than you. God alone, I know, should be enough for me, but he seems to distance himself from me, and chase me away from his heart. But he is the sole repository of these sorrows which consume me. To whom then do I turn? Ah! I hope in him with all my hope, persuaded that he does this for my own good. Implore him, then, that I may not have the misfortune of displeasing him in all of this, and that it is all for his greater glory.

For Holy Thursday we have made a delightful chapel.[10] I should not say it, because it was my work; but my pride, which you

---

[9] "... dans une triste assiette," as in the previous letter.

[10] The "holy Thursday altar" (or, more commonly, Altar of Repose) is a tradition still observed in many Catholic parishes. During Holy Week, a side altar is elaborately decorated, usually in white and gold with candles and flowers, to receive the Eucharist during the Easter Triduum. This *jolie* altar is in deliberate contrast to the stark and minimal appearance of the church, especially on Good Friday and Holy Saturday, the period when the Eucharist will be distributed to the faithful at services but when Mass may not be celebrated. The Eucharist reposes in this temporary altar after the (Holy Thursday) liturgy of the Lord's Supper until it is returned to the tabernacle at the Easter Vigil. And see note 213, below.

well know, should not surprise you. We passed the night before the Blessed Sacrament. I thought well of you and I imagined that you were, perhaps, before Jesus Christ alongside me. But not in Saint-Pallais. O Heavens! My weak hands, by the power that God has given me, erected that altar on which that lamb immaculate, that lamb without blemish rested, out of love for me. I spent three days adorning this place where Jesus Christ stayed. But my heart, the heart which every day becomes a new altar where he wishes to repose — do I take the same care to prepare it, so that it is not a thoroughly unworthy dwelling place for him? This chamber of my heart; is it tidied and swept clean of the things of this world? Oh! I fear it is not. Pray please to our Savior for more and more perfect dispositions to approach the sacrament of his love. Oh how I desire that every heart be set ablaze with a tender devotion to this mystery of his incomprehensible love! Ask this for yourself too, if I am not mistaken, to whom he has sparked this same holy desire; and in the various trials, sorrows, and humiliations that he sends you, find refuge in the holy wounds of the Savior divine. Go and draw from these sources of life the strength necessary to endure the contradictions which God in his mercy visits upon you.

I would like to know if you have come to your senses and are saying your breviary at a more reasonable time. The bad habit you have acquired of postponing your prayers has made you stay up too late: it is not good for Monsieur the Curé, if I may say so. If I were nearby, I would persist in scolding you, in your own interest. Through mere carelessness,[11] you deplete your health by depriving yourself of the sleep you need.

Please do not show anyone my letters. You know the world: you always join prudence to simplicity. Pay careful attention to those in whom you confide, and do not open your heart to every sort of person: this is the advice of the author of *The Imitation*.[12] I will say no more to you on the subject.

I commend myself once more to your prayers. I do not forget you in mine, though they are feeble. May we love God together on this earth as he deserves to be loved, so that one day together we can praise and bless him in blessed eternity.

---

[11] French: "faut d'ordre," "lack of order."

[12] Thomas of Kempis, *The Imitation of Christ* 8.1, trans. F. de Lamennais (Paris 1859): "N'ouvrez pas votre cœur à tous indistinctement"; "Do not open your heart indiscriminately to everyone."

I am sending you the second invocation couplet: you have the first. They are less expressions of what I actually feel than what I would wish to feel. It is as though I am one of those trees which, after they flower, produce only a great deal of bad fruit that uselessly covers the ground. May you become, Monsieur, a mysterious fruit, ripened in the field of the family's father and worthy of being stored in the holy granary for eternity. I ask for you God's good grace; ask the same for me. My God! How I feel in my soul the great desire to love God so much! Pray for me, that I may obtain this sacred love, may his divine ardor consume my soul and yours, that we might die for love of him who dies for love of us.

The Confraternity of the Blessed Sacrament at Saint-Pallais is no more, due to the small number of associates and their small amount of devotion. As a consequence we no longer have either exposition of the Blessed Sacrament or Benediction on the second Thursday of the month. Oh, how sorry I am for that! Is it possible that the faith is so feeble?

Other tasks call me: it is time to finish. I am in our Lord, yours and mine,

Your respectful and obedient sister,
Eustelle.

X. Invocation a l'Esprit-Saint	**Invocation to the Holy Spirit**
Air: *Sur cet autel, le Roi de gloire.*	*On this altar, the King of glory.*
Esprit-Saint, descends dans nos âmes;	Holy Spirit, come into our souls,
embrase-les de tes ardeurs;	enflame them with your passion;
fais-leur goûter ces pures flammes,	let them taste your purest flames,
blesse-les de tes traits vainqueurs.	and wound them with your saving strokes.
eclaire-nous de ta vive lumière,	Light us with your living light,
Divin Esprit consolateur;	Divine Spirit, our Consolation.
viens ranimer l'esprit de la prière	Revive your spirit in our prayers,
dans notre cœur,	in our heart,
dans notre cœur.	in our heart.
O Marie! O notre modèle!	O Mary, O our model!
Epouse de l'Esprit d'amour,	Bride of the Spirit in holy love:
du haut de la gloire éternelle,	from everlasting glory's heights
reçois nos accents en ce jour.	hear our prayers upon this day.

Garantis-nous, ô notre unique asile,	Guard us now, O holy refuge,
des traits de l'Esprit séducteur;	from the wiles of the Seducer.
rends à ton fils, de plus en plus docile,	Bring to your Son, ever more willing,
tout notre cœur,	all our heart,
tout notre cœur.	all our heart.

LETTER 4

Eustelle is charged with preparing the rooms for ill persons receiving the Eucharist; Our Lord must know the choice he makes for her to honor him worthily in the Sacrament of the altar; Desire; Gratefulness; Tranquility; Overture; Forty hours; Union of prayers.

February 7.

Monsieur the Curé has just revived a practice in the parish that existed before the Revolution. When the Blessed Sacrament is brought to the sick, a person is appointed to go ahead to the home of the person who is to receive the sacrament to prepare, in a suitable manner, all that is required for the visitation. You have sometimes noticed, I am sure, how little care was taken, especially among the poor, to ensure that everything is prepared in a decent manner, befitting the holiest of our sacraments. So now there will be, in each village of the countryside, a person charged with this function. And you can guess who was chosen in Saint-Pallais! I hardly believe myself to be worthy of this job, but you know I accepted it without complaint. I bless the Lord a thousand times that, despite my unworthiness, he chooses me to play a role, even a small one, in the grandest, most august ritual of our mysteries. How much gratitude do I owe him for all he grants me in this occupation! Given my place in life, what more could he offer me?

Accustomed as I am simply to share with you what happens in my soul, and assured that you would not abuse my confidence, I will tell you that, a few days ago as I made my act of thanksgiving after Holy Communion, I felt a lively stirring of joy flowing in my soul, something that has not happened in a long time. It seemed to me that our Lord made me understand, in a most particular way, that he wanted me to devote myself completely to honoring him in his sacrament of his love, that I should make this my sole, my exclusive labor; for, while there are souls that may serve him faithfully, he finds only a few that accord him this interior devotion which alone is able to form true worshippers in spirit and in truth. Concerning this calling, I show our Lord the depth of my misery, how I am unworthy of such a predilection, an unworthy sinner. But he made me understand the infinite riches of his mercy, that he loves to bestow his gifts on his weakest subjects, when he found them committed to the execution of his plans. Oh, with what feelings is my heart penetrated after so many favors! What can I say, imperfect as I am![13] Bless the Lord with me. How can I have all the love he deserves? How can I love him and make him loved with the love he has for himself? On this subject, I am but a feeble heart, a feeble voice. How little to offer back for all these benefits, especially for the benefit of the Eucharist, a benefit I am permitted to share in every day! The thought of this makes me tremble and at the same time awakens my thanksgiving. What a terrible price to pay! Do I comprehend the price of such a signal favor? Ah! God grant me this grace. I will join you in blessing him for preparing us, through his power, his wisdom, and his goodness, for the heavenly, life-giving bread which he sent from Heaven to nourish us in the desert of this life. What eternal acts of thanksgiving are owed to him, in Heaven and on Earth, for all his infinite gestures of generosity.[14] Ah, let us try to make up, as much as we can, for the coldness and indifference that so many Christians have towards him in our days. Oh, how delightful it is to deprive oneself of the company of creatures and so to enjoy instead the delights of conversation with him! How he repays and even rewards us for this deprivation, if that is what it is! As if all the advantage is on our side, as if he somehow needs our feeble homages to enlarge his glory and increase his happiness! I rejoice to God for your zeal for this holy practice. Make sure then that everyone you talk to consecrates themselves to the love of the divine Savior, and pray for me that he will send me the grace to do the same.

Our Forty Hours prayers are now just over.[15] We have the Blessed Sacrament exposed almost three days because of the

---

[13] French: "Le moyen d'y répondre, étant aussi imparfaite que je le suis," "the way to respond, as imperfect as I am."

[14] French: "pour toutes ses infinies libéralités," "for all his infinite liberalities."

[15] Forty Hours (recalling the forty hours between Jesus's death and resurrection) continues to be an observance in many Catholic parishes, a time

feast of the Purification, the anniversary of the Confraternity.[16] Our Lord sent me many graces in those holy days; I had lots to do there.

May our Lord give you perfect holiness. Become the great saint that I desire you to be. I join you in praising, blessing, and loving the divine heart of Jesus in the most holy Sacrament of the altar. Before the altar: that is our place, our home, our *chez nous*; let us abide there now, waiting to be welcomed into our glorious home, where we will abide for all eternity.

I need to be encouraged by your good counsels, for I am so weak! Do not refuse me. Command me then to love God, whom I have so many reasons to love. My God! Is it possible to be so cold towards him, who is so aflame with love for me? I cannot cease talking about that love.

Receive, Monsieur, my assurance of the respect with which I am, in our Lord, your sister,

Eustelle.

LETTER 5

The good dispositions of a person excite her joy; Consolations; Love for love.

April 23, 1838.

May the peace of the Lord be with you; may you possess in all your doings this lovable peace; may it be for you and in you a continuous celebration, wherein your hungry and thirsty soul may quench the hunger and thirst you have for the God of all justice, in which alone is found the bread of the elect and the source of the living water that springs forth to eternal life.

I do not see a great need to write to you in this moment, having nothing out of the ordinary to share with you. However, it is N*** who provides the occasion. The news of her change which you announced to me and which gave me great joy made me write to her to express my great satisfaction. I bless the Lord a thousand

period when the Eucharist is continuously displayed for public devotion. In the Middle Ages and after, the Eucharist was often moved to the Altar of Repose during Forty Hours; see note 10, above.

[16] The Confraternity of the Blessed Sacrament; see Letter 3.

times and call on the Lord to send her perseverance. And you, Monsieur, pray to the good God for her.[17]

I know that you are not quite fully in control of your will to do what I have charged you to do; you will do it in Heaven, as I will. In the meantime, let us obey God and those who represent him down here.

Many people, both men and women, approached this year for the Pasch, which brought great happiness to Monsieur the Curé. Praise God! I ask him with all my heart to send them the grace to continue.[18]

In this moment, my soul both rejoices and suffers at the same time. I rejoice because the Lord makes me feel his divine Presence and fills my soul with consolation; but this is only the upper part. Interior sorrows and temptations ceaselessly upset and trouble the lower part of the soul. And I am always in fear that these consolations are false and come from the devil. Nevertheless, I abandon myself entirely into the arms of God. He will do with me what he wants. I place the care of my salvation into his hands. Many days ago, alone before our Savior, on a kneeler in the chapel of the Blessed Virgin, I sensed within myself an abundance of consolation of which, no doubt, I was unworthy. I did not forget you. I begged our Lord to pour into your soul something of the consolation which I had received. Oh, how good is the God of Christians to those who love him! And that prophet was right to say that, from here on Earth, God would make them drink from the torrent of his delights.[19] Let us therefore render him love for love. Oh, that I would love to open my heart here and pour out what seems to me to fill it. But duty calls and, if time permitted, I would not cut off my letter.[20] Let us love God! I sense a sort of relief in repeating these words: Let us love God! Yes, let us

---

[17] This paragraph and the broad timeframe seem to reference one of Eustelle's apprentices who began to emulate her piety. See Thompson 160–61.

[18] The paragraph alludes to parishioners returning to the church to complete their "Easter duty," the obligation to go to confession and receive Communion at least once between Ash Wednesday and Trinity Sunday.

[19] French: "il les ferait boire au torrent de ses délices," echoing Psalm 36:9: "et tu les abreuveras au fleuve de tes délices." Compare the Vulgate: "torrente voluptatis tuae potabis eos." The word choice of "torrente" suggests that, as elsewhere, Eustelle is showing familiarity with the Vulgate.

[20] French: "C'est un besoin pour moi, et, si le temps me le permettait, je n'en finirais pas," "It is a need for me, and, if time allowed me, I would not end it."

love him on Earth until the end of our days, and die loving him with this love.

I can tell you though that I told him everything that happened in my prayer, and the particular graces that I received from our Savior. Ah! If you knew how frequent they are! I will speak to you about all of this.

I send you this little tracing of my thoughts, which are not, certainly, unknown to you. God grant that they be sincere, as are, I hope, my intentions. Abide and live in the divine heart of Jesus, to whom be honor and glory for ages of ages.

I have sent you a song; it is the song of the holy Virgin of which I have spoken to you. Truly you will soon have enough of my scribblings[21] to make quite a little collection.

I am, with respect, your sister,
Eustelle.

LETTER 6

Desire to increase divine love; She devotes the month of Mary to a cleric's deliverance from his terrors; Peace; Light; Thanksgiving; A holy friendship is a treasure; Temptations; Union with God; Detachment from creatures; Vow of humility; Thoughts of God: sweet refreshment; Ascension; All her thought is for the tabernacle; Confidential letters; Couplets.

May 9, 1838.

May the Spirit of our Lord come before you and always accompany you, in all your actions, that you may bear fruit worthy of eternal life, through our Lord Jesus Christ.

My wishes for you are always the same, that is, for the sole purpose of his greater glory, desiring only his dearest interests, the desire to see reigning in every heart that sacred fire which he came to bring to Earth and by which he wishes to set the whole universe ablaze. It is especially your heart I wish to see consumed by this sacred fire, only for the glory of our common Master. I know that you hold this fire, perhaps more than you know yourself; but you know that we can increase it more and more until we have reached the last stage of perfection that one could reach in this life. It is this degree of perfection which I desire, of which I am unworthy, that

[21] French: "barbouillages," "daubs, smudges."

I wish for you with all my heart, so that you can love him for me and for all of those who do not know him. Oh, how I rejoice in God and for God because, in that degree of perfection, you are specially charged both to love God and to make God loved. And, believe me, I do not cease to beg the Lord to send down an abundance of his heavenly blessings on the souls committed to your care, so that, in this life they become, as Saint Paul said of the Christians of Corinth, your joy and your crown, until, in Heaven, they become so many jewels forming the diadem that God reserves for your faithfulness.[22]

Our month of Mary is very beautiful this year: Monsieur the Curé offers lessons which are attended by a very large number of people. On this, I tell you I have done these exercises for your intention, wishing to solicit a great grace for you. I will not tell you what it is until you have received it. You have no idea what it is. The Blessed Virgin once obtained a similar favor for a saint whose name I will not say, because if you knew the name you could guess the grace. It is neither a particular virtue achieved nor a fault corrected: have no anxiety over it. Only join your prayers to mine, and continue to have the tenderest love for Our Lady, more and more complete confidence in her, and, I hope, despite my unworthiness, that God, to whom I make my request, will deign to hear me and grant what will be for her greater glory.[23]

Let me tell you now about the state of my soul. How good is our Lord to pour on me so abundantly the gifts of his mercy! How he knows how to calm the tempest and send calm and peace in its place! This peace, of course, is not a perfect peace; that can only be in Heaven: only there will it be perfected. For three weeks the Lord has showered me with his consolations. The lights and

---

[22] Presumably a reference to the "imperishable crown" of 1 Corinthians 9:25: "Or quiconque lutte, vit entièrement de régime; et quant à ceux-là, ils le font pour avoir une couronne corruptible; mais nous, pour en avoir une incorruptible"; "Now whoever competes lives by their regimen, and for these, they do it for a corruptible crown, but for us, to have an incorruptible crown." The sentiment and language more closely resemble 1 Thessalonians 2:19: "Car quelle est notre espérance, ou notre joie, ou notre couronne de gloire? n'est-ce pas vous qui l'êtes devant notre Seigneur Jésus-Christ *au jour* de son avènement?" "What then is our hope, our joy, our crown of glory? It is none other than you, who will be before our Lord on the day of his coming."

[23] Note to the French original: "It seems that the grace which Eustelle solicits for the cleric is his deliverance from terrors of divine justice [des terreurs de la justice divine] from which Saint Francis de Sales was freed by the protection of the Blessed Virgin."

graces which he sent into my soul sometimes so suffocated it that I yearned for my soul to make me cry out to everyone, "Love God!" Sometimes the very yearning exhausts me. I seek to satisfy this desire at the foot of the holy altar, calling on our Lord to light the sacred flames of his love in the hearts of persons who have the humility to come to me to ask my feeble counsel. You know there are very few people to be found with whom to share these sentiments: we must be careful in this. A faithful friend is a rich treasure, says Scripture; but discovering one is difficult.[24] Mary found such a treasure in Elizabeth, her cousin. How frequent were their conversations! What confidences they shared! What wise counsels from the prudent Virgin! Their virtue only increased in these holy exchanges. When they separated, their friendship did not break because God was the beginning and end of it.

How I regret — God's will be done — not being able to open my heart to you as often and as fully when I could, back when you were at Saintes! God willed it so; to him be blessings. It can only be for the best. Do not think that, because of this, I do not share with the Lord all that happens in my soul; not to inform him, for he knows already, but that he share his lights with me, when I am bereft of the counsels of those placed here on earth to stand for him.

In speaking to you of the graces which God accorded me in prayer, I want also to speak of the temptations which I endured at the same time. The more the Lord manifested himself in the superior part of my soul, the more I felt sorrows in the inferior part, without understanding why; I knew only that by them, God wanted me to recognize my weakness and make me understand that, despite his favors, it is he alone who merits glory for, without his help, the slightest breeze would batter me, knock me over.

What I have told you in relation to the graces that God has accorded me must not give you a better opinion of me. In these matters I am nothing; I feel it every moment. Pray for me: you see the price I will need to pay for all these benefits. Oh, how I fear! But I place my confidence in God, and after him, in Mary. Yesterday after communion, I experienced a most particular calm. I had absorbed myself in the union which must exist between God and us, who have the happiness of nourishing ourselves every day on the flesh of his adorable Son. The understanding was given to

---

[24] Echoing Sirach 6:14.

me in that moment, in a powerfully clear manner, what it meant to be in perfect union with God. I have never understood it so clearly. Oh how the soul veritably loses itself to subsist in God when it possesses this most desirable union! How far am I from this union! But I desire it all the more. Ask God to grant it to me, and I ask the same for you. Let us detach ourselves from creatures; let us empty ourselves of all that is not God. Let us see him alone in all created things, and soon the Lord will grant our wishes.

On the Feast of the Ascension, I renewed the vow of humility that I had made a year ago. Pray to the Lord that he make me faithful to the practices which he imposes on me, faithful to the end of my life. This virtue is most necessary for me on the path on which God is leading me. You have seen yourself, perhaps, how I begin to lose humility as I dilate my sentiments to you so readily. But then, if you did not know me, I would not act in this way. Only you know so much, and I wish I could tell you more. I feel relief in my heart because you know me so well, and I can speak with you completely at ease about the love of my God.

What can I tell you in conclusion? I think of the God who always thinks of me. Let us think of him always. How sweet and consoling the memory! Oh Father, how sweet the refreshment in our sorrows is the thought of the presence of God! What delightful recreation to be in his presence! Now it is with him that I pass my recreation. There is no greater happiness than to be there, on Sunday, alone with him; and, notwithstanding the desire I have for everyone to worship Jesus, it pains me to see people coming to the church bothering me in my solitude. And when I am alone before the altar, I often think about you as well at the feet of the Savior; and I beg him grant your wishes, uniting us in blessing him. Such childlike devotion! What do you think? If people other than you heard me, they would mock me, but I believe that God does not mock me, and that is enough for me. As you wish for me to belong to God, that also is my wish for you. To God, then, always, more and more to God in our times; to God in eternity; to God for eternity, where we will enjoy every good thing and rest in the essence of Father, Son, and Holy Spirit. So be it.[25]

I am, in our Lord who is our Brother, your unworthy sister.

Eustelle.

---

[25] French: "Ainsi soit-il"; here and elsewhere (e.g., letter 15) Eustelle uses this in place of "Amen."

P.S. I will tell you that today, the Feast of the Ascension, Father Briand preached at Saint-Pallais. The celebration was very beautiful, and there were lots of people there. I myself was a little fatigued; I stayed at church all day, tending to my little occupations. Oh how good to be there! Why would anyone not stay there all day, since Jesus is always there? I must tell you that the solemnity awakened in me the greatest desire for Heaven. All my thoughts center on the tabernacle where, despite my unworthiness, it opens every day for me; holding, in the feeble species of bread and wine, he who is the joy of the blessed in Heaven. In his presence, I experienced a foretaste of the paradise of delights whose promise we are given in Holy Communion.

I say again what I said before about my letters: understand they are for you alone. My God! What other things I have to tell you! Could I stop myself?[26]

So onward![27] Let us love him whom we have so many reasons to love. And pardon me as I allow myself to make this recommendation to you. It does not suit me, but you will excuse my simplicity.

So you do not want me to send you the verses that you added to the hymn: *I see the august tabernacle opening*? Is this because the verses are your own composition? Such humility! I am a bad example to you.

Please write to me. I do not know what I am writing anymore. It is after midnight; my quill will not write anymore and I am falling asleep. Good night.

LETTER 7

God's favors; The happiness in conversing with him; The Spirit of the world; Eustelle complains about the trust placed in her; She passes part of the night at the foot of the Blessed Sacrament; Exhortation to holy love; Temptations; She desires the purity of the angels.

June 8, 1838.

Approach Jesus Christ, who is the living rock; and you yourself, like a living rock, rest on Jesus Christ to build a spiritual edifice,

[26] French: "Est-il possible que je ne le puisse pas!" "Is it possible that I cannot?" The context here seems to be Eustelle imagining not being able to trust her correspondence's confidentiality.

[27] French: "Allons!" "Let's go."

in which to offer God sacrifices that are pleasing to our Lord Jesus Christ.[28]

How good is the God of Israel to those who seek him,[29] desire him, and in all things conform their will to his! How good is the God who is pleased to pour out, in such great abundance, the gifts of his mercy on those whose hearts are filled with the desire to attach themselves more and more to him, despising perishable things and renouncing both the world and themselves! This is wholly the effect of his grace, for we find nothing in our own accounts but our very great unworthiness. Can I hope for these graces from the Lord, whom I serve so imperfectly, who responds so poorly to the countless benefits that come to me every day? My whole life ought to be one continuous act of thanksgiving and gratitude. And you, who are the dispensary of the favors which God has granted to me, deign to bless him and give thanks to him with me. God wills that no self-love ever creep into what I am telling you about this. It seems best that I tell you all of this simply, and sometimes, so that you might reassure me in these matters, because I always fear that the Demon might involve himself here. Also, I need to add that I feel an indescribable joy in conversing with you in this way; I would not speak so with anyone else except my director.[30] What a consolation to be able to devote oneself to the loving God! Why ever converse with anyone else? What happiness for me, when I find someone I can talk to like this!

There are two people for whom I urge your prayers in this moment; they are very well moved to turn to God, but the spirit of the world holds them captive and prevents them. I take all possible

---

[28] Closely echoing 1 Peter 2:4–5: "Et vous approchant de lui, qui est la Pierre vive, rejetée des hommes, mais choisie de Dieu, et précieuse. Vous aussi comme des pierres vives êtes édifiés pour être une maison spirituelle, et une sainte Sacrificature, afin d'offrir des sacrifices spirituels, agréables à Dieu par Jésus-Christ." "And you approaching him, who is the living rock, rejected by men but chosen by God and precious: you also are living rocks to be build up to be a spiritual edifice, and a holy priesthood, to offer sacrifices of spirit pleasing to God through Jesus Christ."

[29] Echoing Lamentations 3:25: "L'Eternel est bon à ceux qui s'attendent à lui, *et* à l'âme qui le recherche," "The Eternal is good to those who wait for him and to the soul that seeks him."

[30] This letter is dated during the tenure of Father de Laage de Saint-Germain, who took over the parish of Saint-Pallais a year earlier. It should therefore be safe to assume that the cleric mentioned here is Father de Laage.

interest in their souls and I grieve for their lack of courage. They told me yesterday, in tears — which made me happy — that they believe they lack the courage to follow me. Pray for them: your charity must extend everywhere.

On this occasion, I will confess to you that I feel another pain. It is that so many persons place their trust in me: you know that there are those who speak to me of their inner life and others who ask advice of me. Why do they pay themselves with counterfeit currency? I fear that this sort of thing will bring me pride. At the same time, it seems to me that the pure intent of the glory of the good God is what animates me in these dealings; but still I suffer from the regard that I cannot help seeing people have for me. Ah! This is only because they do not know me! God grant that I am in his eyes just what I am in the eyes of the world. Ask God that I only do what he asks of me and that I behave in these circumstances with great simplicity and humility. And tell me, once again, what you think about all of this.

What I have wanted for so long has finally been granted me: to spend part of the night in solitude in the church. How happy I am to be alone in the presence of our good Savior! I could never wish to be separated from him! Oh the joys I taste, the lights I receive at the feet of the Eternal, especially in the silence of the night! There I am illumined by the feeble light of the lamp which, consuming itself before God, makes me realize that I too must burn and be consumed in his presence, to honor, by my complete annihilation, the grandeur and sovereignty of his Being. What an honor for me to have been able, in these solemnities of the most blessed Sacrament, to construct the altars on which he deigns to rest as a blessing for us: and to bless you, too, because I asked this of him. Oh! the graces and new favors accorded to me during these holy days! I have prayed to our Savior that you have a share of these spiritual goods that I feel flowing so abundantly into my soul, sure that you can make better use of them than I. I can guess what you must think of what I am saying here, but it is the truth. Bless then with me the God so good, so magnificent, for I can now cry out, like the prophet David: *My heart can no longer hold the feelings that fill it: it is to the King of Heaven that I dedicate my songs.*[31]

---

[31] Psalm 45:2.

I just received again the holy blessing of our Lord. Why should he stop with me?[32] I pray once again that he pour out his blessings and benefits on us and on the whole universe. Love him for you, and love him for me, who do not love him as I ought.

In everything I have just said, remember my unworthiness, my miseries, and how imperfect I am; at every moment I would offend God if he did not support me. In this moment I still feel violent temptations, though they are not as frequent as before. May God grant that I come away from these temptations with a clean conscience, and that his glory result from it.

About the temptations, I must tell you that, at this moment, the Demon raises up new ones for me, which bother me a lot. I want to share this with you, that you may see how evil he is, this monster from Hell. But I understand his ruses and hope that he will not seduce me. I will speak to you about all of this in person. I assure you that this does not trouble me at all, that none of it surprises me. Pray then for me, that these troubles do not become greater and that I will not succumb to them. These are two temptations opposed one to the other and yet they come together.

I have sent you the life of Saint Rose;[33] imitate her, and you will be a great saint. This is what I wish for with all my heart.

The permission you have obtained for me to touch the sacred vessels[34] has already well served me several times, the sacristan being absent. It has been assigned me to prepare what is required for the holy sacrifice, which I did with great joy in my soul, despite my unworthiness. I love to think that, like the Blessed Virgin, I am employed in the service of the temple, as far as my vocation permits, and this thought only renews my gratitude. But to be worthy of such holy labor, I must have the purity of that Blessed Virgin, and I am far from having that. O my God! I do not think enough of the account I must render of all these favors given me

---

[32] A crux; French "Pourquoi a-t-il donc fallu le laisser?" "Why did it have to be left?" The surrounding sentences suggest that the meaning here is that God's graces should not be reserved for Eustelle alone.

[33] This book is most likely Jean-André Faure, O.P., *La Vie de Sainte Rose, du tiers-ordre de S. Dominic* (Marseilles, 1692). This is one of the first biographies of Saint Rose of Lima (1586–1617).

[34] Laypeople were generally not permitted to touch the chalice or paten, the gold vessels of the Eucharist, though the bishop could grant exceptions for sacristans and under other circumstances. The prohibition disappeared after the Second Vatican Council.

for my salvation; my mind is full only with enjoying the happiness that the labor brings me. May the Lord deign to adorn me with a purity like that of the angels, to approach so close to and receive so often the God of the angels, so that I may come to bless him forever and ever.

I pray you awaken me by your counsel and by the sentiments of your heart more and more to love him for whom we should sacrifice ourselves entirely and without reserve. It is by that utter sacrifice of ourselves that we achieve a taste, in this life, of that unchanging peace which still is no more than a prelude to the divine peace that will flood our souls in the long and unending eternal ages. I wish this for you, believe me, with all my heart. Pray! Pray for me, for I pray every day for you, more than once a day, for you.

I am off to Mass. Au revoir.

I am always, in our Lord, your obedient sister,
Eustelle.

LETTER 8

It is better to ask for conversion than for good health; Do not wait for the last days of your life to prepare for death; Dying as a fruit of holy love, the commencement of true life.

N.d., 1839.

May God be with you!

Have the kindness, Father, to offer Mass next Thursday, if you would, for a sick person who wishes to regain her health. For my part, I regard her cure as humanly impossible and, while asking God for the cessation of suffering, I believe it is better to ask for the graces of conversion for which she has need, so to prepare her to reconcile herself with God. It is in this final tribute, that separates us from everything here below, that we are made to perceive and understand eternal things, things of unchanging eternity. Oh! how good it is not to wait for the last moment to prepare for this! On the contrary, what goodness it is, after a life full of love, to expire in an act of that same love! Oh precious death! To die thus is not really to die but truly to begin a new life. It is up to us to gain this blessing; let us try to achieve it, for it is in our power. Let us go with courage.

I end my vigil; it is not so long as the last one, which lasted until almost one o'clock in the morning. Tonight, only until eleven o'clock. I am going to do my reading, to awaken love for my God. In this reading, by exciting myself in this holy love, I will ask it also for you, for whom I desire it more than for me, because you will put it to better use.

Your humble, simple, and pure servant,
Eustelle.

LETTER 9

Changing situation.

N.d., 1839.

May the spirit of our Lord descend upon you and remain with you forever.

I have been notified of your next change.[35] I am dying to know what you think of it. I have only the time to say this word to you. On Sunday, in my dear sacristy, I will write to you at length. Be well in spirit until the day when we are reunited in Heaven to love together this God whom we love on earth.

Adieu. Your sister in our Lord,
Eustelle.

LETTER 10

Vows of holy love in our exile, awaiting the consummation of that love in our homeland.

N.d., 1839.

May God give you his blessing, not in some measure but in all its plenitude, and according to the extent of his infinite goodness. Ah, may it increase in your heart, that heart, his living tabernacle where he reposes every day in loving mercy,[36] the purest flames of his holy, Heavenly love. I burn with the desire to see you aflame.

[35] This probably refers to Father A***'s transfer to another parish; see Letter 11 below.

[36] French: "avec complaisance," "with complaisance."

Let your desire for me be the same. May it please the Lord to answer us, living this life of love here below, to go to Heaven to see God, to love him and possess him without fear or cloud. There we will endlessly lose ourselves in God, to relive in God God's own life. I wish this for you.

Adieu: I am, in our Lord, who is our brother,
Your sister Eustelle.

LETTER 11

Conformity to the will of God makes us the same as God; Eustelle must go to La Rochelle in a few days; The Presence of God; Preparing oneself to love him forever.

Saintes, July 7, 1839.

That the most blessed and most just will of God be accomplished in everything, surpassing everything.

You have guessed why I place these words at the head of this letter. It is that you know what a gift[37] it is for us to conform ourselves to the will of God. I believe that if we could possess this virtue perfectly, we would quickly acquire perfection, since God and we, in this conformity, would always do the same thing. What an unchanging peace must flow through a soul so truly resigned! What more could we desire? Nothing more, for we would desire only what God desires. Let us try then so to dispose our wills. For me, I need to do this now; if you need to, do the same.

Is it true then that you are to move away from me? God be blessed! Nevertheless, I will it since God wills it. I would like to know if this change pleases you. I suspect it does not: you would rather be at Saint-Pallais. With all of this, you will be much better off than at N***. I too have a trip to make, to La Rochelle; I shall go next week.[38]

When you are exiled on your island, we will not forget you before God. Let us try to reunite one day in Heaven, to love and

[37] French: "quel prix est." The more direct translation, "what a prize it is," seemed inappropriate to the context.

[38] The northwestward journey from Saintes to La Rochelle on the coast is about 80 kilometers or about 50 miles and would take the better part of a day by wagon (at about 5 mph). See below, Letter 17.

praise and bless him who has been such a frequent subject of our talks here on earth.

Many people here are sad that you are moving so far away. But then, God wills it. I am filled with the thought of him, as I finish this letter. In spirit, I am standing with him, in his adorable presence. Never lose sight of it, this holy and divine presence! We ought to be continually before him. We think of those we esteem; we think of them before God, in whose heart we are like a single fish in the vast expanse of the ocean. That fish loses itself as it sinks into the abyss of the waters; in the same way, we must lose ourselves, annihilate ourselves in the infinite being of God, the Author himself, the beginning and the end of our being.

Desiring with all my heart to love the God who is infinitely good, I desire that you do the same. You do love him; but I pray that you love him more, and do the same for me. Let us try to be able to say, one day, in eternity: *We see and taste, in the city of the Lord, of the God of virtues, as we have been told.*[39]

Adieu. Accept my assurance of the respect with which I am always, in our Lord,

Your sister,
Eustelle.

LETTER 12

Wishes for the new year; The honor rendered to the saints returns to Jesus Christ; It is sweet to rest upon the divine heart; Calm after agitations; God inspires Eustelle to open her heart to a cleric; The thirst to love and to make God loved; Faith is weakening; Prayer on that subject.

28 January 1839.

May the blessings of the Lord pour out on all, abundantly and forever.

I ask for that grace for you unceasingly, every day. Please God answer me. But, at the beginning of the year, God is witness to the wishes that I address to him, to see you more and more holy and at one with his heart. May he increase in your heart the measure

---

[39] Echoing Psalm 34:9: “Savourez, et voyez que l’Eternel est bon; ô que bienheureux est l’homme qui se confie en lui!” “Taste and see how the Lord is good; O, happy the man who confides in him.”

of his most perfect love, the most complete detachment from the things of the earth, the zeal to bring glory to him through the salvation of souls: in a word, the fullness of the gifts of the spirit of love.

Monsignor the Bishop sent Monsieur the Curé relics for our church. I am in charge of embroidering the cloth on which they will be placed. It is a good bit of work, but in laboring for the honor of the saints, we honor our Lord, the worthy friend of our souls. It is a way to adorn the house where he lives for us, for me, yes! For me. Oh, how that thought enlarges my love! Oh that this house is not worthy of his grandeur! How attractive his tabernacle ought to be for us, since it houses him who is all love, and all his love is for us! Glory and love be to the divine Master and to his dear brother, beloved of our souls! May he bless you when you are at his feet, set you ablaze when you possess him. Like the bride of the Canticles, let him sleep on your heart. His sleep will put you to rest; his closed eyes open yours; the beating of his heart will make yours beat the faster. Let this echo be an act of adoration and honor.[40]

In this moment when I am writing to you, my soul is happy. After the painful and numerous trials which God alone has witnessed, I am at peace, as much, I believe, as one can be in this life. Ah! Too many, there are too many favors coming to me in this place of exile! Often my soul cannot contain them. Father, I do not believe I am doing wrong in speaking to you this way. I do not think of this as self-love; when I open my heart to you it comes wholly out of the simplicity which you know of me. But I have another thing to tell you.

Father B*** preached Advent at Saint-Pierre. I was inspired by our Lord to uncover my soul to him, concerning my spiritual direction.[41] It was after asking to know the will of God that I was brought to take this step. I asked Monsieur N*** if he would hear my confession[42] and he was immediately ready. I confessed to him three times, and he was good enough to give me all the time I needed for the preparatory prayers that Heaven inspired

[40] Loosely echoing and expanding on the Song of Songs at various points.

[41] French: "pour ce qui concerne la direction," "as far as direction is concerned." This is Father Briand, mentioned above (Letter 6) for preaching on the Feast of the Ascension in 1838.

[42] French: "m'entendre au tribunal de la pénitence," "to hear me at the tribunal of penitence."

me to say. We reciprocally blessed the Lord in the fulfillment of his holy will in this process. And the road that God has laid out for me was not unknown to that cleric. I await a chance to speak to you later about all of this. He considered and analyzed all that I told him and he said to me that, in all of this, he saw nothing other than the Savior's loving predilection[43] towards me. I am not the same any more, to be fixed in this way. I have not been so for a long time! You cannot form an idea of his faith or his love of God. As for me, his words set me afire, and I can see that I have everything to gain by talking to him. I will go to him every two weeks now, to share what is happening inside me. It is not that I suddenly lack confidence in the one who usually directs me: God knows that. But our Lord wishes in certain situations in the soul, that we receive lights from one or another channel through which he communicates. We recognize this by a special attraction, an interior voice that cannot deceive us, because there is nothing in it of the fantasies or foolishness of light, inconstant souls.

Do not forget me in your prayers; ask for humility in me: that is the ladder of Heaven,[44] and the foundation of saintliness. I need it, in proportion to the graces I receive. Oh, how deep and perfect it should be in me! In expressing the sentiments of my heart to you, I feel that it is not yet satisfied: I do not feel relieved of the thirst to love God and to make God loved by others. Why can I not communicate the devouring fire that consumes me! God knows these are my most ardent wishes. Why are they not granted! I am happy when a day does not pass without my doing some service to my neighbor. Glory to God alone. Me, I am nothing, can do nothing. Ah, let us pray then, ceaselessly, for the spark that will shine over the earth and never be extinguished. Oh, how weak it is now; how pale is its glow!

O Jesus, beginning and end of the faith, rain down on the universe the sacred flame, illumine hearts with its divine fire, drive off the shadows of error with its light, bring back to the sheepfold the sheep that are lost, and those that are separated

---

[43] French: "amour de prédilection," "love of predilection."

[44] Echoing Jacob's dream of a ladder, Genesis 28:10–18; also *L'échelle du Ciel* (*The Scale of Heaven*), title of a Latin treatise by Guigo II, prior of the monastery of Grand Chartreuse (1114–80). Prior to the late nineteenth century, the work was often ascribed to Saint Augustine or Saint Bernard of Clairvaux. An edition in French by Mabillon was available during Eustelle's lifetime.

from their heavenly flock. I beg you, O my Savior, by the depths of your infinite charity[45] and by the divine outpouring of your precious blood.

I close by uniting myself in spirit with you, loving more and more our beloved Jesus. How sweet are his charms; how powerful his love! Let us grow in that holy love at every instant of our lives until the day when we abandon this strange shore, when it will be given to us to enter into the everlasting repose of eternal truth. Then there will be no more shadow, and no more need for faith or hope, for all will be perfected. Charity alone! In an ocean in which we will lose ourselves, to bless as one, by his gifts, God eternal. Amen.[46]

My parents and my sisters offer their respects; pray for all of us, and count on my prayers for you.

Eustelle.

LETTER 13

Eustelle speaks with the Bishop; Her sweet rapport with the adorable Eucharist; A life of holy love; The death of a well prepared young person.

August 26, 1839.

May God reward all of you for your negligence.

I would forgive you for your silence if it were due to your mortifications, but I do not believe that was the reason. Perhaps you would laugh at me if I told you what I was thinking about this. But I have to keep that quiet; your charity towards me is so well known!

I spoke to Monsignor the Bishop last week, for he is at Saintes at the moment. I had the honor to go to confession to him, which

[45] French: "par les entrailles de votre charité infinite," "by the entrails of your infinite charity." Echoing Colossians 3:12 "entrailles de miséricorde," "entrails of mercy." More broadly, an attempt to evoke the blood and water that issued from the wound with the lance in the Crucifixion narratives: see John 19:34.

[46] Two notes on this paragraph: Eustelle uses "charité" and "dilection," more "religious" synonyms for "love" that do not share the physical connotations of "amour." Also, the paragraph ends with her first use of "Amen." These and the first person plural verbs seem to suggest that Eustelle is possibly thinking of herself as composing a prayer.

brought me true consolation. I felt the unction of grace from his words and felt their effect in my soul. Blessed be God! I did not tell him everything that I wanted. Monsieur the Curé spoke to him before I did and told him I was not well. That was wrong of him, because Monsignor the Bishop believed him.

The hour approaches at which I present myself before our good Savior. What a precious grace for me, a poor creature, to be admitted into an audience with the King of Heaven and earth!

What sentiments should move me, in the moment it is given to me to be allowed to converse with the sovereign I AM, in the company of the celestial spirits?[47] So close to this blaze of love, should I not be consumed by holy ardors? Why then is my heart so cold? Surely my unfaithfulness is at fault: pray for me.

The Lord floods me every day with an infinity of graces, and how weakly do I respond![48] Ask God to enlarge his love in my heart, as I ask him for you. Love him greatly, the God of goodness; love him for those who do not love him, and for me, who does not love him enough. Oh, my God! How to obtain it, this divine love? I know the means: pray that God grant me the force to put the means into practice. I come together with you to praise and bless Jesus in the holy Sacrament of the altar, where his divine heart is wounded with love for us. Pray that he wound our heart with the same blow, and that, in dying from this wound of love, we may live anew in that life of love that has eternity as its ending. Let us always stay in the divine heart of Jesus and the lovable heart of Mary.

My sister charges me to say a thousand things for her.

A young person to whom you had given her first communion has just died. She died rather suddenly, but she was, I believe, well prepared to die: she had received Communion on the Feast of the Assumption and she fell sick the next day, but she could not go to confession because she could not let Father know.[49] She was very pious. She received Extreme Unction.

Believe me to be, in Jesus and Mary, your
Eustelle. — Adieu.

---

[47] French: "pouvoir m'entretenir avec l'Être souverain," "to be able to converse with the sovereign Being."

[48] French: "auxquelles je crains de ne pas répondre," "to which I fear to not respond."

[49] French: "parce qu'elle n'avait pas sa connaissance," "because she did not have his knowledge."

LETTER 14

To carry the cross with joy; Detachment from all that is not God; A dream; The fire of divine love.

September 5, 1839.

God be with you.

I am glad you are fine where you are. Try to be at peace there. But you know that our Lord, whom you love, will not let you leave there without a cross. Carry it with joy, this lovable cross, following him who, through sufferings and humiliations, is become the model of our true greatness. He makes me feel the weight of the cross, too: bless him forever! He alone is the repository, and, I hope that, despite my unworthiness, he will become the reward. I pray for you every day; pray also for me. In praying for you, I wish only for the greater glory of the Lord, for whom I would sacrifice all that I am. Ask the Lord for me that I am able to detach myself from all that is not him, and I ask the same grace for you. May God hear my prayers!

I am making you a pall.[50] Because you are going to come here, you can take it back with you. I understand it is not easy to find one where you live.

I had a dream that you were dead, and in my dream, I said, "Let us see if Father keeps his word and comes to tell me if he is in Heaven." Well, fortunately it was just a dream.

It is the eve of the feast of Saint Pallais and I must go and adorn my altars. Love God well; make him well-beloved and in Heaven your reward will be to love him perfectly. Ah, when will we love him as he loves us? May God grant my desires on this subject!

Your sister,
Eustelle.

---

[50] A white linen square stiffened with cardboard and usually adorned with embroidery used to cover the mouth of the chalice during Mass to keep out foreign objects. See Letter 25 below.

LETTER 15

Jesus deserves an expression of gratitude in proportion to his benefits; To banish excessive fear; The gold of charity; Holy love consumes Eustelle's heart; Jesus Christ asks perfect detachment of her; Faith alive; Purity required for Heaven; Correspond ceaselessly to the grace; The feast of All Saints; The Eucharist, ocean of all good things.

November 16, 1839.

May Jesus in the Eucharist be all to you in all things.

Your heart understands these sweet and tender words that Jesus, in his love, is pleased to make heard by the faithful soul, when, as he speaks to the heart in the silence of prayer, he deigns to intimate the desire of his own heart, that, taking his delights with her, he wants her to be all in all things.[51] But when he requires, for his part, a reciprocal love, then what emotions should animate our souls, thinking about the ineffable means which he uses to draw us to his love? And, in reflecting on the numerous benefits he has accorded us, can we not apply to ourselves the words he speaks to us through the prophet: *What more could I have done for my vineyard that I did not do?*[52] What more could he do in the vineyard of our souls that he has not done? Yes, for us Jesus has exhausted, in effect, his power, his wisdom, and his goodness. The greatness of our gratitude should expend, somehow, all the power of our souls. Ah, at least let us render love for love to him. But the bonds that unite us to him do not allow us to love him in a common or ordinary way. So let us aspire, every day, to a more perfect love. Let us be fervent, for it is the Lord whom we serve, and the sacred obligations that we have contracted, each in our own state, are the nails that attach us to the cross of our tender Master. How great is our responsibility! But we must not lose confidence. Do not lose confidence, especially those of you who fear too much. The chaff is mixed with the good grain. Pull up that weed: I do not like to see it grow. Instead, love God. I pray always that our Lord fire your heart and mine with his celestial love. I want you to tell me that the sweet flames of that

[51] For "heart," the French of course has *cœur*, a masculine noun. The usual practice of this translation is to use the pronoun "it" when "heart" is the antecedent. Here, however, Eustelle is deliberately using the feminine pronoun with *cœur* as the love object of Jesus, likely evoking the Song of Songs.

[52] Isaiah 5:4.

love consume your heart. It is not that I do not know that you already love him much, much more than I do; but I want you to love him even more. There is nothing in the temple of Solomon that is not covered in the purest gold.[53] So let us cover our souls in the purest charity, so that there remains nothing in us but acts and expressions of our love of God.

The Lord in his mercy always treats me with his kindness. I feel that he wants his love to live in me, but that, if it remains, my weakness will not be able to endure the workings of his grace. Sometimes I think, perhaps, that the Demon is tricking me. I cannot express to you all the consolations that flood my soul in prayer, in Holy Communion. Sometimes I feel exhausted by the desire to make God loved, to love him myself: and when I am not able to do this that I desire, God alone knows how I suffer.

Lately our Lord has made me understand that he loves it when I talk to him; he wants me to enjoy his company, as he enjoys mine, but he demands perfect detachment from me. You can imagine the sentiments that quickened my heart from this intimation. How I love to approach the tabernacle, where reposes the symbol of the love of the one God for mankind, the throne of grace where love effaces the brilliance of its grace!

Sometimes I have extravagant thoughts; for example, I seem to see the holy ciborium approaching me, where the God of love resides, and I picture myself holding it in my hands.[54] O my God what a thought! How real it seems![55] I press the cup of love to my heart... but, what am I saying? Is this favor not granted to me and to you every day? It is too much, too much for this life! Often I pray either that our Lord moderate his gifts to me or that he give me the strength to sustain them. All things seem so clear to me now that I feel that I no longer have the gift of faith. I labor in these final days for the degree of purity that I need to attain to enter Heaven. Our Lord has made me understand this degree: I confess to you that I was rather terrified, believing it impossible to achieve this degree in this life; at best, it is accorded only to a few people to pass directly from this exile to our true homeland. So let us avoid the smaller faults and anything that could impede our possession of the happiness that we expect. God

---

[53] Echoing 2 Chronicles 4:22.

[54] See Note 50 to Letter 14, above.

[55] French: "Que n'est-elle une réalité!" "Is this not a reality!"

does not work on us only now and then; he works unceasingly through his grace, so let us not cease then to work continually for him. Ah, stay close to him, in the sacrament of his love, as close as you can. And I often join with you to praise him and bless him, begging him to shower you with his graces.

My sister wants to tell you lots of things. Our feast of All Saints was very beautiful: there were 146 communions that day at Saint-Pallais. God grant, as I wish, this for all people. On this occasion, the weak health of Monsieur the Curé suffered from the workload, but the contentment in his heart, so full of zeal, made up for his fatigue.

Pray for me, I beg you: I need it. You understand what I ought to render to God for what he has given me. My mind goes again in this moment, to the holy temple where he stays: my heart is transported there. Why can I not be at his feet? Not until tonight! O divine Eucharist! How I love to repeat those words; how my soul finds delight in them! Let us immerse ourselves in this ocean of every good, and, like the bride of the Canticles, let us respond to the shadow of our well-beloved until the day when, asleep on his breast and tearing away the veil that hid him from us here below, it will be given to us to see him, not under the veil of the sacrament, but in all the splendor of his glory, and to stay there for all eternity.[56] So be it.

I am, in the Sacred Hearts of Jesus and Mary, your sister,
Eustelle. — Adieu.

LETTER 16

The power of heavenly love; Eustelle is its victim; it affects her health; Profound calm; Jesus shows himself to her in the form of a child; Eustelle opens her soul to a fervent cleric; Fruits produced in the soul by the divine spouse; Lights drawn from the foot of the tabernacle.

February 26, 1840.

All for Jesus. — May the grace of the Holy Spirit be with you.

Yesterday a person said to me, speaking about you: "Our traveler will not come to us for our Forty Hours." Ah, please come

[56] French: "et cela, dans les profondeurs de l'éternité," "and that, in the depths of eternity."

when you can. What things have I to tell you! May they be to Jesus's glory! He is my witness, the Master divine, that I desire nothing else. Let him be your only goal as well. It is a delight to do all things for him!

O love of Jesus! What power you have over the hearts of those who subject themselves to your delightful dominion![57] How powerful you are! Before you death itself is nothing but weakness.

O Jesus my Brother, let us be bound by the bonds of love, for love alone elevates the soul to its beatitude, Jesus. It is in the adorable sacrament of the Eucharist that the fire of love is found; it is from this sacred source that the waters spring up to eternal life; this is where we must go to quench our thirst. It is to this tabernacle that we must go to find the spotless lamb who alone can restore our souls to the whiteness of their original innocence. Poor Jesus! He is not loved; he is not known! Such blindness! Oh, the stupid hearts of humankind! Why can I not bring all hearts to submit to the yoke of his holy love? O my brother in Jesus! Love him, then; live only for that love, yes, love only for that love. Jesus himself is the well-beloved; he is the dear Brother, the tender friend who urges us to love him. For myself, I tell you I am his victim. I will tell you simply that if Jesus continues his favors toward me, I feel my heart could not withstand the force of this divine fire. For some time now, my health has been affected; I can see this, and I cannot but believe that the love of Jesus, which is sometimes so strong, has contributed. Our Lord told me once during prayer that I am his victim. I understood the sense of his words, and so I abandoned myself to his pleasure, that he might consume me as he wished. Now my soul is calm; its trials have dissipated, and I have no more fears. Jesus reigns in me; I am his and I love him only. O Holy Eucharist! It is you who take me away from myself, you who transport me to the verge of the celestial region. How I love you! You are my delight! You make me die, to live again and better. Let me die at your feet, for death is a gain to me.

Yes, Father, death alone can put an end to the pains I suffer in the desire to love and be loved. Jesus alone is the depository. You cannot imagine the particular graces that he gives my soul in prayer. A few days ago, I saw the beloved Savior in the monstrance taking on the form of a child. In one hand, he held his divine

---

[57] French: "à ton doux empire," "to your sweet empire."

heart; the other hand he held out to me in the most touching fashion. This vision went on for nearly a quarter hour. Later on, I will tell you all about it in detail. I shared all of this with Monsieur N***,[58] who recognized, without any hesitation, that this was the action of God.

Oh, I am happy to have met him. His soul inspires me with the deepest interest because it so loves Jesus. He told me that he gave glory to Jesus for having inspired in me the thought to make my conscience known to him. I bless God myself; there is everything to gain from being close to him. He just left to preach Lent[59] a hundred and sixty leagues from here, but he allowed me to write to him to make the state of my soul known to him, and I rejoice in being given this permission.[60] If you knew his faith, his charity, his humility, his simplicity! He is just what my soul needed.

The holy bride of the Canticle of Canticles said this in her dream, in speaking of her husband: *Let my beloved come into his garden, and eat of the fruit of his trees.*[61] Do you understand what these fruits are; they are the fruits that Jesus cultivates in each faithful soul, when it becomes docile to his tender voice. Take note that these fruits are gifts and virtues which are in you, are our beloved fruits, which, on the Lord's part, are a completely gratuitous act of liberality. How, unworthy as we are, would we be able to merit these gifts? You surely know that there is nothing within me that could attract the fruits that Jesus made to grow in my heart; they are, with the full force of that expression, fruits of my Savior's trees. I wonder only that he chose my soul to do these things. Ah, believe me that the desire for his glory animates me completely, entirely; and if I say these things to you, it is to make known his goodness and glory. Do not say that he does not want

---

[58] I.e., Father Briand.

[59] French: "prêcher le carême," "to preach Lent." This refers to a custom, begun in Rome, of gathering each day in Lent at one of a list of stational churches for prayer and preaching. Father Briand seems to have been chosen to be one of the selected homilists for what is, in effect, a pilgrimage throughout the diocese. See Letter 18 below. 160 leagues is about 300 miles, almost certainly an exaggeration.

[60] Note at this point in the French original: "We have much to rejoice in ourselves, since it is to this correspondence that we have a great number of letters that comprise this collection, whereby we may learn the most intimate dispositions of the servant of God."

[61] Song 5:1.

you to love him as much as I do. Come often to the foot of the tabernacle; you will learn there, from the sovereign priest, the duties imposed on you in your sacred ministry. There too you receive light. Let us go there together: I join myself to you, to love Jesus with you; I enfold your soul, at this moment, in the heart of Jesus. There we think, we adore, we love as though in Heaven, though with less perfection.

Adieu; pray for my soul. And count on my prayers in return for you. Tell me where you are with God. I am out of paper.[62]

Your sister in Jesus,
Eustelle.

LETTER 17

Have more confidence than fear; Interior sorrows are only a part in our sanctification; Eustelle offers herself in sacrifice for the conversion of a sinner and for peace for an agitated soul; Act familiarly with Jesus; Satisfy the thirst that consumes him; It is delightful to talk to one's love; Monsignor the Bishop asks Eustelle to take care of her health.

March 23, 1840.

May the cross of Jesus fortify you; may his grace sustain you.

I long to know if Jesus heals your soul, inspiring confidence in you that is greater and more filial. We do not have, as you know, so much reason to fear as we have reason to rely, more than you do, on the mercy that stems from the love that our good Savior has for your soul. Oh, you love Jesus, I am sure of it; I know it. Do not say that it is his design that you do not love him as much as certain chosen souls for whom he has a perfect love, and from whom he demands a perfect love. Me, I do not say this; I think of it differently. The external sorrows which are the fabric of your days, these are what they are. They are part of the order of the divine will, in my view; consequently, they enter into the plan of your sanctification. So be hopeful then. And as for your interior state — and it is this, I believe, that you are most concerned about — place it once again in the heart of our good Jesus. Pray to his Sacred Heart to recover what you have lost, for he is, you know, the source of every good thing, and he desires only to give

[62] French: "Le papier me manque," "I miss the paper."

these to you. I assure you, I see your heart more clearly than you think; I see both your little virtues and your little imperfections. So make the former grow and pull out the latter. My God! How I desire to see you a great saint, for the glory of our Master! and the pains I feel when I see that you persist! I speak particularly of interior pains. I do not cease to pray, every day, that God take you more and more fully into his heart. I am going to tell you one of my most intimate feelings. It concerns on the one hand the state of the soul of N***, and on the other, the sorrows I see you suffering. Ardently desiring, for the glory of Jesus, to see both of you become what he wishes you to be, I made him a sacrifice of my health and even my life, begging him, not considering the imperfections of the victim, to grant me the fulfillment of my wishes, both for N*** and for you. See clearly what moves me to do this. If you do not find it appropriate that I offered this for your soul, do not trouble yourself over it; and if you see in yourself something displeasing to the Savior, get rid of it at once, with the aid of his grace. What must we not do to be at peace with Jesus? Courage and confidence! Think how good our friend Jesus is! I am content in the hope that I have that Jesus will grant what I ask of him for you. So make yourself familiar with him; give him little caresses: he loves that. Poor Jesus! Ah, my brother: give him something back in compensation for all the indifference towards him by Christians today.[63]

Sometimes in prayer, during Holy Mass, my dear friend makes me hear these words: *I thirst.* O merciful Savior: you are thirsty? You are thirsty? I understand this thirst: you had thirst, in the bosom of your father, before your incarnation; you were thirsty during your mortal life; you were thirsty in the Garden of Gethsemane; you were thirsty on Calvary, and, now, I hear you once again, calling out that you are thirsty. Ah, I understand: this thirst will not be satisfied until the end of the ages.

O my brother in Jesus, let us share the thirst of our dear benefactor, for he thirsts for our heart, he thirsts for our love. How could we refuse him? Ah, I seem to see him, at the base of the tabernacle; he looks at me with goodness and my heart turns to him. O heavenly friend, whom my soul loves! But, O my God! Do I love him enough? Pray then, that I might love him more. Why can I not die in his love! Ah, this is my hope; let us win it for me.

---

[63] John 19:28.

The time conversing with you goes by so fast. It is such a delight to speak of the one we love! How are there so few persons with whom we can speak of Jesus? Why did he separate us? I think of our conversation on Thursday evening, when you were with us. It is only with Monsieur N*** that I can speak thus, but, at the moment, I do not have that consolation. Jesus wished it. One day we will be reunited, not to speak of Jesus but to see him and love him eternally. So love him well then and tell me all about that love. May the good Savior illumine, occupy, and expand our soul.

I went to visit Monsignor the Bishop; he scolded me a lot because he said that my sickness was my own doing. He absolutely wants me to get fat this Lent. And so I obey, because this is what he wants, and I have already begun. Still I thought as I returned home: he does not know the cause of my illness. If only he knew how the love of Jesus treats me!

Think of N***'s cilice. Pray for my soul. Be sure to tell me how you have been since our last talk. Do not fear that you grieve me in telling me of your sorrows. I would know them anyway, even if you kept them from me. I leave you in the hearts of Jesus and Mary, where I take my rest as well. May they bless you and love you.

Your sister in Jesus,
Eustelle.

LETTER 18

Eustelle's charity; The sentiments it inspires in her.

April 6, 1840.

All for Jesus. May the grace of the Holy Spirit be with you.

Tell me if your soul is better and, in general, how you are doing with all your troubles. Why would you be afraid to tell me about it? I have never seen anyone like you. Nothing you have said to me — nothing you could ever say to me — would trouble me, I assure you; none of that would turn you, in my mind, into either a greater saint or a greater sinner. I know that you do not owe me a window on the state of your soul, but you know that I am interested in it only for the glory of God. I want to know you are happy and full of love for him. I would be especially consoled if I knew you as you want to be, how Jesus wants you to be. I pray often that the God I love illumine you, capture and possess you, animate you more and more with the sweet zeal of his glory, and make you alive with the sacred flames of his divine love. May it be the unceasing food for your soul, this fire so sweet. Why can I not share with you what Jesus has given me? But my God! You already love him more than me. It is for you to reveal to me your superabundance.

On this subject, I urge you to go and spend before the holy tabernacle as much time as you possibly can. I know you do this, but do it as often as possible. How charming the tabernacle must be for our souls, since it contains the blessedness of the saints in Heaven, the one and only Good, Jesus, our friend, our brother, our spouse, our all. Oh, how happy we are to be able to love him! Let us love him, then, for as long as it is possible to love him here below.

Monsieur N***[64] is here at Saintes for six days because he is indisposed. He could not continue the Lenten stations that he had undertaken. You can imagine his disposition.[65] Lately he is feeling a little better. I shall go to see him; my soul needs it.

Tell me please about our Lord. I leave you in the heart of Jesus, where I rest with you, to love and bless our beloved.

Adieu.

Your sister in Jesus Christ,
Eustelle.

LETTER 19

The generous zeal of Eustelle; God lets her know that she still has some time to live; A sweet martyr of divine love; Jesus does not want to have secrets from her; Favors granted to her through the Holy Eucharist; Sacred wound; Confidence; Thanksgiving; Need for communication; The spirit of the world.

May 11, 1840.

May the grace of God be with you.

I do not know if you received my letter, and I do not know if you are alive or dead. I forgive you though. I want to have the charity

[64] I.e., Father Briand.

[65] French: "Jugez sa contrariété," "Judge his contrariness."

to believe that your heavy duties were the reason for your silence. For me, I do not forget those I care about, only for the glory of Jesus, for whom I would give my life. So, why do you leave me like this, without telling me how you are doing? You deserve that I no longer pray for you. But my thoughts do not run in this direction. Consumed by the desire to sacrifice myself for the glory of God and seeing my own weakness, not able to share in the work of evangelization and yearning to see every priest a priest according to the heart of Jesus,[66] I have made to the loving God the sacrifice of my health and my life. Begging him to accept this most imperfect of victims, I have unshaken confidence that he will attain the fulfillment of his desires for each of these premier members of the Church. Now I find that I often ask the one from whom the thought came to soon put an end to my sacrifice. Monsieur N***, to whom I relayed this, said in response: "My daughter, the Lord will answer you; I dare believe it." But Jesus made me understand that my time had not come; I had still to suffer for his name. It would be impossible to tell you all the favors which he ceaselessly showers upon my soul. I will simply say that the love of Jesus makes a martyr of me by his works in me. Jesus alone is witness to this interior torture, which is delightful to me all the same. Monsieur N***, who knows all about this, told me it would cause me to die. Blessed be God. I await the day; I am resigned.

Our good Savior, whom I want to love and whom I want for you to love as well, said to me one day in prayer: My daughter, I no longer want to have any secrets with you. Be faithful to me; do not force me to separate myself from you; I desire to confirm you in my grace and my love. At another time, when I was concerned that I perhaps did not have enough devotion to the saints, he said to me, Fix your mind and heart on the sign of my love.[67] That admirable Master knows well how I am faithful to the teaching of

---

[66] French: "pressée de les voir tous des prêtres selon le cœur de Jésus," "eager to see all of them as priests according to the heart of Jesus." The sense of the passage is that Eustelle is explaining that she has offered her suffering and her life for the salvation and purification of priests, confiding in Father Briand that she was willing to give up her life for this intention.

[67] French: "Je veux que le gage de mon amour t'occupe d'une manière toute spéciale," "I wish that the token of my love occupy you in a very special way." The sense and context here seem to be that Jesus is challenging Eustelle to push aside her scrupulosity about venerating the saints and focus on the signs of Jesus's favors to her.

Holy Church concerning the honor, veneration, and confidence one should have towards the saints, and our Lord is the master of giving to each individual soul its own particular yearning and particular graces of different sorts. How many times did he permit me the favor of seeing him under the Eucharistic veil? Several times, after completing my act of thanksgiving[68] and distressed to leave our Lord alone in the Sacrament of the altar, I placed my heart and my affections before him, uniting myself with the joyful spirits who ceaselessly surround the throne of love. Often then, this celestial friend did me the grace of presenting to me his sacred feet to kiss before I had to leave him. This favor is always present in my mind, and it seems to me that I can still see those adorable feet.

Ah, all I could possibly tell you is nothing compared to all that Jesus works in me. What to do with a heart so incapable of returning love for love? But Jesus gave me this heart of mine, and I offer it back to him as it is. O you, whose soul is often present to me, beseech our tender Savior to enlarge it and set it ablaze with a fire more and more ardent. O Father, how can you heal this wound which the love of Jesus made on a heart so unworthy of him, owing to its past infidelities? How could I deserve the caresses of the divine Spouse? Ask him to hear me for the whole universe. Ah, I can say, to his glory, that he often grants what I ask. But the more my desires are fulfilled, the more they are reborn and become more and more ardent. Pray that I never put any obstacle in the way of the designs of the adorable Jesus. And know that, despite my own shame, I do not forget you in the heart of our dear brother. So let your every effort be to arrive at a more perfect union with the divine Savior. He loves you; have no doubt. Respond to that love, but do not worry if you do not arrive quickly at the state you desire. It pains me to see that you do not have a perfect enough confidence, as though you do not know Jesus. O good Savior! . . . our heart belongs to him. I ask him, for you and for me, that, if our blood should flow, that it flow only for him. I love him; he is my witness. Tell me how you are;[69] I will go at once to talk to Jesus; I will converse with him about your soul, and he will answer me.

---

[68] French: "action de grâces." Acts of thanksgiving were individual prayers of thanksgiving for the gift of the Eucharist, typically made in silence for a few moments after the end of Mass.

[69] French: "Dites-moi dans quel état vous êtes," "Tell me what state you are in."

I continue always my dialogue with Monsieur N*** and gain great spiritual advantages from him; with him I am as though with a tender father on whose shoulder[70] I pour out my entire soul. Oh, I bless God for bringing me to find him. I am going to ask him for permission to confer with him every week, for, when my heart is so full, I need to open and empty it, and I can only do this when I am at ease with him. You know well that there are very few people in this sad age who are aware of the ways of the soul.[71] Ah, how I groan before God! Oh, how small is the number of those who truly adore him in spirit and in truth! But Jesus is always the same. Let us make up for them. I join with your supernatural wishes. And one day, after our exile, we will bless the Lord: I have no doubt.

All of your friends here greet you and ask that you remember them in your prayers. Mademoiselle N*** is amusingly troubled in her head; she makes us laugh a lot. But she does not like me because she says I am dead to the world and that, for herself, she still wants to live there. It is truly a comedy. She does not like anyone who would remind her of other sentiments.

Monsieur the Curé's mother is always ill, and he himself is not very strong.

I leave you in the love of Jesus, and I wish that, after this life, he will introduce you into the eternal secrets of his divine charity, so that you can drink in long drafts the living water that is its inexhaustible source. To this desire is joined my firm belief that this very happiness is reserved for you.

Keep this letter in the utmost secrecy. Do I need to ask this?

Your sister Eustelle. — Adieu.

LETTER 20

She asks for news; The effusion of charity.

May 18, 1840.

Glory be to Jesus. — May the peace of the heavenly spouse be with us.

They say here in Saintes that you have been appointed parish priest; I do not know where, or if this is even true. You do not write and so we stay in ignorance. So, please, now, tell us your news.

---

70 French: "dans le sein duquel," "on whose breast."

71 French: "certaines voies."

Let us just see if you will think about doing this, much as I myself think about praying for your soul. Yes, I pray Jesus, the tender and merciful friend, to enlighten you, to set you afire with the sweet zeal of his glory, and to fill you with unbounded confidence in his goodness. I pray that the sacred fire of the tabernacle consume you; let him be the column of fire that leads you through the tenebrous desert of this age; so that, fortified every day with the bread of life, you will arrive, like Elijah, at Mount Horeb, where at the summit you will lay yourself down and where it will be given to you to contemplate Jesus, our dear divine Savior.[72] I commit you to his heart; there you shall find me. It is my sanctuary. Already I hear him, calling us. How he blesses you and loves you!

Adieu: I leave you once more in the peace and love of Jesus, our God.

I am, in our Lord, your sister,
Eustelle,
unworthy servant of Jesus.

LETTER 21

She endures trials, in the example of Jesus Christ; She opens her heart in her troubles; Confidence animates her; She asks for prayers, before deciding to write about something that concerns her; A confession of her unworthiness; It is a delight for her to recount the divine mercies; Illness; She believes that she will live a while longer.

May 26, 1840.

All for Jesus.

May the peace and friendship of Jesus be with you. The interest that I take in your soul and the share that I take in your sorrows move me to write to you, although I cannot give you the consolation in the position in which you find yourself and which, considered from the perspective of the Faith and of Providence, could be an occasion of merit for you and as a reward for Heaven. But let us embrace more perfect thinking:[73] may the glory and the love of Jesus, of that master full of love for us, who tells us that the

[72] The passage references Elijah's journey to Mount Horeb in 1 Kings 19:8 ff. and the pillar of fire in Exodus 13:21–22.

[73] French: "Mais allons au plus parfait," "But let us go to the more perfect thing."

disciple is not above the master, bring you encouragement in the persecutions, pains, and trials that Jesus sends you, that he wants you to accept from his fatherly hand. Have no doubt: this grace of encouragement comes from the heart of Jesus, and, although it is true you have some reasons for anxiety, I believe that you greatly increase them by your own doing. You are who you are by the will of God: why would you want to change that? My advice: when you can, go and talk to Monsieur N***. I do not believe that you are able to open your heart completely to Monsieur the Bishop, and you need to communicate. I urge you to do this as soon as possible. And have no fear; you can confide in him your whole soul. I am sure he will soon dispel all your anxieties and uncertainties. If you only knew how good and full of light he is! It is God himself who wants you to suffer the pain that has so unjustly descended upon you. So then be filled with confidence and love for that Jesus who loves you, who treats you like his friend. Oh, love him! Do not fear him. His love is the remedy for every ailment. Jesus is our center; let us lose ourselves in him, whatever we may be, with all our miseries. He is so good! Oh, what confidence I have, for you and for myself! But I do not only hope: I believe that one day we will praise God together in an eternal day. Do not say you have doubts as, perhaps, you might be thinking now.

I have one thing to tell you, and it is to you alone that I reveal this. And I demand the greatest secrecy from you, as with everything I have said or written to you. Think back to the day you engaged me to write of the diverse workings of God on me. Monsieur N*** told me the same thing, with a cheery tone.[74] I expressed all my repugnance to this, and I do not know how I will decide to respond. You know what a labor this is for me. I told him it was necessary to consult our Lord on this matter, and he was of the same opinion. Please join us in prayer, so that God's will may be accomplished in this matter. Pray to God that, if there is any danger in this to my soul — which I do not believe — that he let me know so that I can avoid a pitfall so dangerous to virtue and so flattering to self-love. Oh Father, please believe fully that if I agree to this request, the only

[74] French: "en riant." Eustelle is remembering when Father Briand and the bishop instructed her to write a memoir of her life, an instruction she disliked and even opposed but which, for some reason, Father Briand made with a sort of show of joviality. Neither the context here nor the biographies provide any further insight into the explanation for this odd detail.

desire that moves me is the greater glory of Jesus in my acceding to the will of my director. There is no need here to tell you about my unworthiness: this you know. You know I am but nothing, even less than nothing; for I sin against him who created me and who, even so, never ceases to pour his graces on my soul in such abundance. But I am unworthy, both now and later, to occupy the thoughts of creatures; quite unworthy I know: I say this without humility. However, if God, who is pleased sometimes to use the weakest of instruments to glorify him, desires that I obey his voice in obeying his minister, then I promise in all simplicity that, for his greater glory and in the desire I have to inspire love for him, I will take on this writing, in which, I hope, Jesus would deign to direct my pen, for I leave all the concern for it to him. I confess to you that it would be with a very lively joy—and the most ardent of desires—that I might have the opportunity to speak of the numberless mercies Jesus has deigned to gift his unworthy servant. It is in this that it would be a delight for me, at my ease, to share the feelings that the love of Jesus, my dear Savior, communicates to my soul. So yes, I confess to you, I do desire this, in this way. This God so good always continues, time and again, to accord me the most special favors in prayer. Pray that I answer this call; pray for what I have just told you, and do not speak of it.

I was sick in bed when I received your letter. I got well around Easter, but by the feast of Saint Eutrope,[75] I had fever and chills, and since that time I have had a bad cough. Last Sunday I was feeling worse but I am better now. I am no longer bedridden but I have a sore chest and am still coughing. N*** says I am better at coughing than at writing. I do not think I am going to die quite yet. I think our Lord wants me to languish a few years before my sacrifice is achieved. Whatever he wants.

It is time to end my letter. What do you think? I leave you then in the wounds of Jesus; may they keep you for eternity. Pray that I may love the Lord greatly, and I pray the same for you. Jesus will answer us, and we will arrive at the port of eternal salvation. God bless you and love you.

I am, in the heart of our physician Jesus Christ.

Your sister,
Eustelle. Adieu.

---

[75] Easter in 1840 was April 19; the feast of Saint Eutropius of Saintes (third century) is April 30.

LETTER 22

Exhortation to open his heart; Eustelle's health weakens her more and more; Submission; Holy love makes her lose sight of the pain.

June 1, 1840.

Jesus lives!

I spoke about you to Monsieur N***; he is more than willing to receive any communications you decide to send him.[76] I urge you to do this and I can assure you from my own experience, that you will receive a healing balm, as I did, from his conversation. May I always benefit from his good advice!

I told you in my last letter that my health has become a little better. But, for the last week, it became very bad. I do not know if our Lord wants to take me at my word. What I mean, you know, is that I have offered my life as a sacrifice to him. His holy will! I want neither to live nor die. Such a great pleasure, but I suffer a lot in my chest, and they give me remedies that do not help very much. All for Jesus. He is so good, so good! Oh, love him and make me love him. Find yourself always in the solitude of his divine heart: I am there with you. May he be blessed and loved in every heart created to love him!

Adieu. I leave you covered in the blood of Jesus. Let me know if you take the steps we discussed.[77] Be well.

All yours in Our Savior.

Your sister, Eustelle.

LETTER 23

The need to fan the celestial flame; How this makes her suffer; She reassures a sorrowful heart; She asks to know the sorrows that she wants to entrust to the heart of Jesus; She glimpses the approaching end of her exile; She hides the true cause of her illness; Openness is the remedy for afflicted hearts; The foolishness of scruples.

All for Jesus. May he bless you and love you.

June 23, 1840.

---

[76] Continuing a thread from previous letters to Father A***, Eustelle is encouraging him to confide in and seek spiritual advice from Father Briand.

[77] French: "Dites-moi si vous ferez la démarche en question," "Tell me if you will do the steps in question."

United to Jesus through the Eucharist, I need to talk to you for a few moments. The feelings that fill my heart, the feelings that Jesus placed there, move me to seek you out for some sort of consolation. It is not that I need consolation: I have too much, and the desires it awakens in my heart cannot be satisfied through my impotence, causing me a kind of martyrdom that God alone understands. It is true that God's understanding of it should be enough for me; but the fire with which it burns me cannot prevent me from speaking and acting. I well know that only Jesus, the author of my suffering, is able to put an end to it. Not that I do not wish to suffer: but I want to say that if I could bring him glory and sacrifice myself for him, my desires would be fulfilled, diminishing the hunger and thirst that he more and more excites in me. O my brother! How the love of our beloved Jesus is blessed cruelty to my soul! But do not think that I wish this for you; it is the excess of my happiness that makes me suffer. How to respond to so much love? Ah, join with me; bless our common benefactor, and believe that your soul is always present to me when I am at his feet. For both your heart and the heart of Jesus, I do not want you to have that desolate thought that one day in eternity our fates will not be the same. I would see my God and bless my God and you, would you be a stranger to this happiness? Why do you so wound the infinite goodness and mercy of this dear, beloved Savior? Why do you want him to lose the one he chose and placed in his Church to labor for the salvation of his dear sheep? Do you doubt this now? I know everything you are thinking at this moment, and I know everything you would claim if you were here near me, but despite all of this, you do not have the will to lose yourself. But these thoughts alone can ensure you reprobation.[78] I know this well: the greatest sinners will not save themselves, though they claim not to want to be lost; they lie when they say this, for it is in their wanting to be lost that they transgress the laws of God and his Church. No, no! Death will not separate us from Jesus; this too I know. We will see one another again, to love without end he who has been so often the subject of our conversations here below. So receive then from the heart of Jesus the temporal and spiritual trials that I pray

[78] French: "Elle seule pourtant peut assurer la reprobation," "This alone can ensure reprobation."

you accept from his love. They are arduous, I acknowledge, but consider the reward. I assure that Jesus will grant what I ask for you. Tell me all of your sorrows, as much as you can. I cannot, it is true, heal them myself, but I can take them to the altar of Jesus, and the confidence that our good Savior causes to be born in me concerning your interests makes me firmly believe that you will receive God's response to my requests for you. Oh, how powerful is prayer on the heart of Jesus! How could he refuse a humble, confident request? Ask him for this precious humility for me; I need it now more than ever. I will tell you about it later: I cannot tell you everything now. Let us love Jesus now, until we are able to speak face to face about our good master. Ask him that I may love him, for I burn and suffer in the desire to love him. How often do I repeat these words which you addressed to me on your last letter: *Before many years, you will see him and love him in Heaven.* In fact, I believe that my exile is, little by little, coming to an end.

To speak in human terms, I suffer all the time. I have a cough that tears at my chest: it has been six weeks now. Last week, I had a lot of work at Saint-Pallais, but it was work for Jesus, and for Jesus, nothing else matters.[79] Everyone torments me: they say that, if I am sick, it is my own fault. Ah, they do not understand what makes me suffer. Monsieur N*** does not agree with them; in this he is alone with you. The good parishioners of Saint-Pallais do not know me: they are not meant to know me. God's works do not reveal themselves in that way. More than ever I will be private, and I never did talk very much. I have to hear all sorts of comments about my health, neither denying nor admitting any of them.

You should follow the advice that I took the liberty of giving you before, to open your heart to Monsieur N***. You would do well to let Monsieur the Curé know: he will appreciate the thoughtfulness you owe him. You could tell him that, not being able to speak with Monsignor the Bishop, as you would have wished, it is your intention to seek the counsels of Monsieur N***. Do this, please. But I fear you will not do this: you guard in your heart pains and anxieties that could disappear in an instant if you gave yourself recourse to the remedy that I have suggested.

[79] French: "et pour Jésus, rien ne se doit compter," "and for Jesus, nothing ought to count."

Write to me at once, if you can, and speak to me of Jesus: it is such a delight to speak of him!

Mademoiselle **** is scrupulous to the point of foolishness; her poor soul carries around all sorts of excesses. She torments herself and will not simply go to God.

And I leave you. Adieu.

Your sister, Eustelle.

LETTER 24

Peace follows troubles; All sacrifices for Jesus; Her imminent end is announced to Eustelle; She cannot bring herself to write about her concerns until the will of God is made known to her; She abandons herself to our Lord; Woe to those who ignore him!—If he is for us, who can be against us?

July 8, 1840.

Jesus lives!—He blesses and loves us.

I am excited to know your news: about your health, but most of all about your soul. Can you not tell me that everything in your soul is as you wish? But if Jesus, whose plans are impenetrable, permits these trials to come to you, know then that they will come to an end and that a perfect peace will succeed your worries, perplexities, and battles. Do not believe that these trials are your fault, but if you truly believe that they are, do not be afraid to make every effort to pluck out, as quickly as you can from the field of your soul, the little nettles that ceaselessly sprout up again and again, preventing the celestial spouse from resting comfortably there. It is for Jesus that our sacrifices must be made; for Jesus, love eternal; for Jesus who, in this place of exile, every day becomes our nourishment and our comfort. Only Jesus, everywhere, always! Oh, I beg you, do everything that is in you to secure peace for your soul. How I would bless our beloved Savior if you would send me this news! You do not believe that I wish you could be without a cross. I believe I know the road on which God is leading you. You will always have certain persecutions, certain humiliations; and what is more, your own personality will bring you some troubles. I only say this because I care about you.[80] O

[80] French: "C'est l'intérêt que je vous porte qui me fait parler ainsi," "It is the interest I bring to you that makes me speak thus."

my God! How I desire that you become a saint! So hurry up and become one, and you can make me one, too. Foolishness aside, let me know of the state of your soul.

Monsieur N***, whom I saw last week, told me that he knew I was going to the other world. I said he was quite a prophet, for my health is always back and forth; sometimes good, sometimes bad. At the moment, I am coughing more than usual, but I don't eat currants.[81] You obey like I do.

Monsieur N*** asks me once again to write about myself. How interesting would that be? I have actually resolved to begin to do this, but then I seem not to have time. Pray that Jesus inspire me. His divine will be done! I am always trying to get in touch with that worthy cleric.

Why have you not done as I have? Come on then: be reasonable: abandon your soul completely to Jesus, to his way and his end;[82] love the divine Savior ardently and cause him to be loved in just this way. Oh he is good! How his charms draw us near! Go often, as much as you can, to the foot of the tabernacle, for it is there that you will find the arms to use to defend yourself. Jesus, so good and so poorly loved! Ask him that we both might burn with the fire of his love. How pitiful are those who do not know him: let us offer prayers for them. And for you, confidence, peace, union.

May Jesus be with your soul, and may your soul be with Jesus. Let your soul stay with him, for he is our everything, our beatitude. Oh, to make him known and loved by all! Do not forget what I have told you: try to be more tranquil. And next time, tell me about your pains.

Adieu: I leave you in the heart of our best friend. Ah, shall we miss creatures if Jesus is always with us? Who could be against us? Yes, he is always with us. He sustains us in this exile; in our home country, he rewards us. It is he; it is Jesus; it is God; it is he who is. Amen.

Your sister in Jesus,
Eustelle, unworthy and poor servant of Jesus.

---

[81] Black currants were thought to be beneficial against scrofulosis (a form of tuberculosis).

[82] French: "son principe et sa fin dernière," "his principle and his last end."

LETTER 25

Second journey to La Rochelle; She informs the Prelate of her wishes and desires; Rules of prudence regarding bodily mortifications; A fatherly welcome; A recommendation regarding humility; Prayer; Growing appeal of the Holy Eucharist; She envies those who love Jesus readily and forcefully; Persecution by the world.

July 26, 1840.

May the grace of the Holy Spirit be always with you.

My trip to La Rochelle is done. It could not have happened without a lot of pains and annoyances, of which it is pointlessless to tell you. I left Saintes on Monday, believing I was talking to Monsignor the Bishop in the evening of that same day, but I was not able to do this until Wednesday evening. Imagine how long that time seemed to me. Finally, though, I got to speak to the good bishop, and I am very happy with our talk, though he did not want everything that I wanted. We talked about my sorrows, my prayer, my vows, and finally the cilice that you know I wanted to wear; on this last topic, he said he did not care about it. I thought it would be easier to get permission to use discipline; as he could see that I was no stranger to any sort of bodily mortification, he spoke to me about all these things at great length. I wish my memory could recall all that he said to me in this regard; I am sure you would be delighted to hear his thoughts on this matter. He is convinced that all the saints were enemies of their bodies and therefore were courageous in mortification, while sinners, cowards, heretics, and men suspect in the Faith[83] are always more comfortable attacking and ridiculing bodily mortifications than subjecting themselves to it. On the other hand, those who come back to God, in the beginning of their return, sometimes have such a great ardor for their macerations that, if they are not regulated in this behavior, they indulge in real excess. The Demon can very well suggest this behavior in order to lead them, later, to take excessive care of their bodies which they had earlier so abused. Moreover, in giving oneself up to such penances (he said), one loses all the merit one would have in subjecting them to obedience. Monsignor the Bishop cited the example of Henry Suso, to whom the Lord made it known that he took no account of the cruel rigors that he had exercised on himself

[83] French: "les hommes suspects dans la Foi."

because, in doing this, he had only followed his own will. Those to whom bodily penances are permitted, either by a confessor or by a wise and prudent spiritual director whose advice they attend to, must strictly observe the rules set up for them regarding both the nature of their penances and the space of time to be allotted to them. So it is determined for them which days and for how many hours each day they are to wear the hair shirt, the cilice, the iron chain; if the discipline is to be done for the space of a *Miserere*, a *De Profundis*, or more or less;[84] what quality the discipline should be: cords of iron chains, with or without spikes. These penances are withheld from all those persons who have the itch to speak about them to others rather than to the repositories of their conscience and from those who are tempted to esteem themselves higher because of these gifts. Such persons are in need of severe humiliation. All of the instruments of penitence ought to be unseen, and the mortifications themselves unknown so that, if there were any concern that they might be caught out or rumored, all these exercises should be suspended except in communities where the rule fixes the hour, nature, and duration of the penance. In general, penances should not be allowed to the simple-minded or to those with feeble and delicate chests.[85] In general, they are advantageous to persons with a strong, thick complexion, with minds inclined to laziness, to sleep. Regarding sleep, Monsignor says that you should neither prolong your sleep too much nor shorten it too much; the reason for this, outside of the resulting disadvantage for health, is that there ordinarily follows from it a sort of incapacity to accomplish one's spiritual and temporal duties. For the same reason, he does not like immoderate privations of food; he wants that, even for the fasts and abstinences ordered by the Church, one should have no scruple over excepting oneself to them, when a wise director has pronounced that one should be exempt from them. Any doubts that arise in these matters should be disregarded, because, when in doubt, you should take the side of your health. I thought I would please you by giving you these diverse details.[86]

---

[84] Psalm 51 and 129 respectively. Eustelle is talking about the prescribed length of time flagellants are to spend whipping themselves.

[85] A concern reflecting the prevalence of scrofulosis and tuberculosis among the rural population.

[86] French: "J'ai cru que je vous ferais plaisir en vous donnant ces divers détails." There is a palpable "edge" to this paragraph, as Eustelle is relating,

I spoke to Monsignor three times during my stay in La Rochelle. I took part in the prayers and in the lectures that he does every evening in his chapel for all of the persons in the house. The next day, I attended Holy Mass, at the conclusion of which the bishop consecrated two chalices which I transported back to Saintes. With all of this, I spoke to him for three quarters of an hour in total; you can only imagine how my soul needed this three-day colloquy. But a bishop is needed by everyone, and I still consider myself very pleased with the favor that Monsignor was good enough to grant me. He is to come to Saintes in the month of August or September, and I must speak with him then. If he does not come, Monsieur the Curé tells me I could allow myself to write to him. I am encouraged in advance by the quite fatherly simplicity with which he received me. He rightly exhorted me to humility, as he began and then as he concluded his advice to me, and my soul feels very good about that. He urged me to pray a lot for my relations who are in need; and he was humble enough to ask me to make my communion for him from time to time. He would like me to ask for humility in at least fifteen of my communions each month. Unite with him and me, that God grants me this sooner.

I long to know how you are on your island, if the bread of humiliation still nourishes you every day. Bless God for these humiliations; they are wholly to his glory. I am not as happy as you are, for, although I have humiliations, they are not as strong as yours. It is just that I am more feeble. I do not really miss them: God is good!

Because you are my third director, I want to tell you a little about the state of my soul. For some time now I have been much calmer; the temptations are strong but not so frequent. This surprises me. Concerning the state of my soul in prayer, especially after Holy Communion, I am afraid, somehow, to tell you how God treats me in these happy moments. My attraction to the Holy Eucharist is always growing, and I do not know how far God will carry it. My heart aches from not being able to respond to God's love for it, and if I am not worthy of loving him, I would consent, somehow, to deprive myself of possessing this heavenly love, so that the Lord might communicate it to other souls who do not know it and who might put it to better use than I would, if they did know it. How many times in the

---

with barely muted irritation, Bishop Villecourt's agreement with the cautions her correspondent Father Bichon had already voiced.

presence of our Lord would I almost fail to make manifest the sentiments of my heart and do so out loud, for I only stayed in the church because someone detained me there. How good God is to love us so much! Let us respond to him.

I do not know how to bring others to the love of Jesus in the Most Blessed Sacrament. Ah, my God, why can I not do more? How happy for you to be able to do more than I can! I bless God for this, and I urge you to redouble your ardor to make God loved more and more. It is not my place to be saying this to you; but, yearning to bring glory to God and being unable to accomplish this as I wish I could, I must pour out my heart to you. Doing this, I feel relieved of the desire that fills my heart. Believe me that, in everything I tell you, this alone is my motive. May God give you all the love for him that you desire, in the sacrament of love. Ask him for me that I may know him and love him more, and that I respond, with the greatest faithfulness, to the countless graces with which he showers me every day. When I think of the privilege he accords me every day, that he comes to rest upon my heart, the thought penetrates me with a sentiment of respect, of love, and of thanksgiving such that, sometimes, I cannot express them to him and my heart is speechless before him. How I need humility in all of this! What account one day to render! And this account: all of us render it. May God demand it of us only in his mercy!

Pray for a young person who is being converted at this time. She needs to sustain herself against the assaults against her by the world to turn her away from her purpose. Already, because she came to our house I have gone after her, telling her she was going to be a nun. If that happens, I will hear all about it[87] from certain people, but I worry only a little about that. I warned her about what will happen, about what is happening now. What a miserable world, whose pestilential breath corrupts the heart! Why does it have to claim so many victims? So pray then for this poor young woman, that she may have courage to render to her religion a testament so true; for true happiness is found only in the peace of a good conscience, not in the corrupt principles of a perverse age.

I easily received permission from the Bishop to touch the sacred vessels. I urge you to take great care of your stole.[88] Please put

---

[87] French: "je m'attends à attrapper quelque chose," "I expect to catch something."

[88] French "étole," the long thin vestment worn around the neck of the priest

tissue paper over the embroidery all around it, so that the flowers are not damaged by friction, which would eventually make the gold rub off. I will have finished your pall by September or October.[89]

I join myself with you in the praise and blessing and love of the divine heart of Jesus, where I am always.

Your sister,
Eustelle.

LETTER 26

Jesus is misunderstood by this perverse age; Eustelle suffers from this and desires to see, at the cost of her life, the knowledge of her God established in hearts; No hope for her recovery from human remedies.

August 19, 1840.

May the peace and friendship of the dear and thousand-times-good Jesus be with you.

I do not know what reflection you can make on these words, not knowing, for a long time, how things go with your soul. I recommend it every day to Jesus, who alone should occupy and possess it entirely, for whom it is every day his sanctuary and tabernacle. May my own unworthiness not be an obstacle to the fulfillment of the vows I make to the Lord for you every day. I wish to know how you are doing, if your soul is a holocaust consumed by the sacred flames of the pure love of Jesus! Oh, how I desire to see it flame upon this earth, his divine fire! Our Lord desires nothing less than this in the sacrament of his love.[90] But how can so few souls surrender themselves to his secret and loving invitations? He is, under the veil of the Eucharist, the object of men's scorn and indifference. Yes, Jesus is veritably the God insulted, the God unknown! There is hardly any faith left today. Where are the practices of the Gospel in today's Christians? O perverse age! Your stupidity astonishes me, terrifies me! O Father, what a subject of continual groaning in a soul enlightened by the Faith![91] Yes, God alone is witness to my

---

signifying priestly authority. It seems likely that Eustelle is talking about an ornate stole she made for the correspondent.

[89] See Letter 14, note 50.

[90] French: "Notre Seigneur ne désire rien tant dans le sacrement de son amour."

[91] French: "gémissements"; variations on *gemir*, "to groan," seem to echo Romans 8:21, "Car nous savons que toutes les créatures soupirent et sont en travail

suffering on this account, and it is his will that alone supports me in the hunger and thirst he gives me for justice. The more he is offended, the more the hunger redoubles and the more my life drains away.

But bless him. May I thus make people forget the many years spent oblivious to his divine law! And on this earth where I languish, that I desire nothing other than to die of love for him and to see, before my final hour, the knowledge of Jesus established in every person's heart. Ah, why am I so far away from doing for my dear Master all that my gratitude inspires me to do? But it is he who wills my weakness. Pray you, his minister, that his reign come to souls where he is not yet established, and ask him, the King, the Father, *God with us*, that he accept the weak and unworthy sacrifice I make to him of my life for the needs of the Church, our mother, and for the conversion of those of his children who every day wound his tender heart by the most unworthy desertion and by their real contempt for his loving commandments. As much as you can, do not leave our adorable prisoner alone in his prison. Knowledge is at the foot of the tabernacle. It is there that I so often meet you, together to love and to groan.

My health is no better; I can hardly work without greatly fatiguing myself. They say I will not recover; Monsieur N*** is of this persuasion. For me, I greatly doubt my recovery: there are too many causes for my illness for human remedies to cure. And at the moment, all the world is tormenting me; they say it is my fault. Oh, how blind we are! In all things, God's will be done! Nothing but Jesus. Monsieur the Curé is feeling better but his mother is more ill.

We are busy, at the moment, whitewashing the church and putting a new floor in the sacristy. How beautiful it will be afterward! But the time approaches when I am to go to our mutual friend. Here on this side, you will be at his feet as well. I join your soul and your desire with all of mine, that our Lord let you taste, in this life, a foretaste of the fruits of the promised land. You are happier than Moses, then, for you see it here by faith, and one day it will be granted to you to reap bountiful divine fruits.

I am, in the Cross of Jesus,
Your sister Eustelle,
his poor and unworthy servant.

---

ensemble jusques à maintenant," "For we know that all creatures groan and are in labor together up until now." *Soupir* is the more common verb for "groan," but *gémissement* occurs 24 times in French scripture, mostly in the Old Testament.

LETTER 27

Encouragement for another position; Eustelle is indifferent to either life or death; Nothing is lacking in her needs; The bishop thinks about visiting her in her illness.

September 3, 1840.

All for Jesus. — May Jesus bless you, a thousand and a thousand times, and love you.

Monsignor the Bishop is at Saintes. Monsieur the Curé has spoken to him about you, and all appearances point to everything changing for you soon. Submit yourself to the will of God in this situation, as with every other. Oh, have no fear, I pray you; the one who gives you the burden can sustain it. As the sovereign Shepherd, he will lead you, you and your sheep, to the pastures of heavenly love. If you are weak, have confidence without limits in our good Savior. Do you not know who he is? Do you doubt of his mercy? No, no: you are, more than ever, a child of the confidence and the love of the God-Man; more than ever, you will count on the goodness of Jesus. He loves you, believe me. Everything will be better than you think. For me, I will not forget you at the foot of the tabernacle; be sure of that. And remember to pray for me too. I know what you will need in your new obligations, and I will keep them in mind before Jesus. Courage, confidence, language, strength, patience, zeal, peace, and union: may Jesus give you everything. And you, now give your everything to Jesus.

This letter was not all written in the same day. Since the day I started writing it, I now feel a little better. Honestly, it is not until now that I had thought I would recover, but today I view that outcome as possible. So I am better, a little better. If I am to stay in this exile, I adore the will of Jesus: and if I recover, the doctor assures me that my recovery will not be long-term. Believe me that I lack nothing at all that could bring about my recovery, but this help does not come to me from Saint-Pallais. The Lord has realized in me the words of the holy Gospel: *Seek first the Kingdom of God and his justice, and all the rest will be given to you as well.*[92] You know well that my needs hardly concern me: my

[92] French: “Cherchez premièrement le royaume de Dieu et sa justice, et tout le reste vous sera donné par surcroît” (Matthew 6:13).

good sweet Master thinks about them: bless him with me. I tell you all these things for his greater glory.

Monsignor the Bishop must come and see Monsieur the Curé; he knew from him that I wished to go and see him but I could not, because of my weakness. "All right then," he told him, "I will go see him myself." Just imagine my surprise! But if I am better in the meantime, I will visit his house myself.

I leave you now because I am fatigued again. Be filled with the confidence and love in the goodness of God. He holds you under his wing for protection:[93] have no fear. Jesus loves you: remain in his peace. Live by him, and rest in his love.

I am, in his heart, your sister,
Eustelle.
Poor servant of Jesus.

LETTER 28

Feast of Saint Pallais; Monsignor the Bishop blesses Eustelle; Her vitality; She would like to write about her concerns under the name of another; Beautiful sentiments upon that subject.

[Between October 7 and 14, 1840][94]

May the grace of the Holy Spirit be with you.

Our celebration of Saint Pallais was most solemn. Monsignor the Bishop preached, accompanied by Monsieur Gaboreau, Monsieur the Curé of Saint-Pierre, Monsieur Briand, and three other clerics. Monsieur the Curé was enchanted: our church was truly magnificent; there was such a crowd that some people were turned away, unable even to pay for a seat. Being in the sacristy after the services, I saw Monsignor the Bishop and spoke to him; he was kind enough to give me his blessing. Our Lord has truly performed a miracle in the work with which I was charged on this feast day. It had been nearly two months since I was able to work and, well! on Saturday and Sunday I worked with extraordinary vitality,

[93] Echoing Psalm 91:4: "Il te couvrira de ses plumes, et tu auras retraite sous ses ailes," "He will cover you with his feathers and you will retreat under his wings."

[94] The feast of Saint Pallais (Palladius) of Saintes (sixth century) is October 7, a date still celebrated with autumn festivals in the region.

which astonished those people who were aware of my habitual feebleness. May Jesus, love eternal, *God with us*, forever be blessed! Ah, how good he is, and how delightful to confide in him!

Monsieur N*** had come before Monsignor the Bishop, and I had the consolation of speaking with him for some minutes, about our divine Master. If my health should quickly improve, he wants me to do what I have told you about.[95] If you come to Saintes, please be so good as to bring him the letters I have written to you; I need you to do this, and you may take them back with you if you wish. Pray that our Savior enlighten us both and keep the greatest secret on this. I intend to do this under the name of another person. If I share this confidence with you, you cannot doubt that my sole motive in this is the greater glory of Jesus. Let me say, as God is my witness, in speaking about all that Jesus has done for me, I think nothing about myself unless to deplore the numerous sins with which I so badly repaid the numberless benefits of the Lord. Oh that I had the repentance, the love, and the language of Saint Augustine, to put onto paper my memories and the yearnings that the Holy Spirit intimated to my soul, his sanctuary, that was too long a receptacle of sin! Pray that, from now on, his will be done in me, the will of the one I love, love not nearly as I should. Love him, therefore, I beg you: love him more than you love him now. Remember the reliance that the Lord wants you to have in him, and cast fear and worry from your heart. Your head is really bad; think about fixing it. I am filled with desire for the perfection of your soul: may our dear Master answer me! Oh, I do hope for this, that I do not resist as you do.[96] Pray for me: my needs are great, because what the God-Man asks of my soul is great. May we, one day, in union with the choirs of angels, sing the mercies of the thrice-holy God! I leave you covered in his precious blood; may it intoxicate you for time and eternity.

Your sister in Jesus,
Eustelle,
his poor, unworthy servant.

---

[95] Eustelle is referring to Father Briand's and Bishop Villecourt's request that she undertake to write a memoir of her life.

[96] French: "Oh! je l'espère: je ne suis pas défiante comme vous," "Oh, I hope: let me not be defiant like you."

LETTER 29

Reproaches; Leaving fear aside for love; Eustelle begins to write of her life; She is doing this only out of obedience to God; Her life is a martyrdom of love; The supernatural force of Monsieur the Curé of Saint-Pallais on the death of his mother.

October 14, 1840.

All for Jesus.

The remorse that your conscience gave you for your negligence in writing to me was, I see, soon quelled. Really, if I am on the earth after you, I will call upon Saint Negligent and I hope that he will obtain for me the grace to be not so negligent. Finally, give me your news. It is your soul that concerns me the most; I made my communion this morning for it. It is not that I am concerned about your salvation, but I fear that your soul is often off its center[97] and that this is your fault. Leave these fears of a slave; set your mind instead on the pure love of Jesus our God; it is such a delight to be in his domain!

I can tell you that, following the will of my director, I have begun to write my life. Monsieur the Curé is aware of this, since Monsieur N*** asked him his opinion about it. I have gotten as far as just before the time of my first Communion.[98] I beg you pray for me about this, that our good Savior himself dictates to me what will be in accord with his heart. Ah, he well knows what moves me to do this: if they did not want it, I would not have done it. You know my soul: it enjoys unspeakable happiness in this act of obedience. It is a delight for me to recount the merciful effect of the love of the God-Man towards his unworthy servant. If only I had the contrition of Saint Augustine and the love of a seraph to express worthily the grandeur of his benefits! O Jesus! give me your heart; give me your love. Be glorified by what I undertake for your glory. Send me words afire and make me understood.

Our Lord is truly too good to me, I assure you. I can feel that he increases, more and more, the flame of his love in my heart. If only you knew, though, how this love makes me suffer! My life is a martyrdom, but a martyrdom most sweet. Oh my brother in

---

[97] French: "hors de son assiette," "off her plate." *Âme*, "soul," is a feminine noun, hence "her."

[98] Ch. 5 of the *Memoir* above, pp. 7–8.

Jesus: ask our tender Father, ask our faithful friend that I may respond perfectly to his plans for me. All of this that I am saying about myself should not make you believe that your own soul is far from arriving at the state where I find myself. I assure that one day, you will greatly love the one and only object of our love: you love the Lord already, more than you think. I am not saying this to flatter you, but through the light given to me, I know that you love him. How could you not, when you trust in God!

I should make you aware, in case you did not know, of the death of Madame de Saint-Germain. Two weeks ago she ended the sufferings of her life. You can imagine the state of Monsieur the Curé, her son. He has surprised us, however, with his fortitude. She died on Thursday night, at about eight o'clock. On Friday and Saturday, Monsieur the Curé celebrated Mass for her. The funeral took place at ten o'clock. On Sunday he spoke to us about her in the most touching terms: he shared with us the consolation that filled his soul in remembering the virtues of his pious mother. He thanked us for sharing his pain, and then he went on with the instruction[99] as always. Pray for her.

I leave you, remaining in spirit with you, in the heart of the one whom we must love so much. To love him in time and to love him in eternity: that is the vow I make, for you and for me.

Adieu: your sister in Jesus, his poor and unworthy servant.

Eustelle.

LETTER 30

She was close to dying; It is at the feet of Jesus that one finds light and power; Submission in her trials.

December 10, 1840.

Glory be to Jesus.

I had thought that you gave up on your old friends. Truly, your silence is inexcusable. When I received your letter I was just at the point of writing to you to give you a good scolding. You are negligent. Monsieur the Curé told me himself he was sorry that you did not answer his letter. And why? I pray you.

[99] French: "l'instruction comme à l'ordinaire," i.e., the sermon or homily at Sunday Mass.

I must tell you I thought I was going to die this year: the doctor said that I could recover, but I am suffering less and do not seem to have the slightest fatigue.

I am going to write to Monsieur N***; I am so happy to be able to open my heart to a soul who so loves our Lord! Oh, a thousand blessings on the good Master for the inspiration given me to make his acquaintance. I have so much to gain in knowing him. It is simply impossible to hear him speak without being set afire with the desire to love Jesus. How deeply he knows the Lord! How deeply he loves him! And you too love him very much, especially in his prison of love. Ah, go! go to be in his company, as often as your labors permit you. It is at the foot of the tabernacle that we learn the science of love; it is the holy armory where we can find in abundance the weapons that serve to defend us. Go and put on his sacred insignia to fight the enemies who present themselves on the battleground of this life. Oh, love Jesus, and pray that I may love him too.

Adieu: find confidence in the pains that Jesus sends you; they are gifts of his love. So embrace them. These sorrows have an end point but their reward has no end.

I leave you in the peace of the good Savior, and am beside you in spirit in the heart of Jesus,

Eustelle.

LETTER 31

Convalescence; Conformity to the will of God; Holy desire for communion; How delightful to talk about one's beloved!

January 27, 1841.

All for Jesus.

I fulfill the promise I made to you to send you news of my health. There is little use to it, but your concern for me constrains me to satisfy you on the matter. Today, Wednesday, I began to leave my bed but could not go out. I hope to go to Mass on Sunday, but everyone tells me I should wait. In this, as in everything else, I entrust myself to the will of the good Savior. Oh, I especially love his divine will, for it is my will. Ask Jesus, our friend, our brother, our God, our everything, that he augment more and more in my soul that perfect submission to his fatherly will, that wants in all its workings only good things for those who are subject to its gentle domain. I am aware of the occasions you have to practice this submission, and I urge you to practice it with all possible perfection. Our divine Savior has foreseen all of the circumstances of our lives. You know that our tender Master himself tells us that only those who do the will of his Heavenly father shall be part of the kingdom of Heaven.[100] Love, bless, and adore the one who is our only nurture.

Tomorrow the moment will return when the God of the angels will come to rest in my humble dwelling. Jesus, the eternal love, the *God with us*, through the most holy of mysteries, will deign to unite himself with his unworthy bride. Oh, despite my submission to his good pleasure, I desire most ardently that fortunate moment that, in advance, makes my soul enjoy the first fruits of the happiness of Heaven. O sacrament of the Eucharist! Only goal of my heart, object of all my thoughts, all that I believe, all that I want: how to express it? Infinite treasure, alone able to quench the thirst of the Christian heart, why can I not, even by the shedding of my own blood, make all creatures render to you the adoration and love to which you are due!

O my brother in Jesus! I share in your fervor. Let us try to compete in love and zeal which the best of fathers leaves to his children. Oh, pray; and I shall pray for you. And later, we shall love him with the same love in the eternal kingdom. Together we shall enjoy the sight of Jesus, the peaceful and good.

I must stop because I am tired. But my God! it is sweet to talk to another about the one we love.

Our dove is doing well; I love her very much.

I want to know you are content, at peace. I leave you but unite myself to you and to the best of friends, the best of fathers. May charity gather us in spirit at the foot of the tabernacle.

Adieu: your sister in Jesus and his unworthy servant,

Eustelle.

---

[100] Echoing Matthew 7:21: "Tous ceux qui me disent: Seigneur! Seigneur! n'entreront pas dans le Royaume des cieux; mais celui qui fait la volonté de mon Père qui est aux cieux"; "All those who say to me, 'Lord! Lord!' shall not enter into the Kingdom of Heaven, but those who do the will of my Father in Heaven."

LETTER 32

Transports of happiness and love for the adorable Eucharist; Eustelle fears she has only one virtue; An improvement in her health.

February, 1841.

May Jesus bless you and enlighten you; may his love consume you.

The yearning of my heart is not limited to you: ah, why can I not see it happening in every heart? Why can I not make every creature render to our good Creator the tribute of love to him that is so delightful to give? O God! What a joy to feel inflamed by the sparks of his holy charity. You are taking the place of Monsieur N*** with me today. It is in your soul that my own comes to lay down its needs. Ah, it is at the feet of the tabernacle of Jesus, our love, where I lay down all my heart and write down these lines to you. Dear good master, O Jesus! It is too much! It is too much for this place of exile. Suspend a little those ineffable delights which leave the soul afterwards just short of experiencing the bliss of Heaven. O my Heavenly friend, you imprison me in a way upon this strange land; but it is at the feet of your altars. Eucharist! O sweet heart of my soul! O my life! O soul of my life! *Eucharist!* How deliciously that word resounds in me! O Jesus! Amiable Jesus! Finish your victim, or bring me to know you, for you are so misunderstood, O treasure buried in the field of the catholic, apostolic and Roman Church![101] If your loving will still keeps me exiled from your beatific sight, then at least give me the means to bring you glory! I feel my unworthiness; all I can accomplish is through this note. Ah, I do not fear my own weakness, because I sense near me your most powerful virtue. Divine word, sojourn in the heart of this weak creature; as you are truly present under the species of bread, increase my faith and strengthen my hope; above all let me enter, more and more, into the secret of your holy charity. Be with me, Jesus! Be with me!

I am obliged to cease, there is no more paper. O you, my brother in Jesus, pray for me to become one in the heart of Jesus, that my piety be true, that I am not tricking the world with the false appearance of virtue.

[101] French: "O Jésus! Aimable Jésus! achève ta victime, ou donne-moi de te faire connaître." Eustelle here sees herself as Jesus's victim, and asks that he either end her suffering or bring her to know him.

I have some poor prayers to offer for you, but you may count on them. I am happy you are content, and I want your soul to be content as well. You understand me.

I attended Mass for the first time last Sunday, and now I continue to go every day. Ah, I was so hungry! I feel so much better that I am amazed, and so is the doctor, who thought I was going to die. Ah, if Jesus has shot me with a fatal arrow, then he is the master of the delayed reaction. God's will always.

Today I am having the chapel washed; yesterday I cleaned the great lamp of the altar. I join these works to yours.

Adieu: I remain completely devoted to you in the heart of Jesus.

Eustelle.

LETTER 33

Love only the tabernacle; Jesus deigns to manifest himself there to Eustelle; Suffering for Jesus is not real suffering.

March 2, 1841.

Glory and love for Jesus.

Thank you for the blessing you sent me. I have just come back from Saint-Pallais, and I made the same blessing for you there. Oh, in turning my eyes towards the ciborium where the one who is our only goal reposes, I asked Jesus, our love hidden there, to enclose us both in this mysterious cup, to drown us and lose us in the source of the living water. O my brother, love only the tabernacle. Oh, be mad with love for the Eucharist. Oh, how I love our Lord, but not solely in his Heavenly glory; it is under this mysterious veil, the feeble little host, that I like to contemplate him. It is at the breaking of the bread[102] that this tender friend shows himself to me. It is also in this way that the Lord deigned to manifest himself to me and the moment of benediction. Oh, the favors I receive from this pledge of love! And how unworthy I am! How I should love him! O my brother, come to Saintes, but let it be to speak with me about that love and to tell me that you love Jesus more than when you left us.

[102] French: "la fraction de ce pain," which in the Mass is "the breaking of the bread" (*fractio panis*), the breaking in half of the principal host just before the distribution of Communion.

I pray this evening for your curé and I desire the sanctification of both of you.[103]

My health is much better, though never very strong; on my second day out, I resumed my duties in the sacristy. This was not without suffering, but suffering in the presence of Jesus is not real suffering.

I must leave you. I am a bit fatigued, because I passed the better part of the day writing what you know about.[104]

Adieu, adieu through Jesus, to Jesus, for Jesus. Him alone, him everywhere, always him.

All yours, through the heart of him who love us,

Your sister, Eustelle,
his poor servant.

LETTER 34

What makes the days good days; The Eucharist, joy of the soul; The movements of sacred love; Generous offerings in her poverty; The work of mercy.

March 30, 1841.

Glory be to Jesus!

Good day, my brother! Ah, I like to believe that you will never have a bad day because you will be set apart by the will of God,[105] because you will be consecrated by the exercise of pure love; by the love of Jesus, the only good, only lovable, the only one worthy of love. Before shutting myself up with him for nine days in his temple, I come to talk to you for a few moments about the delicious joys with which our generous friend inundates my soul, the soul of one who so wants to share them with yours and completely fulfill your most ardent desires. Oh, have confidence; he who has strengthened the pillars of the Church knows how to prevent her

---

[103] French: "et je désire la sanctification de l'un et de l'autre," "and I desire the sanctification of the one and the other." The sentence is unclear, and the least disruptive interpretation seems to be Eustelle's wish for sainthood for both her correspondent and his pastor ("Monsieur your Curé").

[104] French: "à écrire ce que vous savez"; Eustelle is referring to the *Memoir*.

[105] French: "tous seront marqués au coin de la volonté de Dieu," "you will be marked at the corner of the will of God": a very fluid idiom in French.

collapsing. Let us be humble; the God of the tabernacle shows himself to us again and again in the fraction of the Eucharistic bread, and the light we receive there will surely guide us through the desert of this life and to the promised land.

I cannot express to you the happy state of my soul and the workings of pure love in it that are communicated to the body in an extraordinary fashion. I suffer from it almost always, not in my soul but externally: a weakness, an extraordinary exhaustion especially in Communion and in prayer. At other times, the divine fire works upon me with another effect: it communicates to me a particular power, both in soul and in body. And then, when the fire is a little less intense, I become weak and lethargic. Oh, I do not complain of this evil: I am unworthy of it and I ask Jesus to increase his love in me, although I know well that this will also increase my suffering. Do not complain about this: I know how to get along well enough. The fact is that my path, as Monsieur the Curé said to me the other day, is extraordinary, hardly commonplace. And he does not know everything, not as much as you do. I must confess to you a reckless action. I would allow you even to call it reprehensible, which you might unless you consider it the sort of transport that happens without reflection and is therefore excusable because it is not deliberate. The other day, being alone in the Church, I suddenly traversed the whole distance between myself and the holy tabernacle; I dared to go up to the altar and kiss the door of the prison where his love confines him. This is my confession. Let us love Jesus; love him, my dear brother, but love him without anxiety, troubles, or ennui.

Our Lord gave me a little money which I was able to use for your parishes. It is not much: six *lavabos*, two corporals, three purificators, two amices, and an altar set which is quite plain but will serve you. Do not worry about the money I used to make these purchases: it was given to me for the novenas I made, and because I can dispose of it as I want, I choose to use it this way. When I have the chance to send these to you, I will. You should have Monsieur the Curé write to Monsieur Courcelle, so that *Œuvres de la Miséricorde*[106] sends some help to your poor parishes, both

[106] Note to the French original: "*The Work of Mercy*, newly founded in the Diocese of La Rochelle, accepts donations of money, linen, or fabrics, to provide ornaments to poor parishes. In less than four years, more than sixty churches have been provided with items required for worship."

in ornaments and linens and other essential objects. It is easy to qualify for this help if you can show your need. Why not take advantage of this? The N*** ladies, who take care of this with such zeal here in Saintes, welcomed the presentation we made to them concerning your needs. They need only a word from Monsieur Courcelle, founder of the organization, to come to your needs.

My brother was requisitioned this year. Marie did her job obtaining a very high number for him.[107]

Your sister in Jesus,
Eustelle.

LETTER 35

Remembrance requested at the holy altar; She does not want to be happy alone; Invitation to holy love.

April 13, 1841.

All for Jesus.

I am writing to you in haste. I will eventually finish the different jobs with which you have charged me. The work on your stole will not permit me to begin your alb for three weeks. I envision with great happiness that Jesus will repose on the corporals I made for you. Oh, when your words of Consecration[108] bring him down here, think of the humble servant who lives and breathes only for him! Dear master! O my beloved! I am completely transported by your love.

I have a moment more than I thought, and I need to spend it remembering the kindness of this generous friend. I am happy, but I need to share my happiness. I cannot be alone, knowing that all are called to taste how sweet and light is the yoke of the Lord. Oh, my brother! Why do you not surrender yourself completely to the only love that is Jesus? I need to tell you about all that Jesus is doing for my little soul, but my time is running out. Oh, how I love him! Love him more and more. Tell me about your familiarity

---

[107] Eustelle is referring here to the draft lottery for military service. In 1841 her brother Charles would have been 21 years old; interceding for him seems to be Eustelle's sister Marie, age 24.

[108] The French here is simply "votre voix," "your voice," which seemed somewhat oblique.

with the good master. So I leave you in the daily resting place of our two hearts, in the ciborium where Love supreme reposes.

My sister sends you a very simple breviary cover, but I do not want you to be elegant: the disciple should not come before the master.[109]

Your sister Eustelle, servant of Jesus.

LETTER 36

Love as habit is a thanksgiving; Confidence in God; Eustelle envies the happiness of priests; Unaccountable transports in a holy place; Failure; This letter and the feelings it expresses can only be understood in proportion to the love the writer has for Jesus Christ, in his adorable sacrament.

April 19, 1841, the anniversary of my birth.

To God through Jesus.

Today is Sunday; it is one o'clock in the afternoon. I have returned from Saint-Pallais; there I satisfied, just a bit, the hunger for Jesus that always consumes me. My physical strength has not yet recovered from the weakness caused to me by the love of God, along with the happiness with which my soul overflows today. I blessed and thanked Jesus for what you told me. But you have told me that, since our Lord has granted you some favors, you are inclined to ask him for more rather than give him thanks. Never fail, however, in the obligation to give thanks. Now it is certainly true that a child who loves his father with a perfectly childlike love and who receives continual benefits from him does not occupy himself with ceaselessly thanking his father for each benefit. His favors are too numerous to be equaled by our acts of thanksgiving. The child's love for his father, unceasing yet changing, becomes an unceasing act of thanksgiving.[110] This is how we respond to Jesus: love him with all your life, with all you are. Oh, let your heart live

[109] A breviary is a book containing the daily divine office said by priests. The end of the sentence echoes John 15:20: "Souvenez-vous de la parole que je vous ai dite, que le serviteur n'est pas plus grand que son maître," "Remember what I have said to you, that the servant is not greater than the master."

[110] French: "L'amour habituel divers ce bon père équivaut à une action de grâce," "The diverse habitual love of the father equates to an act of thanksgiving." The translation assumes that the "amour" is that of the child, making the sentence connect logically with the following one.

on love alone, on that sacred love alone! So, do not be troubled when you think you cannot thank Jesus enough—and do not think that I am telling you this only to settle your mind; no: I tell you this because I believe it. For myself, I do this very thing: that is, since it is not possible appropriately to thank Jesus for his love for me, I content myself, when I receive a new favor, with saying to him: O Jesus, how good you are! O my beloved, I love you and want to love only you, for all your kindness; I do not want to attempt to offer you thanks, my sweet master, but you know my heart: it is to say thank you that I breathe out to you this cry of my heart: *I love you!*

O my dear brother, let your heart be more confident: you know Jesus, but know him as he truly is; do not trouble yourself with all your occupations: just do them in love. Without Jesus we are nothing, but with Jesus, what wonders can happen! Oh, believe! For abundant blessings are on their way to your flock. I can see the good that Jesus will do through you, and I bless him for this now.

What you confided in me in your letter has a happy harmony with what I am about to tell you. O priest of Jesus, what will you think of the rashness of my love and the extravagant desires which it inspires in me? Would you believe that I never cease to envy the happiness of priests, who can frequently open the holy tabernacle and to take often in their very hands the vessel of love where Jesus reposes. This thought alone gives me enormous exhilaration. I feel it at this very hour: my whole body trembling, and my pen can scarcely trace, at this moment, the sentiments of my heart. I feel a mixture of happiness, fear, and awe, but most of all, love: how can I call it love? It is an inexpressible transport. Do you remember the time when I asked you to open an empty ciborium before me?[III] Ah, I did not tell you then all that passed in my soul; I imagined to myself the vessel full of hosts, consecrated at the sacred altar through the power of the sacramental words, and I said to myself: Ah, if only I were allowed to press this against my heart! That afternoon, that same thought tormented my altered, burning, swooning soul: I burned with a desire that the Church did not

---

[III] A ciborium is a rounded gold cup with a close-fitting lid used to hold consecrated hosts and for distributing them in Holy Communion. During this period and for long after, laypeople were not permitted to touch chalices or ciboria once they had held the Eucharist; see Letter 26, where Eustelle reports that, as sacristan, she received permission from the Bishop to touch the sacred vessels.

permit me to satisfy. I sometimes need to avert my eyes from the tabernacle because I am tempted to go and press my burning lips to it. The holy ciborium produces as well an inexpressible emotion in my heart. I see with eyes of faith our love imprisoned, but at the same time I love to contemplate the sacred species in which it cloaks itself like a mantle of tenderness. I suffer sometimes when there are people in church who bother me in my need to shed great tears, to weep as I will[112] and to utter cries of love. When there is no one in the holy place, I am at my ease, it is true, to give free rein to the emotions that surcharge my heart, but I am in the grip of temptations that could be seen as a sort of madness. My soul is both flooded and scorched; my heart beats violently: I want to cross the space that separates me from Jesus. I aspire to the happiness of being able to hold in my hands the happy vessel that contains Jesus; and which would be a thousand times happier than me, if it could but comprehend its happiness. I would like to kiss it, hold it on my lips, open my heart and place it there. If such a thing could be permitted to me, the most cruel wounds would be for me the sweetest and most ravishing. Sometimes I lose consciousness, and my members stiffen a bit and become cold; I feel my strength diminish little by little, and I have nothing to say to Jesus; the final ardors escape from my burning chest, and a general lethargy takes over my whole body. From moment to moment, I reawaken to my cry: O Jesus! how I love you! Make yourself loved by the sinners whom I recommend to you, O my beloved! My soul cries out for you; I cannot live without you. My dear Jesus! Why am I not permitted to take you with me? I feel the full weight of my unworthiness and yet I am drawn to you by an invisible, invincible force. This force, it is the love that I have for you, the love that kills me.

Sometimes I call out to the joy-filled spirits that surround the invisible majesty of my God hidden under the veils of the sacrament, saying to them: it is not for you that he is here: it is for me. So leave me in this place that you hold so near him. Why do you take me away? Is not Heaven enough for you to contemplate him is his glory? Give place, I beg you, for his exiled lover, who asks only, as consolation for her exile, to approach closer the throne of his love.

I continue now, on Monday, the letter I started yesterday.

---

[112] French: "à mon aise," "at my ease."

In the afternoon of the same day, I returned to the feet of these holy altars. I suffered from a hunger and thirst that I can only try in vain to describe. Only those who have known these feelings can understand their force. I am alone there and, without considering that I could have been surprised, I crossed the sanctuary and went to touch my lips to the holy altar. Oh, how many time did I kiss the altar? What tears flowed from my eyes upon that altar where, every day followed his divine blood!

In the end, my brother, I cannot tell you everything; some things truly cannot be explained. It was almost impossible for me take any food, absorbed as I was in the thought of Jesus and his love. Oh, how I love him! Love him too.

No: our Lord would not hold it against me for the excessive familiarities I have permitted myself. It seems to me that Jesus would allow us more, through exception, if the holy rules he has dictated to his Church might not be generally applied. Surely, I accept these venerable rules with the most profound respect. They would surely be less stringent, permitting us more access to Jesus in the Eucharist, if all of the faithful were ablaze with that purest flame of holy love.

Write to me, please, with all your thoughts on what I have just told you. I am working on your stole and your ciborium cover.[113]

Adieu: the bell calls me. Safeguard the most inviolable secret contained in this letter. Love the God of love.

Your sister Eustelle.

LETTER 37

Charity knows no distance; Sending various church items.

April 25, 1841.

May the peace of the Lord be with you.

Oh, how happy I am to be able to tell you so often about the divine object that captivates and embraces our souls! Although our distance of place may separate us in body, charity knows how to unite us in heart, where we are one. Saint Paul said that all Christians must strive to be one in Jesus Christ.[114] And how much more united

[113] French: *pavillon*.

[114] Echoing Galatians 3:28: “où il n’y a ni Juif ni Grec; où il n’y a ni esclave ni libre; où il n’y a ni mâle ni femelle; car vous êtes tous un en Jésus-Christ”;

are those to whom the Savior gave complete conformity in words, sentiments, and works, and especially to those whom he brings into intimate familiarity with him? Estranged from all the things of this world, I think only of my happiness, which is Jesus; a happiness I love so much to share with you, with everyone, if it were possible.

Œuvres de la Miséricorde has sent you some different items, linens and ornaments. You should write to Monsieur Courcelle to receive things you still need.

I do not have the time to write to you longer; it is ten o'clock at night, and I will take some rest. May our sweet Savior bless you. Love him. And love him for me, as I will love him for you. And speak to me about your soul; I want to know it is happy.

Pay my respects to Monsieur the Curé, if you think it appropriate. Ask him to remember me on the holy altar.

Adieu through Jesus, our beloved.

Your sister who lives only for him,
Eustelle.

LETTER 38

Eustelle is troubled, being denied the clarifications she asked for; Poetical cry of love.

May 19, 1841.

Blessed be Jesus.

Your silence troubles me. I ardently desire to see you and consult with you, to do nothing that is against the rules. The other day, being at the feet of Jesus Christ, I expressed my feelings to him in the verses that follow:

O seul ami que j'adore et contemple,
Divin époux, ô Jésus, mon espoir!
Ah! près de toi, que ne puis-je, en ce temple,
Couler mes jours jusqu'à leur dernier soir!

O my only friend, whom I adore and contemplate,
Spouse divine, O Jesus, my hope!
Before you in this temple, why can I not
pass my days, until my final night.

"where there is neither Jew nor Greek, where there is neither slave nor free person, where there is neither male nor female; for you are all one in Jesus Christ." The Vulgate and many English translations use "Christ Jesus."

Si ton amour me ravit par ses charmes,	If your love so moves me by its charms
Ah! donne-moi de répondre à ses feux:	Ah, permit me to respond to these fires:
Je veux t'aimer dans les croix, dans les larmes,	I want now to love you in the crosses, in the tears,
En attendant de te voir dans les cieux.	As I wait to see you in Heaven.

Ah, my brother! These sentiments are not yet of my soul. The vision he gives of himself to my soul cannot be expressed: there would be too much to say.

I leave you: it is time to go to rest with him near his paternal breast. Oh, why can I not be nearer to his altar? I ask this of Jesus who loves you, who blesses you. And I await you, in his divine heart.

Adieu, O you whose happiness I envy.

Your sister,
Eustelle,
servant of Jesus.

LETTER 39

The happiness of the priestly vocation; The folly of holy love; Do not fear; Jesus is always Jesus; Desires for humility.

June 6, 1841.

Jesus be with you.

Ah, my brother, how do we not die of love? How does the memory of Jesus in the Eucharist not fill our thoughts? Oh I beg of you: let your love be only that unique love of the Heavenly Father; see only him in everything: breathe, act, only for him. Him alone. Him everywhere. Him always! O you priest of Jesus! how fortunate you are! You can love him much more than I, if you would. And I wish for myself as I wish for you to be madly in love with him: for Jesus is our science, our light, our friend, and our bliss in this life. O my brother, my soul is happy, though it cannot say how. So read, read, in this soul what human language cannot capture.

Do not torment yourself in your fear that you do not love Jesus enough. You love him, I am sure. Later, you will love him more. Oh, that your soul be, and peacefully remain, in the arms of our mutual and peaceful friend. Do not fear: Jesus is always Jesus. His fatherly eyes are on you.

Write to me: time is hard for me. Do not hide away your feelings. Ask Jesus to grant me humility. You can see yourself that, after receiving so many favors, I must respond to them by the practice of this precious virtue. Oh, these Eucharistic veils that I love so much: are they not themselves the essence of humility?

Adieu: let us rest united by the charity of the good Savior. Later, in the promised land, that union will be perfected in Jesus. In the meantime, let us live for Jesus that we may die in Jesus.

Your sister, Eustelle. — Adieu.

LETTER 40

Octave of Corpus Christi; Insatiable hunger for the divine Eucharist; Holy and inexpressible languor; Eustelle reasons with herself to try and stop the immoderate ardor of her desires; To shut oneself up in the Holy Tabernacle.

June 14, 1841.

All for Jesus.

Yes, all for Jesus, especially during this holy octave, when are exposed to our eyes the symbols that express and veil for us his real presence. It is principally during this octave that our souls must contemplate him with eyes of faith so penetrating and so be consumed by the ardors of the charity of our tender Father. What joy! Oh how fortunate and blessed to be able, in this place of exile, to love Jesus, and love him especially in the Eucharist. Holy manna! I starve for it, though I can feed on it every day. Every day, my beloved nourishes me with his divine flesh and refreshes my thirst with his precious blood.[115]

Oh, my brother! I suffer an estrangement as an effect of the love that Jesus has given me for this ineffable mystery. My life is nothing but languor: my good master knows this. This languor at the moment is more noticeable than normal. I cannot explain how I feel: no human language is adequate. Have great love for Jesus, my brother, you who obey him every day. Oh, may you be happy, priest of Jesus! Ah, why must these useless desires so consume me, envying a happiness that cannot be mine on this earth? When Jesus has ascended to Heaven, his holy mother contented

[115] French: "et m'abreuve de son sang précieux," "and waters me with his precious blood."

herself to receive him every day in communion, and in the Holy Eucharist, no longer permitting herself the innocent caresses she lavished on the child Jesus. She forbade herself the kisses with which she once covered his celestial face; she does not receive the sacred manna of the Eucharist to press it to her heart before taking it to her virgin's mouth; she does not ask to carry with her, in her body, this memorial of the infinite love of Jesus for humanity, though there has never existed on earth a tabernacle so pure and so ravishing in the eyes of the Savior as is this immaculate lily.

I am rushed: it is our Heavenly friend who occupies me. I have an altar to raise to him. Oh, it is for Jesus: what a delightful thought!

Mademoiselle Deval has two ornaments made for you. If you have the opportunity to receive them, please do.

Adieu: I must leave you in the sacred tabernacle where I shut myself up with you this morning. There let us suffer: let us suffer from love and in love divine. Jesus knows this; Jesus sees us. He prepares for us the place we are to occupy, not in a material tabernacle but in that tabernacle which he himself has made to contain his glory, wherein we will love each other in the depths of eternity.

Your sister,
Eustelle,
unworthy servant of the celestial spouse.

LETTER 41

Trust in Mary, sign of predestination; Jesus lavishes his most special favors on a grateful Eustelle; Her thoughts about the priestly character delight her; Exclamations of a heart afire; To speak of Jesus.

July 1, 1841.

Glory to Jesus.

I want to pass some time with you.

You have been in Angoulême, and you have told me nothing about the trip? Have you come across the iron you need for making the altar breads?[116] You know I have one that Jesus sent me, with very beautiful engraving; I will hold it for you.

Thank you for your Blessed Virgin. She is a great pleasure to me,

[116] A wrought iron appliance similar to a waffle iron used for baking altar breads. They often had engraving within the circles such as a cross or Chi-Rho (χρ).

and I have done everything you asked me to do for you with her. Do not forget to return it to me when you invoke our common mother. Yes, yes, my brother; one day we will be reunited at the feet of Mary; never doubt that, because the confidence we have in her is one of the surest signs of our Heavenly destiny.[117] There in Heaven, on the throne where Jesus her son placed her, she already accepts with love those tokens of affection which it is such a delight for us to offer to her. Her heart so maternal inclines itself to us, to bless us, shelter us. Let us have complete hope in this clement Virgin: her Son has said that he can refuse her nothing.

Let us talk now for a little while about our Lord. You know the way friends like to talk about the object of their affection. Do we not love Jesus? and do we not love to talk about him? I am transported by his love, so transported that I do not know how to express it. How does he lavish me with so many favors? And what do I have to respond to his love, the love of the seraphim and all the assembled choirs of angels? Oh, that I could have a thousand million hearts and a thousand million voices to consecrate to loving Love himself and to making him beloved! Happy, I repeat without ceasing, are the ministers of the sanctuary! The thought of a priest delights me. Oh, my brother, you are one of them, and it is your character that I love in you. Why must this particular madness make me go so far as to envy a vocation that my sex renders impossible for me? Why does Jesus permit such strange regrets to linger in me about things I know well I can never do? Ah, my dear master! He knows well where the desires of my heart lead; he knows for whom are all these movements and sentiments; he knows the motion of my whole soul. Ah, you know this already: it is to the tabernacle, to the sanctuary of love, to the shadowy and mysterious prison, a prison enlightened by a living faith to allow the king of Heaven to be seen there in all his dazzling light. And it is the priest who reproduces it there! Oh, my brother, may this ravisher of souls unveil my soul to you. My soul understands but cannot explain it: I would suffer the less if I could tell you all of it is from Jesus. But you know this already: it

[117] French: "une des marques les plus sûres de prédestination," "one of the surest marks of predestination." The translation adjusts the term because Eustelle is not using "prédestination" in the Calvinist sense but more broadly, to denote God's and Mary's certain but not determinative foreknowledge of our individual afterlives.

is only the extremes of pleasures in love that make me suffer; but far from complaining, I desire it always, and why? To suffer in loving is to love in suffering. O divine Eucharist! You alone know how dear you are to me; you alone are consecrated, and by you alone the powers that animate me are known. Oh, I have need of you! Ah, you make me weak. But still I hold on to you. O beloved Savior! All-lovable, all-desirable Jesus, my beatitude, sweet heart of my soul, deign to bless by your peace and your love, by your gentleness and your power, the one with whom I am conversing here. Ah, give him your sanctifying Spirit, not in a measure but plentifully; consume him in the pure flames of your Heavenly love, so that one day he will be part of your priestly corona.[118]

Oh, how ardently I desire for us to be reunited up there! Oh, pray for me as I pray for you. Above all may your soul be at peace; hold on to it by confidence and patience.

I am not happy that, in your letters, you hardly speak to me of Jesus at all. In this respect, your letters are not worth the five sous that it costs you to post them. You do know I am joking. Tell me how your soul is; you well know why I tell you this, but you forget everything that I say to you.

I leave you in the peace and love of God, whom we all must love. I am with you in his heart.

Your sister Eustelle, servant of Jesus.

LETTER 42

Holy intoxication; A prayer that charity might catch fire.

August 17, 1841.

May Jesus give me his love and his peace.

I am drunk, my poor brother; yes, truly drunk: drunk with Jesus and for Jesus. And what do I need to satisfy my soul in this moment? Jesus? But I possess him already; I touch him; I love him. He is mine, my good, my property, my all in all, and more than that. I say to you simply: I would have liked, this morning, my brother, to share with you the ineffable joys which flooded my soul in Holy Communion. Oh, it was too much for my heart so small. And I return to the feet of the Lord. I will not forget you: be sure of it.

---

[118] French: "et qu'un jour il soit participant de l'auréole sacerdotale," "and that one day he may be part of the priestly halo."

O Jesus, my beloved Master, my sweet honey! My heart cannot live without you; it wants only to be quickened by you. Deign to send me burning sighs; hear my soul in what it asks of you, both for my soul and for the one in whose bosom I place it at this moment. My heart, for him, says more than my pen. For his glory, open yourself more and more to him.

I leave you, my brother. Let us love Jesus together.

Your sister,
Eustelle.

LETTER 43

It is not possible for the life of Eustelle to go on for much longer because of her languor.

September 2, 1841.

Our Lord is abridging the moments remaining for me to pass upon the earth. A constant languor and a long life are impossible. My health is very bad. Oh, you are not unaware of the cause. I would have a lot of work to do but I can accomplish very little due to my weakened state.

Adieu: love Jesus, because he is so good, and that his love not only makes us love him but leads us to make him beloved, for he is our peace, our brother, our friend, our everything. May he fill you with his most precious goods; may he be your strength, your support, your joy, your consolation, your treasure, your life, your death, and more even than all of these, if it is possible.

Your sister,
Eustelle.

LETTER 44

Eustelle's soul constantly turns to Jesus, who is its center; She moans that Jesus is so unloved; She is beside herself because of the favors with which he showers her.

September 14, 1841.

Let us love Jesus, who alone is worthy of our love.

My soul, which is known to you, turns itself more and more towards its center, who is Jesus; it dies a thousand times in the need of him whom she already possesses so intimately. The same hunger devours it always, and always the same fire consumes it. It is this pain that makes me come to deposit in your heart the sentiments about this pledge of the charity of the God-Man.

Ah, why can I not find here where I live a heart that loves, as much as I want, our good Redeemer in the sacrament of his love? Why is his light so eclipsed in the hearts of those in whom it should burn so bright? O deplorable blindness! O the stupidity of the human heart! Ah, my brother, let us pray on this subject, and bless Jesus our Heavenly Friend for the favors which he has sent me. I am beside myself in the joy, the peace, the ineffable pleasures, and the divine rest that our good Master has given my soul. In his beloved presence I sense a manner so intimate that I do not know what to do or what to say to quench the thirst that consumes me. The intensity of his glory is withering; his love delights me, but I can do nothing for him. Oh, how good is Jesus! He is the friend most tender, the brother most companionable, the spouse most delightful; he is the life of the soul, the king of angels, the felicity of the saints; my joy, my light, my life, my desires, my memories, my thought, my vocation, my delights, my beatitude, and more even than that.

Adieu, my brother; confidence, peace, and love.

Your sister, Eustelle, servant of Jesus.

LETTER 45

Eustelle hopes she will be answered; Exhortation to divine love, through frequenting the holy tabernacle.

October 4, 1841.

All in Jesus and for Jesus.

Last Saturday I went to make a visit to Jesus the beloved for you. I am very confident in obtaining all that I had asked him on your behalf. Join with me in these efforts of my prayers and Jesus will grant what you pray for in his glory. You would not believe how much I hope to be answered on your behalf. I have no confidence in myself but in the goodness of him who said *Ask and you shall receive; ask, that your joy may be perfect.*[119] Oh, it is not for me, a poor creature, to give counsel to a man of your character, and exhort

[119] Echoing Matthew 7:7, John 15:11, and other passages.

you to the love of our good master; but this is what my soul needs, a need directed especially towards you, whose dearest interests I love to take, always with God alone in view. Oh my brother, if you knew how much I desire to see you burn with love like a holocaust! Let us consecrate at the feet of the tabernacle every moment that Jesus gives us. Go there to know and to love the unknown God that love holds captive there.[120] There we learn everything by ignoring everything. Think about how close the lovable Jesus is, always; he is in your hands; be heedful of your great honor and go often to give testimony to the tender master how much you understand the honor he has bestowed on you by calling you to a vocation so sublime.

Adieu: I leave you in the ciborium of Jesus. May your soul and mine repose with that of Jesus. Pray for me who does not wish ever to leave this sanctuary.

Your sister, Eustelle, poor servant of Jesus.

LETTER 46

Eustelle moans that she cannot give Jesus love for love; It is impossible to express what happens in her; Sufferings; Tears; Powerless zeal.

October 21, 1841.

All for Jesus.

My soul's need is too great for me not to take advantage of the opportunity to write to you. Our Lord has made my soul suffer greatly, so that I am not to continue this intimate exchange of sentiments with you, which I make for no motive other than charity. O my brother! If only you could ease, just a little, the hunger and thirst which press me. And yet, far from complaining about this martyrdom of love, so sweet, so delightful, so divine, I moan, on the contrary, for the weakness that prevents me from rendering to Jesus love for love. And, far from asking for relief from this blessed suffering, I ask him for a more perfect degree of love, though I well know that, in asking for this, I am asking to suffer more.

To write what is happening in my heart — this is an impossible thing. Dear brother, you cannot understand it, cannot understand what has brought me here.[121] You are going to think that what I am

[120] Echoing Paul at the Areopagus, Acts 17:22-24.

[121] French: "ou, du moins, vous ne comprenez pas jusqu'à quel point ces choses sont portées," "or at least you do not understand how far these

about to tell you is disordered. No, I cannot believe it. Can that force that draws us to Jesus possibly have a source other than him? To calm a little the excessive ardor of my soul, I would need to have the God of the Eucharist always in my heart. Ah, if you only knew how all my being is transported by this pledge of love! You think I am exaggerating, yet what I say is nothing. Last Sunday, Jesus redoubled the pains of my soul, increasing the love that already was consuming me. I was then so overcome that I left the feet of the tabernacle to withdraw to the sacristy so that I might pour out more at my ease the burning sighs that oppressed my soul. I did not know what else to do.

Ah, the adorable, the delicious Eucharist is not to be received many times in one day. I cannot tell you these things without shedding tears, although I take care that they do not wet this paper. And what adds to my martyrdom is the sight of the indifference of the great part of creatures for the God that I love; I am almost tempted to ask him to temper the ardent zeal which inspires me for his glory, this zeal that, even as it brings more pain to my heart, renders it impotent. If it is not possible for you, my wicked brother, to satisfy my most perfectly extravagant desires, then at least have pity on me and ease my pain by talking to me about Jesus. If I could make you comprehend and feel, for just a quarter of an hour, what my soul suffers, you would no longer be insensitive to my pains.

O good and sweet Savior: you are mine and I am yours.

Let us repose ourselves, one and other, my brother, in the charity of this God of love. In eternity, we will love purely, deliciously, eternally. Be all for Jesus.

Your servant, Eustelle,
unworthy servant of Jesus.

LETTER 47

Reproaches; Desires to be consumed by Jesus, the mysterious light of the soul.

November 15, 1841.

Glory and love to Jesus.

I do not want to write you a long letter: you do not deserve one. To go so long without sending me a sign of life: this is unpardonable.

---

things are carried."

And yet I concern myself with the interests of your soul. My own soul is always happy but always overflowing with desires that cannot be completely satisfied except in the heavenly homeland.

It looks like we are going to get another vicar. Bless God in everything.

I have such a weak lamp to light me that I cannot see. Pray that the light of my soul be not so dusky, and that the mysterious lamp that is Jesus consumes it, illuminating it more and more.

Well, that is enough for you, give what you have given me, eh? But I am not angry with you for that. Your soul is always on my mind; be mindful of mine in return.

Your sister Eustelle,
poor servant of Jesus.

LETTER 48

The benefits of time are granted to us only that we might attain those of eternity; Every day we can believe in holy love; Good use of time; Eustelle regrets that the sacramental presence of Jesus is so fleeting.

January 11, 1842.

All for Jesus.

You know my soul, and you do not doubt what it desires for you every day, but specially at the beginning of the new year. Oh, that Jesus, as I hope, grant the wishes I address to him for you, that the day come when we are reunited, never to be parted. Let us yearn together, with all that we are, for that blessed moment when that supreme glory which we now perceive veiled and covered will be revealed to us in a light as of day. The benefits of the Lord are accorded to us that we may attain only this one singular desire. Now, of all those gifts which so flow to us, the gift of life is not the least. Oh, if we had a livelier faith, a firmer hope and a charity more ardent, how grateful we would be to know that, every day, we could grow in the ways of divine love, cementing the union between our divine Savior and our souls. Let us then rejoice, every morning as we awaken, that the day is still given to us to serve so good a Master. Ah, let us put to use, as perfectly as possible, this time so precious and so very short: and since his holy will keeps us still in the shadows of exile, let us stay there as long as he wills it, but let us stay only to procure his greater glory, each of us according to our vocation.

My soul is always happy, my very good friend, always the same for the hidden God, always desiring more and more to attach itself to the one who holds it captive. Oh, he alone knows all that he is to this soul, especially in the Sacrament of the altar. He comes to rest every day in my poor heart. O fortunate moments! What unspeakable happiness! Why do you pass away so quickly? My memory of communion is sweet to me, but at the same time it is painful, too, since it reminds me of a joy that has passed. My love redoubles whenever I think that Jesus, the Holy of Holies, the being infinite and eternal, is reposed on my tongue and then descends into my heart, so unworthy and miserable. I want to receive him again, regretting that his physical presence is so fleeting. And so I rejoice to be able to offer him this pain as a sacrifice every time this thought comes to torment my soul. Jesus alone knows the greatness of this sacrifice. Oh, I hope the sacrifice will be rewarding.

Adieu. I am done. I am cold, but not in my heart.

Your sister, through Jesus,
Eustelle, his poor servant.

LETTER 49

Eustelle is troubled because she cannot put an end to the coldness and indifference of people; Communion is the only support in her languishing life.

N.d. [*Presumably early 1842.*]

Peace be with you.

How good is our Lord to his poor servant! Truly, I do not know how to respond to so much love. I am lost in that ocean of the mercy of the good Savior; his particular favors to me multiply every day. Still, by the aid of the light he has sent my soul, I know more and more how insulted he is everywhere,[122] but especially in his prison of love. It is a sight that saddens me infinitely and I would like to oppose it with all my strength, but I am nothing but impossibility and weakness. O dear brother! If Jesus in the Eucharistic union

[122] French: "je connais, de plus en plus, combien il est outragé de toutes parts, mais surtout dans sa prison d'amour."

does not ease this pain, it will not be possible for me to live with concerns for him so touching my heart. Pray then; let us pray that his love drive off coldness and indifference. Redouble your efforts to love him more and to make him loved.

I cannot write any longer; Jesus's will presses me to another task that relates to his glory.

Adieu: let us stay together in the same heart, and let us have but one thought: to love and to glorify Jesus Christ as we await our union with him on that eternal day.

Your sister, the poor and unworthy servant of Jesus.

Eustelle.

LETTER 50

Solicitude and good wishes; Courage in tribulations; Union of Eustelle's will to the will of Jesus in sufferings; Her interview with her bishop; Advice to write down her concerns; Dangers of extraordinary ways; The modesty of truly perfect souls; Eustelle's reserve.

March 1, 1842.

May joy and peace accompany you always, through Jesus Christ our Lord.

My very dear brother,

How are you in your new household? What is the state of your temporal affairs? Are you starting to get used to things? Does boredom pursue you? Have you enough to live on? Have you found someone to serve you? Who moved you to your household? Is there any piety in the place where you are? And then what is the state of your soul? Oh tell me please: you are not unaware of the interest I have for you, concerning God. If something is troubling you, I don't want to ignore it. Jesus loves you, so do not doubt that his lovable cross follows you there as elsewhere. Courage and patience: these you need. For the rest, your tribulations are in the order of the divine will; I assure you, they contribute much more to your sanctification than to your fall.

I cannot write for very long because I have been suffering a lot for these last two weeks; my chest is very painful. This pain began as a bad headache, which is very strong at this moment. Ah, how I bless the goodness of God towards me! How great his goodness! My soul is infinitely happy because my will is at one with his in which he makes me suffer. Oh, it is sweet to suffer for Jesus! How far am I from wishing for an end to this languishing life! But you know, my brother, that it is only by his grace that I suffer, a loving grace which lavishes on me his wealth of good things. Oh, if I were able to bring glory to this dear master, what would I not do, either in living or in dying? He is, always and everywhere, the same for me, this dear Jesus, this celestial friend. Pray that my soul stay always faithful.

I would have many things to tell you, but they will be for another time.

You know that Monsignor the Bishop preached Lent at Saintes, in the old cathedral.[123] I went to see him twice; he showed me particular kindness and he welcomed me as he would his child; he put me at ease with the gentleness and simplicity of his speech. I was greatly surprised when he asked me why I had not opened my soul completely to him. The various questions he asked obliged me to go into detail about almost every aspect of my inner life. I told him some of my feelings in regard to the Holy Eucharist, but I did not have the courage to make known to him how far my insatiable desires had taken me. How can one talk of such things to a bishop one sees only in haste, to whom one can speak only for a few minutes while making others wait who also need to speak with him? Anyway, the road that the Lord makes me walk did not surprise him; he agreed with everything, found everything good; about everything his thoughts were, without exception, the same as those of Monsieur N***. What seemed most remarkable to me in our first conversation was that he tasked me to do precisely what I was already doing, in regards to the question of writing. I did not tell him, however, that I had already been instructed to do this by my director. To tell the truth, I noticed that, in the second visit I allowed myself with him, Monsignor the Bishop was much more circumspect on this point. He emphasized especially to me that there is often nothing more dangerous than following extraordinary ways. And he seemed strangely to fear that, in occupying my thoughts too much on myself, I was

---

[123] The Basilica of Saint-Eutrope (the "old Cathedral"), on the west (gauche) side of the Charente River, across the river and about a mile on foot from Saint-Pallais, where Eustelle served as sacristan.

opening myself up to that most dangerous of temptations, that of self-love. He kept returning to this concern in several ways. Lest I be exposed to the subtle snares of pride, I saw how he was careful to emphasize what was extraordinary in the divine communications to me. He let me see that they were more common than you think, but they remained mostly unspoken, due to the modesty and reserve of the souls privileged to receive them. No soul has been as privileged as Mary's, yet there is no soul more silent and reserved. She wrote nothing and had nothing written about the divine favors she received, and, apart from the few words that escaped her in those rare circumstances, she left us with no other memorial of her sentiments than the beautiful *Magnificat*.

I had many things to say the Monsignor the Bishop, but I held them in when I heard him say to me thus: this was, I felt, the way a bishop should speak. Wordlessly I blessed the Heaven that the shepherd might condescend to speak at this level with the least of his sheep, but I dared not say any more, lest he believe that I had a disordered eagerness, wishing to appear to be an elite soul. However, Heaven be thanked, I found in my heart no attraction for this vanity that the bishop wanted me to fear. I made him a profound bow and left him, while he commended himself to my prayers.

This letter should have been much shorter. Adieu: all to you.

Your sister, the poor servant of Jesus,
Eustelle.

LETTER 51

The ever-increasing action of divine love; The need to speak always of Jesus; Faith and love; Prudence in her communications.

March 17, 1842.

Love no one but Jesus.

I feel constrained to acknowledge my accustomed need to open up my soul and let loose the ever increasing fire of the dear and thousand-times-good Jesus. I do not know what he wants me to become, but I cannot withstand the ardor of his Heavenly love. As I have told you, this ardor is always increasing, and it leaves me in a condition in which, without a particular disposition of the divine Savior, I cannot live much longer. This fire, continually present, makes me suffer strangely; to quench this thirst I endure, I need always to speak, either by voice or by writing, of the pure and heavenly love that is Jesus; Jesus my life, Jesus my thought, Jesus my speech; Jesus all I see, Jesus all I know; Jesus all I want to know! When he is placed on the altar, when I see either the monstrance in which he is placed or the ciborium wherein he rests, I experience a feeling of awe and love that penetrates and fills my whole being. To feel him so close to me fills me with divine joy; I could die right then. I am especially attached to contemplating the host in the monstrance. There Jesus is revealed to me, and it is then that I express to him my desires for you and for the whole Church. In saying "I express," I render my thought badly, for faith and love are my only language.

I am obliged to renew to you the confession I once made in another circumstance: it is that, when I found myself alone in the church, I could not hold myself back one day from kissing the door of the holy tabernacle. But that is not all: this week I was given permission to ascend to the altar to clean the statue of the Virgin Mary. Now you know that our Lord is there in the tabernacle in that very chapel; well then, do not scold me, I beg of you: being up on the altar to complete the duty to which I was charged, I knelt down very close to the Lord Jesus, embracing the tabernacle in my arms, I gave it a thousand kisses. It was then the turn of the statue of our good mother, our most tender friend, our sister, for that is what I like to call her; I arranged her, adorned her, and, once then again, allowed myself to kiss her face and her hands. Finally, after three hours had passed, I had to leave this place that is so dear to my heart, and return to love Jesus in my simple home. Believe me though: I left him only in body, for his presence filled my soul, flooding it with happiness, joy, and an inexpressible peace.

O Jesus, why do you make me waste away like this, since it is not given to me, in my station of life, to work as you desire, to bring you glory? Do you delight in consuming a mere straw that does not die? O will of my God! You will always be dear to me. I want nothing except what you want. I surrender myself to your good pleasure. I do not want to die if you want me to live.

I am writing to you earlier, my brother, than I was supposed to, to urge you to take advantage of the occasion that presents itself, to send me what I expect. Do not think, however that this is the sole reason that makes me write. No: it is that the pitcher of my heart is full and, despite me, it overflows. So love Jesus well. I am already sure that you love him but I pray God every day that this love increase; make the same prayer for me.

When you have some particular reason to give thought to my letters, please do not read the parts that seem to be extraordinary. How many people, do you think, would take occasion to laugh at things which to me seem not laughable at all; others, perhaps, might think of imitating in certain things, and this second inconvenient group could come to be more serious than the first.

Write to me when Jesus inspires you. Adieu, in time, to meet in eternity.

Your sister in Jesus,
Eustelle,
his unworthy servant.

LETTER 52

She announces, indirectly, her approaching death.

May 12, 1842.

[NOTE TO THE FRENCH ORIGINAL] THIS IS THE LAST LETTER that Eustelle wrote to this cleric. She did not have more than a few weeks to live. One can hardly interpret her handwriting, so much had the nearness of her death made her hand weak and trembling.[124]

May the will of Jesus be as ours.

You may wonder and worry about my long silence; I should tell you I have been sick since Easter and bedridden[125] for a month. I am constantly in bed and feel no better.

Do not let this news alarm you; you must submit . . . you know how much I love talking about our Lord with you, but my weakness forces me to stop. My poor brother, we have our cross . . . Pray for me. I pray for you.

Eustelle, servant of Jesus.

[124] Eustelle died on Wednesday, June 29, 1842, about six weeks after the date of this letter.

[125] Easter in 1842 fell on March 27; "bedridden" translates the French *arrêtée*, "arrested."

[*LETTERS 53 TO 85 ARE ADDRESSED TO FATHER JOSEPH Briand, a notable author and preacher in the Diocese of La Rochelle. Eustelle first encountered him when he preached on Ascension Thursday at Saintes, May 9, 1838; see Letter 6, above. He had already been recommended to Eustelle as a possible spiritual director by her friend, Sister Anastasia.*

Until this point Eustelle had been corresponding regularly with Father Bichon (unnamed in the French editions), who served at Saint-Pallais during the brief period between Father Jouslain's sudden illness at Christmas 1836 and August 1837, when Father de Laage de Saint-Germain was appointed curé of the parish.

This first, informal "director" was sympathetic and encouraging, but Bishop Villecourt and eventually Eustelle herself came to think that he was not sufficiently experienced to direct someone in Eustelle's state.

Eustelle seemed to have a good relationship with her new pastor (and employer as sacristan), Father de Laage, but the demands of his duties and his poor health made him an inappropriate choice for spiritual director. Also, Eustelle worried that Father de Laage had too high an opinion of her (see Thompson 320–21). So she put herself under Father Briand's direction early in 1840.]

LETTER 53

Eustelle blesses Heaven for giving her a guide and support; She promises him complete openness; Desires; Jesus is not known; Prayer; The heart of Jesus appearing completely on fire; Jesus, victim for the sinners; It is a delight to die for him; Wishes and prayers for the fruits of his preaching; The foolishness of the world.

March 3, 1840.[126]

All for Jesus. — May the Cross of Jesus preserve you; may his death fortify you, and may his grace sustain you.

What a comfort to my soul, after years of privation and trials, to be able to open it completely at the breast of a good father, in the heart of a friend of Jesus! What a joy to have found a support in my weakness, a guide on the road that Jesus makes me take! May you be forever blessed while you wait for the joys of the

[126] I.e., Shrove Tuesday in 1840.

Heavenly homeland, and may he give you a fullness of the gifts of the spirit of love.

The love that Jesus has for my soul is known to you; you are the repository of the supernatural favors which he showers on his unworthy and feeble servant. For his greater glory, I want to tell you again about his embraces to which I am accustomed; I want my soul to be known to you, as Jesus knows it; this Jesus whom you love, this Jesus whom I love. O Jesus! whose name is sweet to the soul who knows you! O my father, when will we see him, this beloved Jesus, in the celestial Sion; when will he be our vestment for all eternity?[127]

On the eve of our Forty Hours, I remained the whole day with our good Savior, busying myself with decorating the altar where he immolates himself for me every day, from which he blesses me so often. My attention did not stray from the tabernacle during this whole time. I hesitate to tell you my thoughts, but no: I am to keep nothing from you. I could not help but kneel several times, my forehead leaning on the altar and saying to myself: why may I not throw open this tabernacle? Why am I not permitted to remove the sacred ciborium from it and hold it close to my heart? Oh, I would water it with my tears, crying, O unknown God! O unknown God![128]

You can understand how my soul felt in this moment. Poor Jesus! No! He is not loved because he is not known, and he is not known because no one wants to know him. O my adorable master! Are you not the light of the world who illumines every person who comes to you? I hear you answer me: *The light shines in the darkness, and the darkness cannot engulf it.*[129] But Lord, you can drive away these shadows; your grace is powerful enough and

---

[127] Possibly echoing Romans 13:14: "Mais soyez revêtus du Seigneur Jésus-Christ; et n'ayez point soin de la chair pour *accomplir* ses convoitises," "but put on Jesus Christ and make no provision for the flesh to sate its lusts."

[128] It is remotely possible that Eustelle is here echoing Saint Angela of Foligno who, when she found herself at the square in front of the Basilica of Saint Francis in Assisi in 1291, repeatedly shouted "O Amor non cognitus," "O love unknown." *Il Libro della Beata Angela de Foligno*, ed., trans. [into Italian], Ludger Thier, O.F.M., and Abele Calufetti, O.F.M. (Rome: Editiones Collegii S. Bonaventurae ad Claras Aquas, 1985), 184; for an English rendering see *Angela of Foligno: Complete Works*, ed., trans. Paul LaChance, O.F.M., Classics of Western Civilization (Mahwah, NJ: Paulist Press, 1993), 142.

[129] John 1:5: "Et la Lumière luit dans les ténèbres, mais les ténèbres ne l'ont point reçue."

your mercy is infinite; one single act of your will would suffice. Make it so, O Jesus! and the clouds will disappear in an instant; force those ungrateful and rebellious hearts to see you and love you.

At night on the same day, I had the happiness to remain alone in the church, until half past eight; I would have gladly stayed there all night if I had been free. How good it was to be in that sacred enclosure, amid the silent shadows at the feet of my lovable Redeemer! I did not forget your soul, as is my custom, and related the little that I am able to do for Jesus with the great deal that so many do for his glory. Before leaving the holy place, and as I was just at the door, I turned and expressed to Jesus the sorrow I had in leaving him. My eyes were fixed on him; my heart seemed to want to draw him to myself. In that moment, our Lord showed me, in spirit, his heart surrounded by flames; it was in the Holy Eucharist that his heart represented itself to me. See how good he is, the divine Master! How to respond to so much love? I took my leave of him saying, *tomorrow, then.*[130]

The next day at Holy Mass, after the Elevation, I contemplated Jesus on the altar, in the form of a sacrificial victim. The beloved of my soul caused me to hear these words whose sense is so tender in my heart: *I offer myself for my sinners.* Mark well these words, my father: *I offer myself for my sinners.* They show how dear the sinners are to him. Oh, let us rejoice: however guilty, we are no less the objects of the tenderest solicitude of Jesus. What have we to fear if our repentance thrusts us into his arms? I declare to you, these words of Jesus filled me with confidence, both for myself and for all his sinners. Ah, if they only knew how good Jesus is to them!

What charms does Jesus have for my soul? Divine Eucharist! O Jesus, my dear brother! Sweet honey of my heart, my life and the soul of my life! O my Father, how I love him! How I love to tell you about him! I am soothed in speaking to you about him whom I love.

O my adorable master, you know how I cherish you; you know how I would count myself lucky to die to show you my love. Why can I not also die to make you loved? I desire to make you loved with the same love that you love yourself.

O my Father: only death can put an end to what I am made to suffer for his love. I consider death to be a gain and, like Saint

[130] French: *À demain!*

Teresa, I am not dying to die.[131] God's will be done, and I submit to it. Pray for my soul; I pray myself for yours and for all those to whom you will minister. May Jesus prepare the land on which will fall the seeds of the divine word, and may he deign to make it bear fruit for the eternal life.

Here in Saintes, the world is even crazier than usual during this miserable carnival.[132] Pray to God for these senseless ones who offend him. I pray to him myself to bless you and to love you, and I am, in his adorable heart,

Your obedient daughter.[133]

LETTER 54

Divine love deprives Eustelle of her physical strength; Magdeleine; Flowers and fruits of Jesus, tree of life; The language of perfect humility; Transformation in Jesus; Fasting prohibited; Eustelle spends four days at the feet of our Lord; The Bishop of La Rochelle preaches Lent at Saintes.

March 10, 1840.

All for Jesus. — May Jesus be loved in the divine Sacrament of the altar.

It is Jesus, my Father, through my mouth, who is going to tell you the happiness of my heart, the effects of his love. I cannot myself express to you the indescribable peace which the presence of the tender Savior produces in me. Now as I write to you, I become a holy temple; my soul is united there to the author of all graces, to the God of all holiness, to Jesus, the tender lamb we both love. But how can I say that I love him? Ah, I love him alone. The force of that love deprives me of my physical strength. After receiving the Holy Eucharist this morning, I felt I was almost losing the use of my senses: I did not know where I was. How delightful was that sleep! Those who have experienced it can understand it easily: you have had the experience, you, the friend of Jesus.

131 Echoing Teresa of Avila, *The Interior Castle*, Seventh Mansion, ch. 3.

132 French "ce misérable carnaval." *Carnaval* or *carnival* (Spanish), etymologically "Farewell, meat"; a reference to Mardi Gras, a pre-Lenten festival both in Europe and in the New World.

133 The French text does not indicate that the letter was signed; it may have been hand carried or even delivered in person. The closing reinforces the father-daughter metaphorics that run through the letter.

Love him with me, and ask him that I might love him as you do. I still seem to see before me the heavenly adorers to whom I addressed myself this morning as the bride of the daughters of Jerusalem.[134] Mary Magdalene, the saint loved by Jesus, was not satisfied until she asked the angels at the tomb where her master was; she wanted to see him, talk to him herself; he alone would satisfy her desires; she knew that he alone was the certain source for all that she needed. For me, I was able to speak to Jesus himself; it is Jesus whom I asked to be my support in this languor that his love has made me feel, for he has within himself the flowers and the fruits that can strengthen and nourish my soul. How sweet the fruits; how tender the flowers! Oh Jesus, fruit divine: how perfect you are! How my heart is captivated when I contemplate you hanging on the tree of the Cross. O mysterious tree, in the shadow of which I love to take my rest, how I love your fruit! O health-bringing fruit, your juice has given life to the world, and to my soul which was dead. O Jesus, I live for you; I want to live for you. O love: give me back my life by giving me death. Do I want to see Jesus? I need to see Jesus. Here is my heart; deliver the last blow.

In speaking to you, my Father, of the goodness of Jesus for my soul, do not forget that I am by myself. You know that I can do nothing except offend my Father in Heaven, unless he takes account of my weakness. I do not say this to you out of humility but because it is true. O how unworthy I am of divine favors! Pray that Jesus remove my unworthiness, you who surpass me in faith and in love, for I am nothing more than an ant wishing to begin to climb the mountain at whose summit you rest and from whence you contemplate the sun at noon.

Last Sunday, after reposing in Holy Communion like the beloved Apostle on the breast of Jesus — for almost two hours — I got ready to decorate the altar of the Holy Virgin when, standing before the tabernacle, the thought came to me to kneel down again because Jesus was so near me. In that moment, I felt wholly

---

[134] Almost certainly echoing Song 8:4: "Je vous adjure, Filles de Jérusalem, que vous ne réveilliez point celle que j'aime, que vous ne la réveilliez point, jusqu'à ce qu'elle le veuille," "I charge you, daughters of Jerusalem: do not awaken the one I love; do not wake her until she wants to wake." The Bride is here repeating, half asleep, the Spouse's injunction to the women not to wake her.

transformed in our Lord, so that I was no longer aware of myself: I felt nothing.[135] I had never before found myself in such a state; the adorable humanity of Jesus absorbed my whole being. Surprised by what I was experiencing, I only saw and felt in my limbs those of Jesus. I thought then of the words of the Apostle: *I live, but it is Jesus who lives in me.*[136] I would have liked for you to have witnessed my happiness. You can see what should be my gratitude and my faithfulness, but, my God, how I still suffer because I cannot make Jesus beloved enough. I burn with desire for his glory, and you know my frailty.

You are aware that I am not supposed to fast. So you see what I am not good at: keeping the laws of the Church. What a poor, useless member of it am I! But still I obey. But since I cannot fast, I want completely to reform myself this Lent. Pray for this.

I recently had the good fortune to pass four whole days close by our Savior, but even after this time, the yearning for prayer that our Savior gives me made me complain to our Heavenly friend that the days had passed too soon. It is so good to be at his feet! Why can we not live and die there?

But we must want what Jesus wants. Oh, how dear he is to me! O my Father, I am far from telling you everything that takes place in my soul. I would like to be able to express it to you for I know you love Jesus; I rejoice in the glory that you bring to him; I pray for you, every day, and I also pray for the souls to whom who proclaim the holy word. May our Savior bless your work and, one day may those souls, to whose salvation you contributed, become the most beautiful jewels in your crown.

I made my Communion for you on Ash Wednesday.[137] It seemed to me that, during Holy Mass, that I saw my soul in the chalice so red with the blood of the divine Redeemer. O my beloved! I love you; I dare to say, like the wife, that the tender and touching glances that you let fall upon me draw towards you all the yearnings of my heart.

Monsignor the Bishop has begun to preach Sunday; he is to preach four times a week. There was a great crowd for his first

---

[135] French: "de façon que je ne me voyais plus moi-même; je ne me sentais plus," "so that I no longer saw myself; I no longer felt."

[136] Echoing Galatians 2:20: "Je vis, non pas maintenant moi, mais Christ vit en moi," "I live, no longer me but Christ lives in me."

[137] Mercredi de Cendres (Ash Wednesday) was March 4, 1840.

discourse. I was told that he had to follow the history of the Church. I could not go that first time; I will go as often as possible. I leave you in the hearts of Jesus and Mary. After a few more days of pilgrimage and exile, we will taste the joys of our homeland. United always with our sovereign Good, we will lose ourselves in the ocean of his divine charity, in the depths of his eternity. I ask for your prayers for a person I care about, whom the Lord is calling. Ask Jesus that she be unable to resist the pull of his grace.

May Jesus be with you, my Father. I am in him your humble and obedient daughter.

Eustelle.

LETTER 55

The martyrdom of Saint Eutrope and the virgin Eustelle; Jesus Christ sacrifices himself every day; Jesus thirsts for the salvation of sinners; We ought to partake of that thirst; Desires for the Holy Eucharist, and for perfect humility; Anonymous letters; Plan for the Lenten station.

March 16, 1840.

All for Jesus.—Jesus be with you, my Father.

I just heard the holy word announced by our first Shepherd.[138] What good my soul experienced from the narrative he gave of the constancy and courage with which so many martyrs fought, giving their lives for Jesus Christ; and, because you say that I love only our Lord, I am singularly joyous to hear him speak of our glorious Apostle Saint Eutrope and of my courageous patron saint, Eustelle. How I rejoice to bear the name of that pure and fearless virgin! Why do I not have virtue sufficient to walk in her footsteps? Why can I not, like her, shed my blood for the Faith? For Jesus, to whom I am proud to belong. Oh my Father, let us prepare ourselves, if Jesus wishes. To give your life for him only once: it is still too little. O good Savior! It was not enough in your love to sacrifice yourself on the Cross; it needed to be that you renew your sacrifice millions of times, every day, until the end of ages. What an enormity of charity[139] in God for his creatures!

[138] French: "notre premier Pasteur," a term Eustelle occasionally uses for Bishop Villecourt.

[139] French: "O prodige de charité," "O prodigy of charity."

He alone is capable of such an excess of love. O my Father, how could we not desire to die for love of Jesus? It happens that, some days when I am attending Holy Mass, I see, after the elevation, our divine Redeemer, crushed before his Heavenly Father, yet offering himself anew for the work of our salvation. He seems then to turn towards me with the tenderest of looks and makes me hear these words: *I thirst; once more, I thirst*. For my heart, these words sum up the love[140] that made me understand the charity of the God-Man.

O my Father! Jesus thirsts once more. In the heart of his Father he thirsted; during his mortal life he thirsted; in the Garden of Gethsemani he thirsted; on Calvary, after all the torments and humiliations, he cried out from thirst. Ah, I hear him still in the Eucharist cry out that he thirsts, and I understand why, and for whom, his divine soul is so affected. Poor Jesus! tender, Heavenly friend! Your thirst will not be satisfied until the end of the ages. But, my divine master, can I not share this thirst with you? Is it not to your glory to cause me to feel with you this same ardent thirst that burns in your heart for us? O my adorable Savior! Yes: I too thirst, but it is you who excites my thirst. However, far from complaining about what you make me suffer, I beseech you to augment my sufferings of this kind to bring about my death.

O my Father, I am unworthy of this favor, but I ask that Jesus grant it to me. I have received his blessing; I asked for it also for you. Now I await the return of the dawn; it will announce to me the coming of the Sun of justice in my soul. Oh, how I long to see the tabernacle open! My heart palpitates with desire to possess the one who is its life. O divine Eucharist! How delightful it is for me to unite myself to you! You alone quiet the hunger that torments my soul. You are my good, all I hold on to;[141] I want nothing but you. More than the earth, more than any creature, more than myself. Jesus alone.

O my Father, read my heart: there is something else, but I cannot say it. Jesus knows it and you understand him. The goods that the divine Sacrament works in my soul are so continuous

---

140 French: "Elles furent pour mon cœur un trait d'amour," "They were for my heart a line of love," echoing John 19:28.

141 French: "mon bien, ma propriété," "my good, my property."

that it is impossible to capture them in words. My God! How unworthy I am of such graces! How feebly I respond to the love that Jesus has for me! Miserable creature! I offend him again and again, in every instant, but he sustains me. Ah, ask our Savior if he will grant me the gift of perfect humility; I desire this ardently, and this desire comes only from him. Humility to the soul is as sugar to fruit; try to make it come to me. Thoughts of your soul are often present to me before Jesus, I love to pray for your soul. Pray also for me.

Your letter did me good for, at the time I received it, my soul was suffering a little hurt that Jesus had sent me. Blessed be Jesus. Also pray for a young cleric who has need of our prayers; I will talk to you about him later when you are at Saintes.

The Protestants are strangely unquiet learning that Monsignor the Bishop is preaching Lent at Saintes. He has already received a number of anonymous letters urging him, in a manner almost threatening, to keep silent on controversial matters.[142] He shared one of these letters with the congregation. All of his Catholic listeners became outraged by the language it used to address our first Shepherd. He declared that all he wanted was the salvation of all his flock, but that, while he did not want to hurt anyone, he was not inclined to keep silent on matters that could affect the salvation of souls. It seems that Monsignor the Bishop's plan, in his instructions for this Lent, is to present a picture of all the persecutions and all the victories of the Church, from its cradle to our own days. He begins every day by discussing a detail from the Passion; then he moves on to present historical narratives, ending in a recapitulation, an exhortation and a blessing.

May Jesus possess you, embrace you, consume you, and recompense you in this life and for all eternity.

Thank you for the hymn you sent me. I like it; I have already sung it and taught it to others.[143]

Your daughter in Jesus,
Eustelle.

---

[142] There are a number of possible areas of contention to which this might refer, including lingering disquiet between Catholics and Protestants in the region over Bishop Villecourt's encouragement of devotion to Saints Eutrope and Eustelle, above.

[143] French: *fair chanter*, "made it sung."

LETTER 56

Apparition of the Heart of Jesus surrounded by angelic adorers; Jesus seems to take the place of the priest; Preferring an act of the will and a good desire to visions.

March 29, 1840.

All for Jesus.—May the cross of Jesus be your portion, his love your treasure.

I cannot refrain from recounting to you, my Father, the mercies of the Lord to my soul; it is a need in my very heart. How well does our tender Lord know my weakness! He sees that it is necessary to exhort me[144] through these testimonies of affection and the continual favors which he rains down on me. Oh, that I could return love for love for him! The divine heart of our good Savior was revealed to me a few days ago during Holy Mass, as though in a large and spacious place. His holy heart seemed to me to be larger than an ordinary heart; and I saw it not only filling this space with the fire of its love, but then darting its flames beyond the immense space wherein it was shown to me. Our Lord made me understand in this his desire to set the universe afire. I also saw several angels, in human form, who stood in adoration surrounding his adorable heart. All of the time this was shown to me, my Father, you understand it was my soul. My spirit was as though lost in that ocean of every good thing, and I knew I was incapable of understanding it. O heart of Jesus! O sanctuary of love! We have received this in fullness.

O heart to which all of us must be drawn! There is formed in you the design of our salvation, like the admirable and divine design to stay with us until the end of the ages; it is there, in the sacrament of the Eucharist, that the power, the wisdom, and the goodness of him who is the beginning and the end of our love rest in fullness.[145] O seat of peace and love, be my home! May it be your home as well, Father. I know it is your refuge; may it be the refuge of every heart. O my Father, pray for me that I may never stray from this refuge. You see how the beloved God is so lavishly generous with me; let me be consumed with love for him!

---

[144] French: *me prevenir*, "warn me."

[145] French: "devaient s'épuiser," "were to be exhausted."

A few days ago, I was struck by the grandeur of the sacrifice that was offered. After the Gospel, I looked and no longer saw the priest at the altar but our good Lord, with a solemn manner full of majesty, offer to his Heavenly Father the holy victim that was none other than himself. A God who offers himself to a God: what a sacrifice! I cannot comprehend such a gift.

It was especially at the moment of Consecration that my soul was seized with awe and love.[146] The sight of the God-Man, consecrating his body and blood, filled me with joy and happiness. With what hunger did I long for the moment when the beloved of my heart would come himself to bring me the bread of angels, giving himself to me! I forgot to tell you that I saw two Heavenly spirits serving him during the holy sacrifice; I seemed to see them near him when he gave me Holy Communion. All of this took place, as it were, in my mind, but I think I still see and feel what I experienced in my soul during this precious moment. It seemed to me that it was on the altar of my heart that the sacred host was being offered. I unite myself to this adorable victim, to be sacrificed with Jesus for Jesus: bless him forever.

I have not forgotten what you told me in your letter, to prefer an act of the will and a righteous desire to the images that Jesus produces in my soul; believe me that I am in no way attached to these things, and that the desire for the greater glory of our divine Master alone occupies me completely. I scarcely think about these things except to tell you about them; and if Jesus, who granted me the great grace of opening my heart up to you, demand that I keep the most absolute silence with you on all these things, I will submit myself to this with joy, persuaded that he would do this only for my greater good.

O my Father, pray for me. I pray every day for you. May we arrive together at the end of our voyage. May Jesus bless you. It is in him that I am your devoted daughter,

Eustelle.

---

[146] French: "de respect et d'amour," "with respect and love."

LETTER 57

Mass requested; Prudent privation; A love aflame and generous for the Holy Eucharist; Union of prayers and sentiments.

April 6, 1840.[147]

May the God of hope send you peace and joy, so that your hope grows always more and more through the virtue of the Holy Spirit.

I would like, if it were possible, for you to say a Holy Mass for a deceased member of my family, next week if it is possible. I would have liked to attend, but as far as leaving Saint-Pallais, everyone notices my absence and worries about the cause of it: so I do not leave. If I only knew the day of the Mass, I would unite my intention to it.

During what I was just writing, I was thinking of something else: how subject we are to distractions. But it is not my fault: whose fault it is you know well. Why does he carry his love so far afield, towards such a miserable creature? You know what I wish to say. It is that Jesus is too generous with me.[148] Do not be jealous: there is no reason to be. But my God! My heart is too small for this Jesus who wishes to house himself there. My soul, though it emanates from his infinite being, cannot contain the abundance of pain which intoxicates it and of which I am so unworthy.

I feel a temptation in this moment, to speak with you for a longer time. It is so delightful to speak of the sovereign good, of Jesus!

O my Father, how to tell you the state of my soul, since our last conversation! Do not think that there is any self-love in what I am telling you. It is solely for the glory of Jesus: he is my witness. How consoling it is for me to pour out my soul to you, who understands so well the language of divine love because you love God so much more purely than I, although this love is not always manifested to the senses.

Our good Savior increases more and more my love for the Holy Eucharist . . . What am I to do with such weakness? But he knows my desires which, I assure you, consume me every day. What martyrdom! Ah, I do not ask for it to end; it is too delightful to suffer for the one for whom I would give my life a thousand and a thousand times over.

---

[147] In the French edition, the year of this letter is given as 1841, almost certainly a printer's error.
[148] French: *trop libéral.*

O holy and divine Eucharist! Heaven is nothing for me. Weak and small host, you enclose all that I love, all that I want to love.

O my Father! I cannot express that which fills my heart: let Jesus tell you.

Yesterday morning, I went to the home of a sick person to prepare what is necessary for the reception of the divine Host. Afterwards, I had the happiness of possessing this pledge of peace and love; and my soul felt so strongly his presence that my body felt its effects. I could not help but let appear what was happening inside me. O my good and merciful friend! It seemed to me then that I wanted to affirm what I had done for the Lord, by adorning as well as I could the little altar on which he deigned to rest in this poor invalid's house.[149]

But I think about your soul: he speaks of it to me every day, as well as I do to his heart. Ah, if you could only see it as he showed it to me! Do not be afraid of the troubles he sends: they are according to his will. If your faith were not so strong, you would not have these sorrows. But Jesus likes to see you like this. Could you wish for something more? Be sure then that, despite my own miseries, I do not forget you when I am near that good Master. I love priestly souls: Jesus knows why. Pray that this good Savior accept the sacrifice I have made for them. But your soul will always know the special love[150] of my Savior, since it is the depository of the sentiments that Jesus in his love communicated to me.

So I unite the little that I do through Jesus with all that you do for his glory. Oh, love him for me, who suffer because I cannot love him enough. May he be your repose, your portion after this exile. And let us rejoice, for one day we shall enter the house of the Lord. In him I am

Your daughter Eustelle,
unworthy and poor servant of Jesus.

---

[149] What is being described here is a "sick call," a visit by a priest to the home of an invalid or sick, homebound person, bringing him or her Holy Communion and sometimes also the Anointing of the Sick (Extreme Unction). In former times the invalid's room was prepared in advance for the visit by setting aside a little table for the Eucharist (*Viaticum*) and for candles, oils and other items used in the rites. Apparently from this narrative, a sacristan like Eustelle might visit the house in advance to assure that the room was properly prepared. See Letter 4, above.

[150] French: "aura toujours la prédilection de mon Sauveur," "will always have the predilection of my Savior."

LETTER 58

Desire and confidence for the conversion of a soul; Eustelle bursts into tears at the mere thought of not loving Jesus; Pious memories; The dew of holy talk.

November 8, 1840.

Jesus, nothing but Jesus.

The dear Savior gave me the thought to pass along instantly to you, my Father, to recommend to your solicitude one of his sheep who is quite ill. This person wished to see me; I came and she received me very kindly, but that did not satisfy me. You know my weakness, yet I long for the conversion of this poor soul. And so I unite my feeble prayers to yours, that the all-good Jesus raise her from the abyss into which she is plunged. Do not forget this, I urge you; pray, and I will pray with you. I do not know the reason, but our Lord has the greatest confidence in me when I pray for her, and my soul expands with joy at the thought of her return to virtue.

Our dear and beloved Savior has consoled me in the pain that you caused me the other day when you asked me if I did not want to love him anymore. More than once has my heart swelled with sighs at the mere thought of not loving Jesus. Not to love Jesus? Ah, I feel the pain of that returning again. And you call me quite a child? But this object is so dear to me. O my Father! Why can I not die every day for love of him? But to come back to the malice you have done to me, I forgive you; all my revenge consists of asking our unique love to consume you more and more with the fire of his divine charity. Ah, I ask that you make yourself a holocaust sacrificed for his glory. The evening of that same day, at the feet of the tabernacle, my face inclined towards the altar, I could not help but shed tears thinking about the misfortune I would have if I did not love my dear master, and I proclaimed anew to him that nothing would be able to separate me from his love.[151]

I leave the blessed temple where love resides, and, as I thought how every day I labor for him, it came into my mind that you

[151] This paragraph is perhaps the best glimpse that reader can get of the complex and sometimes acidic relationship between Eustelle and her director, Father Briand. The paragraph notes the sting of his apparently calling her a "child" (Et vous dites que je suis bien enfant!) and accusing her of not wishing to love Jesus more.

too, Father, are also devoted to his greater glory. Yours are much more than my weak labors, but in the end I offered both labors to this Jesus who is so good and by whose side I spend such happy moments. O my Father, I ask that the God of the tabernacle instantly give you more and more of his light so that his unknowable designs are accomplished perfectly in you, so that you can understand more and more the road on which I am placed, and so help me advance on it by God's will.

I plan to go to vespers at Providence[152] on Thursday. I want to collect the dew of the divine word that Jesus pours into souls by your ministry. Ask our lovable Savior to prepare the ground of my poor heart to receive his divine seed.

I leave you, my Father, even as I remain attached to you by the charity of Jesus Christ our Lord. May the blessing of the Father, the Son, and the Holy Spirit descend upon you and remain forever with you.

Your unworthy servant and daughter, the poorest of those of Jesus,

Eustelle.

LETTER 59

The wondrous appeal of the infant God; Suggestions of a lying spirit; A tormented person; Five days passed at the feet of altars; An excess of sufferings.

December 27, 1840.

Glory to God.

My soul, whose workings I like to unite with yours, has associated itself with yours much more in this solemn work where the eternal life which is in the Father is shown to us. Oh, the charm of the infant God! How delightful is his appeal! How good it is to love him in this humble resting place, on this bit of straw where love himself reposes for us! And there are hearts that do not recognize him! Oh, the stupidity of humans! O unbelievable blindness! O my Father, let us pray: ask the grace for me to understand more and more the blessing of the incarnation of the God-Man.

[152] This is likely the Convent of La Providence in Saintes, about a half mile and across the river from Saint-Pallais.

The person you know has not made her Communion. There were times when she wanted to see you again, and other times when she did not. Her mother is quite worried on her account; she fears that her inner torments will be carried to her brain. Please try, with God's help, to calm her down.

I am staying close to our good Savior these five whole days, in the week just ended. He has given me an increase in suffering, for which I bless him a thousand times. Ask him please, that he never abandon my soul that is nourished every day by his divine substance. Oh, how I love the adorable Eucharist! And pray that I may love it even more. May Jesus bless you in his manger: this is the desire of her who is, through his heart, your daughter,

Eustelle, his poor servant.

LETTER 60

Eustelle, during the Holy Sacrifice, believes herself to be in Heaven; Annihilation; Invocation to the Sacred Heart of Jesus for the intention of souls; When will her mortal bonds be broken?—The river of peace.

February 8, 1841.

Glory and love to the hidden God.

Dearest Father, Saturday I wished to assist at the Holy Sacrifice in Heaven: for, the last time I attended your Mass, I found myself no longer on the earth. I saw you abiding where Jesus ascended in the cloudless sky; a multitude of joyous spirits surrounded the august victim, Jesus my beloved, Jesus my love. As for me, whom I would rather not talk about, I am at your feet, my soul lost in the contemplation of the marvels that took place on the sublime altar through the ministry that Jesus entrusted to you. Would that Jesus himself show you what my soul sees in these moments!

Tomorrow, since you wish it, I will ask Jesus that he give you his spirit, not in measured fashion but in plenitude. O minister of Jesus my God, I owe you the whole truth, and I confess to you that I am completely unworthy to associate myself with what you are doing for his glory. If the fullest confidence did not bring me to the heart of Jesus, I would truly fear, due to my deep misery, that I would arrest the action of grace in the souls rather than disposing our Lord to their favor. More justly than Abraham did, I speak to my Lord, though I am but ashes and dust;[153] it is because I am poor that I go to present myself to the All-Powerful; and still my poverty redoubles my confidence.

No, I will not forget you during the Holy Quarantine.[154] I would also like, like Mother Agnes to Monsieur Ollier, to come and listen to you.[155] It will always be that I am with you in the nest of the faithful dove.

O divine heart of Jesus! sacred hearth of eternal love, my knowledge, my refuge, my place of rest, my hope: I love you, I love you, I love you! Oh grant that I may know you more, that I may love you more and more; clothe me with your sentiments and share with me your inclinations, O unique center of all hearts! It is in you, inviolable refuge, furnace of love, that I dare to enclose in safety the souls that make up our little village of Saintes, to turn to the souls of another village which I do not know, but where my sisters are, on whom your divine breath will soon spread through the preaching of the holy word. Oh bless, adorable heart of Jesus, my joy and my life, bless the instrument of your mercies in this regard; grant him, more and more, conformity with your sentiments. His sole purpose is to bring you glory; fulfill his most ardent desires.

This morning Jesus has doubled my love for him: the desire I have of holding him, through the Holy Eucharist, is so violent that my very flesh trembles with joy. Ah, how infinite is the goodness of the Sacrament of the altar! Why must my mortal bonds not yet be broken? Why must I remain so long in the shadows of exile? Because you will it, my beloved Savior! O sweet honey of my soul, my only friend! Because you will it: your good pleasure suffices for me.

I know from experience, my Father, this river of peace that God promised, through Isaiah, to the faithful soul united completely

---

[153] Echoing Genesis 18:27: "Et Abraham répondit, en disant: Voici, j'ai pris maintenant la hardiesse de parler au Seigneur, quoique je ne sois que poudre et que cendre," "And Abraham responded, Behold, I now make bold to parlay with the Lord, though I am nothing but ashes and dust."

[154] I.e., "the holy forty," an archaic term for Lent.

[155] Mother Agnes of Jesus, O.P. (1602–34), was a Dominican nun in Langeac, a visionary and mystic who, like Eustelle, suffered physical and spiritual pains and sorrows. Late in life she came into contact with Father Jean-Jacques Ollier (1608–57), advising him to found an order of priests devoted to priestly education and formation. Father Ollier followed this advice, founding the Order of Saint Sulpice (Sulpicians) in 1645. Their story is chronicled in several pious books which should have been available to Eustelle.

to his supreme will.[156] Oh, pray that my will always be that of Jesus, my God and my all.

How I would like for your Mass to be said at the altar of Mary![157] But maybe it will be at the main altar, if Jesus wills it. And I have one request to make of you tomorrow. I am going to vespers at Providence. I associate myself most closely with you in the heart of Jesus, our love.

Your daughter, Eustelle.
Poor servant of Jesus.

LETTER 61

A tender reproach; Bodily sufferings.

January 27, 1841.

Jesus our love, our only love.

So why did you refuse to preach our Forty Hours? I believe your refusal has brought us bad luck: all of the priests we asked after you also turned us down. Jesus allowed this to happen, but I pray that he touches your heart.

How many things would I have to tell you if my health, which is very bad, only permitted it. But I cannot write for a long time because of a pain in my side that wears me out. I will patiently wait for the time that Jesus allows me to speak to you in person. Until then, my soul suffers in this prison; pray for it. I persevere for you and am, in Jesus, our love,

Your daughter, Eustelle,
poor servant of Jesus.

---

[156] Echoing Isaiah 66:12: "Car ainsi a dit l'Eternel; voici, je m'en vais faire couler vers elle la paix comme un fleuve, et la gloire des nations comme un torrent débordé; et vous serez allaités, portés sur les côtés, et on vous fera jouer sur les genoux." "For thus says the Eternal: Behold, I will make peace flow unto her like a river, and the glory of the nations like an overflowing torrent; and you will be fed at the breast, carried on your sides, and made to play on your knees."

[157] Older Catholic churches may still have "side altars" to the left and right of the main altar. These are usually adorned with a statue of the Virgin Mary on one side and Saint Joseph on the other. Mass celebrants had the option of celebrating Mass at one of these smaller altars for smaller congregations and on feast days of Mary or Joseph or at other times.

LETTER 62

An intellectual vision of Jesus hung on the cross and sacrificed; Silent adoration and love; Jesus always present in Eustelle's heart; A transport that excites in her a vision of the holy tabernacle and the image of Mary.

N.d. [*Based on adjacent letters, the date of this letter should be early February 1841.*]

Peace be with you.

I was sorry, my Father, that I did not tell you of the grace granted to me by our good Savior a week ago during the Holy Sacrifice. O dearest Father, trust in the sincerity with which I open my heart to you, and trust also in the pure, simple, and filial intention with which I communicate myself with you. These are not outlandish feelings that I wish to share with you, but only those which Jesus has given me, despite my unworthiness. I need for you to believe in all that Jesus inspires me to tell you. I say *need* because my soul is like a vase that is too small to hold the great quantity of perfume that spills over its edges. Oh, may you be permitted to enter into what I am not allowed to express, about the knowledge, the visions, and the lights of supernatural things which Jesus gives me! But what good is all of this if I cannot apply myself to respond to it faithfully, with a life completely in union with that same Jesus? *Yes, O my Father, I pay more attention to the desire and the act of will than to all those visions.*[158]

It was last Sunday when, during Holy Mass, Jesus occupied my soul with those same sentiments of which you spoke yesterday, and which you yourself experienced during this august action. As the moment of Consecration was about to come, about five minutes before, I felt my spirit ascend to Heaven; then, from this abode of glory, before the altar, I was shown a ray, or I should say, a pathway of light about four feet wide, bordered with a hedgerow of clouds as white as silver; and on these clouds were a number of Heavenly spirits who seemed to await, with profound respect, the solemn moment when the Holy of Holies would, if I may so speak, cross by this road the immense distance from Heaven to earth,

[158] This passage, italicized in the French original, seems to refer to Father Briand's earlier warning against *amour propre* or self-love, and specifically his instruction that Eustelle stay focused on acts of faith and will rather than on visions and transports. See Eustelle's Letter 56, above, from March 1840, roughly a year earlier than this one, that references his warning.

to humble himself—no, to annihilate himself—for the benefit of his stupid and ungrateful creatures. I cannot tell you how my soul was so enlightened, or how vivid and penetrating was that light that could only be supernatural. It seemed to me, in all that was presented to my soul, that my bodily eyes would have seen less than my soul itself. What I felt was in conformity with what I saw: I seemed to be free from mortal bonds, so clear was the comprehension that came to me. And it is how I am enlightened in all circumstances. So, no self-love: I do not think about it: but I am permitted to see, in your presence, a presence in which I see none but Jesus, and the continual gifts of the Creator God towards me. Oh, I understand them, but this is not to humiliate me any further. Yes, the more lavish Jesus is in his favors, the more humble I am; and the light he deigns to communicate to me, by revealing itself to my soul, serves as well, I hope, to make me know and feel my humility, my fragility, and my misery.

Scarcely was the holy victim placed on the altar of sacrifice, that I saw Jesus hung on the Cross by two flaming executioners; then, a new bronze serpent, he was lifted up between Heaven and earth.[159] He seemed fixed upon the souls that were at his feet, but the greater number of these were there only in bodily form. My eyes fixed on the divine Cross, I prayed to the lovable Savior that he permit me to sacrifice myself with him, and that I not experience the sadness of watching him die without me. What! I cried, my adorable Master, it is only a moment since, through the most prodigious of all loves, you descended to us from that altar: and now already you cannot wait to lavish your sacred blood on us. Your loving heart burns to bear witness to us, all at once, to the insatiable love that consumes it for us. And it was then that every word, every sentiment, gave place to the silence of adoration and of love. Jesus is sacrificed. Judge for yourself, my Father, the state of my soul then. Thinking about the sacred host reposing on the altar for me, I said to our Savior that I only wish to hold him in my hands and give him a million testimonies of love. I heard then, out of the depths of my soul, these words: *Am I not always present with you in your heart? What more do you need?*

Ah, I am happy, dear Father, to confer all of this to you for the glory of Jesus. I have no ambition except for his glory, and since

---

[159] Echoing Numbers 21:4-9 and John 8:28.

my weakness prevents me from doing for him what I desire, I join myself to you in what you do to bring him glory.

This morning before dawn, I went to find my love, my delight, and all my thought: Jesus in the tabernacle. I had to fix something there above the altar: I climbed there, a light in my right hand and, in my left, a crown I was to place on the head of the Queen of the angels. I had just kissed the holy tabernacle and was preparing to give this testimony of love to the statue of Mary, when I heard the main door of the church open. Imagine how quickly I climbed down! I was just in time, for this was a person who would have been scandalized if she had seen me climbing on the altar.[160] Even so, I was deprived of doing all that I had intended. So I spent some time adorning the altar; I was happy to be so close to my God. Oh! every look at the asylum that encloses my love sets my heart ablaze; and my joy is complete, until I possess through Holy Communion that Jesus who is so dear to me.

I know I will go home with a big headache, next Thursday, when I listen to Jesus speaking through your lips; but I will go anyway. My brother is very happy with the books you were kind enough to lend him. Pray, I ask you, for all my family. My sister is truly grateful that you will look after her before God. I am not finished with you, for I have more to say to you. Excuse me, then: it is divine love that makes me speak.

Your daughter, Eustelle.

LETTER 63

Trait of love; Thirst for justice; Delight before the tabernacle; A faith alive and luminous; Heroic zeal; Exhaustion; Powerful attractions.

February 10, 1841.

May Jesus our love bless you, illumine you, consume you.

The favors of Jesus transport me, my Father; my heart is set ablaze, my eyes are continually wet with tears. This jealous God has shot me a deadly arrow: I feel it, and yet I do not die. O how I love his will! Dear good Master! Oh, sweet honey, hidden treasure that so few souls search for! O my Father, let us be mad

[160] It is likely that "this person" is Eustelle's friend, Sister Anastasia; see Thompson 258.

for Jesus, for he himself was mad for us, whose holy madness caused him to die. Alas, my Father, what you say hardly eases my soul; I truly suffer. Jesus expands in my heart the thirst for justice, but I am always held back by my own weakness. Oh, blessed be his will!

My health is a little restored for me, until our love orders otherwise. I went back to my dear occupations in the sacristy: what sweet joy does my heart taste in this labor! I try to do it with Jesus, in Jesus, and for Jesus. Oh, how my time flows with happiness around the tabernacle! O my Father, what humility, what purity not to ask daily to approach the thrice-holy God! But are these virtues in me? Do not think that I give myself over to excessive fear; I know Jesus too well in his goodness to distance myself from him because of my unworthiness.[161] It seems that our Savior wanted to reward the little that I have suffered for him, by a degree of faith so lively and so luminous that I would be ready to give my life to make it known, when this knowledge should only be given to one soul. By virtue of this infused faith, I feel my soul perpetually consumed by the one who is both its author and its consummation. Lost in this transport so sweet, I find every useless conversation insipid, and I seek continually to say *Love Jesus!* Finding almost no one who attends this language, I am forced to make God alone the depository of my desires, and to suffer in the secret of my heart the thirst that consumes me.

If I did not love the will of God so much, it would not be to you but to God himself that I would complain that I have not been able for some time now to speak to you in person of his love and of what this love makes me endure. Do not think, however, that I ask for a cessation of my sufferings, for their origins are so pure. But I find my heart very narrow for the God who fills it. Sometimes I cannot bear its workings: this is the state in which I find myself now.

I must stop: I find myself exhausted. Jesus does not want me to talk to you for a long time. Commend my soul to that dear Savior; tell him I want nothing other than him, that I live only

---

[161] French: "je connais trop la bonté de Jésus, pour m'éloigner de lui sous prétexte de mon indignité," "I know too well the goodness of Jesus to distance myself from him on the pretext of my unworthiness." *Indignité* here literally connotes humility or lack of self-love, a repeated topic in Eustelle's correspondence with Father Briand.

for him, that I want to die for him. As for me, I have nothing but feeble prayers to offer, though you may rely on them.[162]

I am going to draw near to the Eucharist; this thought transports me outside myself. When I am near the sacrament of love, I am without words. Why is it not allowed for me to open the tabernacle and throw myself on the divine Savior like an infant on the breast of her mother! O Jesus! I leave your minister, your friend, and I go to continue beside you our tender conversation.

I pray to him for your welfare, my Father. May his spirit accompany you.

All for you, in his heart, your daughter,
Eustelle,
unworthy servant of Jesus.

LETTER 64

Favor of Jesus; Wishes for apostolic works.

February 16, 1841.

May the grace of the spirit of love be with you.

Do not forget, Father, to send your address to the poor but blessed servant of Jesus. Without your address, how could I transport my soul close to yours and tell you of the ineffable love that God sends you a thousand and a thousand times good.[163] Yesterday I received from the tender Jesus a favor that you surely cannot ignore, but I reserve for another letter to make known to you this new testimony of divine love.

May the one for the love of whom you are undertaking this trip reward you with his most abundant blessings; may his spirit inspire you every day with his divine breath, as you cast the mysterious seed of the divine word onto their hearts.

Your daughter and servant of Jesus,
Eustelle.

---

[162] French: "mais comptez-y bien," "but count on it," a distracting idiom in English.

[163] French: "lui dire l'amour ineffable que lui porte le Dieu mille et mille fois bon," "to tell him of the ineffable love that God bears him a thousand and a thousand times good!" The translation changes *lui* (him) to the second person for the sake of continuity.

LETTER 65

Eustelle complains that she cannot light in others' hearts the celestial fire that consumes her; She kisses the sacred feet of Jesus Christ; She dies from the need to make Jesus loved; No dearer refuge than the holy tabernacle.

March 9, 1841.

May the peace of the Bridegroom be with you, my Father.

If the will of our unique Father requires me to leave the sleep so sweet which I have just tasted at his fatherly breast, his accustomed love permits me to continue near you this delicious effusion of his soul. O my Father! Is it possible that love celestial, who is Jesus, communicates in this way with his feeble creature? Tell me why this bridegroom — so handsome, so holy, so pure — carries so much love to me to admit me to his chaste favors? O God! I feel, I see, I adore, but I cannot speak. O Jesus, my love! You whom my soul alone cherishes, why is it not given to me to reveal the secrets of your holy charity to the universe?

Oh, if you deign to consume me in that fire that is now almost unfelt by the rest of men, then let me light it where it has gone out. This is a need known to you alone.

Today, the ninth of the month, I make my Communion for you and for the souls you evangelize. Oh, our Lord love you; be confident in his help.[164]

So now I want to tell you of the precious favor that our dear Master bestowed on me. Already, a similar blessing has been given to me, and I have told you about it: it is that, after Communion, happy in the goodness of God himself, I suddenly feel my body and soul as though transformed into Jesus. I am so stunned by this transformation that I stay for a long time in an ecstasy of admiration and of silence.[165]

Is it believable that the joys of Heaven could be more lively, more pure, more expansive than those that inundate the soul when Jesus manifests himself in it? And yet this is given to me in exile, only a sliver[166] of the joys of the homeland.

---

[164] French: "comptez bien sur son secours," "count on his help."

[165] This is the first occurence of the word *extase* (ecstasy) in Eustelle's writings.

[166] French: *un échantillon*, "a sample."

Another grace that the tender friend of souls often accords me is that, when I am alone with him and loving, before I leave, to kiss the feet of his altar, he deigns to present himself to my soul and show me his own sacred feet, inviting me to place on them the kiss I was about to give to the altar step. Imagine, my Father, how all of this serves to set me afire more and more for the Jesus I love more than I can say.

And the moment has come for me to rejoin him. O good Jesus, my beloved! O soul of my life! Soon at your feet! Hear now my prayer: Set your priest afire who has no life except one to sacrifice to you. Kindle your frail virgin who wants only to love you or to die . . . who dies, in effect, from the need to make you loved.

Pray, Father, for her who lives only for Jesus, and who loves to unite the little that she does with all that you do for the glory of our common master.

Let us not leave the feet of the tabernacle, when the Lord grants us the ability to come to him and pay court to him. Let us endure, as though we are enclosed with him in the ciborium: it is the prison of his love; let us not abandon him; let us willingly spend there these days of our pilgrimage. When one loves Jesus, there are no more delightful moments than those one passes with him.

I suffer always: praise God. Pain provides a marvelous increase in divine love.

All to you, my Father, through the most blessed hearts of Jesus and Mary.

Eustelle,
poor servant of Jesus.

LETTER 66

Consuming, continual fire; Eustelle prays for all; Holy intoxication; She must continually write or speak of the divine object that enflames her; Submission and her life; Languor and jubilation.

March 17, 1841.

May the charity of the good Savior consume you.

I see myself, my Father, constrained to give in to the customary need to open my soul and to give free rein to the growing fire that consumes it. I do not know what the dear and thousand-times-good

Jesus wants me to become, but I am not able to endure the ardor of his love. This puts me in such a state of mind that, without the particular will of our Lord, it will be impossible for me to live long. But it is not only in Holy Communion or when I am at the feet of the tabernacle that I find myself almost immolated. The fire is continual: it becomes so intense that, in order to mollify and sate a little the thirst that I endure, I must continually either speak or write about the Heavenly love of Jesus: Jesus my life, Jesus my word, Jesus my thought, Jesus all that I see, Jesus all that I am. When I am permitted to see the divine Savior exposed in the monstrance, I am completely transported; I do not then know what I would not do.[167] But when I am thus almost ravished, I am not simply concerned about myself, but I pray for all of those who care about me: judge for yourself what place you occupy then in my thinking. And our little village of Saintes, how I commend you to the tender heart of Jesus! And all the sinners, how concerned I am for them! How I beg God for their sincere conversion. In these moments, I seem to myself drunk with desire and love; my tongue is not able to speak a single word: I leave everything to my faith and to my heart.

The other day, no one being in the church, I could not stop myself from going to kiss the door of the tabernacle. If there was any harm in this, I hope you will forgive me. I will not do it again if you forbid it, though I cannot claim that, in that moment, I will not give in to the same temptation again.

I can no longer pray daily prayers.[168] To contemplate and to love: these are my sole occupations. Then, at the end of that exercise, the fire that consumes me is so vehement that it is impossible for me not to speak about it, to bring everyone I know to the embrace of this celestial love.

Ah, why does Jesus make me thus to linger? Why does he thwart the fulfillment of my desires? Why, since my state in life does not permit me to procure his glory, does he leave me in a dying life, a living death?

---

167 French: "je ne sais alors ce que je ne ferais pas."

168 French: "prier dans l'oraison," "pray during the prayer," possibly vespers or some other communal prayer service. Eustelle's discomfort with group recited prayers is attested elsewhere and is cited as one of the reasons for her hasty departure from the Sisters of Our Lady of Charity much earlier, in 1835: "Her attraction to pure contemplation made her experience an invincible repugnance to the repetition of long vocal prayers" (Thompson 140).

O adorable will of my God! I submit myself humbly to you, for you are always adorable. I do not want to think or say or do what is opposed to your good pleasure; despite the desire I have to sacrifice myself for your glory, I consent to be, in your Church, a useless member, if you have thus decided it.

I am not telling you, my Father, to pray to God for me. I know your charity, but I implore you to ask him specially for the strength I need in the languor that divine love makes me suffer. Oh, with this languor, I am too happy! This love sends my soul into a state of continual jubilation. I do not know what I am. I pray for you, have no doubt.

Ah, we will arrive at safe harbor. Meanwhile, exiled on the river of this present life, let us work to attain the eternal one. Jesus awaits us there to crown his gifts, to crown our own feeble deservings.

All yours, through his heart,
Eustelle,
his poor servant.

LETTER 67

Return to the practice of religious duties; Eustelle burns with the desire to unite herself to Jesus if it is his will.

April 19, 1841, the anniversary day of my birth.

May the grace of the Holy Spirit be with you, my Father.

You are surprised, perhaps, to see me already at your door; but it concerns an important and very pressing matter. A person who has not been to confession since the Mission and who has sworn not to do so until death has now decided to do so most urgently. She is not from Saintes; I need to speak to you about this in person, and then I will write to you which day she can come. I have promised to give her an answer on Thursday.

While waiting for me to be allowed to come to you to open my soul, please pray for her: she is afire with the most ardent love, that love that I still expect will cut short my life's career. I do burn with the desire to unite myself to Jesus in the most intimate and unending manner. I leave you with him, my Father: in his peace, in his light, in his love. May he bless you: this is the most sincere desire of my heart. I am united with you in the love of Jesus, to die and to live as he decides. I am completely transported by joy and love for the God of my soul; I am on fire for the God who has set me ablaze. I do not know how to express this except with the words of the Bride of the Canticles: *Sustain me with flowers and fruits, for I languish in love.*[169]

Your daughter,
Eustelle.
Who lives not but in Jesus.

LETTER 68

Repose in the heart of Jesus, source of knowledge and of love; A tender reproach; Divine fire.

N.d. [*Presumably between April and July 1841.*]

For Jesus, humility and love.

The beloved disciple is not the only one upon the breast of the good Savior: it is also given to this poor servant to repose there with love, to sense the movement of that heart that beats for her. United to this adorable heart, she is nourished by love. It is from there that the anointing comes to her that instructs and enlightens her. Ah, through this heart we know everything that is important to know. I want no other book than this divine heart. There, all the souls that belong to Jesus live the life that he himself lives, in the bosom of his celestial Father. O perverse world, disappear for me! I have found on the chest of Jesus that holy ignorance that is preferable to all the lights of the professors, and the holy folly of the Cross that is better than all the pretended wisdom of the philosophers. I only want one science, that of my Jesus, who teaches me to attach myself only to him, to love nothing but him or for him.

I accuse myself of almost resenting you, my Father, and from here comes my desire to get angry with you. A pretty little admission, is it not? But then why are you so generous? When one gives alms to the poor, ordinarily, it is not a large amount. You

[169] A variant on Song 2:5: "soutenez-moi avec des fleurs et des fruits, car mon âme s'est fondue à votre voix," "sustain me with flowers and fruits, for my soul has melted in your voice."

will force me to keep silent about dear poverty from now on, a matter on which I would very much like to speak to you. As for the rest, I give in since you wish it: I do not want to stray from your recommendation to maintain a holy indifference.[170]

Let us pray that the fire that falls upon the earth, as you say it does, falls more and more; not only in my soul but throughout the universe, to set it ablaze and consume it. Oh, why can I not contribute to kindling it in every heart, at the expense of my life and of my very eternity, if, by some impossibility, I were allowed to renounce it.

I want to speak to you, but only if Jesus wishes. Tell me please if and when I will be able to talk to you.

Your daughter, the poor servant of Jesus, Eustelle.

LETTER 69.

N.d. [*Presumably between April and July 1841.*]

May the peace and joy of the Holy Spirit possess your soul.

I go to the house of bread: my soul is nourished there by the sacred manna that the world does not know. This morning, the good dear Jesus seemed to loosen my soul from its mortal envelope and plunge it into the immensity of his divinity. Oh, how clearly did I see it! It was Jesus the eternal truth, who is my light. Oh, how I desire to consume myself for him. Eh, who am I thus to fix the attention of his merciful love?

Two thoughts occupy my soul thus lost in his eternal being: how my nothingness is erased in his totality, like a drop of water is lost in the ocean; like the shadows surrounding the sun of justice.

O my Father, how good it is in Jesus! Everything else is unworthy of a Christian heart enlivened by faith. Pray for her whose soul is connected to yours in the love you have for Jesus. I join together with you, despite my unworthiness, in all of the apostolic works which you accomplish through your zeal for the glory of

170 The best guess about this disjointed paragraph is that Eustelle is responding to disapproving comments from Father Briand on her enthusiastic embrace of poverty. Specifically, it sounds as though Briand is reproving Eustelle for giving away too much of her meager earnings to the poor. We do not have Father Briand's letters to confirm these sorts of speculations.

our common Master. May he restore your health: this is the grace I ask of him. I pray that Jesus cover you with his precious blood, and, since it intoxicates you here below, I desire that it empurple the vesture of glory[171] in which you will be clothed for all eternity.

I am, in our Lord,
Your daughter Eustelle, unworthy and poor servant of Jesus.

LETTER 70

Jesus inhabits, delights and consumes the heart of Eustelle; Thirst for Calvary; Delicious suffering; Sympathy of pious souls; Return to God; Humility.

[*THE PERSONS MENTIONED IN THIS LETTER, L'ANGE INFIRMÉ (the Crippled Angel), l'Ange de Saint Jean (the Angel of Saint John), and l'Ange de la Terre (the Angel of the Earth), have not been identified. From the context it seems that all three were pious women living in this part of France and given colloquial names like Eustelle (l'Ange de l'Eucharistie). It seems further that Father Briand was connected to all of them. Also, see Letter 83 below.*]

July 24, 1841.

May the joy and the peace of the Holy Spirit be with you.

Your letter comes in so timely a moment, my Father, tempting me to speak to you for a few minutes. I receive it as I return from the holy place where, as you say, reposes the stranger, the unknown, the exile. Yes, my Father, he is my existence; he is that which I cannot say: God grant that you understand. My soul is outside itself, but it is in peace, because the good, the amiable, the all-desired Jesus inhabits it, delights it, and consumes it. How does he do this? I do not know. In the Eucharistic union, Jesus reveals himself, makes himself real to us in an incomprehensible way. Sometimes I jolt up as though to embrace him. Oh, how the good Savior burns in me with zeal for the glory of his Heavenly Father!

How the thirst for Calvary excites my soul! And in all of this I am but a poor, weak girl, helpless and incapable of anything.

[171] French: "empourpre le vêtement de gloire," "make crimson the garment of glory."

Bless him: this is all I want to be, in it is his will. I suffer from the injury of his love.[172] Oh, how delightful is this suffering! It makes me die and revive all over again. I want, in this moment, to be part of the reverent company where you find yourself, and to be able to kneel a second time at the foot of that holy image, in the presence of which I poured out my soul and shed many tears. His cherished features stay always in my memory, but they return especially when I pray for you and for *the Crippled Angel.* Tell this good young lady that, though I am not worthy of loving her, I dare to show her a lively and sincere affection. May the God of the tabernacle send her a full recovery. Yet I told her, at the same time, that I would not ask God to lessen her cross; oh, certainly, is it not so precious? Jesus gives it to her with so much love.

My soul was bruised with pain and yet filled with joy by the news you have brought me. A priest the enemy of Jesus! Of the God he has so often consecrated? Oh, terrible misfortune. Oh, how feeble is man! O Jesus, sustain us. I pray, oh yes, I pray, that Jesus give him the highest degree of repentance and love. And how happy I am to learn of his unequivocal return to God.

I leave you, my Father; the voice of the one I love calls me to his feet. I go to concern myself also with Mary, to decorate her altar in testimony of my gratitude. How good she is, this sweet Mother! If you feel like reading this letter to *the Angel of Saint John*, you have my complete permission. I fear, however, that my lack of humility in this writing will shock her. But since I have so little humility, I would not be upset if she learns of my deficiency.

May Jesus gather our souls in the fire of his love, in his home unknown to so many. There we can talk to each other, love as though we were in Heaven.

Testify to your *Angel of the Earth* my feelings of respect and affection, and know, my Father that I am always,

your devoted daughter Eustelle,
poor servant of Jesus.

O Jesus my beloved! I love you, I love you, I love you!

---

[172] French: "la blessure de son amour."

LETTER 71

The heat that consumes Eustelle's heart increases her sufferings; Jesus appears as a mystical lamb; His shining humanity is revealed; Unheard of favors; Invitation to visit Jesus Christ often; The promised land.

August 3, 1841.

Blessed and loved be Jesus, our love.

Do you not find me very indiscreet in writing to you so simply and on such little matters? Well, it is your goodness, joined to the will of Jesus, that makes me so bold. My Savior does not want to be the sole depository of the goods with which he has flooded me, of which he is himself both the principle and the author.[173] Poor creature! My sins have made me deserving only of Hell, but nonetheless the love of the God-Man has enriched me with a thousand favors. Since yesterday, when I had the consolation of speaking to you about the good and sweet Savior, my heart has felt so ablaze that today the little strength I had has left me. The heat that consumes me inwardly so overwhelms me that I find myself suffering more. Long live the Lord, and let him be praised!

I would try in vain to express to you the state I was in this morning during Communion and before this happy moment that alone appeases my desires. At the moment of Consecration, Jesus my beloved, ignoring my poverty and my misery, revealed himself to my soul in the form of a mystical lamb, whom I then saw sacrificed on the altar. At once he caused me to hear these words: *It is for my sinners that I sacrifice myself.*

Then after receiving my Savior, the bread of angels, friend of divine chastity, I saw him once more in his humanity, resting peacefully in the sanctuary of my soul; luminous rays shot out from the glorious body, filling the skies where his holy majesty reposed. I was able to cry out with the bride of the Canticle: *Come and lay down, my beloved, for our bed is covered with flowers.*[174] *O my Father, these flowers are not my flowers; they are God's alone.* Oh, ask this beloved Jesus whom I love, that he recount to you the tender effusions of his love, and what my soul feels when

[173] French: "et dont il est lui-même le principe et l'auteur," "and for which he is himself both principle and author." Eustelle is saying that Jesus is both the principle of goodness, "principe [du bonheur]" and himself the principal gift.
[174] Echoing Song 1:15: "aussi notre couche est-elle féconde," "and our bed is fertile"; Vulgate is "Lectulus noster floridus."

the divine bridegroom leads me into his mysterious cellar.[175]

Let us agree, my Father, that I am very unworthy of the favors of my Jesus; the reason for his love for me can only be found in Jesus himself, in the love he bears for me. At the same time understand how much I desire to love and bring others to love this God who alone is so lovable. I dare to tell you as well that, in describing so inadequately these desires that consume me, I feel it diminishing, in a way, what I suffer in the interests of our good master. I am so transported in this moment as I write to you that if I did not hold myself back, I would cover this paper with a thousand extravagances. Oh, let us love, then, the one who is love itself. You hurt me by telling me that, once, you did not love him; I assure you, on his part, that you love him very much. Oh, I am sure of this. So permit me to invite you, with a timid respect, not to leave our divine master alone in his prison of love but pay him visits as frequently as you can. Ah, tomorrow then, lay my desires and my weakness at the feet of the august victim.

For me, I consent to suffer, always to suffer. O my Father, I am ending, and my soul is not satisfied. I think of the Eucharist and feel my heart on fire anew. Ah, believe the sincerity of the sentiments I have poured into your soul. I dare to say, if I am beguiled, it is Jesus who has beguiled me. [176]

I ask you to pray for someone who has offended our Lord: do not forget. And another person just came to me to speak of her conscience: I shudder to think of what she told me. O this perverse century!

I leave you in exile, but with Jesus. How good, Oh, how delightful it is to have such a companion! We are now only glimpsing the promised land, but already he makes us taste its fruits. This foretaste sustains our weakness until the time when the veil is torn, when the shadows dissipate, when faith gives place to the eternal, perduring[177] love I desire for you.

I am always, in the love of our divine Master,
your daughter Eustelle,
unworthy and poor servant of Jesus.

---

[175] Echoing Song 2:4: "Il m'a menée dans la salle du festin," "He led me into the banquet hall"; Vulgate is "Introduxit me in cellam vinariam." These two phrases show fairly clearly that Eustelle is referencing the Vulgate.

[176] French: *trompé*.

[177] French: *inamissable*, "enduring," "not subject to being lost." The unusual word is distantly related to Calvinist doctrine of the perfectibility of man.

LETTER 72

Eustelle does not ever want to leave her solitude, that she might take care of Jesus.

August 20, 1841.

Jesus alone.

It is the will of my Jesus that I go out tomorrow. I say it is his will because, without that, I would like to guard my dear solitude; alone, I take care of him, my felicity in this place of exile. I will come to see you, if it is possible for you to make yourself available. As for now, I bow down before the feet of my God, to adore him, to love him. Why can I not simply die there? I will renew in his presence all my sacrifices. It is sweet to sacrifice oneself, when it is done in obedience.

And I find myself most happy to be, through Jesus, your devoted daughter,

Eustelle, his poor servant.

LETTER 73

Jesus! the cry of love; The mysterious, intoxicating ocean; Correspondence of the heart of Jesus with that of Eustelle; What she confided in him; Hunger and thirst.

August 20, 1841.

Jesus! Jesus! Jesus! Nothing but Jesus!

I just received a letter from Mademoiselle N***; I had strongly advised her to follow your advice, and I am persuaded that she will do so.

Jesus! Jesus! Jesus! This is the cry of your soul and the cry as well of mine, my soul that Jesus delights to take to himself more and more.[178] And so he permits me to take to myself the words of the wife: the king led me into his cellar.[179] Oh! how I am submerged in that mysterious ocean that so intoxicates me! Such sweet refreshment! But at the same time such a consuming fire! Eh! How is it at once to live and to burn like this? My dear Father, your heart is

[178] French: "se plaît à consumer," "is pleased to consume."

[179] Song 2:4.

greater than mine: so you love this love for me, this Jesus whose beauties so transport me. I tell you the sentiments that quicken my heart, because I need always to discharge this superabundance in my heart. It seems as though Jesus himself is battering my heart: each beat of his heart speaks his love for me . . . so why cannot the beats of my heart be so many acts of love and thanksgiving to him?

In just a moment, I will go and lock myself in with him; I will speak to him, in humility, confidence, and abandonment, about the holy ardor which he breathes into me. I will speak to him about the poor sinners that he wants to save, and about the Church, his bride and his mother. Oh! I will speak to him about you, too, my Father; speak to him about me as well, when you hold him in your hands. And think too how my soul envies your privilege.[180] And if my desires are extravagant, at least know too the pains they make me suffer.

I join you, my Father, in the secret of the heart of Jesus. Let us abide together in that holy dwelling-place, where the fogs of earth cannot touch us, where love alone occupies all our thoughts and sentiments.

O dear good Jesus! I hunger and thirst. I long to be near you, and yet I possess you already, for I can feel your beloved presence. It occupies me and satisfies me. It is enough for me.

Your most devoted daughter,
Eustelle, poor servant of Jesus.

LETTER 74

Holy love sometimes takes away speech; Her intention to exhaust herself for him; Trust in Mary granted.

September 7, 1841 [*Tuesday*].

All for the love of the most lovable Jesus.

My Father,

My young sister who brings you this letter will return at noon, if you judge it appropriate to give me a word of response.

[180] French: "combien mon âme envie votre bonheur," "how my soul envies your good fortune," referring to the priest's power to confect the Holy Eucharist and to hold Jesus in his hands. "Privilege" seemed more appropriate than "good fortune" for "bonheur" here.

Did you find me a little quiet on Monday? This was because the suffering love of the most lovable Jesus filled my heart, and it made my heart suffer greatly; but what sweetness it is so to suffer! O my Father! The experience deprived me of speech; I thought of him who is my life, my thought, my memory. Today, I could speak again; but I spoke only of my holy love, of Jesus and for Jesus my beloved, whom alone I love. I cannot shed my blood for him, but if I cannot shed it, I want to use it up, dry it out, consume it. I want, as far as I am able, to dedicate my voice, to use it up, and, in using it up, to make known him who is not known; the one whom you know, my Father, whom you love, who is your life's work, the one whom I know a little through his grace, whom I love, for whom I live and for whom I long to expire. Oh, this night, at the feet of the tabernacle, I begged him to tear from my breast my poor and miserable heart and to place it in the golden tomb where he himself is imprisoned, until I am alight with his divine fires. I begged him to accept all the acts of love that my soul formulated for him, and I prayed for my soul and for the souls who are dear to me.

I must tell you that I bought an altarcloth for the altar of the Holy Virgin; I have a great desire to make this offering to her but I lack the funds. So on Sunday I prostrated myself at the feet of the altar of our common Mother; I explained to her, with a simplicity full of confidence, how I longed to decorate her altar for the feast of Saint Pallais.[181] Mary heard my prayer; the next day I had the funds for it. See how good she is! Do not say that the love I have for her adorable son causes me to forget the holy Mary. Oh, I love her like a true daughter ought to love the best of mothers.

Think of my soul at the holy sacrifice, in the moment when Jesus so good comes in response to your voice.

I wrote today, all day, as you know.

Your daughter in Jesus,
Eustelle.

---

[181] October 7.

LETTER 75

Eustelle announces that she will open her heart to her bishop, who ought to know all of his sheep; His judgments must come first; Eustelle takes a trip in the company of Jesus Christ.

September 19, 1841.

Jesus be with you, my Father.

I would not go to La Rochelle, you know, without a reason that would require me to make the journey. For the tabernacle suffices for me; every other thing is without any interest for me. Oh, how Jesus wants to separate me from all created things; how I would bless him! But I bow down before his will so holy and so just. Do you fear that my health will suffer from this course of action? You have so much charity. Ah, Jesus has many means of weakening my bodily strength. If I were only allowed to tell you what he did to my soul, just last week! Ah, my Father, let him teach you himself. I understand that I must die if I am to love him as I want to love. Are you afraid that Monsignor the Bishop will make me talk too much? The Lord himself will give me the power to tell him everything that brings him glory and that is advantageous for my soul. I am not afraid of speaking inappropriately. There is a time to be silent and a time to speak.[182] Why should I fear opening my heart to him who represents Jesus for me on the earth? God will inspire him to ask me what is necessary for him to know, and he will dictate to me what is appropriate for me to answer. So I should rather be on my guard against a sort of timidity that would render me silent before our first pastor, for whom it is to know and to direct all his sheep. Even though Monsieur the Bishop might be, on certain points, of an opinion contrary to yours, I am sure you possess enough humility to prefer his decision to that which you would have given me yourself. It is, I believe, the Holy Spirit who demands that I take this step, so I will make this trip even though I have no other reason to do so. It would take too long for me to give you sufficient reasons for this decision.[183]

---

[182] Echoing Ecclesiastes 3:1–7: "un temps de se taire, et un temps de parler."

[183] Note in the French original: "The firmness that Eustelle shows here, and her perseverance in not departing from the resolution she had taken to submit her ways to her Bishop, show how distant she was the doctrine of Molinos and his partisans, who rejected reliance on episcopal authority

Tomorrow, at five o'clock in the morning, I have arranged to receive the divine companion on my voyage, Jesus Christ himself; I arranged to receive him before I leave. I will be sorry to undertake this against your will, but I am sure I will cause no distress by following the will of our adorable Jesus. Please be persuaded that I would be in despair if I ever displeased you.

All for you in the love of Jesus.

your daughter,
Eustelle,
his unworthy and poor servant.

LETTER 76

Jesus is with Eustelle in the exile of this life; Concern for the salvation of others; Happiness in being able to make Jesus beloved; Despair; The science of the Tabernacle.

September 21, 1841.

Glory and love to Jesus our God.

My Father,

Our Lord, I believe, has answered the prayer that you addressed to him on my behalf. I had seen disappear my hope of soon seeing the beautiful day of the eternal realm. Do not think I am sorry that this is his will; if I am in exile, then he is in exile with me; yes, he is with me, like he was in the boat with the Apostles, and this thought fills me with an indescribable consolation. O my Father, ask our tender Savior that, if he leaves me in his Church, I will not be a useless member there. The desire to save myself concerns me less than the desire to save others. Why must I be so helpless? Pray, then, I beg you, that our beloved God soon satisfy these burning desires by which his divine charity more and more consumes my soul. I cannot define just what is happening inside me, but I know that shafts of fire fly out from my heart at every

in spiritual matters. On this subject, see the Bull of Innocent XI, *Coelestis*, especially the condemned 66th proposition."

[The note affirms Eustelle's institutional orthodoxy and her respect for the hierarchy, especially Bishop Villecourt, who, in the spirit of full disclosure, was instrumental in bringing together Eustelle's *Recueil* mere months after her death.]

moment that are consoling to me, even as they are also greatly painful. Oh, if Jesus, the Heavenly friend of my soul, were but loved — if his ungrateful creatures simply misunderstood his benefits less somehow — then the zeal which they excite in me will be satisfied, and I will feel that the unquenchable thirst that devours me will subside. I rejoice in suffering, but I yearn for the adorable love to be known. If you could know how good he is to me still! I would have liked to see you, to tell to your soul a new mark of his love for me. His charity transports me. Ah, love him then, and sacrifice yourself to make him loved; make him loved in the hearts of those who, this week, will come to the bread of the mystery through your holy words.[184] You are going, no doubt, to speak of the one we love; Oh, that I might hear these words of life!

It is my intention in writing to you to ask if, however miserable and profane, I might be able to listen to you once or twice at Providence, and what would be the days.[185] If my presence somehow becomes an annoyance or my attending displeases the community, please let me know.

I have encountered a person who wanted to make her confession on Saturday but did not, because she was told that you would not be going to the confessional. She is in great need of your counsel; you know the ridiculous and extravagant thoughts that occupy her mind. Last week, from what she told me, she was in a state bordering on despair; she went so far as to think of ending her life. I talked to her for a long time and gave her some ways to diminish her melancholy condition, but she does not seem to want to use these ways. I admit that I felt a lot of pain seeing her in that state and I have promised to spend Wednesday with her, but I do hope she can speak with you before Saturday. So I beg you, by the very viscera of the charity of Jesus Christ, to be so good, as soon as possible, to try to bring peace and tranquility to this soul; my own concern for her makes me confident of your charity towards her.

---

[184] French: "faites-le donc aimer à ces cœurs dans lesquels, durant cette semaine, va tomber si souvent le pain mystérieux de la sainte parole," "make him loved then by those hearts on which, during this week, shall fall so often the mysterious bread of the holy word." The sentence seemed to require simplification.

[185] Father Briand is apparently giving a series of instructions to the residents of the Convent of Providence; as a layperson, Eustelle might have needed his invitation to attend.

I go now to visit our celestial and adorable master; I hope for a hearing that is favorable to your soul and to mine, for our two souls are dear to one another. I ask him there to give me more and more of the science of the tabernacle; for me, it is all I wish to know. O my Father! It is such a delight to speak of this God but, you know, it is better still to talk to him than to talk about him. Unable to express what is in my soul, I will expose it to the eyes of eternal truth; I will warm it in the goodly heat of the sun of justice. Oh, how good is God, my attraction, my love, my hunger: put an end to my desires! What you bless you set ablaze and consume, until that day of repose, when vision shall succeed faith, when joy shall succeed waiting! Until then I stay with you in the tender heart of the peaceful and loving Jesus.

Your daughter Eustelle,
his unworthy and poor servant.

LETTER 77

Pure gold; The Eucharist, Eustelle's life; Death, the object of her wishes.

October 24, 1841.

Everything in Jesus.

My Father,

I had planned to go and knock on your door on Monday, to ask you for a light. It is not that the one whom I love so much leaves me in need: he is so good! Yet I am so unworthy of his kindnesses, but I am ambitious: the more that is given to me, the more I want to have. Let me obtain, I beg you, the pure gold of holy love. I have heard you tell me that you do not love enough to obtain for others that which you believe you do not have yourself, but I know the opposite to be true. I go to the feet of the tabernacle, and there I will be in the good company of the heavenly bridegroom of our souls. Oh, Eucharist! It is my life; it is all I know, all I see; but it pains me not to have enough love, although it seems to me that I am transported to the adorable Jesus. Why can I not hold him in my arms like Saint Gertrude or Saint Anthony of Padua,[186]

[186] Saint Gertrude the Great of Helfta (1256-1308) was the author of a popular prayer to the Child Jesus. Saint Anthony of Padua (1195-1231) is generally depicted holding the Christ Child.

and protest to him a thousand and a thousand times that I am smitten with his love? O death, my good friend! Come and give me the object of my desires.[187]

You sent me word that you would come to see me in my illness, but I do not want to put you to that bother: I feel as though I should be well enough to go and see you. If you do not want me to make the journey I submit to your will. If you are coming, though, please tell me at what hour. Truly you have great charity.

I leave you in the heart of Jesus: he is my refuge during this night, until the dawn returns; I unite myself to the Heavenly spirits and to the adoration that Jesus himself perpetually pays to his Father for us, in the mystery of his incomprehensible charity.

Your daughter in Jesus, the poorest of his servants,
Eustelle.

LETTER 78

One must die to love truly; Eustelle's languor; She is wholly submitted to the will of God; Holy folly preferable to the wisdom of the world.

October 27, 1841.

Jesus always.

Since his holy will closed the door of his temple to me, I come, dear Father, to beg you to open that of your soul. I feel an inexpressible need for the fire with which Jesus consumes my heart. It is always the God of the tabernacle who once more sets my love afire. Tell me, dear Father, what more could Jesus do for me. Oh, let him tell you what my soul is to him. Being at his feet the other day, I said to him, Lord, I die from the need to tell you how I love you. Ah, these words repeated a thousand and a thousand times cannot satisfy the insatiable desire I have to love him more and more. O minister of my God! One must die to love in truth. But, O will of my Jesus, it is to you alone that I attach myself.

And yet, my Father, I can tell you that I suffer greatly, but what blessings are these sufferings! I languish: often I borrow the

[187] French: "O mort! O ma douce amie! Viens donc me rendre à l'objet de mes désirs," "O death! O my good friend! Come and give me the object of my desires." The translation assumes that all three short sentences are apostrophizing Death.

words of the bride of the Canticles, asking that Jesus sustain me with flowers and fruits.[188] You know what these flowers and fruits are. Besides the ones you know, I want also those of the Cross, of persecutions, of humiliations, and of contempt, but beyond all of these, I love best of all the most holy, most pleasant flower of his divine will. No, despite whatever I might be or do for Jesus, I want only the satisfaction of his good pleasure. When will he allow me to speak to you to convey to you the ardor of my pious desires? Some of these desires, I know, cannot be realized in this life, and yet it is my Jesus who excites these desires. What does he want from me? That I leave the earth?

Ah, look at me here, ready to fly away to the homeland to prostrate myself at his feet, to throw myself into his arms, intoxicate myself with his delicious love. What does he want from me? That I remain banished? Ah, I consent to that too, but let him satisfy my desires or let him temper their burning ardor. But what am I saying? I do not want the ardor to be tempered: for, if it gives me suffering, it also gives me happiness. O you worldlings![189] If you heard my words, you would call me mad. I am: I admit it. But leave me to my madness and keep your wisdom for which I will never envy you.

I leave you, dearest Father, to repose in the divine heart of Jesus. There one can know everything by ignoring everything. Remember my soul: it is entirely devoted to you in our loving Redeemer.

Eustelle,
poor servant of Jesus.

LETTER 79

All creatures are insipid to her; Yearning for the Heavenly homeland; Transported by the sight of the vessel containing the Eucharist and by the thought of the heart enclosed in it; Tears; The cradle of the infant Jesus; his charms; his sleep.

November 25, 1841.

Glory and love to Jesus in the Eucharist.

With what regret have I just left the feet of the tabernacle, my Father! With what sadness, even though already resigned, am I

[188] See above, Letter 54 of March 10, 1840, also echoing Song 8:4.
[189] French: *Mondains*, translated as "denizens of the world (le monde)."

separated from the supreme Good, my God and my all! Oh, how painful it is for the soul that tastes only Jesus to lend itself to created objects! And how does my soul suffer from being unable to be rid of all that seems dead to it! O good divine pleasure, you alone make me enjoy what makes me suffer, and those occupations to which I give myself up for Jesus are sweet only through you.

Nevertheless, my Father, I am tired of creatures; it is infinitely sweeter for me to talk to God and about God.

Tonight, the divine Master made me understand something of the joys of Heaven; I felt, through an intellectual vision,[190] powerfully drawn towards the Heavenly homeland where the soul sees Jesus, where it lives by his divinity and his eternity. Oh, awaiting that eternal day, I leave off, enclose, and hide in the lover's wound, in the heart of my Jesus, in the God of the Eucharist . . . what do I leave there? — my soul and all its powers, my heart and its burning desires, all its affection, my thoughts, whatever they are, my memories, delightful and painful both, and all my weakness. Oh, Jesus knows all of this, and how painful it is to me when I think how I cannot glorify and love him as my ardor directs me.[191]

This morning, the hidden God was carried to a sick person, and I came along. I had gone there before to prepare a little altar. Seeing the holy ciborium resting there, O how I wanted to be able to press it to my miserable heart. The mere memory of this makes me shudder. Jesus and you too are aware of the pain that comes to my soul from this cruel privation. So I am content to lay bare my immense desires in the presence of my God. And when my work as a sacristan permits me to kiss the holy corporal on which he is laid,[192] O God! it is such tenderness to my heart! What an outpouring of happiness, joy, and love!

This love has given me a violent headache this morning; the thought of the goodness of our Lord come to the home of this poor, sick man, and the thought of his grandeur brought as though to

---

[190] French: *vue intellectuelle*, "an intellectual vision," that is, a mental vision without images. See *Memoir*, chapter 21, note 63, above.

[191] French: "quand je songe que je ne puis le glorifier et l'aimer comme j'en aurais la passion," "when I think that I cannot glorify him and love him as I would have a passion to do."

[192] A corporal is a white linen cloth, usually about a foot square and typically with a small red cross embroidered at the center bottom. It is spread out on the altar before the canon or Eucharistic prayer; the chalice and paten are to sit on the corporal during the Eucharistic prayer.

nothing under such a fragile species,[193] made me shed many tears. O hidden God, often unknown to those who are consecrated to you, why is the power not given to me to express what my soul understands of your Eucharistic love! I just received a new favor of this love of the angels: it is that, in Holy Communion, my soul was represented to me as the cradle of Jesus. It was during my prayers of thanksgiving that he showed himself to me, at the age of six. What divine sleep! What a beautiful face! Such a perfect peace in all his movements! And, despite being asleep, he seemed to be aware of me. I can see him now: to borrow the sentiments that you expressed in the Canticle of Canticles, which you adapted to the Holy Eucharist, let me repeat these same words with you: "Sleep, sleep, merciful and peaceful friend, sleep: do not be afraid that I will wake you, for your sleep calms me; your closed eyes open mine; every beat of your heart echoes in my heart, and that echo is my act of adoration and love."[194]

After so many benefits, very dear Father, silence, love, and admiration are my soul's ordinary acts of thanksgiving; I offer Jesus my powerlessness in response to his benefits; I consecrate my life to him which is consumed little by little. Speak then of my soul to this love whom I love, O my Father, when this same love is made flesh in your hands. Oh, then I would like to lie prostrate near you, made into nothing, my eyes fixed on the victim of our love. Relish, I say, relish alone this incomprehensible happiness, and may Jesus in these precious moments engulf you in his divine fires.

Pray for me; though I do not like that word, "me." I do pray for you. I burn in the flame that transports me; and yet, I am very poor, extremely poor. I very much like to talk about poverty; and yet I do not always practice it. Why? I can tell you simply enough: I am afraid that there is no remedy for it.[195]

Your unworthy daughter and poor servant of Jesus,
Eustelle.

---

[193] French: "et le sentiment de sa grandeur anéantie sous de si fragiles espèces," "and the feeling of his grandeur annihilated under such fragile species"; "annihilated" (anéantie) or "brought to nothing, eradicated" seemed inexact in the context. See the next sentence: Jesus's grandeur is *hidden* (caché), not annihilated, in the Eucharist.

[194] The general sentiments here evoke the language of the Song of Songs, but the passage has no direct parallels in the Biblical text.

[195] A confusing sequence of ideas, both here and in the original. Eustelle may be distinguishing between actual financial poverty and the virtue of being one

LETTER 80

Plenitude of heart; Jesus is her all; The Eucharist has no more clouds for a lively faith; She wishes to die at the feet of Jesus; Jesus hides from evangelical workers the results of their labors.

December 10, 1841.

May Jesus live in every heart.

Here, my Father, are the verses on which you are to write the couplets that you had the kindness to promise me.[196] I pray our Lord give you the thought not to forget about them.

Esprit-Saint, prêtez-lui vos ailes;	Holy Spirit, spread your wings,
Descends, Esprit consolateur,	Descend, O Consoler Spirit,
Et viens, des voûtes éternelles,	Come from the vault of Heaven
Verser tes feux dans notre cœur.	And pour your fires into our heart.
Ah! si, du sein de la lumière,	Ah, if from the bosom of light,
Tu vois, à mon heure dernière,	You see in my last hour,
Pâlir le flambeau de la foi, (*bis.*)	The torch of faith begin to fade, (*repeat*)
Esprit d'amour, éclaire-moi. (*bis.*)	Spirit of love, enlighten my way. (*repeat*)

But why leave the rest of the page blank when my heart is so full of the need to pour itself out? Since I left you at the feet of our good Savior, the adorable master has not ceased firing his arrows at me and, if he continues, I will not be able to withstand their effect. O my God! how these transports of Heavenly love are martyrdoms for the soul that they affect! But how lovely is this pain! Ah, if I am not allowed to use my own feeble voice to proclaim the ineffable love of the Redeemer God to the whole universe, then at least let it be given to me to entrust my whole soul to you; and to speak to you, my Father, of him who is the

---

of "the poor in spirit," "les pauvres en esprit" (Matthew 1:3). Catholic teaching is that poverty of spirit has less to do with the amount one owns and more to do with one's attitude towards material things, with celebrating self-denial and want. It may be this paradox that Eustelle sees as having no remedy.

[196] The translation retains Eustelle's apparent distinction between her own *verses* (vers) and the *couplets* which Father Briand has promised "to write upon them." The original French appears alongside the translation to show Eustelle's work with meter and rhyme. By including them here, she seems to be reminding Father of his apparent promise to rework them into couplets.

only good, the only tender, the only lovable, the only one worthy of being loved: of Jesus our father, our king, our friend, our companion in exile, our everything.

Oh, how beautiful is Jesus, love uncreated. But now he is so misunderstood, so forgotten, even so despised! I come from his sanctuary: ah, in what disposition does he put my soul in those precious moments? To tell it is impossible. All that I know is that my spirit has no other thoughts, my heart no other sentiments to express in the presence of this God three-times-holy. Ah, my Father, you know it, you to whom these secrets are not unknown: the Eucharist has no more clouds for a lively faith. O sacrament of my God! how essential you are for my soul! O Jesus, how I love the cloud that shrouds your holy majesty! O my Savior! I am no longer close to you; I want to say, close to your sacrament, but my heart constantly turns to you, its dear object! I see you under these fragile species surrounded by a multitude of Heavenly spirits who are my friends because they love Jesus and I love to be with them.

O my Father, I would like to be permitted, every day, to fasten my lips[197] on the sacred host. What a thought! Ask that he grant me this alone, despite my unworthiness: the invaluable privilege to expire at his feet, at the feet of the tabernacle where my tears have flowed so many times, at that tabernacle I have chosen for my home until the day of eternity.

O you my Father, who loves more than I do the God of the Eucharist, show me the way to love him more; ask the God of charity to make me penetrate more and more the secrets of his love. And rely on my own feeble prayers. But I do not like to hear you say that you are not where you are supposed to be. Oh, if the will of God calls you somewhere else, you will certainly not resist it.

Be at peace; I see well your zeal: you want to convert souls by the thousands, as Saint Francis Xavier did.[198] Have patience: if the Lord shrouds your works in a cloud that seems to take away your view of their results, he does this only to increase your final reward.[199]

Your daughter in Jesus,
Eustelle.

---

[197] French: "coller, chaque jour, mes lèvres," "stick, each day, my lips."

[198] 1506-1552; early companion of Saint Ignatius Loyola at the University of Paris and co-founder of the Jesuits; legendary missionary to India and Japan.

[199] French: "il n'agit de la sorte que pour en augmenter le prix," "he does it only to increase the price."

LETTER 81

Confidence of the priest at the holy altar, to obtain the conversion of sinners; Eustelle groans at her own impotence; Jesus wants her to suffer always; Visits to Monsignor the Bishop; He approves her intellectual visions; The bishop's Lenten instructions.

February 23, 1842.

Glory and love for the unknown God.

Jesus, then, is allowing me to speak with you for a moment now that my fever has passed. Nothing is sweeter to me than the divine language. I know already that Jesus is in you. Tell me, my Father: do we know where you are, the Savior beloved, my martyrdom, my death, my life! Who is there to repair his rejected glory? He is most assuredly within you. Oh, that through you his worshippers gather in spirit and in truth! May you be victim together with him: may his *sinners* be *your sinners*. O my Father, it is given to you to bring them, every day, to his altar. What confidence must come alive in you when, taking into your hands the infinitely holy Lamb of God, you present him to those whom he calls, with affection so full of mercy, *his sinners*! I join myself to your zeal for the salvation of the souls you nourish every day with the Bread of the holy word. Ah, if I cannot preach, why can I not, at least, pray well? For me, ask for the virtues that will bring Jesus to answer me. All my being, it seems, breathes only zeal for his glory. Why do I not have a thousand lives to consecrate to him, a thousand sacrifices to make for him?[200] O my Father, unite, unite to yourself this little bit that Jesus makes his poor servant able to do; unite them to the works that the interests of the ineffable Master make you undertake. Ask him that the sacrifice of my powerlessness satisfy the desires by which he is pleased to consume me.

What can I say to you now about my soul? Is it divinely happy? Words cannot express my happiness: only Jesus could teach you that. His love is always what moves me completely. Physically, I am always suffering. He promised this to me, and this is how. On some days, I am heart to heart with him: I recall the request made to him by the virgin Agnes concerning Father Ollier, and like her,

[200] French: "Pourquoi n'ai-je pas mille vies, pour les lui consacrer comme autant de victims," "Why do I not have a thousand lives, to consecrate to him as so many victims."

embracing his lovable and super-adorable will, I ask him that, if I am not able to procure him glory, if I am not useful here below in the world, would he be good enough to call me to himself.[201] And then that adorable Savior made me hear these words: *It is my will that you suffer again and always*. It was with touching and tender goodness that our Heavenly Friend intimated to me this desire of his heart and, by his grace, led me to accept with love these sufferings and the prolonging of my exile.

Though I am unworthy of your thoughts, please, my Father, do not disdain the needs of my soul, when Jesus, traversing the immense distance between his humanity and ours, becomes flesh and rests in your beloved hands. How must your soul feel in such a solemn instant? Oh, human language cannot express it. Since I am not able to participate in this privilege, ask Jesus that he give me, more and more, knowledge of the most ineffable mystery.

Why don't you let me do this Lent what you let me do last Lent?

Something else to tell you. I have just come from Monsignor the Bishop, who, as you know, is come to Saintes to preach, as he did two years ago. He graciously accorded me a conversation that lasted three quarters of an hour, the second I have had with him. You do not doubt what was the subject. Even now I am still amazed. From my first visit, before I had said anything to him, he asked me why I had not made known to him, more particularly, the spiritual life I was leading.[202] He approved of my not revealing my soul to lots of people, but said that I should reveal everything to him because he has received from Heaven the necessary power and authority to judge and make determinations on the state of souls. Forced to answer, I told him that, out of the fear of self-love, I do not like to speak freely to him about what passes in my interior. Monsignor the Bishop was not deterred by this; I was obliged to provide some details in regard to my prayer and the effects it produces upon my soul and my body, and of the love that Jesus communicates to me. I had to speak to him of the special graces that our Lord accords me, specifically mentioning only three: the apparition of our Lord during

---

[201] French: *suradorable*, "super-adorable." A reference to Saint Agnes of Jesus, O.P., and Jean Jacques Ollier, founder of the Sulpician Fathers: late in her life, Mother Agnes supported Father Ollier's vocation through her prayers and encouragement, much as the ailing Eustelle sees her relationship with Father Briand. See Letter 60, note 155, above.

[202] French: "la voie par laquelle je suis conduit," "the way by which I am led."

my interior pains; when he represented himself to me again during prayer as he was when Pilate, showing him to the Jewish people, said to them, *Behold the man*;[203] and one last favor, which I have already told you about, that took place at the moment of Consecration.

What do you think, my Father, that Monsignor the Bishop thought of these, as against what you yourself decided? His sentiments conformed to yours: and he added that, in what I had said to him, he saw nothing sensible[204] and recognized them more as supernatural workings, and that from them I should not be fearful of delusions, provided I had not prepared and disposed my imagination to give birth to these images of mind. This is not my situation; I can say that I have never gone before what the Lord has deigned to work in me. Everything was always unexpected to my surprised soul. When these things happened to me, I thought only of humbling myself before God, of annihilating myself and loving him. Suddenly the picture that struck me presented itself to my soul: nothing had prepared my soul for these favors. It was God who did everything, and my imagination and my desires were constantly kept separate from them.

So you see, my Father, how our Lord allowed the judgment of our First Pastor to be a repetition of yours. He has recommended to me that I write carefully and religiously[205] all that concerns my spiritual life: the transformation of my still earthly affections to pious ones, and then to a supernatural state. This is precisely what you yourself have suggested. I told him, in a few words, of my communications with you and the sentiments you have expressed. He seconded your decisions and seemed to me quite disposed in your favor. He had never spoken to me as he did in these two conversations of the intimate union with the soul of Jesus, of the tokens of the good Savior's familiarity[206] with the soul. I tell you I did not

---

203 John 19:5.

204 French: "rien de sensible," "nothing of the sensible"; sensible, having to do with the senses. The bishop is distinguishing Eustelle's experiences as "intellectual visions" and not apparitions or delusions.

205 French: "avec soin et avec un enchaînement régulier," "with care and with regular sequence."

206 French: "des familiarités de ce bon Sauveur avec cette âme," "of the familiarities of that good Savior with that soul"; "token" is my addition, to avoid the odd-sounding plural of "familiarity." It is unclear whether Eustelle is saying that Bishop Villecourt is speaking of his own soul's familiarity with Jesus or is speaking generally.

put him on this path. I was preparing to tell him many things in our second conversation, but I found him extremely preoccupied with the concern that I might think myself something special because of the favors that the Lord has accorded to me.

"My child," he said to me, "there is always a great precipice alongside the most signal benefits of divine mercy. It is for this reason that, when the Apostles returned to Jesus to tell him of the marvels that they had done, the Lord took great care to tell them that it was at the highest point of his glory that Satan had been cast down from Heaven into Hell."[207]

Monsignor the Bishop added that self-love could, in an instant, put the Demon in the place of Jesus in a soul. He gave me many examples which so struck me that they filled me with anger.[208] First, he shared the example of a very pious and contemplative person who was intoxicated by the esteem she thought she inspired, and became a visionary to the point of ridicule and was mocked as fully as she thought herself to be admired; then another example, of one who pretended ecstasies and ravishments and deceiving a respectable cleric into believing she was a saint; and lastly, the case of a young woman of the diocese of Sens, who pretended to have discovered the state of souls, assigning some to Heaven, others to Hell. She also dabbled into being a prophetess: one year, she managed to procure four or five hundred francs, which she used to buy wheat at a very high price, saying that there was going to be great shortage and scarcity; but, in the year that followed, the harvest was so abundant that such a low price for wheat had not been seen in a long time. In addition this woman then predicted that she would be the foundress of a religious congregation, but she died a short time after making this prediction. And a priest, for one, very virtuous and a confessor of the faith, had blind faith in this girl. He had written, inspired by her, a huge jumble of her reveries. There were claims in it, Monsieur the Bishop said, that simple reason should have condemned as contrary to common sense and to delicacy. Her ecclesiastical superiors, when they heard all that was being said about this creature, took steps to test her humility and obedience, learning quite soon that she possessed neither of these two virtues. Her death took place under appalling

[207] The reference here is Jesus's brief dialogue with the returning disciples in Luke 10:17–18.

[208] For a description of this scene, see Thompson 311–12.

circumstances, and yet certain adepts who were infatuated with her continued to regard her a saint. There were even processions to her tomb and marvelous tales told by those who chose not to give up the falsehoods that they first believed about her.

Then Monsignor the Bishop finished what he was to say to me, engaging me and depending on me always to walk the simple path, and assuring me that doing so would not prevent the Holy Spirit, if he wished, from leading me along another road. I know I need not tell you, my Father, with what respect and obedience I followed all that he was so good to say to me. And I noticed that he smiled at me when I told him of certain not-too-reasonable desires I had at the sight of the altar and the holy tabernacle.

"It is enough," he told me, "that you receive Communion every day. It is good to love Jesus Christ, but our love for him must always be accompanied by profound respect. The Church does not permit even the priest himself, through an improper familiarity, to neglect the veneration that is due to the most holy and most adorable Sacrament of the altar; and he is not permitted to open the holy tabernacle without wearing a surplice and stole and with one's head completely uncovered."

Hearing these words, I felt their full significance. So I stopped myself from telling Monsignor the Bishop about all the extravagances to which the transports of my love for Jesus in the Blessed Sacrament have brought me.

The topic of the Lenten instructions that Monsignor the Bishop is preaching here at Saintes is virtue placed in parallel with vice. He is showing that, if there comes any happiness in this life, it comes through virtue, while every misfortune comes from vice. The instruction is always preceded by a short exposition on one of the commandments of God. A lot of people attend, mostly men.

You have maybe never received such a long letter. Do not forget me at the feet of Jesus. Oh, how happy he has made me this morning! The sleep of my soul is so sweet that I would have like to have awakened in Heaven, in the arms of Jesus our love. Good Savior, when will I fully enjoy you? When will I know your divine essence? That day will come, let us hasten its coming by our desires.

I leave you, dearest Father, joined to me in Jesus, our all; may he bless you, as does the one who, despite her unworthiness, dares to call herself your obedient daughter,

Eustelle,
poor servant of Jesus.

LETTER 82

Eustelle's life is no more than a death; Perfect submission; Inexpressible desires to possess or contemplate Jesus without cessation; He lives more than she in Communion; Beautiful movement of memory; Vision of the heart of Jesus; Next departure of the prelate.

March 12, 1842.

O Jesus, dear spouse, you whom my soul cherishes: speak.

I return, Father, to my accustomed language. My God, I desire to identify myself, more and more, with the object of my love! Ah, my life is nothing more than a death. But how to depict this state of the soul? I can only stammer imperfectly, forced to rely the more on my words and the less on my love. And why? Because my heart cannot love as much as it desires. Oh, how painful is this barrier of incompetence! However, Lord, I bless you for it: and despite the many and painful sacrifices it imposes on me, my will, which wills only as you will, acquiesces, in all it is, to your lovable and good pleasure. Yes, my beloved Jesus: I rejoice, not only in what it makes me suffer from the zeal of your glory — and you alone know how far this martyrdom goes — but again in my incapacity, my uselessness in your Church; for doing your will is my sole ambition, my thought, my labor.

See, dear Father how my poor life passes: in desires whose violence is inexpressible, and in continual spiritual acts of submission. Ah, to satisfy the love that is its principle, I would have to be able to sacrifice my life millions of times. Where am I to go? To Heaven? Jesus does not want it yet. And what to do? Contemplate Jesus under the veil of mystery? Oh, at least, if these fragile species that veil him were more often and longer in my possession!

If only it were given to me, even if I could not taste these divine species, at least to contemplate and adore them ceaselessly![209] Useless wishes! Ah, if you but knew, my Father, all that Jesus is to me in this mystery! How my soul sees him; how he reveals himself to my soul; how he clothes and scorches me with light!

[209] French: "S'il m'était donné, sinon d'en jouir, mais de pouvoir les contempler sans cesse," "If it were given to me, if not to enjoy them, but to be able to contemplate them ceaselessly." The translation assumes that the plural *les*, "them," refers to the two Eucharistic species of the previous sentence and that *jouir*, "enjoy," denotes receiving Holy Communion.

Ah, my Father, I do not have what Jesus communicates to you, and I suffer from it. My intelligence is the Holy Eucharist.

O love of my soul, my dear Jesus, my beloved, my sweet honey! O that I were able to press you to my heart! I know, dear good master, that through the divine Communion, I possess you intimately; your presence makes itself felt to me in an ineffable manner, so that it seems that you live more in me than I live in myself. But though I house the Holy Eucharist like another tabernacle, I wish that you might not visit my soul for such short times; my heart wants to possess you without end, without interruption. You flee from me so quickly, my beloved, to shut yourself up in a prison that cannot know the treasure it holds: the God of love for whom I groan, because he is my life, my joy, my peace, my all!

Heavenly Friend, *the looks you let fall on me draw towards you every movement of my heart*. O my tender brother! The expressions that I use do not say all that I see or all that I sense, all that I understand of the mystery of your love. And yet, O Jesus, I am nothing but a puny creature, a worm, filthy mud, and an instrument of your death, through my iniquities. Jesus, sacrificed: how am I worthy then to participate in your favors? Jesus, my God! Forgive my temerity. But it is you, it is your love, that makes so bold. O infinite goodness! You seem to ignore my wretchedness as you lavish your benefits on me. O Jesus! O Jesus! My soul is consumed in you, by you, and for you.[210]

These are not only the innumerable graces that Jesus sends to my soul, that so excite my love and my remembrance: there is also the love that leads him to humble himself to communicate to me, such a poor, such a little creature. O infinite charity! Only you know the reason for the love you have for me, for everything in me is capable only of pushing you away.

I will tell you, my Father, that, soon after receiving our love, I must leave his Eucharistic presence. I feel a pain so strong that I do not cease gazing at the holy tabernacle even as I withdraw. When there is no one in the church. I testify to him, in the most ardent

---

[210] This passage is quoted, with ascription to Eustelle, in Abbé Paul de Terris, *Nouveau Mois du Sacre Cœur* (Avignon, 1893), 249–50. The book is a compilation of prayers to be used during June, the "Month of the Sacred Heart for the conversion of sinners and the salvation of France," devotions which began in 1833. The passage is also quoted in another devotional anthology, Frère Philippe, *Méditations sur l'Eucharistie* (Paris, 1889).

expressions, my bitter sorrow at leaving him alone there in his prison of love. A few days ago at his feet, I asked him, since it was his will that I should separate myself from him, would he then deign to enclose me in the ciborium on which I so love to meditate. I begged to him to unite my heart to his divine heart, to transform it through a sort of transubstantiation. Then the divine Master showed me his heart filled with incomprehensible marvels that I well understood but cannot describe. He also showed me my own heart, united to his by an indissoluble bond.[211] Soon I saw my heart melting, flowing and being lost in that furnace of love, so that afterwards I only saw the infinitely holy and adorable heart of my Savior. Jesus himself assured me that I am, night and day, present in his holy tabernacle. This grace greatly consoled me, only increasing my love.

Ah, my dear Father, tell me that, every night, you too retire your soul to the golden prison where Jesus dwells; I do the same, and so I always meet you in this holy refuge. As I fall asleep, I whisper these words, which you well know:

Avant l'aurore,	Before the dawn,
Il paraîtra;	he will appear;
Demain encore,	again tomorrow,
Jésus viendra.	Jesus will come.

Then, in the morning, as I arrive at God's house, I say:

Ce n'est que dans ce temple	It is only in his temple
Où mon cœur est heureux:	That my heart is happy:
Mon amour y contemple	There my love contemplates
L'objet de tous ses vœux.	The object of its desires.

Then, having arrived at the tabernacle, I continue:

Ah! voilà mon asile;	Ah, This is my refuge;
Voilà mon vrai Bonheur	Here is my true happiness;
Adieu, monde futile.	Adieu, useless world:
Jésus a tout mon cœur.	Jesus has all my heart.

Despite my poverty, I pray very much for you, my Father, and as well for the souls which you evangelize. This is all that I can do: to offer some prayers that Jesus will not reject. He is good! So good! So good! My confidence in him is without bounds. Ask him to render to me according to his heart.

---

[211] French: "Le mien me fut aussi représenté uni à ce cœur sacré par un lien indissoluble," "Mine was also represented to me united to his Sacred Heart by an indissoluble bond."

Next week I go to present myself to Monsignor the Bishop, because he needs to go to La Rochelle for the consecration of the holy oils, which, as you know, happens on Holy Thursday.[212] Today, March 12, he has conferred the subdiaconate and diaconate on many seminarians of Angoulême. Before ordaining them, he gave them a very spirited instruction on the marks and proofs of a true vocation. His sermons at Saint Peter's are always very well attended and do a great deal of good. We would have liked that, like two years ago, he would spend the Easter holidays here at Saintes; but La Rochelle this year is his preference.

My health is very bad; I am in constant pain; but it makes me greatly rejoice. Be reborn in Jesus with me. I owe him a great obligation. I leave you to go to his feet. I ardently desire to die for his love.

Your daughter, in his heart,
Eustelle,
his littlest servant.

LETTER 83

Jesus transports her soul outside itself.

N.d.

May Jesus consume you during the holy sacrifice.

My Father,

I knew you were going to Saint-Jean: please kindly express to the *Angel* of this place my thoughts full of tenderness and respect.[213] How I long to see her, to talk with her about all that we should love! Jesus transports my soul outside itself through his love. I will come to see you, if my visit is not embarrassing to you. In this regard, do as our Savior wants. I am, in his tender and divine heart,

Your daughter Eustelle,
poor servant of Jesus.

[212] This diocesan ceremony still takes place in the episcopal see (the home church of the bishop or archbishop) on Holy Thursday as part of the Chrism Mass. In 1842 Holy Thursday fell on March 24, almost two weeks after the composition of this letter.

[213] See Letter 70, above.

LETTER 84

Eustelle is happy in thinking that the end of her exile approaches; (She did not have more than a week to live.)

June 21, 1842 [*a week before Eustelle's death*].

Jesus is all.

Very dear Father,

The sentiment of hope that you gave me yesterday, how happy it makes me! I thought only of it. To be united with Jesus perpetually: such happiness! United to this Jesus, for whom my soul is so hungry! Dear spouse and friend of my heart, you are my whole life. Dear object towards which my soul takes itself with unequalled vivacity, how I love you! My dear Jesus, how I love you! O dear half of my soul, I want to die for you!

The doctor just left; he did not find me any better; he just ordered a very painful remedy.

All for Jesus.

Eustelle.

LETTER 85

The last letter of Eustelle, written after she was administered Extreme Unction.

N.d. [*Probably June 27 or 28, 1842, a day or two before Eustelle's death.*]

Jesus alone, him everywhere, him always.

Worthy friend of the dear good master, O my Father! The wish of your soul for your unworthy daughter has come to pass. Jesus has come for her. Imagine my happiness! Ah, he was not content to abandon this, his tabernacle.[214] His love made him cross once more the threshold of his temple, where he had given me many days of delight. But what so afflicts me now is that, between the

[214] French: "Ah, il ne s'est pas contenté de laisser son Tabernacle," "Ah, he was not content to leave his tabernacle"; the context makes it fairly clear that Eustelle is referring to herself here as a tabernacle. Thus, she is describing receiving the Eucharist (called the Viaticum when administered outside a liturgy) and the "last rites" or Extreme Unction, now called the Sacrament of the Sick, prayers and anointing with holy oils brought to the home of a person nearing death.

church and my home, there are so many souls that refuse the tribute of respect and adoration to which he is due. Poor Jesus! O God misunderstood! I possess you; my soul is happy . . . O my Father! Bless him: the tears that Jesus caused me to shed this morning have tired me a little. But that Heavenly friend repairs all. I must stop: being so feeble, I feel that writing this hurts my head. Jesus be with you. Come and see me when you can. Thank you for all your attentions. May the Lord reward you a hundredfold.

I do not know if it is Father's intention often to bring me the Eucharist. Please, kindly pass along my thoughts on this point.

All to you in Jesus our beloved. Remain in his love.

Your daughter, through his heart,
Eustelle,
littlest of his servants.

[*LETTERS 86–88 ARE ADDRESSED TO "ESTHER," APPARENTLY a novice of the Sisters of Our Lady of Charity (the "White Ladies") of La Rochelle, where Eustelle spent about two weeks as an aspirant in about 1834, when she was about twenty years old. Letter 88 refers to Esther's profession of vows, so it should be possible to infer that she entered the community roughly when Eustelle did. Eustelle's referring to Esther as "daughter" seems to imply that Esther was somewhat younger than Eustelle; at about twenty Eustelle might have been a little older than the typical entrant.*]

LETTER 86

The Lord repays every sacrifice; Prefer the company of God to all others; Revive yourself with the thought of Heaven.

February 26, 1836.

Dear daughter, we were deprived of the pleasure of having you with us on Sunday evening, but God willed it, no doubt, and I am very sure that you have resigned yourself to the will of this good master. He will not leave this little sacrifice without reward. After all, the loss is not a great one, and detachment from creatures is much preferable to the pleasure we might take in their company.

We prefer that of God alone: his conversation has no bitterness.[215] I thought that, having had the pleasure of receiving him this same day, you knew how to best use the opportunity to talk with him and offer him this little act of self-denial. We shared in it as you did, and conformed ourselves to his good pleasure. Dear daughter, it is on the Cross and by sacrifices that those who would be all to God are nourished. Do not be discouraged; think of the reward reserved for you and revive your hope by this salutary thought.

We drew tickets; I will send you yours. Adieu, dear Esther,

your humble servant,
Eustelle.

LETTER 87

Meet in the adorable heart of Jesus.

To the same person.

December 10, 1837.

It is my turn again, my good Esther: this evening I will go to make a little visit to our Heavenly neighbor, and I will tell him something for you. I hope I will find you in the abode of his divine heart. When you were at Saintes, he was closer to me than to you; now you should feel no jealousy since he is closer to you than he was to me. Let us love him then, very much; let us love him: all for him.

Your devoted Eustelle.

LETTER 88

Testimony of affection; Protection of a monastery; Privileges of the brides of Jesus Christ, far from the dangers of the age; Eustelle's project; Her poverty; Exhortation to holy love.
To the same person.

9 June, [*1837?*].

All for Jesus.

Dear Esther,

Since Monsieur the Vicar, having come from La Rochelle, must make a visit to your community, I asked him to bring along this

[215] French: "sa conversation n'a point d'amertume."

little letter: it will recall the interest I took in your soul when you were nearby, and Jesus is witness to my continuing concern for you. Yes, at the feet of the tabernacle, you are often present to me, just as he is who, in the refuge of peace where you live, shares your joy and peace. There, Jesus makes you grow in the shadow of his divine protection: there, he floods your young hearts with ineffable delights. Fortunate children, he has given you abundantly to share the favors reserved for the Heavenly bride; wives of the divine lamb, you are led into the intoxicating cellar of his love.[216] Rejoice that he has kept your lips from the poisoned cup of Babylon. To love God, to bless him: this is your delicious occupation; to love and bless Jesus, our Brother, our Heavenly Friend, what a role to share![217] He is our center; it is in him that we should mortify[218] ourselves every day. Let us annihilate ourselves before Jesus; let us die for Jesus who is our life: by this we will render to him what we owe; by this we will glorify him. Oh, how sweet it is to love him, especially at the feet of the tabernacle! Like the bride in the Canticles, love to repose yourself in his shadow. Ah, ask the good and merciful Savior that I may love him more, more purely, more ardently, without deliberation,[219] without measure, to make up for in the future my past ingratitude.

Dear Esther, I plan to go to La Rochelle for your profession, if it is the will of God; but God has made me so poor that I do not have enough money. It is Jesus who reduces me in this way. Love and practice well humility and poverty. Jesus loves these two dear virtues so much that we also should delight in them.

Angelina tells you a thousand things: pray for her. I leave you, my good friend, along with your companion, in the sweet heart of the good and peaceful Jesus. Shine silently in that refuge of love and peace. There, supported by Jesus, await in delight the end of this life, like the night before the new dawn, after which eternity will shine. I almost dare not to ask you to pay my respects to Mother Superior, finding it useless to recall to her memory such a useless and puny creature.

Adieu. Your friend, Eustelle,
unworthy servant of Jesus.

---

216 Echoing Song 2:4: "Il m'a menée dans la salle du festin," "He led me into the banquet hall"; Vulgate is "Introduxit me in cellam vinariam."

217 French: *quel partage!* "What sharing!"

218 French: *abîmer*, "damage."

219 French: *sans interêt*, "without interest."

LETTER 89

Firmness in vocation.

December 28, 1837.

My good friend,

Your friend went several times to your parents' house to ask them to send you your belongings, and to learn what they thought of your decision; she was very surprised at the change that took place in your absence. They are very ill-disposed at the moment, and they do not want to send you anything you need. I believe that, if you stay firm, eventually they will give in to your decision. They will certainly encourage you to return to see them, but take care.[220]

I assure you, good friend, that I know your pain well, but do not torment yourself; patiently await the moment that God has determined for the fulfillment of his designs for you. He will know how to make you triumph over all the obstacles. Leave it to him, abandon yourself entirely to him: you know his goodness, and you have often felt its effects. The grace that you ask for in this moment is a precious one; may God make you understand the whole price you will pay, and may he help you endure the difficulties that arise. This is the cross he imposes on you; let your cross be joined to that of the spouse you have chosen.

For myself, I would envy your fate, if it were God's will. I will pray to him with all my heart until his good pleasure is fulfilled in you, and that your will become one with his.

Ask him for patience and humility for me.

Adieu, good friend: I leave you in the peace of the Lord, and I wish its fullness for you.

Eustelle.

---

[220] French: "Ils ne manqueront pas de vous engager à vous rendre près d'eux; mais donnez-vous en bien garde," "They will not fail to encourage you to draw near to them, but be careful." The rather clumsy circumlocution here might reflect Eustelle's attempt to thread a needle, to assure her correspondent that her parents will not refuse to see her but are not welcoming a visit either. Eustelle's own father René was similarly "ill-disposed" to her decision to become a nun.

LETTER 90

Eustelle's Humility; The better part; Harbor of salvation; The life of the Cross and of self-denial; Sow to reap; Delights of the holy tabernacle; Conquer the world; Sadness.

[*THIS LETTER CAN BE DATED THANKS TO ITS INQUIRY ABOUT the condition of Father Jouslain. Father Joseph-Alphonse Jouslain was curé of Eustelle's home parish of Saint-Pallais in Saintes from 1834 to 1836. The letter was written between Christmas 1836, when Father took violently ill at Midnight Mass, and Christmas 1837, when he died. After becoming ill, Father Jouslain was removed to the Sisters of Charity in La Rochelle for care; this is the same community that Eustelle joined for two weeks in 1834, at Father Jouslain's urging, and the same community where the "Esther" of the three previous letters professed.*]

May the cross of Jesus be your portion and his love your treasure.

My good friends, you wanted me to write to you, so I hasten to satisfy your desire. However, you will not gain much advantage from my writing; to my little bit of virtue, I add an absolute incapacity to awaken it in others. What can a poor person living in the world tell you, one who strives to detach herself from it, it is true, but who often feels drawn to earthly things out of the inclinations natural to the children of Adam? Again, what can I say to you who, separated from the perverse world, dwell now among the brides of the Lord? What a sublime gift to which you aspire! Like Mary, you have chosen the better part, and, like her, it will not be taken from you.[221] Oh, let me share your joy with you, now that you have arrived at the harbor of salvation. I do not want to say by this that, from now on, you will be examples of pains, discord, battles, and sacrifices. The religious life is a life of the Cross and of abnegation, a life of death, of unending separation from ourselves and from all created things: in a word, from everything that is not God. But do not be discouraged: the one who sows takes great pains until the harvest; but at harvest

[221] Echoing Luke 10:41–42: "Et Jésus répondant, lui dit: Marthe, Marthe, tu t'inquiètes et tu t'agites pour beaucoup de choses; mais une chose est nécessaire; et Marie a choisi la bonne part, qui ne lui sera point ôtée"; "And Jesus responded and said to her, "Martha, Martha, you are troubled and are concerned about many things. But one thing alone is necessary. Mary has chosen the better part, which will not be taken from her." The passage is often used as a justification for the contemplative or cloistered life.

time, with what joy does he reap the fruits of his labors! Likewise, the cross is a good tree that bears excellent fruits,[222] but it is principally in the heavens that we can taste its sweetness. Courage, then, and perseverance in what you have undertaken. Remember for whom you have undertaken it; remember that, in comparison to what God has done for us, we have done very little; nothing, even, compared to him who is everything. Ask our divine master that all be done to you according to his good pleasure. O my good friends, do you want a way to obtain from God the graces that you need, the graces which he himself desires to give you with so much love? Go to the feet of the holy altar; arrange yourselves around the sacred tabernacle, and, like the dove, moan in the presence of the one whose love holds him there captive and imprisoned. O that dear home! How precious it should be to us. If the good master finds his delights in us, as he assures us he does, why do we not find ours in his company? Ah, he himself claims that he is not visited!

Let us make recompense to him,[223] as much as we can, for the coldness and indifference of so many Christians. What favors are hidden away in his divine heart! And he burns with the desire to share them with us. Go! Present yourselves at the entrance to the heavenly channel. Jesus the lamb, pure and unblemished, friend of virgins, your friend, your most devoted friend: he will care for you, lead you into rich pastures.

Pardon me if I allow myself to speak of things that you know and see much better than I do. However, insofar as we hold these sentiments in common, permit me to tell you, very simply, my thoughts. So, love this good Jesus; thank him for his choice of you over so many others. Pray for me; bless the Lord for me; help me to give thanks to him for the lovable crosses he sends me. Truly, I say, nature complains:[224] ask God that his grace bring final victory; ask him that, if it is his will that I remain in this world, doubtless to atone for the incalculable faults I have, that

---

[222] Echoing Matthew 7:17: “Ainsi tout bon arbre fait de bons fruits; mais le mauvais arbre fait de mauvais fruits,” “Thus, every good tree bears good fruits; but every bad tree bears bad fruit.”

[223] French: *Dédommageons-le*, “let us compensate him.”

[224] Probably echoing Romans 8:21: “Car nous savons que toutes les créatures soupirent et sont en travail ensemble jusques à maintenant,” “For we know that all creatures groan and together are in labor even now.”

he accord me the grace to win over the world, the devil and this miserable myself.[225]

I can tell you simply that I am the same. Right now as I write to you, it is almost eleven o'clock at night and my soul is sad and troubled, perhaps very reluctant to unite with God in the Holy Eucharist. Pray for me.

People you know have entrusted me with all their affectionate memories of you.

If you write to me, send me news of Father Jouslain.

I leave you in the love of Jesus and Mary. Mary! My wish is that this love consume us all.

Adieu. Your humble and most obedient servant.

Eustelle.

LETTER 91

Request for prayers; Openness of the heart to inner pains; Cross; Death.

N.d.

[THIS LETTER CAN BE DATED NO EARLIER THAN MAY 1838, when Eustelle first encountered Father Briand, who is mentioned in the last paragraph. The correspondent, "Agatha," is not Eustelle's biological sister: her name was Marie, called "Angele." Given that the "Adieu" in paragraph three is addressed to "mes bonnes amies" (plural), it can be inferred that "Agatha" was a member of a community with whom she would have shared Eustelle's letter. This convent is likely the Sisters of Charity of Letters 86–91. Neither Mademoiselle Rosalie nor the unnamed companion embraced by Eustelle has been identified.]

May Jesus be our love. All for Jesus.

My dear sister,

Many people have asked me to recommend them to your prayers, and I join myself to them in making this request. I have great need for them. Do not refuse me this help; ask God to grant me pardon for my numerous faults, and for the grace not to fall into them again. Oh, let us avoid sin, God's evil and our own.

I have resumed, good Agatha, the project of which I have spoken to you concerning my inner life. Next week, I plan to open

[225] Echoing Jesus's three temptations in the desert: see Matthew 4:1–11.

my heart a second time in that matter. Oh, how I need strength for this, and God alone can communicate it to me. Ask him for the light I need.

Blessed be God for all the crosses he has deigned to send me. I am unworthy of them, but I hope that they may not be taken from me. Do not speak of this to anyone. I embrace your companion. Adieu, my good friends, whose happiness I envy.

Mademoiselle Rosalie has died: now she enjoys the rewards of her virtues. Her death was as edifying as her life. It was Father Briand who recommended her soul to him.

Your friend Eustelle.

LETTER 92

Family news; Prayers requested; A wish for holy love.

N.d.

May the peace of God be with you.

Your sister has asked me to write you some lines, sending you canvas for shirts. It is your uncle who sends them: you should thank him. Do not forget to write to him for his birthday: he will be flattered.

Your brother has written to your parents: he tells them that, although he did not write to you, he did not forget what you had said to him. Pray that the good Lord preserve and increase in him the good sentiments he has given him. May I also recommend N*** to you; pray for her; I very much want to see her abandon this miserable world; I ask this of God with all my heart. That would mean one more soul safely in port.

Adieu, good friend; say lots of good things about me to your companion: she knows how much I love her in Jesus. And do not forget me before God: my needs are always the same. May the love of Jesus reign in your heart; may that love increase in you, every moment of your life, until your last breath.

How sweet it is to die, when we have as our judge the one we love so uniquely!

Adieu, your affectionate,
Eustelle.

LETTER 93

Trials; These make one feel the price of the favors that follow them; Grace proportional to obligations; Confidence; generosity; Invocation for the monastery of Providence of La Rochelle.

N.d.

All for Jesus.

Well then, my good sister: has the good Savior not yet made an end to his rigorous but loving trials?[226] Does his love still postpone your moment of happiness? So: he has given you these trials to make you better realize the cost of the favor which he prepares for you, wanting to raise you to the dignity and sublime quality of his bride. Understand, them, dear girl, the grandeur and diversity of your obligations when you enjoy such happiness. Surely the grace of the Heavenly bridegroom is already so abundant in you, so that it will be easy for you to win the heart of this beloved husband. Oh, how much confidence you must have in him! How his love alone must wholly capture your soul! Oh, how your whole being ought to become a perfect holocaust offered to his glory! Oh, then the tabernacle ought not to have a cloud for you, and Jesus have no more secrets from his new bride. If, however, his good will differs from that sweet felicity, submit yourself, dear girl, to his good pleasure; receive from his good and divine heart the arrow that pierces yours, for it is always love that guides him, the dear master. Oh, how good he is! How delightful is Jesus's goodness to our heart! And especially in the divine Eucharist, where he annihilates himself for our love. O Jesus, stranger, unknown, exiled in this mystery: take us captive, just as we take you captive. On all these good souls united in holy community, where you have welcomed two friends whom I love only for you, spread your most abundant blessings. To all the members who make up this family of virgins, and to each of the sisters individually, give them the plenitude of your Spirit. Oh, consume them as just so many victims who love you eternally.

Dear girl, I am curious; I would love to know when you make your vows. How long it seems to me since I saw you! What

[226] The paragraph is based in the traditional metaphor of the nun as the bride of Christ. For example, many religious communities of women continue to require novices to wear wedding dresses in the profession ceremonies and many nuns wear gold wedding rings after profession.

consolation I would feel in seeing you good ladies again, for whom I feel such affection! Please write me a little note as soon as possible, if our Lord gives you permission.

Pass along my respects to Mother Superior and to all your ladies. I know Sister Saint Vincent de Paul is there with you.

Adieu, good friend. May Jesus bless you; that is the wish of her who is your friend and sister.

Eustelle,
the poorest and most unworthy of the servants of Jesus.

LETTER 94

Submission to the divine will manifested through the Director; Reward assured for the patience in the Cross.

February 24, 1840.

May Jesus maintain and increase in your soul the virtues he gave birth to, and that the most vibrant of these virtues be love.

I see, with great pain, your concerns and your privations, but consider well that the guide of your soul has given you this trial only through the inspiration of the one who so fills it with his spirit and his love. You waste time tormenting yourself like this, and this behavior prevents you from moving forward in the love of Jesus. Now, I hear you tell me, "Is not Holy Communion a powerful way to advance there?" Undoubtedly: but perfect conformity of the will to the will of God is the seal of perfection. Our divine master is come upon the earth only to do the will of his Heavenly Father; he assures us himself that his Father's will is our food and that he regards as his brothers and sisters those who have faithfully fulfilled it.[227] And recognize this adorable will in those who represent Jesus himself. Believe me, you will have more merit in submitting yourselves than in receiving Holy Communion, even if it were every day. We often seek ourselves and find ourselves in the use of the sacraments. However, far be it from me to pass judgment on you; I am not saying this for you,

[227] Echoing John 4:34: "Jésus leur dit: ma viande est que je fasse la volonté de celui qui m'a envoyé, et que j'accomplisse son œuvre," "Jesus said to them: My food is that I do the will of the one who sent me, and that I fulfill his work."

but to bring you to believe that our beloved Jesus, despite these privations, does not leave you without consolation. Go to the feet of the tabernacle, pour out your soul in his presence: there he will witness all your desires, count all your sighs; he will record all your tears, and these desires, these sighs, and these tears will, one day, become the most beautiful flowers in your crown.

Cease then to afflict yourself, for there is imperfection in that, and Jesus does not want it. Rather love this good Master: he has so many rights to your love. Oh, it is a delight to love him, especially in the Cross. Unite your love to his own, and participate in the sacrifice of yourselves; stay there constantly attached to the Cross by the nails of humility, chastity, and obedience. One day, Jesus will break you free to share with you his joy and his triumph in Heaven. Then, no more shadows: we shall see him as he is, immerse ourselves in him as our eternal beatitude. Amen.

This is quite a long letter, I hope. I do not have time to talk to you; I have to finish up until Thursday, when I shall have the pleasure of seeing you. Farewell and good luck until then. At this moment, I wrap your soul in the divine heart of Jesus. This is also where you will find me: it is so good there!

Do not have any concern about the subject which you confided in me and counted as a secret. I have the greatest interest in your soul, and I would like, for the glory of Jesus our everything, to see you become a great saint.

Your friend, Eustelle.

LETTER 95

All in Jesus and Jesus in all; The ways of prayer are not the paths for every soul; It is very easy for those who love God; Thanks.

March 2, 1840.

All for Jesus in the Eucharist; you are all in all things.

Your heart understands the sweet and tender words which Jesus in his love makes the faithful soul hear, when, speaking to it in the silence of prayer, he deigns to make it understood that, just as he wishes to be himself all in all things, the soul must also make every effort to reach this divine life where it will see Jesus in everything and everything in Jesus. It is faith alone, a real and practical faith that allows us to taste, here below in the world, the first fruits of celestial happiness. An excellent way to get the fruit of this faith is prayer. The Holy Spirit tells us that *the world is covered in desolation because there is no one who reflects in his heart.*[228] How right you are to devote yourself to this holy exercise. But is it to me that you should turn to learn what leads to the gift of prayer? Do I even know if I can pray myself? In this regard, I am only a poor neophyte, like those young bees who, just hatched, want to leave the hive and fly like their mothers but who, because their wings are not yet well-formed, fall to the ground. Even so then, desiring to condescend to your humility, I rely on our good Savior to inspire me with what will be his will regarding what you are asking about.

You know that not all souls are led along the same path, and so there are different directions for them. Thus the flowers of a garden require different cultivation, according to their species and quality. Jesus, the divine gardener, gives to our souls gifts that are unique to it, to achieve in it and through it what it is to be in the order of divine wisdom. My intention would have been to pass along to you here some means of prayer; but I will wait until you are less hidden from me and you can make me understand your wishes. You would not refuse me this, at our first conversation. Then I will tell you more certainly what I believe to be most useful to your soul. Jesus wants you to love him very much; with him, prayer is very easy to do. Be of good courage, and go to the tabernacle. Moses resorted to the Ark when he had need, and his needs were granted; how much more will you be heard by him for whom that ancient tabernacle was only a figure? It is there that we find the proper weapons to defeat the enemies of our salvation. It is the tower of David, the true Temple of Solomon, where his glory resides, where he gives us the proofs of his wisdom and his love. So love then that King so filled with love; oh, live only for that love; begin in this life the vocation you will have in eternity. When will we see the day that shall crown our love? While awaiting the time I can thank you in person for your charity, I pray our tender Savior repay you by pardoning you the

[228] Jeremiah 12:11: "toute la terre a été ravagée, parce qu'il n'y a personne qui y fasse attention," "the whole earth has been ravaged because there is no one paying attention." The Vulgate is closer to Eustelle's phrasing: "quia nullus est qui recogitet corde," "for there is no one with a heeding heart."

loss of sacrifice that you have caused him: I am in no way happy about that: so may Jesus forgive you for your excess of charity and forgive me for my lack of discipline.[229]

I see you where I have placed you: how well you are there! Abide there: I enclose myself with you.

Adieu until Tuesday. Love until then. May Jesus be with you.

Your unworthy servant,
Eustelle.

LETTER 96

Jesus sometimes hides himself out of love; Not everything that displeases us proves that we are guilty; To live in holy love; Eustelle believes herself unworthy of love and of being chosen as instructor.

March 26, 1840.

All for Jesus.

May the cross of Jesus be your portion, his love your treasure.

Like the sun sometimes shows itself to us only for a moment and then covers its brilliant light from us, so Jesus often shows himself to the faithful soul and then leaves it as though enveloped by clouds. He acts thus according to the designs of his unknowable wisdom. Do not think you are entirely to blame if our divine master treats you with this sort of rigor, for these rigors are nothing of the sort but, believe it, true kindnesses. You would like always to be fastened to the adorable heart of Jesus to draw there the milk of his consolations; realize, however, that this is the food of infants, no longer yours. I believe that you do not abandon yourselves enough to trust, and that you are too concerned about what is happening in your soul. Doubtless, if you see something

[229] French: "En attendant que, de vive voix, je puisse vous remercier de votre charité, je prie notre tendre Sauveur de vous récompenser, en vous pardonnant la perte du sacrifice que vous lui avez causée: je ne suis nullement contente de cela; que Jésus vous pardonne donc votre excès de charité, et à moi mon immortification." The translation is as literal as it can be, leaving a sentence that seems cryptic at best. It sounds like Eustelle may be — very ornately — thanking the correspondent for an extended visit, which Eustelle sees as an act of charity towards herself and also lost time for the nun, lost time worshipping God. Thus the final phrase smilingly asking God's pardon on both of them.

there that could displease that jealous friend, you must get rid of and pluck out even the smallest useless weeds that take up space in the field of your soul. It is the will of the divine gardener who wants only to cultivate the trees and make them bear fruit. At the same time, do not believe that everything that is displeasing in you comes from your fault: this is a trap of the Demon. Do not think that way and have more confidence: humbly let yourself be led by him who is the way, the truth, and the life.[230] Leave your soul, with all its miseries, at the tabernacle. Jesus will consume them in the divine fire of his charity. To tell you what I think, I believe that Jesus, our Heavenly friend, wants to lead us on the path of love. Oh, what a privilege to love such a lovable Savior! I would like for people to think only of loving him, never fearing him: he is so good! His love is so sweet! Love only this love; breathe only this love; live only in this love. Do not let yourself be discouraged; you have no reason to worry. Believe it: it is a test to which Jesus subjects you. You will understand later the good that these sorrows produce in you. Peace comes after troubles, calm after the storm: so after our exile comes our homeland. I am thinking, in this moment, of the last thought of your letter on the instruction of Monsignor the Bishop;[231] but, without slander, I can hardly believe that the poor person you have chosen for your friend is worthy of your trust. She is thoroughly unworthy, believe me. I recognize your choice with pain, because it is only in the eyes of Jesus, nothing more. Oh, ask our Lord that she die immediately in the memory of creatures, being unworthy of occupying their thoughts. A poor half-broken reed, which the slightest wind blows down to the earth![232] It is up to you to correct me for the faults that you recognize in me: I charge you with this work of charity; do it for the love of Jesus, for his glory. I join myself to you, in heart and spirit, to know and love more and more the good Savior in the adorable Eucharist. I transport myself, in this moment, to

---

[230] John 14:6.

[231] Note to the French original: Monsignor, on the occasion of the friendship of Saint Basil and Saint Gregory Nazianzen, had made his audience feel the value of a friendship founded on virtue, recommending that they seek from God the grace of finding true friends, and conform to their friends' salutary advice.

[232] Perhaps echoing Matthew 11:7: "qu'êtes-vous allés voir au désert? Un roseau agité du vent?" "What did you go to see in the desert? A reed disturbed by the wind?"

his feet: he is alone, but he is thinking of us. I see him kindly stopping his gentle glances at us as he raises his divine hands: this is to bless us. May this blessing be the pledge of all which he wants to give us one day, calling us to blessed eternity. I will tell you the rest tomorrow evening.

Adieu.

Eustelle,
unworthy servant of Jesus.

LETTER 97

Baptism of blood; Confidence and love; Cast off sadness and worry.

April 22, 1840.

All for Jesus.

In talking to his disciples some time before his Passion, our tender Savior expressed the sentiments of his heart in these words: *I must be baptized with a baptism; how pressed I feel, until this baptism is accomplished!*[233] He was speaking of the Baptism of Blood which was to happen in the day of his immolation for the salvation of men.[234] O true friend! How well do these words show us his love, this love on which you rely so little, my good friend. Jesus is not pleased with you because you lack the confidence in and perfect submission to his holy will. Seek therefore the God of comforts and not the comforts of God.[235] Then you will love him for himself and, according to the words of the Evangelist, he will reveal himself to you and make his delightful home in you. Oh, how his heart burns with love for yours! How he desires that you serve him with peace and calm, without turmoil, in the trials that he makes you pass through. Why then are you sad, since you possess such a good and merciful friend? He is sleeping now, lying on the altar of your heart. He reposes in peace; so why would you want to trouble his sweet and peaceable slumber with the agitation

---

[233] Luke 12:50.

[234] Baptism of (or by) blood, *baptismus sanguinis*, or martyred baptism is usually defined as complete remission of sins in a righteous but unbaptized Christian person who dies confessing the faith. The term had its origin in the early Church, when catechumens awaiting baptism by water were arrested and executed before they could receive the sacrament in the traditional way.

[235] Cf. Letter 130, below.

you bring to your own heart? Oh, be with him, that he may be with you. Humility, patience, conformity: may his love, which is so pure and so sweet, fortify, purify, and increase these virtues. Despite my profound wretchedness — ah, if you only knew — I will not forget your soul while I am near Jesus: you may count on it. I want you to be what I wish myself to be. I pray that our Lord hide you in his sacred wounds: may they hold you there in peace for eternity.[236]

Adieu: I leave you.

Eustelle.

LETTER 98

Jesus a prisoner for love in the adorable Eucharist; Recognition and confidence; Sacred meeting.

May 18, [*1840: the letter does not list a year in the French original; 1840 is presumed. May 18, 1840 was a Monday.*]

All for Jesus. Since Jesus loves you always, love him more and more.

How sweet are the attractions of Jesus in the Eucharist! How forceful and powerful they are to attract hearts! Who could resist the love that makes him thus, a prisoner of love for his creatures, with a love that endures to the end of ages? To be sure, it will only be at the end of time that Jesus will leave his tabernacle; until then, his charity will hold him captive in the secrets of this ineffable mystery. There, Jesus will be the friend, the faithful companion and the guide to the soul in exile who ceaselessly, like the moaning dove, sighs far from its homeland. In the Holy Eucharist, Jesus is its Heaven, its joy, its force, its blessedness. Ah, let us die in love and gratitude for this divine and mysterious benefactor. All for Jesus! Nothing else satisfies us; death to everything that is not Jesus. Human considerations, proper satisfactions, points of honor, interests — even spiritual ones: all must be sacrificed to the love of that love who is Jesus, our dear Savior. With what touching care has he prepared these consolations for you, the little satisfactions you enjoy where you are and which surpass all your hopes. Ah, Jesus takes care of his friends, and you are of that

---

236 Somewhat loosely translating the French: "et je désire qu'elles vous rassurent pour l'éternité," "and I desire that they reassure you for eternity."

number. So be full of confidence in him. Love! Love! Nothing is sweet but Jesus: he is our center and we are made for him. Ah, be hungry for this bread of life; relish it. It makes virgins grow; it embellishes the brilliance of their chastity. Cherish your spouse and rest in his heart.

I am coming to see you on Thursday. You know the oratory where we can meet together, although far apart: it is a wound in the heart of Jesus, the sanctuary where divine charity burns. We must sink down in these fires and die to live again in Jesus. Oh, this wound reassures me for eternity: it is my refuge, it will be the shield with which I will pass through the darts of the enemy seducer.

They bring me your second letter. The happiness of your soul gladdens me. Blessed be Jesus.

My letter is not long, but I will make up for it on Friday.

I leave you in the peace and in the friendship of Jesus. Of Jesus! Oh, savor this word! May he bless you a thousand times.

Adieu. Your friend, Eustelle,
unworthy servant of Jesus.

LETTER 99

The road to Heaven is that of the Cross; It is through Jesus that we die to ourselves; Follow the counsels of the director.

June 14, 1840.

All for Jesus.

May the Cross of Jesus be your portion and his love your treasure.

It is in the presence of Jesus our God that my soul will place in yours the sentiments that the good Savior will deign to inspire in it. Incapable as I am to tell you anything good by myself, I charge him to guide my spirit and my heart.

The divine master tells us that there are many mansions in his Heavenly father's house.[237] See which one you would like to inhabit. Do not condemn your motives then as stemming from trivial interest, for they are spirit-filled and permissible, benevolent and agreeable. Such a good God will lead us to the most perfect place, persuaded, as we must be, that it is Jesus's will that we

[237] John 14:2.

live like him and for him.[238] It is through this so precious and desirable resemblance to Jesus that we acquire the true liberty of the children of God. But we do not arrive there without pains and troubles. The road to Heaven is that of the Cross: one must climb Mount Calvary to arrive at Mount Tabor.[239] We must be cast down in order to rise and reign. Try, therefore, to achieve this goal by receiving with peace, submission, and love the sadness, trials, and troubles that come to you from the heart of our common Father, a heart full of love. Oh how he loves your souls, placing them so under the press of tribulations! Have confidence, faith, and love. May your miseries and your very weaknesses, far from discouraging you, lead you to throw yourself with holy trust into the bosom of the one who wants so ardently to save your soul and who, on the Cross, complained of the thirst which his love made him endure for us. Courage, then, faithful soul, for Jesus is with you. It is for him that you die to yourself, overcoming the inclinations and desires that do not conform to those of the tender Savior. It is right for you to say that you would be willing to open your whole soul to me, but you know you do not have to do this. All you need is a little more simplicity. And, believe me, in my eyes you are neither more nor less. If you find faults in yourself, well, I have mine too which, through the resources of my self-love, I keep hidden away. Follow the advice of the angel whom God has given you for a guide: he knows what you need.[240]

My eyes are on the side of the tabernacle where Jesus resides; I pray he turn his gaze to you and pierce your heart with the

---

[238] French: "Voyez quelle est celle que vous voulez habiter, et, sans rechercher ce motif d'intérêt, quoique spirituel et permis, celui de bienveillance et de complaisance, pour un Dieu si bon, devrait vous porter à ce qu'il y a de plus parfait, persuadée, comme nous le devons être, que, pour Jésus, il nous faut vivre comme lui et pour lui," "See which of these you would like to inhabit, and without studying the motive of interest, although spiritual and permitted, is benevolent and complacent, for a God so good ought to bring us to that which is most perfect, persuaded, as we must be, that, for Jesus, he makes us live like him and for hum." I have interpreted the sentence as addressing her correspondents' uneasiness at questioning their communal life, the "mansion" the Father has chosen for them. Elsewhere, in Letters 97 and 98 for example, Eustelle acknowledges some of the sisters' dissatisfactions and questions with their community while urging them to accept what God has given them.

[239] Mount Tabor is believed to be the site of Jesus's transfiguration.

[240] As the headnote to the letter suggests, "angel" here probably refers to the correspondent's spiritual director.

marks of his love. Ah, when I am alone at the feet of this Heavenly friend, I seem sheltered like an infant in the arms of his mother. O Holy Eucharist! Consolation in our exile, when united to you here below, we achieve, through you, eternal union.

I pray our Lord place your heart and mine in his adorable heart, although I am unworthy of this favor. May he bless you from the depths of his sanctuary: this I pray to him.

Adieu.

Your friend Eustelle,
poor servant of Jesus.

LETTER 100

That Jesus be known and loved: Eustelle's singular wish; Testimony of tender affection.

July 24, 1840.

Blessed be Jesus in all things.

May the merciful master pardon me for the pains which my words caused you.[241] He knows, however, how far the meaning you gave them is from my heart. God's will alone, given my unworthiness, could make it possible for me to endure not being of some use for the salvation of those souls for whom I would give my blood. I call Jesus to witness the desires and ambitions of my heart. Oh, that he might be known! That he might be loved! Look into and accept my heart, and hear my prayer.[242] Ask this same Jesus to tell you my wishes for you. Far be it from me to seek the esteem of creatures. Jesus! Nothing but Jesus! And for Jesus, to my neighbor: charity! Promise me not to think for an instant of filling your soul with such painful reflections. For me

[241] Thompson (268) identifies this letter as written to Eustelle's friend Anastasia. Eustelle had spoken of how painful it was for her to leave the Church after a period of adoration at the tabernacle, and how the pain increased when, on her way out of church, Eustelle found someone waiting to talk to her. She complained of this to Anastasia, forgetting that it was often Anastasia herself who was waiting for her there. This letter, Thompson suggests, begins with Eustelle apologizing for her inadvertent snipe at Anastasia. Thompson quotes the letter in its entirety (ibid.).

[242] French: "Qu'il agrée ce qu'il sait, et qu'il m'exauce," "Let him accept what he knows, and hear me." This seemed too oblique for the context.

who, despite my faults, never thought that a visit from you could be an annoyance, I fear these suspicions will lead you to visit less often. For the love of the good Jesus, my wish is for you to love him more than I do myself: if it is his will, please do not deprive me of what I love for him, in him, and through him. To God, yes! All to God, through the bond of the most perfect charity. To God in time; to God in eternity. Yes, we will be God's and in God, to bless and love Jesus our God; to cover ourselves and lose ourselves in the life eternal that is God. Always, more than always, all for you. Christians love him for eternity. And may Jesus reveal to you the rest of my thoughts.

Eustelle,
poor servant of Jesus.

LETTER 101

Eustelle's humility and confidence; Exhortation to these virtues; They lead to holy love.

N.d. [*Probably late summer, 1840.*]

All for Jesus, through Jesus, and in Jesus.

It was not for me that I felt sad last night. It was for you: I was afraid you would not be allowed to go out again. It is not that you should not be permitted to direct your steps to my poor home, but rather, what help could you find by relying on an arm of flesh, too weak even to sustain itself? Though I am unworthy, vile ashes and dust, pray, pray, that Jesus, love eternal, bestow on me his sweet and merciful regard. Oh, how he lights up my heart! Oh, may he kindle in my heart, a heart created for him, that pure love of him who is its force and principle. I need that fire to consume the innumerable flaws that wither my soul, which each day Jesus makes his sanctuary and his temple. My weaknesses humble me without discouraging me, for I know they are of our dear Savior. I count upon him and he does not disappoint my hopes. Good friend, have the most tender trust in his goodness. He refuses nothing from that good virtue joined with humility.

Confidence in Jesus. O crèche! O Cross! O sacrament! O love of Jesus! These are the reasons for the confidence of Christians; these are my reasons for confidence and your reasons as well. Take care not to hurt the gentle and peaceful heart of Jesus by failing in this holy and benign confidence. Oh, live in peace all the days of your exile. Affirm, more and more, the designs of the Lord for you. Set yourself to die to yourself, to your will, to your judgment, to your pleasures, and to your inclinations, and clothe yourself entirely with the new man,[243] with Jesus our God. These sacrifices, these victories over yourself, put you in possession of divine charity. The spouse will give you entry into his cellar,[244] where he intoxicates the souls who are dear to him. There, he *will set his charity upon you*;[245] that is to say, he will eliminate the flaws which are found so often in this gold which must be so pure. Hasten then to burn with this divine fire just as I burn, because this sacred fire does not set enough hearts aflame. Jesus alone can appreciate what I suffer for this. Pray that I will be the first to put into practice what I write to you on this subject. Now is it my job to preach?

I leave you. Soon I will visit this Heavenly neighbor and present him your adoration. Adieu: be at peace, for Jesus is with you. He will lead you by the hand into the promised land, and I hope that, happier than Moses was, you will not see it only from afar but you will be allowed to enter and to collect the milk and the honey that come out of the stone, which is Jesus Christ.[246]

Eustelle.

LETTER 102

Happy the soul that learns the tenderness and humility of Jesus; The holy tabernacle is his school.

October 1, 1840.

Glory be to Jesus.

Take courage, my good friend. All for Jesus. Do not grow weary in the exercise of holy humility and sweet simplicity. Do not be discouraged by the difficulties that the Demon never ceases to

[243] Echoing Colossians 3:10: "revêtu le nouvel homme," "clothed in the new man."

[244] Echoing Song 2:4. See note 175, above.

[245] French: "*il réglera en vous la charité.*" Italicized in the French original; possibly a very loose echo of Psalm 91:14.

[246] Eustelle is alluding here to Deuteronomy 32:51–52, the Lord's refusal to allow Moses to enter the Promised Land because his faith wavered at Meribah.

bring forth in this painful path of nature; know that humility requires sacrifices but brings perfect peace and perfect liberty to the faithful soul. Our divine and all-good master, truth eternal, tells us to learn from him, not the working of miracles or raising the dead, but meekness and humility. How happy the soul possessing these virtues! Jesus abides there: it is his tabernacle, the throne where he takes his rest, his garden of delights.[247] Yes, it is the humility in that soul that makes Jesus take pleasure in it; what torrent in his heavenly communications does not intoxicate this soul? Humility brings the soul to feel the sweetness of Jesus's presence, introduces it to the treasures of his divine heart, this sacred refuge from which rise to the Eternal God profound adorations, incomprehensible love, and acts of infinite price. Oh, unite yourself more and more deeply to this tender Jesus, to your dear brother, to God with us. Enclosed within your heart, think, adore, and love the only one worthy of love, Jesus all good. I rely upon his promise: he will grant you the fruits of the wishes that I have articulated for you. I ask him, in this moment, to give you more and more the science of the tabernacle: I ask this for myself and for the others. Pray also for me, for my needs are great, but I count on the price of my ransom. Adieu: until Jesus wills that I may see you. In the meantime, remember to love him.

Eustelle,
his unworthy servant.

LETTER 103

Do not deprive yourself of Holy Communion due to vain worries.

October 14, 1840.

All in Jesus, through Jesus, for Jesus.

I do not know if it is because you do not have permission to receive Holy Communion or if, because of some turbulence of conscience, you are depriving yourself of it on your own: whatever these troublesome thoughts may be, I place them tonight in the tender heart of the good Jesus, whom you love more than yourself. Oh, how good is this God, so full of love! How divine are his

[247] Probably echoing Song 4:12–16.

attractions![248] How he deserves all our love. Pray, my good friend, that he become known. Oh, how I know him myself, such a good and tender friend. Do not scold me for what I write to you: it is Jesus who wishes it; it is for his glory. All yours, through Jesus.

Your friend, his unworthy and poor servant,
Eustelle.

LETTER 104

How sweet it is to live and die for Jesus; We arrive there through tenderness, patience, and detachment; Languor; Wishes.

November 13, 1840.

All for Jesus.

May the divine bridegroom possess your soul.

The time seems long to you, yes? because I have been negligent in writing to you. Forgive me: I miss having the leisure. But I wish today to repair that fault by talking to you about the singular object of our wishes and desires. You know well what I mean. Your heart must bloom with joy to think of this God full of love, this Father so tender, this Jesus, the admiration of the angels, the crown of virgins, and your own if you want. Oh, how sweet it is to live for this Jesus, to expire in Jesus! To reach this desired end, which so readily changes tears into joy, which transports the soul from exile to its homeland and from sorrows to eternal rest, you must respond, with love and with all possible generosity, to the gaze, full of mercy, that Jesus, our dear and only benefactor, has for you. So be humble, gentle, patient, detached from everything. Search for nothing but Jesus; worship only Jesus, look only for Jesus. Let us not fear sacrifices, whatever they may be: they are for Jesus, God with us, our heavenly friend, our everything.

I was near him a few days ago, and you were there too: I prayed that this tender Savior enclose us in the secret of his tabernacle and consume us there with love for him.

---

[248] French: "Que ses charmes sont divins," "How his charms are divine!" As elsewhere, the translation might mute but not erase Eustelle's characteristic borrowing of the tropes and vocabulary of romantic love, of which the ultimate source is the Song of Songs.

Good friend, I grow fatigued and so I need to stop. See what I want. My health has not been good this week, and I am still waiting for the doctor. Last night and today, though, I coughed less and my chest was not quite as painful. But I cannot do anything. Jesus wills it: may his divine will be blessed and observed! I leave you covered in his precious blood; I wish that he would empurple the vestment of glory with which he will clothe you on that day that he leads you into the heavenly Sion.

Adieu. All to you in Jesus.

The unworthy servant of the dear Savior,
Eustelle.

LETTER 105

It is on Calvary that the lovers of the Savior are born; Eustelle wishes to die at the feet of the tabernacle.

[*THIS SEEMS TO BE ONLY SURVIVING LETTER ADDRESSED to this person, apparently a lay woman and acquaintance of Eustelle, who wrote to her with some urgency asking her about her fitness to receive Communion.*]

November 14, 1840.

All for Jesus.

Dear Lady,

I wrote to you Friday evening, and today, Saturday; I have just received your letter to which I am at once responding to satisfy what you have asked me. I know that you are permitted to continue receiving Holy Communion; if necessary, however, you could speak with Father N***. So then, either make your communions as you have been permitted to do, despite your concerns, or go and talk with Father. I believe that the Demon has prevailed over you this week; take care then not to lose the fruit of the trials to which the Lord is subjecting you right now, for they are the flowers of his Passion with which you should make a bouquet to place on your heart with joy, delight, and love. Oh, recognize more deeply the interest that Jesus so good has in your soul by acting as he does towards it. It is on Calvary that the lovers of Jesus are born; it is there that he presents them with his crown of horror and pain. Let us love, good friend, to follow[249] the desires of the heart of Jesus; let us join to the Cross everything he sends us, everything we are. It is then that, in the order of his good pleasure, we will come to the day when it will be given to us to receive with joy the fruits so sweet of the mysterious tree on which we have been redeemed.

I leave you at the feet of the throne of mercy. May Jesus, from on high on his adorable Cross, let a few drops of his precious blood flow onto you.

I slept a little better last night, and today I coughed less. I am going now to the Church of Saint-Pallais, my dear abode. Pray that, having stayed there so much, I might expire there, at the feet of the tabernacle of love, for him, the one whom love makes victim and prisoner.

Adieu: all to you through his heart.

His poor servant,
Eustelle.

LETTER 106

Have no fear; Humility; Confidence; Faithfulness to Communion.

November 18, 1840.

Blessed be Jesus.

Yes, you must bless him, this all-amiable master: the behavior he shows towards your soul is the result of his mercy and his love. Why then do you sometimes slacken the confidence you have in him? Why give yourself over to worry? It is not enough that he has made you receive these testimonies of his goodness; embracing his designs, you must humbly submit to his divine will, assured that Jesus, like a tender father, watches with love the children whom he loves and whose happiness and felicity he desires fervently. Oh, little sister of Jesus, love this tender brother: do not fear but humble yourself; at the day of his coming, he will call to himself only the simple ones, the little ones; he will raise only those who have humbled themselves.

[249] French: "Aimons, bonne amie, à seconder les désirs" "Let us love, good friend to second the desires."

I am happy that our Lord has provided so well for your spiritual needs; I bless him with you; be grateful for these with a more and more perfect fidelity towards him.

If you would like to pay me a little visit, you will find me, in secret, in the heart of Jesus.[250] It is there that I urge you to unite with my soul: it is there that I desire to be consumed and where I wish all souls to be consumed with mine.

My health is pretty much still the same; I had a bad cough yesterday, which I attribute to my needing to talk a lot. Today, the cough is less severe and my chest less painful. All is Jesus's will. The doctor has not come again to bleed me.

Be at peace: stay where you are if it is our Lord's will. Be resigned, and do not miss your communions: and since you have a director, take profit from him.

Adieu. I forgot that today is your birthday, so I wish you well. You know the wishes I have for you, may Heaven grant, I hope. May you soon see all your own wishes fulfilled.

Adieu: all for you in Jesus our God.

Eustelle,
his poorest servant.

LETTER 107

Self-denial; Jesus wants us to accept him; Humility, virtue of virgins; Die here below to live in Heaven; The state of her health.

[*EUSTELLE'S TONE AND INTERACTION WITH HER CORRE-spondent here seem strikingly unlike those of other letters in this group. The undercurrent of discomfort and even disapproval is palpable, though we cannot know how much of the language may be jocular. The phrase towards the end of the letter, "faiseuse de reproches" or "[feminine] maker of reproaches," is particularly striking. A fairly reasonable guess is that the correspondent here is a novice struggling with final vows, perhaps especially chastity, which might account for Eustelle's comment about burning the book she wanted. In all, the letter is a reminder of Eustelle's powerful relationship with these women; the sisters seem to*

[250] French: "dans le secret du cœur du doux Jésus," "in the secret of the heart of the sweet Jesus." I have rendered "dans le secret" adverbially, as "secretly," or "in an ineffable manner."

rely urgently on Eustelle's little letters and the advice and encouragement they provide.]

December 18, 1840.

All for Jesus.

You are wrong to blame me for what you say is my keeping too long a silence towards you: in addition to it being the holy season of Advent, when we must subject ourselves to greater mortification, I must tell you that our Lord did not want me to write to you. So do not blame me. I understood the harsh trial to which you were subjected, but I can only bless his paternal rigor which wants to test your love and asks that your response be pure and resigned. Humble yourself: this is the whole of the science of a virgin who has chosen for her spouse the God-made-man, one who is poor, suffering, who must end this mortal life in abasement and humiliation. All of this he suffers out of love for a virgin whom he loves with a predilection and for whom his tender heart still feels the thirst of Calvary. Oh, do not be ungrateful to the spouse of blood. Love him as he loves you. Enclose your whole soul in his heart. There, live in his life, and learn to die to live in his realm so beautiful, magnificent — the realm of Heaven, where he rewards you in God for the privations, the trials, the sacrifices, and the tribulations of all kinds.

Tomorrow, finally, the penance ends that was imposed on you by the angel of eternal Sion. Rejoice, for the winter is passed, and the dew of Heaven will fall on you: the lovable Jesus will double his favors. Humble yourself: this is the thanksgiving he expects for his generosity towards you. Oh, how delightful he is! Oh, how good he is! Die rather than fail to love him.

I burned the book you asked me for: you will receive the gifts you want. I will not come back between now and Christmas.

My health is not very good today: my cough and the pains in my chest continue, and I am not as strong as before. I am waiting for a bloodletting: do not be angry, my lady.

I thought of you this evening, at the feet of the Lord. I have to stop: I am tired. Adieu, bringer of reproaches.[251] I leave you in the heart of Jesus. It is in him that I am your friend.

Your unworthy servant,
Eustelle.

---

[251] French: *faiseuse de reproches*, "reproach-maker lady."

LETTER 108

The presence of God gives birth to humility and is the soul of prayer; Do not be discouraged by the difficulty it presents; We will get there in time; Spiritual culture; What is asked of us.

N.d.

[*THIS IS ONE OF THE MORE REMARKABLE LETTERS IN THE* Recueil. *It contains no greeting, no personal notes, inquiries or wishes, and no valediction except Eustelle's request for prayers for her own humility. Its tone is insistently didactic from beginning to end, and its figurative language is denser than that of any other of Eustelle's writings. It almost reads like Eustelle's response to a request for an instruction on prayer.*]

To the glory of Jesus.

To attain a disposition to holy prayer, it is essential to work to acquire interior mortification, which consists of routing those little natural desires: for the more we take care to empty our souls of ourselves, the more our Heavenly spouse will fill them. When we want to fill a bottle with some precious liquor, we usually take care to clean it first; in the same way, our souls need to be pure to be filled with the perfume of the gift of prayer. Come to Jesus stripped of yourself; hold on to his feet like his beloved Mary Magdalene. Prayer is the elevation of our hearts towards God: and the knowledge of who God is and what we are is enough, in his presence, to maintain the most profound humility in us. Also, Jesus Christ said, *The Kingdom of God is in you.*[252] When you pray, accustom yourself to seeing our good Savior present in your soul and resting on your heart. Before him, then, be like a sick plant exposed to the benign effects of bright daylight; like a beggar at the door of a rich person; like a drop of water in the expanse of the ocean; like nothingness lost in wholeness. Say as the blind man of the Gospel did, "Lord, I want to see."[253] It is the divine Eucharist that should be, above all, the subject of your prayer. When your heart is one with this Savior God, the sight of this favor must occupy your soul and enfold it in heavenly love; remain calm and peaceful before Jesus, like a statue that its owner would have

---

[252] Luke 17:21.
[253] Luke 18:41.

placed in a niche. Listen to Jesus and answer him interiorly, for he understands your language. Love him tenderly, without fear, without worry; let yourself be imbued with his love; sometimes, desires are enough in prayer, and the most perfect confidence the fruit. Finally, do not be driven off by the difficulties that you encounter in this labor of prayer;[254] the Demon well knows the good that comes from it, and so he tries to turn souls from it. But have great courage: love greatly. It takes time: the gardener who sows is not ready to harvest the fruits: he waits for the seed he entrusted to the ground to become an offspring, and for it then to grow. Then he inserts the graft, for otherwise it would be a wildling; he gives it, if necessary, a stake[255] to support it. The gardener takes care of it himself and prunes it when the time comes. It is only after all of these various treatments that the tree finally produces the flowers that later become fruit. It is the same with our souls. The gardener who cultivates them is Jesus, but he requires us to cooperate in our cultivation. This cooperation is easy, for grace is there to assist us. So count on his help, and love prayer, for this is the source of the union with the Savior God; grace alone is the perfect way to Holy Communion. So delight in this union, begun here on earth, and make it the pledge of the eternal union that I wish for you.

Pray to our good master that he give me a little humility; I need it to heal my pride.

Adieu. Your friend,

Eustelle,
poor and unworthy servant of Jesus.

LETTER 109

Come to Jesus like a child to her mother; Submission to the divine will.

N.d.

Good lady, you can postpone until tomorrow the consolation of reuniting yourself with the sovereign good of your soul, with

[254] French: *dans cet exercice*, "in this exercise."

[255] French: *tuteur*. The word can also be translated "tutor," making it reasonable to imagine that Eustelle is playing on the word and nodding towards her own "tutorial" relationships with the spiritual directors who supported her in earlier years.

Jesus, to whom you are betrothed and whose wife, later, you will become. Come to him like a child to the breast of her mother; come, intoxicate yourself at the pure source of divinity.

As for my health, ask not for what you want but for the divine will, to which I submit for life or death, for time and eternity.

All for Jesus, your friend,
Eustelle.

LETTER 110

Sacrifice for the love of Jesus.

N.d.

My dear good friend, it is the most adorable will of Jesus that you do not come to see his unworthy creature. I am not telling you this to add to the little sacrifice imposed on you, but I believe that, even if you had asked for permission yesterday, it would not have been granted to you. Be submissive, and wait for Jesus to make it possible.

Oh, how good Jesus is!

Eustelle.

LETTER 111

Take Communion and advance in charity.

N.d.

[*THE CONTEXT FOR THIS SHORT LETTER IS ESPECIALLY unclear. The second sentence suggests that Eustelle is somehow taking responsibility for her correspondent's receiving the Eucharist, though it is hard to imagine a circumstance in which Eustelle's "permission" would make sense. Alternately, it is possible that the correspondent's family is opposed to her vocation, and other letters have shown that Eustelle has continuing contact with the families of young women in the novitiate; see, for example, Letters 89 and 92.*]

Glory and love to Jesus in the Eucharist.

Child of God, you can continue to unite yourself with the sweet and peaceful friend of our souls. If required, I give this permission.[256] Continue then, above all, to advance in holy charity. Always, always: divine love and humility.

Your friend and unworthy servant of Jesus,
Eustelle.

LETTER 112

Privations are the test of a strong soul.

N.d.

Glory be to Jesus, our God.

Dear lady, in rereading your letter, I think I understand the reason for your grief. Our Lord has treated you, not like one who is weak and childlike, who needs the milk of consolation, but like a strong and generous soul, hungry for privations and sacrifices out of love for him. It is Jesus: before washing you in his divine blood, Jesus wanted to test your love and submission by inflicting on you this harsh but useful deprivation: not feeding you so often with his divine flesh and drinking not so frequently of the cup of his precious blood. Oh, have faith that, despite this trial, which is only for your own good, the well-beloved Jesus has his eye fixed on your soul, to enrich it imperceptibly with graces and favors. Later, the trial will be over and Jesus will reward you with new favors. I wish that you seek him only in all things, and die to every thing that is not him. So I leave you covered in his adorable blood: may it intoxicate you, at once both satisfying and deepening your thirst.

Adieu. Eustelle.

LETTER 113

The rays that come from the heart of Jesus are always full of love; Eustelle abandons herself to Jesus in his poverty.

N.d.

All for Jesus.

[256] French: "Je répondrai de cette permission, s'il le faut," "I will answer for this permission, if it is necessary."

My good friend,

Do not despair that Jesus is testing you; this is a testimony of his love for the souls he holds dear. These traces come from his divine heart and, if they may be hurtful, they are full of love. You must love to suffer if you wish to become the bride of Jesus crucified. It is in the school of Calvary that the lovers of Jesus must be formed.

My good lady, love; but let it be by suffering, if that is what the tender master wishes. Perfect conformity to the divine will is the most accomplished degree of perfection. If you cannot come to see me before Sunday, I will come next Thursday. Thank you for asking if I need anything. It is not up to me to provide: it is in the Lord's power. It is his affair; I do not involve myself in it.

As for my health, it is always the same. I had lots of coughing today, but it is the season. My shoulder pain has been a little less hurtful but it still bothers me.[257]

I leave you in the secret of the tabernacle; stay there awaiting when the eternal tabernacle shall be open to you.

All yours in Jesus. Your friend,

Eustelle,
unworthy servant of Jesus.

LETTER 114

Light and strength drawn from the heart of Jesus; Love crucified; Humility, obedience and submission; Give back to Jesus for the ingratitude of men.

December 13, 1841.

All for Jesus in the Eucharist.

The beloved disciple, intoxicating himself with the purest of joys at the breast of Jesus, received there, at the same time, an abundance of light and power. So let us go and repose ourselves on the heart of Jesus, not only for the sweetness and light that it gives us, but also to learn the ways of love crucified. It is only through this last knowledge, followed by its practice, that it will be given to us to enter into familiarity with Jesus and to receive

[257] French: "mais je suis toujours oppressée," "but I am still oppressed." This seemed too strong, given that she has just said that the shoulder pain had lessened.

the special marks of his tenderness. But in vain do we aspire to these favors if we are not very humble, with perfect obedience and submission in every circumstance. The supernatural graces are only the fruit of one's total death to everything that is not Jesus. So, let us die as long as Jesus wants and how he wants. When it is given to us to unite ourselves to the divine word in Communion, it is then that love brings about the consumption of our whole being through the ineffable union that elevates the soul above the fogs of the earth and lets us contemplate only that radiant sun reposing in us through the Eucharistic mystery. Oh, since this fire descends from Heaven to the earth, let the earth then be consumed by it![258] Let us expand our love, since so many souls expand their offenses and ingratitude. Let us be aware of how the divine soul of Jesus suffers, ever in the prison where he hides himself for love. Let us leave there our heart, our thoughts, our memories. Let us love in suffering, suffer in loving, and it will be sweet to die.

I have been writing all day: I am fatigued and I have a great headache. Therefore I stop now, leaving you united, in heart and mind, to the loving heart of our dear Jesus, my mercy, my pardon, my victim, my existence, my all, my God. Oh, if you seek out wisdom, you will find it first and ever in the sacrament of his love.

May he bless you, our merciful and peaceful friend. This is what she desires most ardently, she who is, in him and through him, truly devoted to you.

The unworthy and poor servant of Jesus,
Eustelle.

LETTER 115

The demon profits from our exaggerated fears; We must despise him and his suggestions.

April 1842.

Be at peace: the visit you made could not expose you to evil. In the thoughts that come to you, remember always the malice of our common enemy. You are so fearful and uncertain: these things he

[258] Echoing Luke 12:49: "Je suis venu mettre le feu en la terre; et que veux-je, s'il est déjà allumé?," "I am come to bring fire to the earth; how joyous it would be if it were already alight?"

sees.[259] Despise him and also his suggestions. Again, be at peace. I go to be with him whom I need to be at rest and peace,[260] so that I can then work with more zeal. Always yours through his heart.

Eustelle,
his poor servant.

LETTER 116

Why is the whole earth not ablaze with divine fire?—Eustelle's wish; She envies the happiness of priests.

December 13.

To Father ——, Curé of ——.

All for Jesus in the Eucharist.

Yes, it is for Jesus that I send these few hymns; I send them so that, when they are sung, Jesus's mercies, and especially his love in the adorable Eucharist, are celebrated. Nothing pleases me more than what relates to the Eucharist, this sign of peace and love. Oh, by this ineffable means, the fire of Heaven falls upon the earth. But why is the earth not consumed by this fire from Heaven? Divine and spiritual fire, the eyes of flesh do not see you. O minister of Jesus, to whom I like to speak because you represent him for me: this fire is not felt by the great number of men because they do not know where it is, the one there for us on his altars. He is the love of the angels, the Word of God, so good and yet almost universally misunderstood. Dare I say it? This is even the case of many of those consecrated to him. You can hear, I think, what I am saying? Oh, here there is something to mourn! And the more reason to love, more and more, this tender master, in proportion to the ignorance, the indifference, and the coldness that Christians have for him these days!

O merciful and peaceful friend, good Jesus, my mercy, my pardon, my victim, my sole existence, my life, my God, captive for me in the ciborium where you find love! Where else could we claim to find happiness except in you, through you, and with

[259] French: "Vous êtes si peureuse et si ombrageuse qu'il en a profité," "You are so fearful and so enshadowed that he has profited from this."
[260] French: "Je vais joindre celui près duquel j'ai besoin de prendre du repos," "I will join the one near whom I need to rest."

you? Bless with your peace and your love this one of your priests to whom I address these lines. Oh, send him your Spirit, not in a measure but in fullness. May the flock that you have entrusted to his care respond to his paternal tenderness, and one day become the most beautiful flower in the crown with which your blessed hand will encircle his forehead, on the day of your blessed eternity.

I always dare, priest of Jesus, to make this same prayer to you for my soul: I intend always to make this prayer at the solemn moment of Consecration. How happy you are then! I envy your happiness. Oh, Jesus knows all the rest of this. So pardon me this extravagant thought: I have many others that would surprise you no less. Jesus be my witness that all I say to you is from the simplicity of my heart. Pray, and ask for humility for me.

I did not note all of the melodies for the songs I am sending you: it is not that I do not know them, but I did not know how to identify them for you.[261]

I know perfectly the person in question: I am pleased to communicate with her sometimes, because I see that she wants to know and love our Lord very much. She is weak, scrupulous and susceptible to temptation; but her will is strong and, after all, she is better than she shows herself to be. Give her counsel sometimes; talk about Jesus to her: it is he whom she loves. I have great hope for her in the future. May the tender Savior keep her and make her grow in knowledge and love! The whole of wisdom is there. I rest united with you, Father, in the adorable heart of the sweet Jesus. Oh, let us stay ceaselessly in this sacred refuge of eternal love.

Your unworthy servant and that of Jesus,
Eustelle.

LETTER 117

Feelings of gratitude; Hundredfold; God is not known in his mystery of love.

September 2, 1840.

All for Jesus.—May the peace and friendship of Jesus possess our souls.

[261] The letter apparently was accompanied by some hymn texts. Eustelle evidently composed these lines "to the tune of" one or another familiar melodies whose actual names she does not know. See, for example, Letter 3, above.

Dear ladies,

I do not doubt that our good Savior, this God with us, welcomes and repays the charity that quickens your soul a hundredfold, and that, as the reward for your faithfulness in making this precious virtue bear fruit, it will be given to you to achieve its perfection, its consummation, in the eternal kingdom of the good and merciful Jesus. I cannot rightly express to Jesus the good wishes for you that my gratitude for your kindnesses makes me feel;[262] but, at the feet of the tabernacle, I like to believe that he understands. It is there, it is there in the Eucharist that he awaits us to teach us. Why do we not, all of us, give him the love that his extravagant charity deserves! Yes! Jesus is good, but he is not known, and me? I seem only to increase all the more the number of those who fail to know him.[263] Pray! This is the only wisdom that we should value, this wisdom that is madness in the eyes of the world: what happy madness given us by the pure love of Jesus our God!

If the eternal mercy, where all of our hope lies, strips my soul of its mortal bindings and then reveals to it the joys of the homeland, then believe, oh believe, that the memory of your goodness to me will come with me to the Lord. Christians love for all eternity!

May Jesus reward you for what you have contributed to the service of his Church, his bride. May he bless you and love you. I leave you in his adorable heart; there we abide until our entry into the promised land. O, the goodness of the God-Man! We only glimpse the homeland from afar, but already he makes us taste its fruits.

Your unworthy servant, the poorest of those of Jesus,
Eustelle.

---

[262] French: "Je ne puis dignement lui exprimer les vœux que me dicte la reconnaissance due à vos bontés," "I cannot worthily express to him the wishes that gratitude for your kindnesses dictates to me."

[263] French: "et je m'augmente que trop le nombre de ceux qui le méconnaissent," "and I only increase too much the number of those who do not recognize him." Throughout this letter, Eustelle seems to be expressing her frustration at her inability to bring souls to know Jesus.

LETTER 118

On the same subject; The sweet place of charity.

[*THESE TWO LETTERS (118 AND 119) AND LETTER 148 BELOW seem strikingly different from others in this group. Both share a dense, elaborate sentence structure, extended metaphors, and insistent, effusive compliments. Both letters are addressed to a single female correspondent, called "Madame," seemingly in keeping with their self-conscious diction and tone. It is possible that the addressee is the Mother Superior of the White Ladies of La Rochelle, with whom Eustelle spent two weeks as a postulant. Other letters in the group seem to hint at Eustelle's uncertainty about how she was remembered by the Mother Superior, a feeling that may account for her odd self-presentation here.*]

November 10, 1840.

Glory to Jesus.

I am struck with feelings of the liveliest and most respectful gratitude for the countless kindnesses of your tender and heroic charity. Given my powerlessness to give proper voice to my gratitude, I cannot but admire the economy of divine Providence, of the Father we have in Heaven, whose tenderness is so prodigious towards his children. Here and now, vain praise and flattery are far from my thought, for I know, Madame, that you do not like incense: it is sweet enough for you to do everything for Jesus. I bless him a thousand times for the measure of charity with which he has already filled your soul. I pray to him every day to reward your labors with a more and more perfect increase of that virtue of his divine heart, which is so sadly missing in these days, the virtue of divine charity.[264] Ah, why does this sacred bond not unite every heart? It is so sweet to be in his empire![265] Let us

[264] A perilous passage. French: "Ici, loin de moi la pensée des vaines louanges et de la flatterie: je sais, Madame, que vous n'aimez pas l'encens: il vous est trop doux de tout faire pour Jésus, et je le bénis mille fois de la mesure dont il a comblé votre ame, le priant, chaque jour, de récompenser ces œuvres par un accroissement, de plus en plus parfait, de cette vertu de son divin cœur, de cette vertu si méconnue de nos jours, la divine charité."

The translation divides this into three sentences, sacrificing some of Eustelle's immediacy for a more measured exposition. Assuming that incense is a metaphor for cloying praise that interferes with good works, the translation treats the implicit subject throughout as divine charity.

[265] The word choice here may be meant to evoke the Napoleonic Empire, one not founded on divine charity.

pray that this wish from the heart of Jesus may be fulfilled soon. Also, I fervently wish that he grant the wishes formed for you by one who is so indebted to you, and who, unable to give you return for your charity, raises instead her poor and weak prayers to Heaven to rain down spiritual consolation on you, while we await the eternal day of the beatific vision. Then God will be pleased to flood his elect with a torrent of delights.

Your unworthy servant and the littlest of those of Jesus,
Eustelle.

LETTER 119

Wishes for spiritual happiness.

[*SEE THE NOTE FOR THE PREVIOUS LETTER, LETTER 118.*]

November 11, 1840.

All for Jesus.

Madame,

Gratitude is the virtue of good and well-born hearts.[266] We owe this gratitude to God, for he is the author of the numberless benefits that fill us every day, both from grace and from nature. But this tribute can and should also be paid to those whose benevolent and industrious charity so pleasingly follows, with so much love, the impulse of divine inspiration, in imitation of the divine Model given to us, Jesus so good.

Madame, it is not possible for me enough to recognize or appreciate your kindness to me. Please God make up for my helplessness. I do dare, though, unworthy as I am, to elevate to him the voice of my prayer, and the confidence that his goodness inspires in me makes me not only hope but strongly believe that he will accept the wishes that I address to him each day. These wishes, Madame, are only that you may know happiness in this life by the bonds of faith, hope, and charity, uniting you to him who is the author and end of these virtues, Jesus, whom we joy to believe, will become our reward for eternity.

266 "La reconnaissance est la vertu des cœurs bons et bien nés," a French version of the unattributed Spanish proverb "Ser agradecido es de bien nacidos." Eustelle may or may not be conscious of the classist, even elitist implications of the saying.

Accept, Madame, the respectful sentiments with which I remain your unworthy and poor servant, the poorest of those of Jesus,

Eustelle.

LETTER 120

Jesus, the science of the saints, the treasure of souls; He wants to be placed, like a seal, on our heart; He sighs only for our happiness.

18 March [*1840?*].

Jesus: him alone, him everywhere, him always.

I leave him at the tabernacle of his altar, this God unknown to the greater number, this Jesus whose divine charms have so many attractions to bring souls to the fire of his holy charity. Ah, how we should love him, this dear and thousand-times-good master! It is the science of the saints, without which we can know nothing, without which our souls are lifeless, without which our hearts, seats of his love, are without warmth. Happy the soul that is faithful to the secret touches of this generous friend, this tender father, this king so full of love! This holy charity, it shows through the most tender of experiences the truth of these divine words: *I will discover myself to her.*[267] O how the soul immerses itself, as though sinking into this ocean of celestial delight! It rises, from light to light, from splendor to splendor, into the noonday of the Divinity. There, everything created disappears before it, because Jesus, love eternal, this God with us, inhabits, captivates, embraces, consumes, and then unites the soul to his own heart by ties stronger than death. Place me, says the divine bridegroom in the Song of Songs, place me like a seal upon your heart on your arms.[268] Just as these words express so well the dear master's desire that we be one with him alone, in a holy union that he came to seal in his blood! How he thirsts, this lovable Savior, for our thoughts, our sentiments, our affections. Ah, what does he need of our homage, of our hearts so cold? Is he not sufficient in himself? Can we feeble creatures add

---

[267] Echoing John 14:21: "Celui qui a mes commandements, et qui les garde, c'est celui qui m'aime; et celui qui m'aime sera aimé de mon Père; je l'aimerai, et je me manifesterai," "He who has my commandments and keeps them: it is he whom I love. And he who loves me will be loved by my Father, and I will reveal myself [to him]."

[268] Song 8:6.

anything to his happiness? Ah, my Jesus, I know you: you have loved us to the point of your death and, in forcing us to love you in return, you want only to make us happy. So all the advantage is on our side. Could we then refuse his tender solicitations? Can we turn our eyes away from this perfect model and return them to the perishable goods of this present life? Oh, love of Jesus, give us, here below, a glimpse of the promised land. But what am I saying? He has already given us to taste its fruits.

Pardon me, Mademoiselle, if I do not write any more to you: Jesus, whom you so desire to see, gives me no more time. And besides, what can my feeble thoughts produce?

All yours, through the most loving heart of our sweet Savior.

Your unworthy servant,
Eustelle,
the poorest of those of Jesus.

LETTER 121

The goods of this life are nothing before Jesus.

To the same.

N.d.

May the peace of Jesus be with you.

I am sending you some offerings that were given to me for the seminary, along with the book that you were kind enough to lend me. It is very beautiful; why am I not following its picture in my own conduct? How is it not given to me to die for love of him who is its subject? O futile, transitory goods! You are but nothing, dust, before Jesus, and he alone is worthy of capturing my heart; he alone is my speech, as he is my thought: let my every day belong to him![269] I ask him, Mademoiselle, to enclose your heart in the ciborium of his love. May he enlighten you, bless you, consume you.

All yours, Mademoiselle, through his adorable heart.

Eustelle,
his poor servant.

[269] French: "et toujours je veux que son jour me suffise," "and always I want for his day to suffice for me."

LETTER 122

A blessing on holy enterprises; The sweetness of holy love.

To the same.

N.d.

When I saw you yesterday, I forgot to give you what I have sent you today through my little apprentice. May Jesus bless you, you and your enterprise. But I have no doubt he has already done so. May this worthy friend of our souls draw you close with his divine charms, animate you more and more with his Spirit, and consume you in his love!

It is so sweet to love him! To love him is to begin to know, in this life, the joy of heavenly bliss.

Receive, Mademoiselle, the assurance of the respect with which I have the honor to be your unworthy servant.

Eustelle.

LETTER 123

Heart of Jesus, chamber of holy love.

To the same.

N.d.

If our Lord permits me to come into town this week, I hope to have a chance to come and see you. It is so good to talk about his merciful love! I rest joined with you, Mademoiselle, in the safe refuge of his divine heart. It is the sacred chamber where burns the love that will save our souls. Rest there, until our day of unclouded vision.[270]

Eustelle.
Poor and unworthy servant of Jesus.

[270] French: "jusqu'au jour de la vision intuitive, " "until the day of intuitive vision."

LETTER 124

To the same.

Song of Divine Love.

Quand votre amour vient m'animer,	When your love came to bring me life,
Mon Dieu! que mon ame est ravie!	My God! how it stirred my soul!
Pourtant, combien, sans vous aimer,	But how many moments of my life
J'ai passé d'instants de ma vie!	I have passed without loving you!
Rien n'est doux loin de vous,	Nothing is sweet if distant from you,
O mon céleste Epoux!	O my Heavenly Spouse!
Adieu, monde, je t'abandonne:	Adieu, world, I leave you behind:
C'est à mon Dieu que je me donne.	It is to my God that I give myself.

May Jesus inspire you, bless you, fill you and hold you fast. May he be, in everything and always, the fire that quickens you.

More to you than to myself, Mademoiselle, through Jesus our love.

The poor servant of Jesus,
Eustelle.

LETTER 125

The divine will, our Paradise on earth; Accept trials for the love of Jesus; The death of the righteous is only a sleep; The Eucharist, our refuge, our all.

June 28, 1841.

[*THE IDENTITY OF THE DECEASED PRIEST IS UNKNOWN. He was apparently close to the community of the Sisters of Charity; it seems likely that he was either a chaplain or a stricken diocesan cleric entrusted to the sisters' care, as Father Jouslain was in 1837.*]

All in Jesus and for Jesus.

Your hearts embrace these words, my good ladies: the all good and merciful Jesus makes you understand all their meaning and, as a result, you enjoy the peace that comes from complete submission to his holy will. Oh, how good it is, how righteous, how adorable! Oh, how happy it makes us, this will of our heavenly Father who is goodness and justice together![271] It is in submission to his will that our paradise on earth must be, and it is this submission that will ever lead us on to our only goal, Jesus, our eternal beatitude. May we accept divine consolations in Jesus and for Jesus. But let us not become attached to these consolations, for they are only the prelude to the tribulations that follow, which come to us every day from the love of our adorable master. Oh, I seem to see him throwing these sorts of trials at us from his divine heart; they are painful but no less are they testimony of his tenderness towards us.

Let us accept then, for Jesus, separation from one whom we hold most dear; for Jesus, one who paid nature's ultimate cost; for Jesus, joy amidst the tears. See, my good ladies, see the one whom our Lord called to himself, whose loss you so rightly regret: see him, I say, with the eyes of Christians, and you will see him resting at the breast of the eternal glory, rejoicing in the goodness of God himself and praying for his dear children. For our Lord said of Lazarus before his tomb: he *is not dead; he is only sleeping.*[272] Ah, well then: this good Father is only sleeping, and this sleep only affects his body: for, as concerns his soul, he lives at rest in endless felicity. Let us envy his happiness, then, and constantly send him our wishes and desires.

In his pains and difficulties, Moses always returned to the tabernacle of the Ark, and God heard him. So let us also go to the tabernacle, not that of the old law, which was only a figure, but to the living tabernacle, of the God of the Eucharist, of the God unknown, of the heavenly friend, the king, God with us. Oh, let our souls learn to appreciate what this God has done for his creatures. How ineffable is this love of Jesus, under the shadows of the sacred species, shadows that do not exist for lively faith, and which the loving soul well knows how to break through to contemplate the God it adores and who brings it delight! And so

---

[271] French: "Oh! qu'elle nous rend heureuses cette volonté de notre Père céleste qui est aux deux," "Oh, that it bring us happiness, this will of our heavenly Father who is both." "Both" (deux) almost certainly refers back to the apposite goodness and righteousness of the preceding sentence.

[272] Echoing John 11:11: "et puis il leur dit: Lazare notre ami dort; mais j'y vais pour l'éveiller," "then he said to them: 'Lazarus our friend sleeps, but I am going there to wake him up.'"

it is at the feet of this refuge that our pains, our tribulations, and our miseries must be left; it is to the God whom love holds captive that we must immolate ourselves. Oh, may our life be then an image of the sacramental life; let us preserve him in our soul, as he is preserved under the species of bread; let us have no thoughts, no feelings, and no memories but for Jesus in the Eucharist! Oh, the loving soul is the pledge of peace that sees nothing and wants for nothing but for Jesus in the Eucharist, the sacred furnace that illumines it, embraces it, holds it close, transforms and consumes it in God and for God.

The will of our good Savior requires that I end this conversation with you, my good ladies; so then, what are my final frail thoughts to you? Pray for her who is hardly worthy of your memories. And I will pray for you and for him who is separated from you only for a time.

I leave you in the wound of the most lovable heart of our dear and thousand-times-good Savior; may you stay united by his holy charity, awaiting, if it is his good pleasure, when I am able to express my thoughts and my admiration for you in person.

The poorest of the servants of Jesus,
Eustelle.

LETTER 126

Eustelle speaks of her health, her gratefulness, and of holy love.

To the same ones.

July 19, 1841.

May peace and joy be given you by Jesus Christ.

Dear ladies, my good friends,

I seem to hear that one of you has complained of my negligence in not writing and not giving you news of my health. But is it useful for you to occupy your memories with so little a thing? Oh, turn your memories entirely to him who is alone worthy of them. Nonetheless, to satisfy your charitable concern, I obey. I am in a lot of pain since my too short stay with you, when you lavished so much care on me. May our good Savior repay you a hundredfold in this life, by a more and more perfect increase in charity, that charity which you imparted to me. Ah, may hope and divine love be with you, my good mademoiselles, soul of your souls. The God we serve is a good father, a father so good that not only is he lavish in his benefits, but lavish also of himself. Ah, you know how...

Return his love! Live for him, of him, and in him. Let us fix ourselves to the home where his love first fixed him.[273] Let it be there that we arrive on the last day, we who in life have cast ourselves at the feet of the tabernacle.

I finish: and Mademoiselle **** is already saying, "how short it is!" Please convey, my young ladies, my affectionate respects for Madame your mother and for Father.[274]

I remain united to you by the bond that makes saints. May Jesus perfect this union, until the day when we will be one with him, just as he is one with his heavenly Father!

Your unworthy and most affectionate,

Eustelle,
servant of Jesus.

LETTER 127

Apparent rigors, actual kindness; Recourse to Father de Montfort; Submission; Eustelle promises her prayers.

December 5, 1841.

All for Jesus.

I was aware of the different trials which it pleased the Lord to send to your respectable family. I completely sympathize, but, at the same time, I consider as well the mercy and love he has sent her; these are sad trials but ones given in affection. It is a tender father who is seen to chastise the children he loves; what might seem harsh is truly a kindness.[275] O divine faith, light emanating from the one who is both its source and end: it is you who make us understand the cost of the crosses and hardships. Let us therefore

---

[273] French: "Fixons notre demeure où son amour l'a fixé le premier," "Let us fix ourselves to the home where his love first fixed him."

[274] Referring to "M. le Curé," the convent's chaplain.

[275] French: "rigueurs apparentes, et bontés véritables," "apparent rigors, true kindness."

delight in our conformity with the good pleasure of God; it is the golden ladder by which we ascend to Paradise. Oh, how peaceful is the soul that only wants what Jesus wants!

I heartily approve of the idea of a novena to Father de Montfort: I have boundless confidence in this Servant of God,[276] and what redoubles my confidence is that there is a person for whom a novena to Father de Montfort was offered and then experienced great improvement, although his sickness was judged to be incurable. A candle was burned before an image of this holy priest each day of the novena. But I believe it would be better if the candle were burned at his tomb, and you could certainly do this.[277] Our Lord knows how much I desire the return of this good health that is so precious. Let us therefore always submit ourselves to his will so holy, so just, so adorable. I dare to join my feeble prayers to yours, my lady, that these graces be accorded you. May it be God's will that my own unworthiness not be an obstacle to the fulfillment of your wishes. And please, Mademoiselle, offer my most affectionate thoughts and memories to all your family; equally pay my respects to Father: may he be kind enough to pray for my soul at the feet of the altar of the God who hides himself out of love.

Also, please say a thousand things to the good Mariette, who is no doubt good, but who needs to work harder to love, more and more, the one whom she loves already: Jesus so good and yet so unknown and so weakly loved.

And poor Marie-Anne, how is she doing? She is still suffering, I think. May she bless the hand that strikes her: may she humbly submit to the will of our Heavenly father; may she patiently suffer these evils which prepare her for the immense weight of glory, and which, after she has conformed herself to our good Savior, will make her worthy to see him there where we no longer will suffer, where rest follows labor, joy follows sadness, where Jesus God himself will wipe away the tears of his servants and do so always, for eternity.

---

[276] Saint Louis-Marie de Montfort (1673–1716), priest, preacher, spiritual writer, especially of works on veneration of the Blessed Virgin Mary. He was beatified in 1881, making "serviteur de Dieu," "Servant of God," the proper ecclesial term for him when Eustelle is writing this.

[277] Saint Louis de Montfort died and was buried in Saint-Laurent-sur-Sevre, about fifty miles north of La Rochelle.

Please accept, Mademoiselle, my respectful sentiments. I remain united with you in the most loving heart of our tender Savior, in this sacred home which saves souls.

The unworthy servant of Jesus,
Eustelle.

LETTER 128

Confidence; Without the Eucharist, our souls are without power or warmth; Jesus awaits us, to crown us at the portal of eternity.

To a nun.

N.d.

All for Jesus.

What do you say of my long silence, dear sister, since I had promised to write to you much sooner? But I do not forget your soul, at the feet of our good Savior; but I worry for your soul, knowing how easy it is for it to fear too much the one your soul should so singularly love, the one who so perfectly loves it.[278] I know that the dear Master places you on the cross, but he does not want this to diminish your love. And is it not this pure celestial love springing from his tender heart that presses you again and always with love, to approach with your lips, or rather with your heart, the loving chalice of his passion?

To tell you what I think, I believe that the good and loving Jesus

[278] French: "mais elle m'inquiète un peu, sachant combien elle est facile à trop craindre celui qu'elle devrait uniquement aimer, celui de qui elle est si parfaitement aimée," "but she concerns me a little, knowing how easy it is for her to fear the one whom she ought uniquely to love, the one by whom she is so perfectly loved." The translation becomes ungainly because Eustelle makes the sentence work in French by exploiting the feminine pronoun for *âme*, "soul."

The particular point of this letter, to dissuade the correspondent from her excessive fear of God's justice, may suggest that the correspondent is Eustelle's friend and confidante Sister Anastasia, a nun of the convent of La Providence stationed at a school in Saintes. In his brief sketch of her character, Thompson notes that she "suffered from exaggerated fears of the justice of God" (201), which is what initially drew her to seek Eustelle's counsel. After Eustelle's death, Anastasia wrote down extensive recollections of their conversations.

has pierced you with these painful experiences; but, dear sister, I also believe that you make these trials worse. There they are: my thoughts.[279] You do not know our Lord as he is.

But for what do I truly blame you? For not giving your soul more often the sacred nourishment of the divine Eucharist, the pledge of the tenderness and the charity of a God, the food without which our souls are without strength, without warmth, without life itself. Oh, if the light of the angels illumined our souls, what labors could we do? And why is there so much ice, in the midst of so much fire?

Love, sister dear, to leave your tribulations at the tabernacle where our adorable captive lives; his divine voice will be heard in your soul, bringing it peace: dear peace, ineffable peace, which becomes a foretaste of the eternal and immutable peace of the holy city.

Oh, how I would like to know the state of this, your soul, of which I am speaking! Could you tell me if it is more at peace? Oh, may our Lord grant the wishes I express for you, for your whole community, and for the young students which our Lord has placed in your care. May the good master, in whose love I leave you, bless you, sustain you, enlighten you, inflame you, and hold you captive, just as you hold yourself captive in the sacrament of his love!

Please, dear sister, offer my affectionate sentiments to all of your ladies, if you judge it appropriate.

Exiled on the shore of this present life, let us labor to attain that life of blessed eternity. It is there that Jesus waits for us, to crown his gifts, and thereby so crowning our feeble merits.[280]

Eustelle,
poor servant of Jesus.

---

[279] French: "Tenez, je vais vous dire ma pensée," "Here, I will tell you my thoughts."

[280] Echoing Saint Augustine, Exposition of Psalm 103 §7: "Ergo coronat te, quia dona sua coronat, non merita tua" "Therefore he crowns you because he crowns his own gifts, not your merits" (§7.20). *Expositions of the Psalms 99-120 (Vol. III/19), The Works of Saint Augustine,* trans. Maria Boulding, O.S.B. (New York: New City Press, 2004), 85-86. Thanks to Andrew Larson for identifying and sourcing this quotation.

LETTER 129

Jesus ardently desires to unite us to himself through prayer; Do not limit yourself to types of prayer that do not suit you; Imperfection of distress and trouble; Frequent visits to the holy tabernacle, at least in your heart; First fruits of Heaven.

To the same person.

August 4, 1840.

I will lead her into solitude, and there I will speak to her heart.[281]

How these sweet and tender words must bring us hope and confidence, these words by which Jesus in his love makes the soul hear how much he desires it for himself![282] How they express the sentiments of his adorable heart, and the desire to fulfill in us the request he made to his Heavenly Father in these words: *My Father, may those whom you have given to me be one with me, just as I am one with you.*[283] O grace ineffable! O divine union which Jesus wants so ardently to perfect! The most powerful and quickest way to bring this about is prayer. In these intimate communications, treating familiarly with God, the illuminated soul purifies itself, detaches itself, and elevates and unites itself to Jesus, its beatitude. Pay more attention to the heart than to the understanding, and give preference to the act of will, the desire of the heart, than to inner visions. Humbly love our Lord, and he will make himself known to you. I have already advised you to be satisfied with the kind of prayer you have begun: this is the will of the dear and thousand-times-good master. Do not make any effort on your own to represent him in his humanity or in any other way whatsoever.[284] If our Lord wants to allow you to participate in his divine caresses, acquiesce to this humbly and lovingly, without ever losing sight of the depth of grief and of sin that all of us bear, after the choice of our first parent. Be

---

[281] Hosea 2:16.

[282] The language of romantic desire here explicitly echoes the quote and context of Hosea, whose monologues were directed to his wayward wife.

[283] John 17:24.

[284] The language of these three sentences very closely echoes that of Letter 56 to Father Briand, dated March 1840 (about five months earlier), where Eustelle acknowledges very similar cautions from her confessor about forming or encouraging visionary experiences in prayer.

on guard against the instigations of the Demon, but know that you fear him too much. It is he who inspires this excessive fear in you; it would be his plan to make you abandon the kind of prayer to which you have been applying yourself, prayer that is making you advance admirably towards God. There is a lot of imperfection in the worry and trouble that you sometimes experience; and in this the Demon is already winning. Oh I beg you, for the love of the good and peaceable Savior, devote yourself as much as you can to loving him and making him loved. Go to his feet, as often as you have leisure; and when this joy is not permitted to you, transport your heart into its prison of love and stay there in the ardor of you desires. Dear sister, how I would like to love him as Saint Paul did, as Saint Francis Xavier did. Why has it not been given to me to travel, as they did, to distant lands to make this Jesus known, now so tragically the object of dismissal and ingratitude from almost all humankind! O poor sister, let us then seek to compensate this true friend, this friend so neglected. Think always of the benefit of the Eucharist, and let it be the sole occupation of your heart, the ambition of your soul, your joy, your repose. The Eucharist alone can soften our exile, it alone gives us a taste of the first fruits of the promised land, waiting for the veil to be torn and the dawn of the eternal day to shine, where we will see, will possess, will love . . . whom? This you know. . .

Your sister, in Jesus, his unworthy and poor servant,
Eustelle.

And a note to the same person:

Dear sister, despite my unworthiness, which ought to move me to keep my silence rather than teaching others, I am sure that our Savior approves our conversations, in which our hearts enflame each other more and more with the pure love of Jesus, our spouse. On this subject, have no worries: have only humility and love. I understand what you are saying. Continue and advance always in the chaste favors of the beloved who wishes, more and more, to captivate your soul. Take refuge in his heart; I am with you, to love him and bless him. Tonight he must bless us. See how good he is! I will go to see you this evening, without fail. Adieu.

LETTER 130

External good works do not diminish interior values; Do not torment or worry yourself; Simplicity; Seek God, not his consolations; Open the heart to Jesus; Peace; Contentedness; Love; Humility.

April 6 [*1841? This being the final letter of the group, it seems likely that it is dated after the preceding, hence 1841.*]

Blessed be Jesus.

I regret not writing to you; Jesus, no doubt, did not wish it, since he did not give me the time. The state of your soul pains me, but it is only your fault a little bit; you have a lot more worry than you should have: this, through lack of trust in God. Live alone: it is required. But never get the idea in your head that you are going against the inspiration of God when you apply yourself to good external works. We can indulge in these good works and still maintain humility, a meditative spirit, and the presence of Jesus. For a soul truly united to this Savior God, no occupation should be capable of distracting it. It is because we are so weak that we so easily lose the moment our soul finds itself in during our thanksgiving after communion.

Do not concern yourself, then, if people do not want you going out so often: be obedient, and, if it is permitted, go out, without troubling yourself with thoughts of vanity that come to you; everyone has these. Oh, often you lack simplicity in your spiritual labors. Think well on this. Next, I do not want you to be uneasy about your vocation; as you fret about it, the Demon gains more than you imagine, even as you believe you are doing right by concerning yourself about it. And when, at Holy Communion, your soul is arid, give it over into the heart of Jesus, and seek more the God of consolations than the consolations of God.[285]

But perhaps you will say to me, "Often it is my fault." When this happens, gently, peacefully, lovingly, and without troubling yourself remove what you see in yourself that is displeasing to the God of your heart. You should think only about loving. Just as physical fire consumes that which is exposed to its force, so also the divine fire, with the cooperation of your will, must annihilate everything in you that could oppose the absolute establishment of the all-loving reign of the divine Savior. I seem to see our

[285] Cf. Letter 97, above.

all-amiable master, from the depths of his tabernacle, addressing to your soul these sweet and tender words: *Open to me, my sister, my love, my spouse: I am your beloved chosen from a thousand.*[286] This is to say, he whom you must prefer to anyone else. You are my sister: I took on your humanity out of love for you; you are my friend whom I want to beautify by my grace: all because I love you.

Ah, make yourself attentive and faithful to these solicitations of love but do not be discouraged by the difficulties and the time it takes for you achieve this love. Have courage. And once you have made your confession, try not to become disturbed and thus deprive yourself of a visit by the King of Kings.[287] Be more easygoing to those around you. seek only the divine will, finding it in the will of your director. Fill yourself with trust and love and humility. These virtues will make you one with Jesus in these times, and become the source of an eternal union. Amen.

I ask that you remember before God the poor soul of the one who, despite her unworthiness, dares to call herself the poor servant of Jesus,

Eustelle. — Adieu.

LETTER 131

Equality and serenity in character; Eliminate the old man.

All for Jesus.

Understand perfectly the meaning of these words. Trust me: do not apologize; never show any sentiment of coldness but only peace and benign patience.[288] From the tale you told me, you have not failed in charity: have not a thought about it.

[286] Song 5:2: "Ouvre-moi, ma soeur, ma grande amie, ma colombe, ma parfait," "Open to me, sister, my great love, my dove, my perfection."

[287] Eustelle is speaking here of a degree of scrupulosity that would deter someone's coming forward to receive the Eucharist in Communion.

[288] French: "ne montrez jamais le moindre sentiment de froideur, mais toujours la douce paix, la bénigne condescendence," "never show any feeling of coldness but always sweet peace, benign condescension." Given the next sentence, the context here seems to be that Eustelle is calming her correspondent (possibly Anastasia) about a work of charity that seems not to have gone well. In the event, Eustelle says, one should neither apologize nor turn away coldly but approach the situation with peace and patience. The translation opts here for "patience" because "condescension" carries negative connotations in English that were not present in Eustelle's French.

My health is always the same.

So try to eliminate the old man from your heart.[289] Beware of yourself. The love of the sovereign love, the ineffable and delightful Jesus, is recompense for your pains and your sacrifices; he will inundate your soul in this life with the plenitude of his uncreated charity, and then annihilate it in the divine holocaust during the eternal reign of the dear, the good, the all-amiable Savior.

Adieu: I am always yours in his blood, and I leave you with his love.

Eustelle,
poor servant of Jesus.

LETTER 132

Point of singularity; Resignation; Seeing a doctor; Love is a fire that purifies.

April 27. [*The year is not given; the surrounding letters in the collection are all dated in 1840.*]

The peace of the Jesus the spouse be with you.

Blessed good friend,

To speak frankly to you and in the interest I bear for your soul, I do not like the singularity of your costume. Remember to put into practice all that you told me at the end of your last letter, that you desire to do everything that would please Jesus, and when, in Holy Communion, his presence is eclipsed in your soul, then, it is then that you must accomplish this good purpose, submitting yourself humbly and peacefully to the conduct that the good and merciful Savior has towards you, testing and purifying the love that you have for him. Oh, how a soul that is pained and resigned is agreeable to Jesus, when it does everything that is in it to avoid being guilty of any voluntary act of infidelity! But if you do, do not worry: the doctor is there to cure you. Love greatly, and the sacred fire will reduce all of the imperfections in your piety to cinders.

[289] "The old man" (vetus homo) occurs three times in the Epistles, notably Ephesians 4:22: "Savoir que vous dépouilliez le vieil homme, quant à la conversation précédente, lequel se corrompt par les convoitises qui séduisent," "Know that you must throw out the old man, as we have said previously, the one corrupted by lusts that seduce." See also Romans 6:6 and Colossians 3:9.

I cannot converse for long with you: I am going to need a little rest: nature requires it. Right now, you are sleeping. My wish is that the heart of Jesus watches over you and that it be open to you when you awaken, just as I desire that he be with you at your waking to the eternal day.[290] May Jesus bless you and love you. I am sending you twelve sous for the person from the Propagation of the Faith.

Adieu: the unworthy and poor servant of Jesus,
Eustelle.

LETTER 133

Self-love easily corrupts all our actions; Acting calmly; Encouragement to Holy Communion.

July 1840.

May the Cross of Jesus be your portion and his humility your companion in your actions.

For the soul truly interior and united to Jesus, love eternal, should there be any occupation that distracts from the sweet and loving attention to the divine presence? All our actions, whatever they may be, can take on an entirely divine merit from the perfection with which we do them. But as soon as agitation or worry or haste becomes your motivation, losing before them the supernatural motive, self-love quickly corrupts these good works. This is the cloying incense of the Demon, which Jesus rejects. So it is necessary for all of us, as we begin some task, to purify our intention and perform it for Jesus, in Jesus and for Jesus. He is the prince of peace; his throne is peace; he loves only peace: in Heaven and on the earth, and he gives it to men of good will.[291] Everything we do, let us do it with calm and peace, with gentleness and tranquility; and let us remember that we are doing for Jesus our God, our father, our Heavenly friend, the companion of our exile.

As you look at your miseries, do not be discouraged; rather, animated by dear and sweet confidence, may your soul detach

[290] French: "comme je désire qu'il vous soit propice à l'ordre du jour éternel," "as I desire that it be favorable to you at the order of the eternal day." The translation reconstructs the sentence rather drastically.

[291] Echoing Luke 2:14, the proclamation of the angels at the Nativity.

itself, purify itself, rise above everything that can dry it out, so to unite itself in this life in anticipation of its principle, of its beatitude, of Jesus, love unknown. O my adorable master, be loved or let me die. If my voice is incapable of expressing my love, then, at least, awaken my heart and set it on fire with your pure flame. You alone, you alone will see the fire that consumes me.

My good friend, tomorrow, without fear, approach the altar of the lamb; go and satisfy your hunger, quench your thirst. It is the love of the God-man who calls to you; it is Jesus, the dear friend, the unique benefactor; he opens his heart to you, so hasten to enter there and you will find there the fullness of all good things. I leave you now and pray Jesus will bless you. I go this very moment to his feet, and I pray that these lines I have written[292] to you may be to his glory. The holy tabernacle: this is where all my desires are centered.[293] I go to speak to Jesus about your soul, and I ask him to beautify it in advance of the visit he will make to it tomorrow. I thank you a thousand times for your charities. Adieu, your friend,

The unworthy and poor servant of Jesus,
Eustelle.

LETTER 134

Frequent communion unites us to Jesus; it destroys pride, the poison of souls.

N.d.

All in Jesus and for Jesus.

Be careful not to fall into the trap laid for you by the Demon, suggesting to you the idea of leaving off from frequent communion, and receive it only as often as so many others do, others who, perhaps, might not be saved. You are too weak; the communion you receive once a month cannot hold fast in your soul the divine model that

[292] French: "que je vous ai tracées," "that I have traced." *Tracer* is a verb Eustelle has used before to refer to her own writing; here as elsewhere the word might suggest that she is crediting Jesus with the words of her letter, herself only tracing the words.

[293] French: "Le saint Tabernacle, voilà où se bornent tous mes vœux," "the holy tabernacle, see where are all my wishes are limited." The translation assumes that "bornent" is used to mean "contain."

you must constantly retrace in yourself, and your very redemption requires you to conform to this divine model.[294] Our Lord said in the Gospel these words directed to his Heavenly Father: *O my Father, may those you have given to me be one with me as I am one with you.*[295] Behold in these words the Savior's desire. How they describe the most perfect union! So, do not think that you can acquire this union by distancing yourself from that which establishes it, maintains and preserves it, and which makes it grow in time to preserve it in all eternity. To make a reckoning with God, as you would be doing by adopting this course of action, would be to constrain him to take back his graces from you. He has the right to expect from you a life most perfect, a love most generous. And under the pretext of destroying pride, you would neglect the means of destroying it. Humility, humility, humility and confidence. Destroy the self-love that is within you and bring yourself to humility.[296]

I want you to renounce your ideas; they bring me pain.

Adieu: belong to Jesus through Jesus.

Eustelle.

LETTER 135

Jesus, the husband of virgins, the flower of the field and the lily of the valley; The spirit of sacrifice and thanksgiving, especially for the adorable Eucharist; Courage; Patience.

August 4, 1840.

Glory be to Jesus.

I am the flower of the field, and the lily of the valley,[297] says the husband to his beloved. This bride, this singular dove, expressed

---

[294] French: "Vous êtes trop faible, pour que la Communion de chaque mois entretienne dans votre âme la vie du divin modèle que vous êtes obligée de retracer en vous: imitation sans laquelle on ne peut être prédestiné." "You are too feeble, so that the communion each month maintains in your soul the life of the divine model that you are obliged to trace within yourself." The translation takes some liberties to make the sense more transparent.

[295] Echoing John 17:24: "Père, mon désir est touchant ceux que tu m'as donnés, que là où je suis, ils y soient aussi avec moi," "Father, my desire is for those you have given me, that where I am, there they may also be with me."

[296] French: "et, pour cela, communiez avec humilité," "and, for this, communicate with humility."

[297] Song 2:1.

in her turn, the holy love with which she was filled: *My beloved,* she says, *chosen from among a thousand, he is white and red.*[298] You understand very well who this husband is who wishes to lower himself to become yours and that of every virgin soul, every soul which, captivated by his charms, sees and loves only him. He is the *flower of the field.* The flower of the field is simple, uncultivated, just as the author made it. Jesus, our spouse, is as the virgin's womb of Mary gave him to us. And he is the *lily of the valley*: he loves the humble soul, little in his eyes, alone, that loves to breathe in the sweet perfume exhaled by his divine virtues. He is *white and red*: the white of innocence, purity and sanctity; and he is red on the Cross for love of us, empurpled with his adorable blood; and it is by this crimson that our souls recover the radiance that we lost in the fall of our first father.[299] How crimson are our souls when they leave the sacred tribunal! See! See what you must do for such a spouse so good. First of all, he wants of you the spirit of sacrifice in all you do, but you should not want to arrive at this all at once. Patience, conformity. Peaceful waiting. Love to pray, and to stand respectfully in the presence of the Savior, fasten the eyes of your soul to the favors of his love. May the Eucharist above all hold captive your heart and its affections, your urges and your inclinations. Oh, that you may come to appreciate this ineffable joy! May Jesus himself bring you to know all that the tabernacle contains. I ask him to make of you a holocaust, a burnt offering for his glory.[300] But have courage; do not be despondent. Patience, one more time. Our exile will end, and death, our dear sister, far from bringing us a real death, will make us begin real life, a life with God, in whose breast we will abandon ourselves for a happy eternity. *Amen.*

I remain united to you in the heart of the good and tenderest Jesus, to whom be honor and glory throughout all the ages.

Your sister in Jesus, his unworthy and poor servant,
Eustelle.

---

[298] Song 5:10.
[299] A reference to original sin.
[300] French: "Je lui demande pour vous qu'il vous rende un holocauste immolé pour sa gloire," "I ask him on your behalf that he make you a burnt offering sacrificed for his glory."

LETTER 136

God tests us because he loves us; Let us love him; Acceptance of the Cross; More generosity; State of her health.

September 10.

All for Jesus, our love.

The heavens are not always clear and calm; roses are not born without thorns; and the lily itself, in all its dazzling whiteness, often fears the blasts of weather. And so it is spiritually for the soul that loves Jesus; exiled for now from its home country, trials, dejections, anxieties, and tribulations of all kinds come to assail it; but they come to detach it and purify it in keeping with the designs of the eternal wisdom of the Redeemer God. Ah, these trials are nothing other than signs of Jesus's love, a love eternal, for his creatures. Jesus! you are not known; you are not loved. When will our soul, of which you are the heart, be lost in you, O heavenly friend, whom the angels contemplate in wonder, consumed in love? O good friend! Courage and confidence: the fatherly eyes of the dear Savior are on you. Adore, bless and love him. Remove from the sanctuary of your soul whatever may displease the one who so often comes to stay there. Humbly and lovingly acknowledge the dispensing of crosses that this dear master asks you to accept, as compensation for those many souls who refuse to approach and place their lips to the mysterious chalice of his Passion. Think not about the bitterness of this chalice, for its sweetness prevails. Love, but love as you suffer, because this is what the beloved Savior wants. As we arrive at the evening of life, it will be the conformity we have to the divine model that will be our consolation.

Have a little more generosity, please; after all, the gain will be all on our side.

I leave you covered in the divine blood of the God-Man, this God-with-us. Oh, tell him that I love him and that I want to love him more.

My health is always the same; my headaches hurt me a little less,[301] but my chest is painful. Do not be alarmed. My health will be restored to me: I have a good mediator.

[301] French: "mes mouches me font un peu moins de mal," "my flies hurt me a little less"; *mouches* emended to "headaches." See Thompson 172 for references to Eustelle suffering from headaches.

Adieu: I am fatigued, but it is for Jesus that I am the unworthy and poor servant.

Eustelle.

LETTER 137

All for Jesus, who only punishes out of love; Energy for God and against the Demon; Giving all to the one who gave all to us.

October 7, 1840.

[*THIS LETTER SEEMS EXCEPTIONAL IN SEVERAL WAYS: FOR its sense of urgency, its formality, and its unusual lack of gently complimentary language towards the correspondent. Unlike other letters, here Eustelle imagines Jesus directing his reproaches specifically to this mademoiselle, urging her very directly to amend her life. Another exceptional feature is the letter's concluding without a mention of Eustelle's frail health, perhaps suggesting that the correspondent did not know her well.*]

All in Jesus and for Jesus.

My very good Mademoiselle and friend,

I fervently wish that our good and sweet Savior bring you more and more to understand the words whose meaning is so sweet to the soul that loves Jesus well. Yes. *All for Jesus,* the eternal Word, God with us. Everything comes to us from him: joy and sorrow, health and sickness, good times and adversities, consolations and desolations. Why not say, in all these situations without exception, *All for Jesus*? Oh, how dear is a soul to the heart of this good master, when he sees that it only wants what his own most holy will desires, when, submissive and resigned in the various trials through which it pleases him to make it pass, the soul rests humbly in the designs, sometimes painful, it is true, but always loving, that Jesus has for it.

Ah, this God-Savior punishes only out of love. The Demon is jealous of your soul; he looks out to deprive it of the good he has lost himself; beware of the thoughts he often sends to you, thoughts which will lead you away from the path of truth. When these thoughts come, examine them to see if they conform to the Gospel: if so, follow them; otherwise, courageous resistance is needed. Remember that, to enter into glory, it is necessary to deny yourself. So have then more energy and generosity for God; consider all he has done for you and then look to see if what you do for him is worthy of his love. Would you abandon him and add yourself to the number of those who insult him? Go to the feet of the tabernacle: it is there that the God of love resides, the God despised, the God whom love continually immolates for his unworthy creatures. From his prison of love, he makes us hear his sweet and benign voice: O faithless souls, he seems to say to us, what can I do for you more than what I have done? Can my mercy go further? My power, my wisdom, my goodness are exhausted here; what more can I do to earn the right to your love? It is to you, Mademoiselle, that he addresses these reproaches, that brim with goodness and love: could you be insensible to them? Your heart is made for love, but to love the sovereign, the singular good. Oh I beg you, give to your soul, which is the friend of Jesus, what it received from him: its faculties, its operations, your heart and its affections, that from now on everything in you is for Jesus. And he too will abandon all that he has for you: his merits, his grace and his love; he himself will be the promised reward for your virtue.

I rest joined with you in his adorable heart. It is there that you must leave your pains and sufferings; it is in this place of peace that we must await that fortunate moment of our deliverance, of our entry into the true promised land that I wish for you.

Your unworthy servant, the poorest of those of Jesus,
Eustelle.

LETTER 138

Exhortation to Communion

November 13, 1840.

[*THE LANGUAGE HERE SOUNDS LIKE EUSTELLE MAY BE corresponding with a newly ordained priest. The correspondent here is not Armand Guerin, the seminarian with whom Eustelle corresponded beginning about a year later, in autumn, 1841.*]

All for Jesus.

I have done your commission, servant of Jesus: you can, in total confidence, peace, humility and love, unite yourself to this Jesus, so good and yet so little known. As you approach the sacred hearth where burns the fire that saves souls, I wish to know you are consumed like a holocaust. Peace, joy, light, confidence, union. May Jesus give you all; and you, give yourself, in return, totally to the God whom you hold under the Eucharistic veils.[302]

I leave you, waiting to be reunited with you at his altar. Oh, all is here!

Eustelle,
his poor servant.

LETTER 139

To be all to Jesus, who wants to be all to us; Seek only him; Her sad state of health.

October 12. [*No year: the description in the final paragraph suggests perhaps 1841.*]

All for Jesus.

Yes, all for Jesus: in joy and prosperity, in health and sickness, in consolations and desolations. Everything comes to us from Jesus, from his heart, from his love; and we must accept all of it and bring it to his heart, for the sake of his love. Let us aspire constantly to the happiness of a soul that is in this blessed state.[303] It is such joy to act only for Jesus, to think only of Jesus, to see only Jesus, and to serve only Jesus, our beatitude, our all in all. *My God and my all!* the seraphic Saint Francis would repeat, all night long. Let us work to repeat, with sincerity as deep as that of the great saint, these sweet and loving words: *My God and my all! My God and my all!* The world is God and all of his followers.[304] O Jesus, adorable captive in the Eucharist, you take delight with your creatures, and they move away from you! O life eternal! Your love makes us your everything, and us, vile nothingness, we do not want you for our

---

[302] French: "au Dieu que vous captivez sous les voiles eucharistiques," "to the God whom you capture under the Eucharistic veils."

[303] French: "Aspirons sans cesse au bonheur d'une âme qui est dans ces heureuses dispositions," "Let us aspire without cessation to the happiness of a soul that is in these happy dispositions."

[304] French "Le monde est le Dieu et le tout de ses sectateurs"; a fairly elliptical expression. Eustelle seems to be expanding on the repeated "mon toute," "my all," suggesting that the world for the true lover of God consists of nothing more than God and God's followers.

own; we prefer, to quench our thirst, the foul water of human consolations! We love riches, and we do not want to seek out your riches, true riches. Oh, Jesus, give us light: it can come from you alone. Become, we beg you, the sole object of our desires, since you will be the source of our reward for all eternity.

My dear good friend, see how wrongly I write: let not my soul go wrong as well.[305] Ask for me humility and love, the dear love of Jesus, our Heavenly friend, our brother, our all. Be tender, patient, submissive, and humble; and love will be given to you in return. This is the will of our divine master. Repeat these little words, so deep in meaning: *All for Jesus. All for Jesus* throughout our life; *All for Jesus* at death; *All in Jesus* for eternity.

You have asked for news of my health: it is not very good, humanly speaking. I cough all the time; I suffer in my chest and cannot sleep. All for Jesus: I can offer him only these miseries: bless him. I would very much like to know how your soul goes.

Adieu: your friend the unworthy servant of the sweet and good Jesus,

Eustelle.

LETTER 140

Purify your intentions and act without scrupulosity, in the interest of souls.

N.d.

[*NOTHING IS KNOWN ABOUT THE CONTEXT OF THIS LETTER. The tone and urgency suggest that Eustelle is responding to a serious incident or problem, one which she is less than comfortable talking about. Given her connection to the Sisters of Charity of La Rochelle, it is possible that Eustelle is encouraging a nun counselling a novice who has been propositioned by a man: this is only a guess, of course.*]

All for Jesus.

For Jesus, everything that you are going to do; for Jesus the pain that will try you, I think, in the things which you will have to experience, which you have told me about. I imagine your

[305] French: "pourvu que mon âme n'aille pas de même," "provided my soul does not go the same way." The sentence is probably referring to Eustelle's deteriorating penmanship. See Thompson 366.

dread,[306] but it must be done. Purify your intentions before you begin; then, in all simplicity, for the sake of the glory of our divine master, listen to what this person will tell you. Let her say all those things so painful for a virgin who has made an unchanging determination to purity. Then tell her how she should make her accusation.

These things are certainly not agreeable to talk about, but take courage: it is for Jesus, for that Jesus so good and so worthy of our love. All for him, all in him, all through him. Remain always in his charity. I remain joined with you in the bonds of his love.

Eustelle,
unworthy servant of Jesus.

LETTER 141

Prayer is the key to Heavenly treasures; Life is a blessing, since we can offer it to God.

N.d.

Jesus. Him alone.

Our Lord wants you to prevail over this reversal, which has brought you such pain, no doubt due to the zeal you have for his glory. So have confidence: this labor which he has begun will be achieved in the time prescribed by his mercy. Pray: this key of Heaven will open the treasury of Heavenly favors for you, as it will for the person you care about before God.

Love him who must be your all; consider nothing outside of the order of his sovereign will. May it be your paradise on earth, this divine will without which we would be nothing and could never know or love God, our Creator, our Savior, our giver of rewards.[307] Oh, what a blessing then is life, since we can devote it completely to the sublime work of God. Let us love, we poor creatures: love God. Love Jesus, his eternal word as himself; love Jesus, the splendor of his glory, the King of angels, the felicity of

[306] French: "Je crains votre imagination," "I fear your imagination." Imagination here probably refers to the image-making faculty of the mind, which makes the little sentence mean something like "I fear for what you can imagine might happen."
[307] French: Rémunérateur, "Rewarder."

the saints, and the ruler of men![308] Jesus our science, our life, our beatitude! O best of friends: love; live to love; love to die; die to live again in the glory of the eternal city, the city of love, pure, perfect and unchanging love.

I leave you, my good friend: I am pressed by the will of the good Savior.

Adieu: I pray our Lord to enclose your soul in the ciborium where his love reposes. Oh, where wonders happen! Let us try to be part of that.

Your friend in the bond that makes the saints,

Eustelle,
who lives only for Jesus.

LETTER 142

Jesus uses our misfortunes to train us in humility; In the calm, prepare for the storm; Defiance of self; confidence in God; Study and imitate the God of the tabernacle.

October 13.

Jesus, only Jesus; all for Jesus.

If Jesus makes you feel all that you are, my good friend, then bless him,[309] for he wants to train you in humility and, to do that, he uses your own individual heartaches. Know that you need to prepare, in times of calm, for the storm that is to come after. Place no trust in yourself, and place all your confidence in the one who is all love and who is placed by that love, to sustain those souls that are little and humble in their eyes. And more, study ceaselessly the God of the tabernacle. There, we understand all by unknowing all.[310] To please this God-with-us, we must be certain that our life is but a continuation of his eucharistic life. For this, we must be humble, hidden, mortified — I speak especially of the interior life — detached and consumed by love. This is the

[308] French: "le dominateur des hommes."

[309] French: "Si Jésus vous fait sentir ce que vous êtes, ma bonne amie, veuillez l'en bénir. . . . "

[310] French: "Là, on apprend tout, en ignorant tout," "There, one understands everything by ignoring everything." The translation opts for translating *ignorant* as "unknowing," a concept and term common to mystical writings and, it would seem, more apt for this context.

only way to arrive, like the one who must be the object of our imitation, at the glory which is the reward for a life hidden in God.

I have no more time to give you; it is my God, the dear half of myself, who allots it. Let us submit, you and I, to his good pleasure. Believe me, good friend, the one most devoted to you in the abode of faithful souls.

Adieu: to Jesus through Mary.

Eustelle

LETTER 143

Do not separate yourself from Jesus because of trinkets.

N.d.

All for Jesus.

Do not deprive yourself of Holy Communion without reason, for it is the life of our souls. Would you let your soul die for mere trifles, to which great and generous souls pay no attention because they abandon themselves with a feeling of trust and love, to the one who knows too well the fragility of human nature? He wanted to put on our human nature out of love for us, to make up for our helplessness and to expiate the fault that our nature causes us to commit. Courage and confidence: think about what I just told you. If you believe that, in speaking to the Bishop, you will be more eager to receive Holy Communion, then you should go and speak to him rather than deprive yourself of the supernatural bread that your soul needs. Oh, do not abstain so readily from such a great good: from the only good which the faithful soul can see, adore and love, because it comes from him who is both its principle and its center. Eucharist! At this very word, the lover of Jesus expands and blossoms; her hunger is awakened, her thirst increased, redoubled; she rushes towards Jesus, she wants to see him under the veils of mystery. Like the bride in the Song of Songs, she says, not to the daughters of Jerusalem but to the blessed spirits that surround the tabernacle, with whom she is joined in their adoration and love: *Surround me with flowers and lift me up with fruit, for I languish in desire and love.*[311] My wish, O friend of Jesus, that this same love of the bride of the Canticle

[311] Song 2:5.

inspire from you language that so pleases the divine husband. But have no fear: approach him. And think of my soul, which belongs to Jesus: think of its miseries and its unworthiness and, through your prayers, obtain for it pardon for its numerous faults.

Adieu: I am all for you, the poor servant of Jesus,
Eustelle.

LETTER 144

See all in God; Courageously resist the Demon; Humility, submission; Seek happiness only in God.

December 9, 1840.

All for Jesus. May the peace of the good Savior be with you.

Courage, friend of Jesus, in the pains and tribulations that you endure every day, the enemy of your salvation; he joins to himself your other enemy—you yourself. Redouble your energies amidst the difficulties that you face. When it comes to some act of renunciation or some sacrifice, view these, with the eyes of the one living faith, as the will of the Lord in everything that happens to you. Never say it is bad luck; it is nature that wants this or that, that determines one or the other outcome. The infinite providence of our Father God most high dispenses in his wisdom, for the good of his children, the various miseries of this present life, all of which can serve to acquire for us goods that are imperishable and real if we know how to turn our trials to good. Therefore I urge you to triumph generously over the tempting spirit by constantly resisting his malignant maneuvers. It is for Jesus, your father, your friend, that you will take up arms. Ah, how sweet it is to enroll in his holy militia! It is no base metal that should adorn us on the day of our eternal reward but a halo of glory. What is it I am saying? It will be Jesus, our God himself, who will be our crown and our reward.

So be humble and submissive and you will find peace and joy and happiness. Do not fool yourself: you will find happiness only in God; to look elsewhere is only deception and foolishness. Jesus alone, Jesus always, all for Jesus: it is he who must be the object of our ambitions and our desires. Try then to find in him your delight, your repose, your happiness, for this present happiness is the prelude and the foretaste of a perfect and immutable happiness that God has reserved for his faithful servants.

I leave you, though I remain united with you through the charity of our good Savior.

Yours,
Eustelle,
poor servant of Jesus.

LETTER 145

Simplicity and purity of intention; Drink at the source of pure charity; Despise vain thoughts.

N.d.

All for Jesus.

Simplicity and purity of intention are the spiritual wings of the faithful soul, with which it must take off and raise itself to God, its beatitude. Jesus loves simple souls; he makes himself known to them; he makes them enter into the intimacy of the secrets of his love; he makes them drink, in anticipation, from the wellspring of life eternal. O, how changed you are by that water! Jesus invites you to this, as he once invited the Samaritan woman.[312] Go then to the altar of his love; it is there you can drink, in long draughts, from the source of pure charity. Find yourself as often as you can at the feet of this tender and peaceable friend. Make up to him for the ingratitude he has been made to suffer from the great number of his children. Try to be more faithful to his sweet and benign voice; and burn with love for the love eternal, for Jesus, our God.

Do not trouble yourself over the vain thoughts that come to you: they are but flies that buzz about our ears but do not sting.

Keep to your place in the church, without troubling yourself about whether anyone is looking at you. Abide in Jesus: be still and distant from every object other than him.[313] Adore, love, pray. Always keep to this sweet occupation, and they will come: the evening of your life, then the dawn of the eternal day and the beatific vision. Then Jesus will adorn your brow with an immortal diadem.

---

[312] John 4:4-30.

[313] The advice here, to stay at the feet of the tabernacle and not to care if anyone is watching, echoes Eustelle's own behavior: for example, see Letter 7 above.

Adieu. I leave you in the precious blood of the God-Redeemer, the purifying blood that engenders virgins.[314] Pardon the form of my letter. It is the poverty of Jesus.[315]

Eustelle,
his poor and unworthy servant.

LETTER 146

Have no will other than the will of God; Helps.

N.d.

[*UNLIKE NEARBY LETTERS IN THIS SEEMINGLY RANDOM group, this letter seems to be directed at an actual acquaintance rather than to an occasional correspondent. Its occasion is a postponed visit and it closes with a terse and frank report of Eustelles's failing health. There are also traces of personal affection in the complimentary closing.*]

All for Jesus.

Yes: all for Jesus, in all that concerns you, just as in all that concerns my own self. For Jesus, for this dear master, the deprivation of your being able to come and see me, a little pleasure at best for you. Also for Jesus, my sacrifice of not being able to speak with you. Blessed be Jesus. Later then if he allows it. Oh, how good it is to be of one will with him for whom his Father's will was his nourishment.[316] So let us always be submissive, resigned; and the peace of the God-Man possess our souls; his love will reign there because Jesus makes his abode there. Love him, this dear Jesus who is so good; he is the well of our love: why deny it to him?

Our Lord is truly so good to provide for the needs of his unworthy servant. You want to send me wood for heat; send me instead wood to spark holy love. It is Jesus's will, and I submit.

---

[314] French: "sang purifiant qui fait germer les vierges," "the purifying blood the germinates virgins."

[315] Here Eustelle is probably referring to the poor physical appearance of the letter: the pen, the paper.

[316] French: "Oh! qu'il fait bon n'avoir qu'une volonté avec celui qui faisait sa nourriture de celle de son Père." With this rather labored sentence, Eustelle is carefully expressing a central idea of her thought: that, Jesus in Gethsemane, accepting the cup of his Father's will as his *nourriture*, is the model for the Christian "who is of one will with him." The sentence thus subtly links the subjugation of the individual will to union with Jesus in the Eucharist.

Remember that Jesus was poor, and I must walk in his footsteps.

My health is not good; I suffered a good deal yesterday and this morning as well.

Adieu, I am all yours in the heart of Jesus.

Eustelle,
his unworthy servant.

LETTER 147

Open your soul to your director; Practice mortification when you abstain, according to the circumstances; Her health.

N.d.

May the peace of the good Savior possess your soul.

I cannot, my good friend, write very much to you: I have no time. Speak to Monsieur the Curé about your wish, and then about the inclination of your soul, but let it be in the confessional. First of all, ask him if this last thing is useful, and if he approves it. For the way to do it, make yourself known, just like when you speak to me about your soul. Say that these are your thoughts, your feelings, your inclinations, and your tendencies, especially as they concern self-love.

And if Jesus, whose love is sometimes sorrowful but always loving, leaves your poor soul in the Garden of Gethsemane, be careful not to complain, for he is with you. During this trial, have humility, confidence, peace and love.[317]

If you can avoid going to the distribution of the prizes, then do not go; but if your companions are going, and if by not going you will appear peculiar, then go.

On Thursday I will make the communion that you ask of me.

My health? It is always in the hands of my only everything, of my sole existence, of Jesus so beautiful and so good. His dear and good will is always to make me suffer a little, sometimes a little more. He wishes it: his will is my paradise.

Adieu: I am united with you in the bond that makes saints.

Eustelle,
poor servant of Jesus.

---

[317] "Humilité, confiance, paix, amour, durant cet état," "Humility, confidence, peace and love, during this state."

LETTER 148

The love of Jesus eases this exile; Our divine Savior does not want us to be attached to nothings.

N.d.

Blessed be the sweet and good Jesus.

Believe me! Ask to make Holy Communion on Saturday, and make it with confidence, peace and love, towards the only friend of the exiled soul. We only feel half in exile when we love Jesus, who is love eternal. Be more humble and more simple in going to him: he does not like little souls that attach themselves to nothings, sometimes neglecting what is essential. I pray our divine Savior give you his grace, his light and his love. I am sorry to be so pressed for time; I know you can see it in my writing.[318]

Adieu: yes, to God entirely through charity, through the bonds by which I remain united to you in the furnace of the lovable heart of the good and merciful Jesus. Our Lord thanks you for what you have sent me; he did once again what he did at the wedding at Cana, for those who had no wine.

Eustelle,
poor servant of Jesus.

LETTER 149

Pious workings of charity discovered; Acknowledgement.

N.d.

[*IN TERMS OF STYLE AND TONE, THIS LETTER IS STRIKINGLY similar to Letters 118 and 119 above, which may have been addressed to the Mother Superior of the Sisters of Charity of La Rochelle, where Eustelle briefly stayed as an aspirant. The unnamed gift she is acknowledging in the second paragraph could be literally anything, but given the date and the contents of surrounding letters, a reasonable guess is a pile of wood for her fire.*]

February 8.

318 French: "vous devez le reconnaître par mon écriture," "you must recognize it by my writing." As elsewhere, this could refer to the letter's brevity, style or physical presentation (penmanship), or, more likely, a combination of these.

May the grace of the Holy Spirit be with you, Madame.

I bless the Lord for the degree of charity with which he adorns your soul, and, despite my indignity and the poverty of my prayers, I dare to ask the Lord, confidently, to return you a hundredfold in this life, the reward of the actions which are the result of it, and more and more to increase in your heart the precious treasure so unknown in our days, divine charity.

You may have thought, Madame, that I would not recognize the person who left *you-know-what* in the room I occupy; but our Lord made me understand your pious charity. May he be blessed, and may he deign himself to make up for the insufficiency of acknowledgement that I owe you, Madame, for your charity. I confess myself to be unworthy of the paternal care of our Heavenly Father, of this God who provides with so much love for the needs of the little bird; who adorns with such richness the lily of the valley and the flower of the fields.[319] Ah, all together, let us thank him for the blessings with which he continues to shower us. Even in our trials, let us look with wonder on his designs, for the hand that strikes us is always guided by his tender heart, and if the trial that hurts us is painful in nature, let us remember that a great weight of glory must be the price, and that Jesus, love eternal and God-with-us, undertakes to wipe away the tears of his servants, and to become himself their repayment during the long duration of the eternal ages.

Receive, Madame, the assurance of my respect and my submission. Your unworthy servant, the poorest of those of Jesus,

Eustelle.

LETTER 150

God counts all our pains to reward them; The Eucharist, divine magnet, the source of power; Eustelle prays for those who persecute her.

September 21.

May peace, joy and love be given to you by Jesus Christ.

I ardently desire, dear young lady, that our sweet and amiable Savior give your soul the continuation and the increase of that

[319] Song 2:1; see Letter 135 above.

cherished peace that you possess, which emanates so wondrously from this wellspring[320] of mercy and love. Rejoice! Your heavenly Father, from whom nothing you do is hidden, faithfully tallies your sacrifices, your privations — in a word, all your pains: and why? that he himself may be the dispenser of your rewards, in the abode of his celestial glory.

O admirable invention of the charity of our God! O precious and yet unknown means of his love and tenderness! O divine Eucharist! Jesus, all my love! It is by this divine magnet that he attracts, that he illuminates, that he penetrates and binds our will to his own, all-holy, all-adorable, in the different circumstances in which his paternal kindness sometimes places us. Oh yes, this is the essence of the divine mystery, of the bread of angels, of this Jesus a thousand and thousand times good, who gives our souls his power and his virtue, so that we can acquiesce, humbly and peaceably, in that which his love commands and wishes for us.

May our souls be responsive[321] to the impression of the sweet and tender voice of the divine Spouse; may they move, exuberant[322] yet peaceful, towards this unique goal of our affections, the goal of every soul that loves the Savior God.

Jesus, my love and my only life, often shoots traces of his love in every direction from the arc of his divine heart. He sometimes uses the bad dispositions and the sarcasm of creatures for this purpose. How good is Jesus to treat me like this! Please bless him; also pray to him to enlighten the persons who speak out against me, and to forgive them. My soul yearns full of energy, with everything that is in it, after the persecutions and contempt of creatures. It wants to be known only to God and it wants humans to ignore it; it takes care to hide itself from all eyes; Jesus alone fixes his attention on it; Jesus alone holds its thoughts; it is fixed on Jesus alone; Jesus alone occupies it.

Hold a memory in your thoughts, and believe that, at the foot of the altar, your soul will not be forgotten in mine, weak and imperfect as it is. I pray that our sweet Lord Jesus make you more and more worthy of him, worthy of his acceptance and love, and finally worthy of his beatific view. Let us be humble and detached,

---

320 French "principe," "principle."
321 Translating "dociles."
322 Translating "impétueusement."

and may Jesus our beloved pour out on us, like a torrent, the abundance of his heavenly goods.

All yours, my young lady, in the bond that makes the saints. Jesus, nothing but Jesus; all for Jesus.

Eustelle,
poor servant of Jesus.

LETTER 151

Jesus wants us to unite intimately with him; We cannot live without his love; The devouring thirst of Eustelle.

19 March.

Place me like a seal, upon your heart, upon your arms.[323]

Your heart knows these tender and loving words, the wish of the bridegroom whose heart beats with love for the soul that he wants to confirm in his grace and friendship. How well they express the thirst with which the sweet Savior consumes himself for the soul, especially in the sacrament of his love, where the God of the angels, the well-beloved Jesus, reveals himself to the souls and shares his most intimate secrets. Let us ask of this heavenly spouse that, in joining himself by this token of his love, he will deign to let flow in our souls a spark of this infused faith which in its brilliance leaves behind neither shadow nor darkness. Oh, how sweet it is to know Jesus in this mystery! Oh, how delightful it is to rest upon his heart, the wellspring of so much love![324] Let us love Jesus! Let us love Jesus; let us breathe no other love; let us live only for this love, for this is the will of our dear master.

Ah, good lady, this Jesus consumes me with desire to see him loved; it causes me pain that he is so unknown. Relieve in me, at least a bit, the thirst that devours me,[325] by immolating yourself in the fire of divine love, for the one who is the principle and source

---

[323] Echoing Song 8:6.

[324] French: "principe de tant d'amour," "the principle of so much love."

[325] French: "Soulagez, en quelque sorte, la soif qui me dévore," "Relieve, in some way, the thirst that devours me." The sense and context here seem to require translating "en quelque sorte" as "to some extent" or "even a little" rather than "in some manner" or "somehow." Eustelle has just described her pain at knowing the world does not know Jesus, a pain that would be lessened to some extent by the redemption of her correspondent here.

of that love: for Jesus, and especially for Jesus in the Eucharist. O my tender Savior! O faithful friend! O you who loves my soul![326] O Jesus, my beatitude, my all in all. Consider in your mercy the fervent wishes of your unworthy bride and hear her sighs and supplications on behalf of all those souls lost from the path of truth, the way which is yourself. Your divine heart needs to see them made subject to the sweet empire of your holy charity. One word alone, my dear brother, and my thirst will be satisfied, my desires fulfilled. Ah, if you deign to alight in my heart the zeal of your glory, deign also not to allow my unworthiness to prevent its sweet and saving influence.

I leave you, friend of Jesus, at the foot of the altar, to continue this peaceful, delightful conversation. The faith is no longer beclouded for the lovers of Jesus: the beams that illumine them are brighter than sunlight, and the sweetness of his beloved presence transports them, captivates them. Returned to his feet, I will not forget you. Ask this God Jesus to tell you my wishes for you and for your family. There, in his heart, join your heart to mine as we seek out the fire that must consume them for eternity. Jesus awaits us at the eternal port.

All yours through this good Savior, his unworthy servant,
Eustelle.

LETTER 152

Invitation to the love of Jesus; Jesus finds only coldness everywhere.

March 30.

Mademoiselle,

Do not be concerned about the preacher you want to hear. Jesus takes great care of it. He does not forget his friends, this good Jesus, this unique master, this generous friend. Ah, Mademoiselle and good friend, love Jesus; live for Jesus; die for Jesus, our eternal happiness, our unchanging beatitude. O love: who could not love you! Who could resist your divine attractions? Who could refuse her heart to the divine charms of your holy charity? O Jesus, my

[326] French: "O toi qu'aime mon âme!," "O you whom my soul loves": note the familiar pronoun, "toi." The balance of the paragraph uses *tu-toi* in addressing Jesus.

life, the soul of my life: O my uncreated love, convert, purify, join and transform the hearts of all creatures. Oh, may they breathe only the heavenly flames of your pure love.

Good Mademoiselle, I join myself to you to quench, if it is possible, the thirst for love of our sweet Savior. Oh, let us pray that he will be known, especially in his prison of the tabernacle. Oh, how good it is there; what power it is to attract souls! Eh, why is he permitted to die for love, not just once, but a thousand and a thousand times as day, by this infinite fire that yearns to spread its flames abroad but which finds everywhere only coldness and ice?[327] So pray then for the intentions of this dear master: they must be your intentions too, for a wife must not separate her interests from those of her husband.

May Jesus be with you, for his glory, until your last breath. Let us dispose ourselves, in this our exile, to merit by divine grace the rewards of blessed eternity. All yours in the bond that makes saints.

Your unworthy servant,
Eustelle,
the very poor servant of Jesus.

LETTER 153

The soul is sometimes darkened and tested; This is how Jesus strengthens the soul; Be submissive when he sends you privations; He is not known.

To the same person.

N.d.

May the Cross of Jesus be your portion and his love your treasure.

The sun, pure and brilliant at its rising, mounting from splendor to splendor until midday, is often, as the day wears on, obscured

[327] French: "Eh! pour-quoi n'est-il donc pas permis de mourir, non pas une, mais mille et mille fois par jour, d'amour, pour cet incendie infini qui voudrait communiquer ses feux, mais qui ne trouve partout que froideur et glace?" "Eh, why is he not permitted to die, not just once but a thousand and a thousand times a day, of love, for this infinite fire that wants to broadcast its flame but which find everywhere only coldness and ice?" A dense and elliptical sentence: the translation assumes that Eustelle is mourning the fact that the redemptive death of Jesus, reenacted in the sacrifice of the Mass, sends out "flames of grace" that are met only with indifference.

by somber clouds that, eclipsing its brightness, seem to rob the earth of its sweet and goodly light. Just so it is for the soul that Jesus loves: wanting the soul all for himself and after having it taste the milk of divine consolation, after intoxicating it with a torrent of divine pleasures, he often makes it pass through the crucible of tribulations, tests and privations of every kind. In this, he acts like a tender and chaste spouse who wants to assure the fidelity of his wife. Jesus is the spouse of our soul; he desires, with love, that the soul is his all-lovely, his dove, his one and only; it is from this desire that, time and again, he reveals to it the signs of his love.[328] Now these signs of love are sometimes saddening; but they are for this no less loving. Oh, let us proclaim, with the bride of the Canticles, that Jesus *is our beloved, chosen among a thousand!*[329] Oh, could we ever wish, in Heaven or upon the earth, for one more lovable, better, more tender than Jesus, our eternal beatitude!

My good demoiselle, if this dear and worthy friend deprives you of his Eucharistic presence, seek him in the tabernacle of your heart, for he is always there, living, glorious. If the inestimable happiness of nourishing yourself with his sacred flesh every day is denied to you, remember that it is the divine master himself, by the power of the one for whose word and life he is, who wills this privation to give your soul new merits through those very acts of renunciation which your soul moves you to practice.[330] Have courage and confidence; Jesus is with you. Bless him for making himself known to you. I wish and I beg of him more and more to augment, to deepen, our knowing of him. There is nothing so rare, in this age we are in. No, the adorable Jesus is not known, a

---

[328] As noted above, the French *l'âme*, "soul," is a feminine noun, which gives passages like this one a romantic, even erotic undercurrent: French: "Il agit, en cela, comme un tendre et chaste époux qui veut s'assurer de la fidélité de son épouse. Jésus est l'époux de notre âme; il désire, avec amour, qu'elle soit sa toute belle, sa colombe, son unique: c'est pour cela qu'il décoche, de temps en temps, sur elle, les traits de son amour." "In this, he acts like the tender and chaste husband who wants to assure the faithfulness of his wife. Jesus is the husband of our soul; he desires, with love, that she be his all-lovely, his dove, his one and only, and this is why, time and again, he reveals to her the traits of his love."

[329] Song 5:10.

[330] The sense of the sentence seems to be that the correspondent should not dwell on being unable to receive daily Communion and that she should trust that Jesus is sending her compensatory graces in recognition of her acts of renunciation.

thought that causes me untold suffering.[331] Ah, pray Jesus send us his light. Pray that I myself not be in that number of the blind, or like those who know the law but do not observe it.

At the moment I write to you, Jesus is alone in his tabernacle. Why am I not at his feet? Because his holy will says otherwise. At least I can be there in spirit, and I beg him to express to your soul the fullness of his spirit of love. So love greatly the dear and thousand-times-good Savior: he wishes you to pray for his unworthy servant: she has great need of prayer.

I leave you in the peace and love of Jesus, your love. When shall come the evening of this life and the order of the new, eternal day?

Your unworthy servant, the poorest of those of Jesus,
Eustelle.

LETTER 154

The Cross is the stairway by which one mounts to the city of God; To suffer with Jesus

August 25.

May the Cross of Jesus be your portion and his love your treasure.

The first wish my heart forms for you is that Jesus our dear Redeemer bring you to comprehend[332] the inestimable riches held in the mystery of his sacred Cross. Truly, the Cross is, for the Christian soul, the stairway by which one arrives, surely and readily,[333] to the City of God; it is the banner under which we must love to be sheltered; it is the august sign which must prepare us, at the last day, for the glory of the elect of Jesus. Oh, how we should cherish this adorable sign! Let us remember, though, that our love must not be limited to the material Cross of Jesus. It was not only the God-Man's physical sufferings that made him cry out in thirst but also that his holy soul was lost, especially to sinners past, present and future. Oh, if it were given to us to understand

[331] French: "cette pensée me fait étrangement souffrir," "this thought makes me suffer strangely."

[332] French: "donne à votre âme de comprendre," "give to your soul to comprehend."

[333] French: "sûrement et facilement," "surely and easily." "Easily" seemed an inappropriate adverb modifying the taking of one's cross.

then the thoughts and desires of Jesus! How could we not suffer for love of him whom love made to suffer so much? Oh, the pains, the trials, the sacrifices, whatever they may be, would seem light to us, if we had just once truly entered the inner Jesus, tender and submissive! Courage, patience, confidence: the hand of God that strikes you is directed by his heart, and he loves you. Yes, he loves you, so may his love be your treasure. Be his dove, his one and only, through the purity and wholeness[334] of your love. And may this love be the sweet bond that attaches you to his precious Cross. Jesus, love infinite, will be there for you, and with him you will climb, degree by degree, to the sacred mountain where the immortal crown reserved for fidelity awaits you.

I have lost my rights: your spiritual father has returned.

Adieu: love Jesus well, love him exceedingly. I leave you in accord with his holy will: do whatever he wishes.

Your unworthy friend, poor servant of Jesus.

Eustelle.

LETTER 155

When Jesus presents it, accept the chalice of bitterness; Why is he misunderstood and abandoned?; Acknowledgments.

March 25, 1841.

The holy will of God.

Madame, my good friend,

These tender, benign words, how consoling they are for the soul that Jesus makes pass through the crucible of tribulations! How strongly they are felt in a heart illumined and ignited with the sparks of a pure and lively faith! Oh how full of love that soul, suffering but resigned, cries out: *The will of God! all for Jesus!* And it is that faith, of which Jesus is the origin and the endpoint, that makes the soul at one with the divine will, the one alone capable of bringing the soul, in this life, to taste the unnamable sweetness of Heavenly felicity. Oh Madame, if it is the good pleasure of the divine master to bring the loving chalice of his passion to your lips, do not refuse to drink the few drops that he has left for you

[334] French: *l'étendue*, "extent."

there. Oh, seek in this sharing in his sufferings, to quench the thirst with which his heart is consumed for you. How good is this dear Jesus! But why is he so unknown? Why can we not see him here and now, as he is?[335] Why do we leave him alone, so often and for so long in his prison of love, I mean the tabernacle?

As I end this conversation with you, Madame, I hear his tender voice calling me to his feet. There, despite my weakness and my unworthiness, I will ask him to send down on you and your family his most abundant blessings. I will pray to him also to return your health to its original vigor, to fill you with resignation and hope: resignation to the crosses which he sends you, and hope that you will soon recover, for his greater glory, the physical vigor you need to continue the chain of good works whose final link connects you to eternity. Exiled, meanwhile, on the shore of this present life, let us work to achieve that eternal happiness. Jesus awaits you there, to crown his gifts by crowning our feeble merits.

I thank you, Madame, for your charity towards me. If Jesus has restored my health just a little, although it is still weak, ask him that it be used only for his glory and love.

I leave you in the power of the divine will; may you remain united in the charity of the good Savior. All yours, Madame, through his divine heart, your unworthy servant, the poorest of those of Jesus,

Eustelle.

LETTER 156

The milk of consolation is for beginners; After the trial, however, come calm and peace.

To a young lady.

N.d.

May the peace and friendship of Jesus be with you.

Our Lord no longer wants to act with you as though with a weak and timid child, to whom he usually gives the milk of the sweetness of his consolations, and giving in to everything asked of him. For you, to whom he wants to give nourishment more solid,

[335] French: "Pourquoi ne le voit-on pas où il est?" "Why can one not see him where he is?" It seemed that the sentence needed some expansion.

he permits, once and again, privations and sacrifices. He wants this so that, in dying to yourself, you will live only in him. These seeming rigors are true good gifts. If Jesus, who loves you, has allowed that Communion be refused to you this morning, he will reward your sacrifice tomorrow. Rather than crying, bless Jesus. Desire only what Jesus wants, and treat all that happens to you as coming from his divine heart. And so I leave you to rest, until tomorrow, in the arms of the good Savior, who will soon sleep on your heart, as a child on the breast of its mother. I wish and ask him to enlighten you and to set you ablaze with his pure and chaste love, and that, dying in the power of this divine flame, you may, in the house of glory, see, bless, and love Jesus, our Beatitude.

I am so pressed for time that I do not know what I have written to you. Another time I will be more fruitful[336] in my reflections.

Pray for your friend, the unworthy servant of Jesus,
Eustelle.

LETTER 157

Loving in suffering; The benefits of Jesus are proportional to the generosity of the soul; After exile, the homeland will come.

To the same person.

N.d.

All for Jesus.

Yes, for Jesus are the different trials through which he makes you pass; for Jesus, for this lovable Master, comes this privation of even spiritual consolations, if his heart which you love desires it. Ah, these are the traits which, though painful in nature, are for the faithful soul the deposit of the love he has for it. Since our Lord, whom you have chosen for your portion, has presented to you the chalice of bitterness, how could you refuse to bring your lips to the cup of mystery? Ah, every day he presents to his Father a picture of all that he wants to suffer for love of you. So then, ardently love the dear and thousand-times-good Savior but, since he wishes it, love him in suffering. Do not keep accounts with him, for you can

[336] French: *féconde*, "fecund."

never do too much with him.[337] The more perfect your generosity becomes, the more his benefits are multiplied for you. In the midst of your pains, look to Heaven, which is Jesus, who promised to be himself your recompense. Oh, then how sweet it will be for you to have endured some tribulations and through them to have gained some traits in conformity with the divine model. Our Heavenly Father has said, in the mouth of the Apostle, that he will save only those in whom he finds some resemblance to his Son.[338]

So then, take courage: Jesus will be with you in your pains. Love in suffering and suffer in loving. The end of our exile is near; then shall come the homeland, where we will have only to bless, only to love, and only to enjoy our sovereign good, Jesus our love, our happiness, our eternal beatitude.

Adieu: the unworthy and poor servant of Jesus,
Eustelle.

LETTER 158

Humility and mortification for those who wish to advance in prayer; It is there that the sacred fire of Heavenly love is ignited.

August 4, 1840.

Glory and love to Jesus, our God.

Would you be kind enough to ask our Lord that I be the first to practice the advice that I dare to offer you on prayer, being myself only a little way along in this holy exercise? First of all, there are two virtues without whose practice it would be difficult, not to say impossible, to ever reach a good and solid degree of prayer: humility and mortification, and I speak of humility of the heart and not that which is only in words. As to mortification, I mean not exterior mortification, although you should not reject it (for all the saints practiced it), but interior mortification, the enemy of self-love, that brings us true freedom of spirit. Yes, you must purify the heart to be able to comprehend the things of Heaven;

337 French: "Ne comptez pas avec lui; jamais vous n'en pourrez trop faire."

338 Echoing Romans 8:28: "Car ceux qu'il a préconnus, il les a aussi prédestinés à être conformes à l'image de son Fils, afin qu'il soit le premier-né entre plusieurs frères," "Those whom he has foreknown, them he has also predestined to be in conformity with the image of his Son, so that he will be the firstborn among many brothers."

you must be pure to converse with the God of the angels: you must be detached from everything that is not Jesus to be worthy to enter into his divine secrets. Jesus reveals himself to generous souls and accords them his divine friendship. Have then the spirit of sacrifice in all situations; know that it is for the one who does not keep accounts with us,[339] whose adorable heart burns with the desire to see us entirely his own. O you who constantly receive the most touching proofs of his tenderness: what should you be feeling, how great your ardor should be towards this merciful Savior! Oh, with what faithfulness ought you to renounce everything that could make you distant from him, after all these favors given you? *The one who receives me*, says this dear master, *must live for me.* And it is so sweet to live for him! The gain: is it not all on our side?

I implore you then, by the charity of the God-Man, do not allow reservations in the immolation of the victim. Love, and make loved, the one who is love. And for love, devote yourself to prayer: talk with Jesus. What a privilege! Yes, it is in prayer that the sacred fire that I desire for you is ignited; a fire which, I hope, will only increase for the Heavenly Sion, where love infinite, Jesus our God, will consume you to live again always, always, in this ocean of love.

May Jesus be with you; may he make you obey the one who holds his place here below.

Do not show this letter to anyone. Only one other may see it; you know who.

All yours, in the heart of Jesus, filled with fire, his unworthy and poor servant,

Eustelle.

LETTER 159

Aspire to a life of sacrifice; For great souls, Tabor is on Calvary.

February 10, 1842.

May the Cross of Jesus be your portion and his love your treasure.

The beloved disciple rested on the chest of the Savior: there not only did he penetrate the divine secrets which he would make manifest to the world; also there he received those grand

[339] French: “pour celui qui ne compte pas avec nous,” “for the one who does not count with us.” And see the previous letter, Letter 156.

sentiments which would sustain him in the apostolic work that Jesus was soon to entrust to him. Following the example of this faithful disciple, let us not seek the sweetness and rest of holy love, or at least let us not attach ourselves to them; let us aspire with all our soul to a life of sacrifice, to the love much more true, more sure, and more perfect of Jesus crucified. For these great souls, Tabor is on Calvary.[340] Let us rejoice then, spouse of the suffering God; he subjects you to these privations only to raise you to infinite glory. What else matters, as long as we possess him? This favor should ease everything for us, make us ready to suffer everything. Picture to yourself this Savior-God, who, from the center of his sanctuary (which is your soul), lovingly presses you to receive, with even more love, the traits which his heart full of love reveals in yours. Then, listen to him addressing these tender words to you: *You must love me as I love you.* How then could you not envisage, with joy and thanksgiving, the good divine pleasure which delights in setting you afire? Seek Jesus then; but let us seek him where he wants to be sought, where he truly is.

I wish for and ask that our divine master nevertheless compensate you for these pains and tribulations, but not that he remove them. I implore him to make you understand your full reward,[341] so that the all-lovable will of God all-good may be your peace, your joy, and all your felicity. The Eucharistic love must teach you all things, for all things are there.

I have been writing all day, and I am tired.[342] So I end this conversation, which I beg Jesus to bless. May he captivate your soul; may he become its everything. I pray for you in this way; please pray for she who unites herself to you through the love of the sweet and divine heart of Jesus our love, in whom I rest at one with you, being, through him, more for you than for myself.

Monsignor the Bishop has arrived, today, Thursday, in our village.[343]

Your unworthy servant, the poorest of those of Jesus,
Eustelle.

---

[340] Mount Tabor (or Sinai) is the traditional site of the Transfiguration of Jesus; see Matthew 17:12.

[341] French: *prix*, "price." The translation expands the sentence to show that, here, *prix* should be taken as "reward."

[342] Cf. Letter 162, below.

[343] In his introductory letter (pp. xliii–l, above), Bishop Villecourt recalls that he visited Saintes in February 1842 to preach a series of Lenten sermons.

LETTER 160

Eustelle invites him to answer his vocation, to visit the holy tabernacle, the source of true science; Humility and love.

To a student in the minor seminary at Pons, in the diocese of La Rochelle.

October 23, 1841.

All for Jesus.

I love to believe that your soul comprehends these tender words, child of God; oh, all for Jesus, for Jesus in the Eucharist.

You understand, student of the sanctuary,[344] that the God of the tabernacle is my word, my very thought. Dear child, I want to speak this language to you, because I believe that I know Jesus, the sovereign priest, wants to give this yearning. I know it: he already makes you taste these charms. So then devote all your efforts to recognizing these signs of his mercy and love that are upon you. May your generosity and your love respond to these favors: hasten to visit the tabernacle of the *unknown God*, the God who wants to make himself known to you. There, as I have told you, you will grasp everything, unlearn everything. There, at the feet of the tender Master, of the peaceable friend, one tastes, in anticipation, the celestial joys. Ah, may then your young heart fall in love with the one whom this asylum of love contains! Study above all the incomprehensible humility that this God-Man teaches us and always take these words as your motto: *Humility and love.*

You, whose hope I envy: pray for me. Ask of the God who captivates hearts to captivate mine completely. He is too miserly, said a great saint, for whom God is not enough.[345] So let him

---

During that extended visit he recalls speaking to Eustelle on February 23. See also Letter 81, above, which details their conversations during this visit.

[344] The addressee of this letter and of Letters 161–63 is Armand Guerin (c. 1827–c. 1850), a seminarian from Saintes for whom Eustelle developed a special fondness. Cardinal Villecourt remembers him in a letter (quoted in Thompson, 167), citing his childlike innocence and noting that, after ordination, he survived Eustelle by only a few years.

[345] "You greedy misers, what will ever satisfy you if God himself doesn't?" Saint Augustine, Sermons on the Old Testament 19.5, in *The Works of Saint Augustine: A Translation for the 21st Century*, III.1, trans. Edmund Hill, O.P. (New City Press, 2009), 383. The saying turns up now and again, in Meister Eckhart and, in French, in the life of the French Carmelite Blessed Mary of

suffice for us, and we will see his recompense for what we have given up for him.

My prayers are little and poor, but still I offer them for you.

Do not make any more stains on your ratchet,[346] and above all, do not make any indelible ones on your soul.

All yours in Jesus,
his poor servant,
Eustelle.

LETTER 161

Holy dialogue which aims to excite divine love; No human language can express the effects produced by the adorable Eucharist; The vocation of priests; Preparation; Advice; Trials; Helps; Sending hymns.

November 15, 1841.

May the Cross of Jesus be your portion, and his love your treasure.

I leave the feet of the tabernacle, where Jesus gave me the thought to continue with the tender conversation that I have begun with you, child of charity. What a grace, what a consolation it is, this dialogue of souls, this exchange of our most private and secret sentiments![347] The sweet outpouring of the soul to its Creator continues through our union, through our dialogue, which leads us to love God together in one love. Yes, one love together: this is to say, a love that must be all-giving, heroic, ever constant, all-consuming. This for us, the love of the unknown God, the God who hides himself from our senses so that he does not overwhelm us with the brilliance of his divine presence, his dazzling light. O miracle of love! Divine Eucharist! It is not possible for me to offer words for the visions, the lights, the sentiments that Jesus intimates to my soul as I partake of this ineffable mystery. When

the Incarnation, 1566-1618: "Trop est avare à qui Dieu ne suffit." It is likely that Eustelle found the quote here, despite her ascribing it to "a great saint."

[346] A white tunic resembling a surplice, the short white vestment altar servers wear over a cassock.

[347] French: "Oh! qu'il est utile et consolant ce commerce des âmes qui donne de réunir les plus intimes sentiments!" "Oh, how useful and consoling, this intercourse of souls bringing together the most intimate sentiments!" The French original is less overtly erotic than a literal English translation would be; also, *utile*, "useful," seemed pallid in context.

I say that it is not possible for me to express it, I mean that there is no human language that can capture what Jesus alone can know and say. What a gift from God to humanity![348] And how to offer him recompense? For he himself is the only gift that humanity can worthily offer back to God, the only gift that is in perfect harmony with his supreme majesty. O my dear child, how happy you must be! Recognize your great happiness: Jesus, love eternal, *God with us*, has chosen to raise you, one day soon, to the august and awesome dignity of his ministry. The very thought makes my soul rejoice for you; then it saddens me: Jesus knows.[349]

You are aware, I know, of the dispositions and virtues you must cultivate in yourself so that you might be prepared for the anointing you will receive that will empower you to take into your hands the pure and spotless victim. The angels that surround the tabernacle are present to adore and to love but not to consecrate. Do not stray from the path you have begun to follow. Do not be afraid of reversals: you will have them, but to what trial would you refuse to submit to gain such a reward? He who calls you will support you, enlighten you, instruct you. Ah, for this, go to the tabernacle, the armory of the holy: there are arms there to defend yourself and achieve your triumph.

Our Lord sends you the two songs that you asked me for, and three or four others that he composed himself. It is to the tune of *Contemple en silence*; but you know the song has two melodies. It is to the lesser-known melody that I put the one I am sending to you.[350]

I leave you, rescued in the blood of Jesus.[351] You know where: in the ciborium where rests your love and mine, in the dwelling of his divine and all-lovable heart, from which we receive everything and to which we must turn in every need.

---

[348] French: *hommes*, both here and in the following sentence.

[349] Eustelle is alluding to her admitted envy of the sacramental powers reserved to the male priesthood; see, for example, Letter 36, 40, 116, and elsewhere.

[350] See below, Poem II, for the text referenced here.

[351] French: “Je vous laisse, ô prix du sang de Jésus,” literally “I leave you, O price [or prize] of the blood of Jesus.” The French idiom “prix du sang” translates as “blood money” or payment to the family of a homicide victim. The sense then is that the correspondent’s (Armand Guerin’s) priestly vocation is being presented as a recompense or gesture of gratitude for Jesus’s redemptive death on the Cross.

And pray for the one who, though so unworthy, dares to call herself the poor servant of Jesus. Love Jesus well. I think of him always, Always Jesus.

Eustelle.

LETTER 162

Vision of God; No turning back; Examples; Perseverance; The price to pay for failing in one's vocation; Commune; Act only for Jesus; Build up; Virtues; All for Jesus.

To the same person.

February 10, 1842.

All is nothing and dust before Jesus.

It is so that you may serve him in greater love, child of his mercy, that the all-good Jesus has placed you in this asylum of peace where you spend your first days. It is because he wants to give you the pure gold of perfect love that he removes you from the world and its vanities. Take care never to turn back; may the examples that our Lord sometimes places before your eyes become a powerful motivation for you to hold more and more to your original resolution. I ask of our Lord, with all the energy of my soul, to give you perseverance until that day when it will be given to you for the first time to hold the sacred victim sacrificed upon the altar. O child of God, may you understand — more than ever I could understand — the great height of your destiny. There are, no doubt, some difficulties here in this solemn moment, but take courage: the one who has called you will know how to smooth these out. Ah, what accounting would you have to make one day if, through your fault, you lose your vocation!

Go to the tabernacle: there is the armory of the apostolic soldier. There Jesus himself will be your invincible weapon. Oh, love well this good and lovable Savior. Try to unite yourself to him, more and more, in this pledge of his tenderness. Heaven is there; everything is there. Make your every thought, sight, breath, and action for Jesus alone, for Jesus, our only all. May your example serve to make him loved; may your talk be always of Jesus and Mary. Humility, peace, confidence, love, and oneness with the divine: Oh, may Jesus give you everything and in return, may you give all to *your* Jesus. May he remain *your Jesus*, sanctifying you; *your* Jesus, consuming you; *your* Jesus, blessing you.

Remember my soul in the presence of our love; ask him to communicate to me his Eucharistic love. When you want to find me, it will be in the adorable heart of the one through whom I am completely devoted to you.

I have been writing all day: I am fatigued.[352] Monsignor the Bishop arrives today, Thursday.

Eustelle,
poor and unworthy servant of Jesus.

LETTER 163

Eustelle, consumed with fever, asks a redoubling of love; To be deprived of the tabernacle is a great sacrifice to her; The Eucharist; Breathe only for her; Surges of the heart.

April 12, 1842.

Jesus, nothing but Jesus, Jesus for our hearts.

The supreme will, whose loving designs I adore, while depriving me of the happiness of speaking about the unique object which should captivate our heart here below, has instead permitted me to put on paper the sentiments that consume my soul, sentiments of this Jesus so sweet and so good. Dear husband, heavenly friend, how do you express your actions in our hearts?

The ardor of fever consumes me at present, and in this I ask the One beloved of the angels to redouble also in my heart the ardor of his sacred love.[353] Oh, that these ardors might come together in a holocaust consumed all the sooner. This evening began a painful privation for me, making me suffer my inability to go to prostrate myself before the tabernacle of the God who hides himself there out of love. Will of Jesus, you are my paradise, despite the sacrifices

[352] See also Letter 159 above, written on the same day. That letter ends with a similar remark, that Eustelle is fatigued from "writing all day," suggesting that her correspondence in the last months of her life may have been more extensive than what is represented in the *Recueil*.

[353] The sentence is a gentle play on *ardeur*, "ardor," "passion," "fervor," "intensity," etc. With a literal physical fever, about two months before her death, Eustelle finds that one of her favorite metaphors, heat, fire and immolation, comes to literal, physical life.

you demand of me. Dear child of God, these sacrifices are great: no one except those whom Jesus has chosen can have even an idea of them. I suffer in my body, but my soul suffers incomparably more through what our Lord brings it to feel in its zeal for his glory.

My God, what a martyrdom! But it is sweet, oh, so sweet. Jesus makes me suffer with much joy, and peace, and happiness. Oh, how attracting is his Cross! How lovable it is! How precious! The Eucharist is the essence[354] and the memorial of the august mystery of the Cross. Adore, love, and comprehend, so far as you are able, this ineffable sacrament: the science of Jesus, the love of Jesus crucified.

Ah, brother of Jesus, child of Mary, let yourself be consumed by the Eucharistic flame. To the Eucharist bring all your soul, your heart, spirit, thoughts, sentiments, words, actions, intentions, love, breath, and taste: in a word, let your whole being, your totality be only a continual sacred flowing towards that unknown Jesus, hidden so lovingly in the prison of the tabernacle. Oh, may he be always our joy, our peace, our goal.

Whenever the choice lies with you, approach the holy table more often, to savor its honey so sweet. Perhaps, in a few days, I will be deprived of uniting with Jesus. God's will be done. I submit to him with all that is mine; but, even with my submission, tears already wet my eyes.

Ah, my dear Jesus! May you come inside my poor abode, only until I can go to yours: you will come and annihilate all that you are, in the poor recesses of my heart. O Jesus, your love brings me to silence, but my heart is not hidden from you: it lives only for you and it will die only for you, at your feet, in your tabernacle.

Dear child, your generous resolve leads me not to conceal completely from you the state of my soul: although my letters are not worth this, if you have the idea to read them to one of your classmates, use real prudence in choosing them. Oh, it would be infinitely better if the memory of me disappeared entirely!

I cease; I cannot write any more, with such a strong fever. Oh, how good is his fire, joined with that of Jesus, yes?

All yours through his heart: the poor servant of Jesus,

Eustelle.

---

[354] French: *abrégé*, "abstract," "abridgement." Eustelle clearly does not mean that the Mass is a shortened version of the Crucifixion but rather a mystical reenactment.

LETTER 164

Gratitude; The attraction of humility.

To Monsignor the Bishop of La Rochelle.

[*THIS LETTER WAS WRITTEN ABOUT THREE WEEKS AFTER Eustelle's first visit to La Rochelle and her first, transformative conversation with Bishop Clément Villecourt. In advance of this visit, her pastor at Saintes, Father de Laage, had written to the bishop to advise him that he felt Eustelle's health and economic position could not support the level of physical self-mortification that she wished to exercise; for the text of this letter see the Appendix to the Memoir, Appendix 3. Bishop Villecourt apparently agreed with this assessment and counselled Eustelle in August 1839 against using the cilice. He also warned her, perhaps oddly, of the temptation to pride or* amour propre, *as Eustelle calls it. Accordingly, Eustelle's subsequent letters to the bishop are tightly fixed on reporting her progress in humility to the bishop. Note: "Your Grandeur" was the honorific often given to bishops in this period; cf. "Your Grace," "Your Excellency."*]

September 11, 1839.

May the grace of the Holy Spirit be with your Grandeur.

Monsignor,

Please pardon my indiscretion and permit me to write a few lines to your Grandeur.

The good my soul gained from the holy advice which you had the charity to offer me leads me to offer my heartfelt gratitude to you. To have the honor to be guided by your Grandeur in the ways of humility, that virtue of which God makes me know the true worth, and for which he deigns to give me a particular attraction! So I do recommend my soul to your memory before God, Monsignor, that he may the sooner fulfill the wishes of my heart by granting me the gift of this holy virtue that I love, of which my present practice is so small and so imperfect. I look forward every day to better fulfilling my sacred commitment to the practice of this virtue.

Please, Monsignor, pray on this subject for the one who joins her sentiments of respect with those of the most profound veneration, and with the honor of being of your Grandeur,

the humble and obedient servant and daughter,
Eustelle.

LETTER 165

An outpouring of confidence; Two peaceable desires: to be ignored and to enjoy a more intimate familiarity with Jesus in the Holy Eucharist.

[*THIS LETTER APPEARS ONLY IN THE SECOND AND THIRD editions (1848, 1850) of the Recueil. Like the first (1843) edition, these editions were presumably overseen by Bishop Villecourt, who would resign as ordinary of La Rochelle in 1856 and retire to Rome. The language here generally resembles the somewhat strained elegance of Eustelle's other letters to the Bishop. No editorial explanation is offered for its appearance in 1848 and 1850 or for its subsequent disappearance.*]

October 25, 1841.

May the grace of the Holy Spirit be with Your Grandeur.

Monsignor,

The more than paternal kindness with which you have welcomed me redoubles my confidence and excites my boldness; it moves me, despite my unworthiness, to take the liberty to write these few lines to you, for my soul desires to express to you its true need.

I have not forgotten, Monsignor, the important advice which you had the kindness to give me, urging me to *seal my soul to everyone except Jesus*. But, moved, I believe, by the actions of this same tender master, am I not permitted to open my soul to one who represents my Lord to me, one with whom I love to speak as though with him?

Two desires consume me; and yet if it were God's will, I would renounce them both. I desire only what the Lord desires for me, and desire it only out of love for him. So I am at peace in these desires; they do not disturb the peace that intoxicates my soul.

Oh! what is it that could disrupt the ineffable peace that Jesus alone can give? Hell? The world? Sin?[355] Oh! Jesus so good teaches me that, by stripping myself of all that is myself and then clothing myself in his spirit and his inestimable merits, I need fear nothing.

It is not that I believe myself to be thus vested in his divine spirit, but still I have great confidence. No, I do not want to fear anything, not even this Jesus who must judge me.

---

[355] The list of three here perhaps evokes the traditional "three temptations," *mundus, carus, diabolus* or "the world, the flesh and the devil," but the standard French rendering is "le monde, la chair, le diable."

And this world, by the most holy and adorable will of my Savior, casts its own judgments on me from time to time.[356] But what does the judgment of mere creatures matter to me? The kind regard of Jesus is enough for me. And truly, I do not even desire his divine gaze, finding myself already overpaid for what I do for him.[357] Oh, Monsignor! If only the universe might ignore me, as I try to hide myself from its attention. But Jesus's will be done in everything!

The God of the tabernacle is my only thought, my continual occupation, my only knowledge, my sole existence. Oh, there, Monsignor! There, one learns everything, in unknowing everything.

Please, Monsignor, remember my poor soul when, in that most august sacrifice, Love unknown rests in your hands.

Dare I, Monsignor, tell you the thought that fills my mind? This thought? It is my wish to hold him, the Lord, in my hands, as you do: to clutch him to my heart, and finally to press my unworthy lips to the sacred host. In truth, the extravagant thought of being deprived of this, this fantasy that flies against all common sense, causes me nonetheless so uncommonly to suffer.

Pardon me, Monsignor, for wasting your time reading this from me. It is not out of humility that I tell you this; for, truly, I am unworthy to take up anyone's thoughts. But please, Monsignor, ask our Lord for true and perfect humility,[358] for me, for his greater glory.

Deign, Monsignor, accept the respect and profound veneration with which I dare to call myself, in our Lord,

Your unworthy servant and daughter,
Eustelle,
poor servant of Jesus.

---

[356] French: "me lance de temps à autre plusieurs traits," "throws me lines now and again." The following sentence seems to make the sense here clear.

[357] French: "me trouvant trop payée d'agir pour lui."

[358] The phrase echoes advice given to Eustelle by Bishop Villecourt in a letter of September 16, 1839, quoted in the Introduction to the *Recueil*: "Courage, chère fille: travaillez, sans cesse, à acquérir la vraie, la parfaite humilité; mais ne croyez pas qu'on y soit parvenu, parce qu'on en sent le désir. Il y a une distance infinie entre le désir et la possession," "Courage, dear daughter; work ceaselessly to acquire true, perfect humility. But do not believe that one has achieved it simply because one feels the desire. There is an infinite distance between desire and possession."

LETTER 166

To protect herself from any illusion, Eustelle is disposed to open her heart to her bishop; Her soul is at peace; Simplicity; Her heart cannot contain the fire that consumes her; Persuasion of her unworthiness.

To the same person.

[*THIS IS THE FINAL LETTER EUSTELLE WROTE HER BISHOP; this letter is dated on the second Saturday of Lent, about five months before her death. Eustelle is aware that the bishop is scheduled to come to Saintes to preach a series of Lenten sermons beginning on March 5, about two weeks away.*]

February 20, 1842.

All for Jesus in the Eucharist.

Monsignor,

As Jesus our beloved has permitted you to understand the path on which he is conducting me, please allow me to inform you in a particular way—as far as I am capable—about a group of things about which I have already had the honor of discussing with you.

You already know, Monsignor, the reason that led me to keep silence in regard to the graces with which Jesus so good has deigned to favor me. Now, I wish simply to open my heart to you, and submit it completely to your judgment. My soul is in a state of perfect calm, but I fear nonetheless illusion, so dangerous, so subtle, and so easy in these sorts of matters.

Rest assured, Monsignor, that this fear I speak of does not diminish in any way the unalterable peace which I now enjoy; in fact, I find myself completely powerless to trouble myself about anything.

Pardon me, Monsignor, if I permit myself to interact with you so freely: but as I see only our Lord in your person, it is not possible for me not to speak to you as though to the Lord himself.

For a long time, Monsignor, I have wished to open all my soul to you, but doubtless the divine spouse did not permit this sooner, and as I love nothing other than his holy will, I have submitted myself to this privation.

Further, Monsignor, I do not seek to satisfy for myself any desire to make known the favors with which the Lord has deigned to accord to his unworthy servant; Jesus being the only author of these gifts, it is also for him alone that I wish to speak to you in all simplicity.

My poor heart cannot contain the fire which our Lord has been pleased to house there, and it often seems to me that my heart is going to burst open, so violent is the force of this love.

I admit, Monsignor, that, had our good Savior had not sustained me, my frail health would not have been able to withstand these vehement transports. Moreover, had he not restrained me, what extravagances would I not have experienced externally! Oh, I did some things that only my dear Jesus knows about! Do not try and guess them now, Monsignor; I want to share them with you only when you know the full extent of my inadequacies.[359]

Believe me, Monsignor: in all things I sincerely hold the conviction of my own unworthiness and, consequently, it would be impossible for me to attribute to my own worth even the least of the graces I have received from our lovable and well-beloved Savior.[360]

If I were not afraid of troubling you, Monsignor, I would dare to ask you to permit me to speak with you one day next week. Please, Monsignor: if you deem it appropriate, be kind enough to respond to Mademoiselle de Saint-Legier.

Good Jesus, my God! You alone know how I love you. Oh, it is only for you, O my well-loved, my mercy, my pardon, my victim, my all! Bless you, bless you, our first Pastor.[361]

Accept, Monsignor,
my respects and my profound veneration.

Your unworthy servant and daughter,
Eustelle.

---

[359] French: "que lorsque vous saurez toutes mes pauvretés," "only when you know all my poverties." The "extravagances" Eustelle is alluding to here include her rushing the altar in the empty church and embracing and kissing the tabernacle.

[360] French: "il me serait impossible de m'attribuer la moindre des graces," "it would be impossible to attribute to me the least of the graces."

[361] French: "premier Pasteur," an honorific title for the bishop.

[*THE FOLLOWING NINE LETTERS WERE WRITTEN TO A MAID-servant who had been intimately acquainted with Eustelle. Near the end of Letter 173, we learn that Marie has someone read and write her letters.*]

LETTER 167

Wishes for a happy new year; Eustelle asks for prayers for the inner pains that she suffers.

December 29, 1837.

My dear Marie,

At the beginning of this new year, I hasten to make up for my negligence in not writing to you. I should have written to you sooner, but a little — or a lot — of laziness made me delay until now. Postponed is not lost.

I make up now for my failing, for which you will forgive me, I hope.

My dear Marie, I wish you a happy new year in temporal matters, in regard to your health but even more in spiritual matters. I wish that the Lord will answer the weak but sincere prayers that I offer him for you on this beautiful day when the he receives the name of Jesus, announcing to us the salvation that he comes to bring to the earth.[362] On your side, do not forget me: I am greedy for prayers, and I feel my need for them. Have the charity to ask God to give me the gift of strength. And I have great need for patience and resignation to his holy will, in the trials through which he wills for me to pass. Let us strive, one and another, to do all things for God, to endure all for God, and so to arrive at the possession of his pure love, the greatest grace that we can receive in this miserable life, as we wait to love him in a perfect way in eternity. Such a comforting thought! Pray for me and believe that I am always your truly humble and obedient servant,

Eustelle Harpain.[363]

[362] French: "dans ce beau jour où le nom de Jésus qu'il reçoit, nous annonce le salut qu'il vient apporter à la terre." The Gospel for December 29 is from the second chapter of Luke, recounting the presentation of Jesus in the temple. Eustelle is thinking of an earlier event, Jesus's circumcision (where he is given the name "Jesus," recounted in Luke 2:21).

[363] This is the only time in her letters that Eustelle uses her family name.

LETTER 168

Eustelle wishes to have the zeal and the fervor of Saint Louis de Gonzague; To conquer oneself: that is true piety; Obedience; Simplicity; Obedience to the director.

February 23, 1838.

May the peace of our Lord Jesus Christ be with you.

Good Marie, thank you for the beautiful image that you were good enough to send me; it represents a saint that I love very much, but whom I scarcely can imitate, given my cowardice, no doubt, and my scanty generosity towards God. Saint Louis de Gonzague,[364] whom it depicts, did not behave in this way: no, always filled with zeal and fervor, he did not understand what it might be to hold something back in his sacrifice of himself. Let us be strong then and hold on: by the grace of God we will conquer ourselves, for it is in this that true and enduring piety consists.

Good Marie, permit me to express the pain I feel for you, knowing the sorrows you have, sorrows somewhat due to your own fault. These sorrows would immediately disappear if you practice the obedience and the simplicity of Saint Louis de Gonzague. I fear that in giving you this advice I am renewing your pain, but believe me, it is in the concern I have for you that I decided to do so. Oh, if only you could conceive of the merciful, the loving designs that the Lord has for you, with what sweet assurance would you throw yourself into his arms! He wishes only for the union of your heart with his own. Oh, I pray you, for the love of our good master, remove everything that is an obstacle to the peace of God becoming established in you: submit yourself to the one who stands for God with you.[365] The Demon is at work in you, and if he finds you unprepared for his temptations, he will lead you far astray. So treat him only with contempt and do not give him an advantage over you.

Adieu, good Marie, pray for me.

Eustelle.

---

[364] Known in the French-speaking world as Saint Louis de Gonzague and elsewhere as Saint Aloysius Gonzaga (1568–1591), Italian Jesuit scholastic, patron of youth and students.

[365] French: "à celui qui vous tient la place de Dieu," "for the one you hold in place of God," i.e., her spiritual director.

LETTER 169

Submission; Obedience; Charity.

N.d., 1838.

May the cross of Jesus be your portion, and his love your treasure.

My dear Marie,

Pardon my negligence: I ought to have written to you earlier. I feel I have no excuse, but I know well your charity. It is a charity that would overlook my little fault which I wish to repair by the occasion which presents itself of Monsieur your Vicar, whose departure is causing us much sorrow here. He is truly a little saint. No doubt he will be perfectly suited to your parish. I hope, my dear Marie, that from now on, everything will be better for you, and that you will be more reasonable than in the past. I speak to you out of friendship, and, I must tell you in all sincerity that what I learned about you saddens me.[366] Know then, following the example of our divine master, to submit and obey, for in him alone will you find peace. May holy charity be the garment of your soul, before God and before neighbor. It is so good to love God! Why do we not consecrate to him all the affections of our heart? They belong to him already in so many ways! Does he not have the right to demand possession of them? Why delay giving him everything? Let us love then the good and tender master, but let us love only him, and love nothing that we would not love for him. How sweet our final hour will be, at the end of a life lived in the exercise of this holy love! With what joy will we see the end of the days of our miserable exile, and shine on us the beautiful dawn of eternity, in which we shall be consumed together in the charity which is the one God! So be it!

Pray for me. I hope to come and see you next summer. You will have difficulty reading this because I am in a hurry. It is after eleven at night.

Eustelle.

---

[366] The following letter provides needed context here. The correspondent Marie is the woman mentioned in other letters, who suffered from a level of scrupulosity that kept her from receiving the Eucharist. See Letter 23 above for a reference to this correspondent.

LETTER 170

The humility and charity of Eustelle; Confidence, submission, love, frequent Communion.

October 2, 1838.

My good Marie,

You must find me very negligent in having delayed writing to you until now; do not think, however, that this was due to indifference. If God desires, and deserves, that we detach ourselves from creatures that we might attach ourselves to him alone and love him alone, then he also asks that we be united, one to another, through a perfect and heartfelt charity. Believe then that I always have for you the sentiments that you deserve; and, as you are my sister in Jesus Christ, accept the excuse that I offer and grant me pardon for my laziness: I admit that I could have written to you sooner.

The trust that you showed in me when you were visiting at Saintes last month, in letting me understand the sorrows with which your poor heart was burdened, makes me wish to know if you are now more reasonable. I would bet you are not. Ah, my good Marie, there is indeed a remedy for these troubles: but you do not want to employ it. Why do you not go to God with confidence? Why do you not give yourself up to his good pleasure? Why not, after him, submit yourself to those who represent him here below? Do you think you know more than they do? Oh, I beg you in the name of your own happiness, come to God in love, not in fear. Oh, if you only knew how much this good Jesus wishes that you would come to behave with him in simplicity and familiarity! He yearns ardently to possess your whole heart, wants to make it his garden of delights. If only you could persuade yourself of this, I have no doubt that you will correct all these vain scruples which, after all, serve only to make you regress in the ways of salvation. The way to achieve this is to submit and not to distance yourself from the sacraments. I admit to you, if I had myself neglected to approach Holy Communion — and if I could have withstood it — I would be in the same state as you: I am talking about my health.[367] So believe me then, and get out of this

[367] French: "Je vous avoue que, si j'avais négligé moi-même de m'approcher de la sainte Communion, je serais dans le même état que vous, si toutefois j'avais pu le soutenir; je parle de ma santé." Eustelle is suggesting here that

state of self-consciousness and unease:[368] you have no reason to distrust someone who only speaks to you from happy experience and who only wants you to feel the same. Unworthy as I am, I ask for you that the good God send you the power you need to defeat these excessive fears; I know it takes courage to rise above the suggestions of the Demon; with God, what can we not do?

Pray also for me. The Lord shares with me, as with you, his Cross: bless him. Oh, I desire that one day, we will be reunited in eternal blessedness. There we will know no harm, no more conflicts.[369] There we will see God clearly, love him without division, possess him without any fear of ever losing him. The goodness of God himself: this is the reward that awaits us.

Adieu, good Marie, may the peace of the Lord be with you. Amen.

I am your submissive and respectful servant,
Eustelle.

LETTER 171

The Lord blesses those who do violence to themselves; Respond to divine love; Peace of the soul, a foretaste of Heaven; Invitation.

N.d., 1838.

Dear Marie,

With what sentiments of joy was my heart filled when I heard the generous resolution of your heart for God! Ah, he does not leave without reward these first steps you have taken to connect to him. The violences which you will have to do to yourself[370] will be accompanied by the help of his grace, and they will earn for you the most beautiful flowers in the crown that will encircle your forehead for all eternity. Then you will remember these

---

she could not have willingly brought herself to deny herself Holy Communion; only her illness could have made this happen.

[368] French: "gêne et malaise," "embarrassment and uneasiness."

[369] Translating "plus de combats."

[370] French: "Les violences que vous aurez à vous faire." It seems unlikely that Eustelle is telling Marie to inflict physical violence on herself; Eustelle herself was extremely reticent about discussing her own acts of mortification, most of which were forbidden to her by the bishop. It seems more likely that she is referring to necessary and painful changes in her way of life (violences) that Marie must be willing to make to advance herself on the way of virtue.

sorrows, these sacrifices, these past violences. And how little all these miseries will seem to you compared to the immense weight of the reward which will then be your share. How grateful you will be to have profited from the means of salvation which the Lord will have given you to sanctify yourself! Dear Marie, profit from them, while these means are at your disposal. Do you feel as though Jesus has thrown open a portal to your heart, as though he desires to take possession of it? Respond to him, then, with eagerness to the sweetness of his love, and do not fear the pain. God will know how to soften it and return calm and peace to your soul: that peace which has for so long been banished from you; that amiable peace that our Lord wished for his disciples and which lets us taste here below the first fruits of heavenly joy, awaiting here, until we are in Heaven, the perfection of peace that will be given to us, a peace that receives its fullness and perfection in God himself.

Despite my sickness, my poor Marie, I pray for you every day; and now I will ask the good Lord for the continuation and the increase of good that he has begun in you. Please, on your side, pray for me: it is not a lie that I need it.

I learned that you are leaving Monsignor the Curé's house, doubtless to go to your own. You would do well to stop by at Saintes; I would like for you to spend a few days with me. It would make me happy. You will certainly not be a bother to me. You can do the cooking: it will remind you of old times. Do not worry about sleeping: it will not be outside. I was longing to have the chance to tell you this: accept my compliments if it was you who hemmed the handkerchiefs: they are finely sewn.

Adieu: all to God, dear Marie.

Your friend Eustelle.

LETTER 172

It is good with Jesus; Separation; Attach yourself to God alone; Do violence to self; The welcome that Eustelle receives from the Bishop; Frequent communion.

July 28, 1839.

May the grace of the Holy Spirit be with you.

Good Marie,

You will think, perhaps, that it has been too long a time since I have written to you, but my occupations have not permitted me to write sooner. Now I wish to make up for that little negligence and satisfy myself: not in person as I would wish if God willed it, but rather by entrusting our conversation in Christian friendship to paper, guided alone by Jesus's charity.

It is in my sacristy, my regular home, near the altar where Jesus rests in his holy company, that I converse with you. How good to be here! Why can I not fix my stay here permanently? Remember the time that you and I spent here together; but let not this memory reawaken your sorrows, for all I wish is that you could be now as you were then. I would like to know if you are being reasonable, since you are so far from me. They told me that you only cry, so it would seem you are not becoming accustomed to where you are. If this is what is happening, I advise you to come back rather than stay somewhere reluctantly.

You know that Father has changed his posting; he has left Saintes, heading for his new destination. He is now far from us, poor Father; thus God separates us from our friends and those who were a help to us, so that we will attach ourselves only to him, so that he will be enough for us. And it is said likewise that he wants us to be enough for him, for he himself tells us that he delights in the children of man. Why so? We would not find our delight in him! He is too miserly for whom God is not enough.[371] Let us try to find in him our joy and our peace. May every thing that is not him be as nothing to us.[372] Good Marie, if you would permit me to offer a little advice, and believe me that it is only in the interest which I have for your soul that I ardently desire for the glory of God, that you advance on the paths of justice and virtue. And you know the means you must adopt on this path you have taken: have no fear of difficulties and the small pains you will need to overcome for this. You know that the kingdom of God suffers violence: only those who do violence to themselves will succeed.[373]

---

[371] See Letter 160 to Armand Guerin, above.

[372] French: "que tout ce qui n'est pas lui ne nous soit rien."

[373] Echoing Matthew 11:12:" le Royaume des cieux est forcé, et les violents le ravissent," " . . . the kingdom of heaven suffers violence, and the violent bear it away."

So come on: take courage and have a little energy: work to love God as much as you can. It is so sweet to love him! Love him, poor Marie, and make him love you if you can. O my God! I command you to love God, I, who am so far from loving him as I desire in my heart;[374] I, on whom his graces have descended with such profusion that it seems he could not grant me more! Pray then, until that day when, after having loved him on this earth, we can love him together in the heavenly homeland.

I have just made the journey from Saintes to La Rochelle. There I had the honor to speak three times to Monsignor the Bishop. The Bishop is a saint, most of all in humility and charity. I was truly surprised at the kind way he welcomed me, because you understand my character and the character of the one to whom I presented myself. Imagine: me, talking to a bishop! And soon I will have this honor again. I can imagine what you are thinking: what did she say to him? *Dame!* that is my secret.[375]

So anyway, I have to finish, because I have to straighten up the sanctuary. There I am alone with the Lord. Have the greatest devotion to his divine sacrament; approach it often. Pay attention to these words: *Approach it often.* It is not without a reason that I repeat this, you numbskull.[376] Write to me soon and tell me how you are, in body and in soul.

Adieu: I leave you in the heart of Jesus: leave yours with him there, so that he embraces it with heavenly ardor. Pray that he accept mine as well; let me make my home there, while we wait to come to stay in the heavenly homeland. There, together with the choirs of angels, we will praise and bless the Father, the Son, and the Holy Spirit. Let it be so.

I am, in our Lord, your friend,
Eustelle.

---

[374] French: "moi qui suis si loin de l'aimer, selon le désir de mou cœur," "I who am so far from loving him, according to the desire of my heart."

[375] Thompson (244) identifies this as a colloquial entreaty to the Virgin Mary (cf. "By 'r' Lady!") and claims it is the only instance of Eustelle using "an expression peculiar to the inferior class from which she sprang."

[376] French: "Ce n'est pas sans sujet que je vous dis cela, mauvaise tête," "It is not without reason that I tell you this, you bad head." Beginning with "Dame," above, this passage is almost stunningly conversational, making it almost a necessity to render "mauvais tête" in colloquial English. In modern French the idiom tends to mean a refractory or obstinate person; given what the adjoining letters reveal about Marie and especially her scrupulosity, it seems sensible to see Eustelle playfully pushing her here.

LETTER 173

Greetings and encouragement; Draw near to the source of all good, the Eucharist; Visit the Eucharist often, at least internally; Patience, resignation; Trials.

October 20, 1839.

May our Lord deign to adorn your soul with the flowers of all virtues, and may the most beautiful and lively of these flowers be his love.

With what profound joy did I receive your letter! It confirmed my perception that you have become more reasonable in Bordeaux than you were during your previous visit. I have blessed the Lord a thousand times, not for your conversion, for you were no infidel,[377] but rather for the sincere determination that you have brought to the work of your sanctification, with greater ardor and perfection. I believe and hope that your present state of mind will prepare you to accept the plans that God has for you, so to taste in this life the ineffable peace that the Lord is pleased to rekindle in your soul, in the presence of this Jesus who, divine as his Father, eternal as his Father, before whom the very universe is nothing more than a point and who, by a single act of his will, could reduce this same universe to nothingness, in the excess of his love humbled himself by taking on the feeble species of bread to become our food.[378]

Dear Marie, it is from this, the source of all good things, that you must draw often; it is from that fount of living water that you must quench the thirst of your soul. Oh, if only the people of the world knew the delicious pleasure to taste the sacred banquet, I have no doubt that they would renounce their false joys to drink

---

[377] French: "car vous n'étiez pas pervertie," "for you were not perverted." Direct translation of "pervertie" seemed to risk deflecting the sense of the original.

[378] French: "J'espère et je crois que les dispositions dans lesquelles vous êtes maintenant vous prépareront à remplir les desseins de Dieu sur vous, et à goûter, dès cette vie cette paix ineffable que le Seigneur se plaît à répandre dans les âmes dociles à sa tendre voix.... Quels sentiments doivent animer votre âme, en la présence de ce Jésus, Dieu comme son Père, éternel comme son Père, devant qui l'univers n'est qu'un point qui, par un seul acte de sa volonté, pourrait réduire cet univers au néant, s'abaisse, par l'excès de son amour, sous les faibles espèces du pain, pour devenir notre nourriture," the longest and most complex sentence in the Letters or the *Memoir*. It is humbling to remember that Eustelle has only five years of schooling and very limited access to books.

in long drafts from the source of eternal truth. And for you, who have tasted this indescribable goodness, hasten then to expand it by Holy Communion, as frequently as possible. Let your delight be in this divine food; may Jesus in the Eucharist be for you your all in all; recognize him, in the sacrament of love, as your father, your brother, your friend, in whom you must confide all your sorrows. Oh, how it pleases him to see one at his feet who knows his misery, who proclaims it to him there![379] How he pours on that soul, so abundantly, the generosity of his love! Cherish, then, when you can talk with him, as often as your obligations permit it; and, if you are unable to quench this desire there, then transport your heart and its affections to the tabernacle where he reposes. When you love someone and cannot see him, at least we think of him, remember him with delight, imagine him. Do this very thing, my dear Marie: in the middle of your occupations, place yourself in the presence of God. Work to achieve the holy union that must exist between you and God alone, for in this is the beginning of your true grandeur. Be patient, resigned in the pains or trials that it has pleased the Lord to send you; try to bear them even with joy and grace; love God and, if possible, make him loved; but love him principally for himself and not solely for his gifts or consolations or rewards. The more your love is stripped of self-interest, the more worthy it is of God.

Apply yourself also to the practice of holy humility. Without this virtue, there can be no true piety. There are many pious persons but there are few that are truly humble. Good Marie, all I have said to you is said in the interest I have for your soul, because I wish for you to become a great saint; I ask this of our Lord with all my heart. Please ask of him the same grace for me; do not deny me the help of your prayers, for I have need. God in his bounty has made me endure very difficult trials: bless him always. Oh, my God: it is because I am weak that I find these pains so great. Ask that he send me more power, more courage, more generosity for him, so that, more faithful in the future than in the past, I can make up for so much time I spent in negligence and lukewarmness.

A few days ago, I had a visit from Monsieur the Abbé, who spent four days in Saintes. As much as his arrival made me happy,

---

[379] French: "une ame qui connaît sa misère, qui la lui confesse!"

his leaving made me sad: God's will be done.[380] He told me how happy it would make him to be at Saint-Pallais. I embroidered a pretty pall for him which he took with him. We spoke of you. He told me that your Holy Virgin was still in his successor's room.[381] I urged him to pray for you; do not fail to do the same for him. Give my respects to the person who reads and writes your letters:[382] I pray for her; ask her also to pray for me. I leave you, good Marie, in the divine heart of Jesus; draw from it, the source of everything, the love that must consume your own heart. May he hold you close in these times, until he consumes you in blessed eternity. I hope that there we will be reunited.

Adieu, good Marie, your friend,

Eustelle. Adieu.

LETTER 174

O, if men knew how to appreciate the divine Eucharist!; The Savior's thirst; The refuge of the tabernacle; External practices; Meditation; Exterior mortifications; True piety.

August 8, 1840.

Glory to Jesus.

Dear Marie,

No doubt you are saying to yourself, Eustelle has forgotten me, with not a thought of what Eustelle promised you. Instead, believe firmly that I do not forget you at the feet of our Savior, and that I often ask him to animate more and more in your soul the divine fire of his love, that love in which he burns for you, that love that causes him to stay with us until the end of the ages, to strengthen his creatures under the veils of the Eucharist. There in the Eucharist, he eclipses his greatness and holy majesty; he gives us an easier access to him.[383] Ah, if men knew better the price of this gift most divine, they would understand how good

[380] French: "Enfin Dieu le veut ainsi," "Finally, God wants it so."

[381] The statue of the Virgin Mary mentioned in Letter 41.

[382] This is the first and only indication that Eustelle's correspondent here cannot read or write.

[383] French: "Là, en éclipsant sa grandeur et sa majesté sainte, il nous donne près de lui un plus facile accès."

it is for them to have Jesus in the Eucharist, and how eager they would be to respond to the desires of our adorable master who, from the instant of his incarnation to his death on the Cross, took no action, made no movement that was not done for us. Near the consummation of his sacrifice, of that martyrdom that was his whole life, he cried out, in a transport of love that consumed him, *I thirst.*[384] Ah, dear Marie, it was not his sufferings that made him cry out for thirst, but instead his violent longing for your salvation, for mine, and for that of all the souls for which he shed his precious blood. Ah, let us try to respond to his unimaginable act of love.[385] I urge you to take your delight in the bread of the angels, as often as possible. In your pains, your trials, hasten to take your refuge in this asylum of peace; take your shelter in the shadow of the tabernacle, for there reposes our tender Father, our compassionate Brother, our celestial Friend, the God of the angels, adored by those in Heaven, on the earth—by all souls enlightened by the luminous ray of faith. Ah, how small is that number! Oh, that I might increase that number by the price of my blood; but, O my God, I am unworthy. Pray for me, my dear Marie, that I myself might be adoring in spirit and in truth.

I urge you not to get yourself too attached to any purely external practices of piety: they are good, no doubt, but they are only the bark of the tree of perfection.[386] Give yourself over instead to meditation, for it is here that Jesus speaks to the faithful soul. Love interior mortification; detach yourself from creatures; become dead to your inclinations, your faults. Be gentle and patient: these virtues please everyone. Love piety, and bring people to love it as well;[387] it is not what the people of world think of it: dark, fierce and constraining, as it is often said. Religion alone elevates the person in thought and feeling; it alone shows the path of true happiness and grandeur founded in the immutable truth which is God. I desire, with all the ardor of my soul, that Jesus, our God, enlighten you, immolate you, and consume you in the fires of his holy charity. And that which I desire for you I desire also for people you know there where you are and, in particular, for

---

384 "J'ai soif," John 19:28.

385 French "son excessive charité." "Excessive" has more negative connotations in English, and "charity" seemed pale in translation.

386 See *Memoir* 18 and note 51 above.

387 French: "Aimez et faites aimer la piété."

those who read your letters: I think about them all the time.[388] May God preserve them and bring them to advance, more and more, on the path of justice and virtue.

I end, good Marie: the time is gone. I hope you can write back soon. Monsieur the Abbé must come to Saintes on business in a month or nearly so: he wrote to me a few days ago, telling me not to die before then. You know that, since you left, I have been and still am in great pain, always in my chest: I do not know what will happen. All I know is that I want only what God wants, I desire neither to live nor to die but rather desire only to accomplish entirely the designs of God towards me.

Adieu, dear Marie: I leave you full of the same desire, I know, that I too share: to love Jesus more and more. In this moment, I enfold your soul into his divine heart. For that is our center: let us remain there always, always. Our exile will soon be over, and the joys of the homeland will be eternal with God. My wish for you.

Adieu, your friend,

Eustelle,
unworthy servant of Jesus.

LETTER 175

Will must work together with grace; Self-love, a bitter herb; Pay Jesus back for the indifference of men; News; Frequenting the sacraments; When will the day of divine union come?

July 14, 1840.

All for Jesus, may he bless you and love you.

You have been quite a long time writing to me, good Marie, and your silence caused me a little concern; and if, on receiving your latest letter you had given me the good news of your return to reason, I would have been much more satisfied. I suffer the pain of seeing that you have not changed, and I would like with all my heart to provide a remedy for that which is effective in you. But this cannot be accomplished without your making an effort. Humility, submission, confidence: complete abandonment to the

[388] This second reference to Marie's readers and scribes signals Eustelle's sense of a broader audience and that this is not now and never was a private conversation.

decisions of the one whom Jesus our Savior has given you to direct your soul. There is a weed in the field of your interior; can you guess it? Self-love. Dear Marie, do not let it take root; pull it up; Jesus will offer you help. Go and seek it, this help, at the banquet of the merciful lamb. Oh, he loves your soul; may your soul, in turn, respond to his tenderness. Seek to make up to him for the coldness, the indifference, and the forgetfulness which so many of the hearts created by him have for him. Oh yes, Jesus is the unknown God, more unknown than you can comprehend. For a soul that loves Jesus, this vision of humanity is enough to render that soul a victim of pain and love. Pray, dear Marie, that I may be the first to console the desolate heart of this good and peaceful friend. I have too little love, after all the benefits I have received. Pray that my life might be as I desire it to be: a continual act of love. I am hurried and cannot converse with you any longer.

I will tell you though that Monsieur the Abbé came to see me during the week of the Octave.[389] his health is not good; I can only attribute the cause of his illness to his need of someone to pray for him: do this. Father Briand has gone to Bordeaux this week to preach a retreat, but not for you.[390]

I leave you in the peace of Jesus, love eternal. Approach the tribunal of penance often, but let it be with calmness, without worry or unease, and with the greatest simplicity. From this sacred pool, go to the holy table, often partaking of the sacred bread that gives life, and which, uniting you with Jesus on earth, will enable you to achieve eternal union with him. Oh, when shall that beautiful day come?

Adieu: all yours in Jesus, your friend,

Eustelle,
unworthy and poor servant of Jesus.

---

[389] As this letter is written in July, the "octave" Eustelle is referring to must be the Octave of Pentecost, celebrated in the eighth week after Easter, between roughly mid-May and mid-June. The octave, a major solemn period in the Church for centuries, was inadvertently discontinued by Bl. Pope Paul VI in 1969.

[390] French: "mais qui ne sera pas pour vous," "but this will not be for you," suggesting that Marie is in Bordeaux but that it is not possible for her to attend the retreat. This could be for any of several reasons: a retreat for another parish or for an exclusive congregation, for men only, for example.

LETTER 176

The heart of Jesus suffers from the indifference of his children; He is generous to courageous souls; Humility is the best way to lead us to pure love; Love Jesus; Visit him often.

[*FINAL LETTER IN THE FIRST (1843) EDITION OF THE* Recueil. *The look and feel of this letter suggest that the correspondent might be one of Eustelle's biological sisters, Angèle or Magdeleine-Anastasie.*]

15 January.

All for Jesus.

My dear sister, I unite myself to you to bless and glorify our Lord, for he gives your soul the thirst for justice and your heart the desire to burn with his heavenly love. Oh, how his divine heart suffers from the coldness and indifference that the children he loves have for him, for whom he offers, a million times every day, his blood and his life! Try then, my sister, by the ardor of your charity, to quench the thirst felt by our dear and thousand-times-good master. Do not fear the sacrifices: Jesus is generous with the souls who do not keep accounts with him; he abundantly rains down on them the riches of his love and his most precious favors; he attracts them, enlightens them, purifies them, sets them afire, and then chains them to his tender heart by bonds that are stronger than death.

The best way, in my opinion, to help us soon arrive at the possession of the pure love of Jesus is humility, the virtue of the God-Man, the foundation of the stairway of perfection.[391] Divine love will never reign where vanity holds sway, because Jesus loves only hearts that he finds empty of themselves and empty of everything that is not him. When we possess this humility, it brings with it this emptying, this stripping. O my sister! It is with this virtue that you can trustingly present yourself[392] to the God of the tabernacle, to Jesus, our father, our brother, our friend, our eternal beatitude. Oh, why do we not love this object so worthy of our love, this Jesus, the joy of angels, the crown of virgins, the admiration of Heaven? I urge you, as often as your obligations permit you, go often to the feet of the sanctuary, pour

---

[391] The medieval English writer Walter Hilton identifies humility as the foundation of the spiritual life; *Scala Perfectionis* (*The Ladder of Perfection*) I:15.

[392] French: "se présenter avec confiance," "present oneself with confidence." The word "confidence" seemed at odds with the theme of humility.

out your soul to his adorable heart, take this sacred dwelling for your own, where, night and day, burns the fire of eternal love.[393] There you will find the light, the power, the sweetest consolations, the most perfect peace. There in this sacred arsenal, you will find an abundance of arms to defend yourself against the attacks of the enemies of your soul. O my sister, may you spend your days there and die there, in the love of the One whose love is captive there.

I leave you, continuing to be united to you in charity. Pray that my soul will ever be in love with him. May Jesus bless you and love you. All yours, through his heart.

His poor servant,
Eustelle.

[*THE FOLLOWING THREE LETTERS DO NOT APPEAR IN THE first (1843) edition of the* Recueil *but are added in subsequent editions (1850, 1860, and 1883). No editorial explanation for the additions is offered. The curious exact repetition of the closing words of Letters 177 and 178 may call their authenticity into question.*]

LETTER 177

Seek nothing but Jesus; Eustelle's gratitude; May the divine and beloved Jesus be known and loved, wherever he reposes in the divine Eucharist.

To Mademoiselle A***.

1840.

Follow your decision to speak to Monsieur L***, since, as you say, you do not feel at liberty doing so with Monsieur D***; go ahead.[394] For myself, I prefer to have only one director, though I do not find anything wrong in your taking this step. Take care not to seek out anything but Jesus, Jesus alone. It is all too easy

---

[393] As a sign of the Eucharistic Presence, Catholic churches still burn a candle, often enclosed in a red glass vessel, near the tabernacle, a light that would have been all the more striking after dark in pre-electric ages.

[394] French: *faites-le*. Eustelle is carefully encouraging her correspondent to seek out a new director, as she herself had done. At the same time, she is counselling Mademoiselle A*** not to be caught up in her relationship with any director but to keep her focus on Jesus.

to find oneself in things, even spiritual things. Take this principle as your own and let it rule your conduct: *All for the pure love of Jesus; nothing else satisfies me.*

I wish you good night, and hope that you will never have a bad one. These nights will serve as proof that the days preceding them were full and fruitful to the heart of the one who so liberally pays those who work faithfully in his vineyard.

Have a thought for one who loves you in Jesus and for Jesus.

Estelle, his poor and unworthy servant.

P.S. May Jesus fulfill my wishes and reward your generous actions and the actions of those people who, regardless of my unworthiness, have the goodness to take care of a creature as miserable as this unworthy servant of Jesus.

Eustelle, all yours through his heart.

LETTER 178

Jesus allows our sufferings to make us humble; Compensate him with love; The ardent desire of holy love.

1840.

All for Jesus.

Yes, it is for Jesus that you should continue your communions, despite the spiritual sufferings that you have described to me. Jesus has allowed these to come to you to make you humble, and to make you understand how much your soul needs his continual help. Replace this faithlessness — for which he has already pardoned you — with a tender and grateful love. It is so good! So good! Live in this heavenly love!

Since you are going to P***, you can reconcile with Monsieur B*** and tell him everything that the Lord inspires in you. But if you cannot do this, take Communion with confidence.

I would love like a seraph the one for whom I would gladly die! Ask him, though I am so unworthy, that this final wish might be granted me.

May he bless you and love you — these I ask him often of you.

Adieu, to God.[395]

Eustelle.

[395] French: "Adieu, à Dieu."

LETTER 179

This letter sent by Eustelle to a little girl of five or six years of age.

Kind regards.

August 1840.

May God bless you, my dear child.

See, I am faithful to my promise, my dear Clémence: and this is to commit you to be submissive and obedient to your Papa and to your good Mama. Be faithful to your prayers, morning and night. Give your heart to the good God, in the morning when you awaken and in the evening when you take your rest. Also mind your good Grandma and your good aunts.[396] And have a great love for the holy Virgin; she greatly loves the little girls that pray to her.

I'm sending you a little picture. When you think of it, pray for me. And I will pray also for you.

Adieu, dear little one. I love you with all my heart.

Your friend, Eustelle.

[*Note accompanying this letter:*]

So that the little girl does not guess who this letter is for, I put it in this envelope, as you see. Give it to her, please. And imitate her in her lively and ardent love for Jesus, our dear Savior, whom I would love like a seraph, the one for whom I would gladly die! Ask him, though so unworthy, that this final wish might be granted me.

May he bless you and love you — these I ask him often of you. Adieu, to God.[397]

---

[396] French: "Sois obéissante aussi à ta bonne Mémé, et à tes bonnes tantes."

[397] With the exception of a missing *j'en sois* (I am) here, the close of this letter from "I would love like a seraph" (je voudrais aimer comme un Séraphin) to the end is identical to that of the preceding letter. Eustelle alludes to the love of the seraphim elsewhere, in Letters 29 and 41.

Cantiques | Songs

I. Pour la Communion.	For Communion.
Qu'il est doux le Seigneur,	How sweet is the Lord
Sur son trône de grâce!	on his throne of grace!
Là, son amour efface	There does his love cast in shadow
L'éclat de sa grandeur.	the brilliance of his greatness.
Qu'il est doux le Seigneur,	How sweet is the Lord
Quand de l'âme docile	when, in a gentle soul,
Il se fait un asile,	He takes his refuge
Et qu'il parle à son cœur!	and speaks to it from his heart.
Devant l'œil de ce Dieu,	Before the eye of this God
L'Ange, à peine, est sans tache;	the very angels fear some stain;[1]
Le Chérubin se cache	the cherubim hide themselves
Sous son aile de feu.	under their fiery wing.
Et l'homme, chaque jour,	But man, every day,
Sous un léger nuage,	under only the lightest of clouds,
Voit ce Dieu qui l'engage	sees this God who connects with him
A l'aimer sans retour.	to love him without any return.
Venez, vous qui pleurez:	So come, all you who cry:
C'est le Dieu qui console;	this is the God who consoles;
Sa plus douce parole	His sweetest word
Est pour vous qui souffrez.	is for you who suffer.
Et vous, pécheurs, venez:	And you, sinners, come:
L'agneau mort au Calvaire	the Lamb that died on Calvary
N'est pas un Dieu sévère;	is not a God who is hard or severe:
Il vous aime: espérez.	He loves you: come in hope.

[1] Literally, "The angel is scarcely without stain." In context, the sense is that the angels feel shame and awe before the Eucharist while humans see only the appearance of bread and wine.

II. Amour et reconnaissance, après Communion.	**In love and thanksgiving; after Communion.**
Air: Contemple en silence.	*To the tune of "Contemple en silence."*
L'amour qui m'embrase Pour vous, bon Sauveur, De sa douce extase Enivre mon cœur. Amour délectable, Tu fais mon bonheur! Combien est aimable Ta céleste ardeur!	The love for you, good Savior, that love that sets me afire from your sweet ecstasy intoxicates my heart. Delightful love How happy you make me! How kind, how gentle your Heavenly ardor!
Près du Dieu que j'aime Redoublent mes feux; C'est Jésus lui-même! C'est le Roi des deux! La foi qui m'éclaire Dissipe la nuit Du profond mystère Dont l'ombre s'enfuit.	As I draw near to the God I love, the fire in me redoubles; it is Jesus himself! He is King of both! The faith that illuminates me scatters the night of deep mystery, makes the shadow take flight.
Je sens sa présence; Le ciel est en moi; Mon ame, en silence, S'unit à son Roi. Chœurs sacrés des Anges Qui formez sa cour, Offrez mes louanges A ce Dieu d'amour.	I feel his presence; Heaven is in me; my soul, in silence, is at one with the King. Holy choirs of angels, you who surround his heart, offer my praises too to the God of love.

III. Même Sujet.	**On the same subject.**
Divine foi, lumière vive et pure,	Faith divine, living and pure,
De tes rayons viens pénétrer mon cœur;	May your rays come to penetrate my heart;
A ton flambeau, sous cette forme obscure,	from your flame, under form obscure,
Je reconnais mon Dieu, mon Rédempteur.	I recognize my God, my Redeemer.
Près de l'autel où celui que j'adore	Before the altar the one whom I adore
Voile pour moi l'éclat de sa beauté,	veils for me the radiance of his beauty,
Guidé par toi, je viens, à chaque aurore,	guided by you I come each day
Offrir mes vœux au Dieu de majesté.	to offer my wishes to the God of majesty.
Le Chérubin, brûlant de votre flamme,	The cherubim, burning in your flame,
Tremble, ô mon Dieu! devant votre grandeur;	tremble, O my God! before your greatness;
Moi, plus heureux, je possède en mon âme,	Happier me, for I hold in my soul
Le bien suprême objet de son ardeur.	the supremely good object of its ardor.
De votre amour, ô Sauveur adorable!	Your love, O Savior adored!
Qui redira les transports généreux?	Who can answer such generous transports?
Pour un pécheur, pour un enfant coupable,	For the sinner, for the guilty child,
Vous abaissez la majesté des cieux.	You humbled the very majesty of Heaven.
A vous, mon Dieu, je consacre ma vie;	To you, my God, I consecrate my life;
Tout mon bonheur sera de vous servir:	All my good is in serving you.
Oui, désormais, de mou âme attendrie	Yes! from this day forward, may you fill
Vous remplirez le plus doux souvenir.	my tender soul with sweet knowledge of you.
En poursuivant des images frivoles,	By pursuing vain and foolish images
J'ai méconnu mes devoirs et vos lois:	I have disregarded my duties and your laws:
Ah! dans mon cœur abattez ces idoles,	Ah, tear down all these idols in my heart
Et fixez-y pour jamais votre croix.	and keep it ever fixed on your Cross.

IV. Pour la Bénédiction.	**IV. For Benediction.**
Air: Qu'il est doux le Seigneur.	*To the tune of "Qu'il est doux le Seigneur."*
O prodige d'amour!	O wonder of love!
Le ciel pour nous s'abaisse:	Heaven itself is humbled before us:
L'homme-Dieu, par tendresse,	the Man-God, out of tenderness
Fixe ici son séjour.	Fixes here his stay.
Mortels, prosternez-vous	Mortals, prostrate yourselves
En sa sainte présence;	in his sacred presence;
Implorez sa clémence:	beg for his mercy, and
Il va vous bénir tous.	He will bless all of you.
Sa divine splendeur	His divine splendor
S'éclipse sous cette ombre;	is eclipsed under this shadow;
Mais ce nuage somber	but the cloud as it parts
Nous conduit à son cœur.	takes us to his very heart.
Qu'offrent de plus les Cieux?	What more could even Heaven offer?
Jésus est dans ce temple:	Jesus is in his temple:
L'œil de la foi contemple	Let the eye of faith contemplate
Son éclat radieux.	His radiant light.
L'autel a mon amour;	The altar of my love;
Le temple a ma pensée;	the temple of my heart;
Ma demeure est fixée	my dwelling stands unmoved
Où Jésus tient sa cour.	where Jesus holds his court.
C'est là qu'est mon bonheur;	All my happiness is there;
C'est là qu'est mon asile.	my refuge? It is there;
Adieu, monde fragile:	Adieu, fragile world:
Jésus seul a mon cœur.	Jesus alone has my heart.

IVa: A related poem.

Drawn from Letter 82 to Father Briand.

As I fall asleep, I whisper these words, which you well know:

Avant l'aurore,	Before the dawn,
Il paraîtra;	he will appear;
Demain encore,	again tomorrow,
Jésus viendra.	Jesus will come.

Then, in the morning, as I arrive at God's house, I say:

Ce n'est que dans ce temple	It is only in his temple
Où mon cœur est heureux:	That my heart is happy:
Mon amour y contemple	There my love contemplates
L'objet de tous ses vœux.	The object of its desires.

Then, having arrived at the tabernacle, I continue:

Ah! voilà mon asile;	Ah, This is my refuge;
Voilà mon vrai Bonheur	Here is my true happiness;
Adieu, monde futile.	Adieu, useless world:
Jésus a tout mon cœur.	Jesus has all my heart.

<table>
<tr><th>V. Même sujet.</th><th>V. On the same subject.</th></tr>
<tr><td>Je t'adore en silence,
O Monarque des cieux;
Ta divine presence
Ici comble mes vœux.
Aux célestes Archanges,
J'unis mes chants d'amour;
Pour prix de mes louanges, (bis.)
Bénis-moi dans ce jour.</td><td>I adore you in silence,
O Monarch of Heaven:
your divine presence here
fulfills my every wish.
To the song of Heaven's Archangels
I join my hymn of love;
In return for my praises (repeat)
Bless me this day.</td></tr>
<tr><td>De ton amour le gage,
O divin Rédempteur!
Est mon seul héritage,
Le nectar de mon cœur.
Pour toi je sens mon âme
Se consumer d'amour;
Qu'à jamais il m'enflamme
Bénis-moi dans ce jour.</td><td>This pledge of your love
O divine Redeemer
is my only heritage,
nectar to my heart.
In you I feel my very soul
consumed in love;
may it ever set me aflame, (repeat)
and bless me this day.</td></tr>
</table>

VI. Autre.	VI. Another.
Le fils de l'Eternel, caché dans ce mystère,	The Son of the Eternal, hidden in his mystery,
Pour nous, heureux mortels, s'immole chaque jour;	sacrifices himself for us, happy mortals every day;
Aimable prisonnier, au fond du sanctuaire,	lovable prisoner, at the center of the sanctuary,
Il attend de nos cœurs le tribut de l'amour.	He awaits the tribute of love from our hearts.
Là, du juste et du faible il est l'appui fidèle;	There he is the support of the just and the weak:
Il leur prête sa force au milieu des combats;	He lends them his strength in the midst of their battles
Du pécheur repentant il anime le zèle,	He awakens the zeal of the repentant sinner,
Accueille ses soupirs et redresse ses pas.	He welcomes his sighs and straightens his steps.
Cher objet de mes feux, pour toi seul je respire;	Dear object of my fire, for you alone I breathe:
Augmente mes ardeurs, ô mon unique bien!	increase my ardors, O my unique good!
T'aimer, mourir d'amour, c'est tout ce que desire	To love, to die of love is the only desire of this heart
Ce cœur qui t'est uni par le plus doux lien.	united to you by the sweetest bond.
Nourri du pain sacré, je suis ton tabernacle;	Fed by holy bread, I am myself your tabernacle,
Mon âme est ton palais, ton temple, ton autel;	my soul your palace, your temple, your altar;
Il n'est rien que j'envie au bonheur du cénacle:	there is nothing that I envy in the joys of the upper room, for
Tu me donnes déjà quelque avant-gout du ciel.	you have already given me a foretaste of Heaven.

Le ciel! O mon Jésus! C'est toi . . . chastes délices,	Heaven! O my Jesus! It is you— chaste delights,
Le monde ne saurait soupçonner vos douceurs:	The world can never know your sweetness
Il me plaint,	They pity me,
ne voyant en moi que sacrifices:	seeing in me nothing but sacrifices, and
Il ignore, grand Dieu! vos biens et vos faveurs.	never seeing, great God! your goods and favors.

VII Autre.	**VII. Another.**
Le voici présent sur l'autel	Here he is present on the altar,
Ce Jésus que ma foi révère:	This Jesus whom I revere;
Par amour il descend du ciel,	for love he came down from Heaven
Et se rend captif sur la terre.	and made himself captive on the earth.
C'est le cher objet de mon cœur;	He is the dear object of my heart;
C'est le doux ami de mon ame.	He is the tender friend of my soul.
Je trouve à ses pieds le bonheur;	I find happiness at his feet;
Près de lui redouble ma flamme.	near him, my love's flame redoubles.
O prodige de son amour!	What a wonder, his love!
O miracle de sa puissance!	What a miracle, his power!
Quoi! dans ce modeste séjour,	Lo! in this, such a modest form
Il me fait sentir sa présence!	He makes me feel his presence.
Prêtez-moi, brûlants Séraphins,	Lend me, you bright-burning seraphim,
Le feu sacré qui vous embrase:	the sacred flame that sets you alight;
Je veux, dans vos transports divins,	Oh, that I could, in these divine transports
Mourir de la plus douce extase.	Die in such sweet ecstasy.

VIII. Pour l'Elévation.	VIII. At the Elevation.
Le voilà donc accompli le mystère	Here he accomplishes the mystery
Qu'en tremblant révère ma foi!	Which, trembling, my faith reveres!
Fils ingrat, j'offensai mon père,	Ungrateful child, I offended my father,
Et c'est lui qui revient à moi!	But it is he who always returns to me!
Je l'offensai...	I offended him...
mais, pour laver mon crime,	but, to wash away my crime,
Son sang divin coule sur cet autel;	His holy blood streams down from Heaven;
L'enfer allait dévorer sa victime;	Hell was going to devour its victim
Jésus s'offre,	when Jesus offered himself,
et m'ouvre le ciel.	and Heaven opened for me.
Pour consoler mon long pèlerinage.	To console me on my long pilgrimage,
Son amour le tient enchaîné;	His love keeps him bound for me;
C'est ici que son doux langage	It is here that his tender words
Doit fléchir tout cœur obstiné.	Must bend every obstinate heart.
Il retentit, comme sur le Calvaire,	As he did on Calvary, he cries out again,
Ce cri puissant qui sauva l'univers:	the cry that saved a universe:
Pardonnez-leur...	*forgive them...*
Ah! pardonnez, mon Père...	*Ah, forgive them, my Father...*
Et ce cri ferme les enfers.	The cry that slams shut the gates of Hell.
Pénétrez-nous, salutaire rosée;	Come into us, salutary dew:
Coulez, coulez sang de Jésus;	pour out, pour out, O blood of Jesus.
Notre âme languit desséchée,	Our life languishes, a dried out husk
Quand vous ne la fécondez plus.	when you cease to nourish it.
A notre cœur rendez son innocence;	Return our innocence to our heart, and
De la vertu ramenez les beaux jours;	may its virtue bring back the happy days.
Ah! quand la foi semble quitter la France,	Ah, when the faith seems to leave France,
Sang de Jésus, coulez toujours.	Blood of Jesus, flow always on us.

IX. Avantages de la Croix.

Je contemple, sur le Calvaire,
L'œuvre d'un éternel amour;
Le rayon divin qui m'éclaire
Est plus vif que l'éclat du jour.
C'est un reflet de cette gloire
Dont s'entoure le roi des rois:
Clarté sainte qui me fait croire
Que mon bonheur est dans la croix.

Mondains, vos honneurs, vos richesses
Ne sont point l'objet de mes vœux;
Gardez vos trompeuses promesses
De plaisirs et de jours heureux.
Le cœur de Jésus est l'asile
Que son amour offre à mon choix;
J'y cache ma vertu fragile:
Tout mon salut est dans la croix.

Tout est consommé! . . . Croix divine,
Tu nous enrichis pour jamais;
De Jésus la tête s'incline;
Il met le comble à ses bienfaits.

Ses yeux éteints semblent encore
Dire au pécheur: *Gémis et crois.*
Tendre victime que j'adore,
Tu nous as sauvés par la croix.

Vainement le monde s'apprête
A troubler ma paix, mon bonheur:
Je laisse gronder la tempête;
Je repose en ce divin cœur.
Oui, je brave, sous cette égide,
Tous mes ennemis à la fois,
Et de souffrir je suis avide,
Quand je vois mon chef sur la croix.

IX. Benefits of the Cross.

On Calvary I contemplate
the labor of a love eternal;
the divine ray that illumines me
is brighter than the light of day.
But it is only a reflection of the glory
that surrounds the King of kings:
a blessed light that makes me know
That all my joy is in the Cross.

Worldlings, your honors and your riches
are not the objects of my desire;
just keep your treacherous promises
of pleasures and of happy days.
The heart of Jesus is the refuge
that his love offers for my choice:
there I hide my fragile virtues
For all my health is in the Cross.

It is finished![2]. . . divine Cross,
You always enrich us;
and as Jesus bows his head
He reaches the summit of his gift to us.[3]

His dying eyes then seem to say
to the sinner, *Moan, and then believe.*
Tender victim whom I adore:
You have saved us by your Cross.

Vainly does the world prepare
to trouble my peace, my happiness;
I let the world's storms rumble
reposing in his heart divine..
Yes, under his aegis I stand tall
against all my enemies altogether
and am ready, eager now, to suffer
When I see my captain on the Cross.

---

[2] Echoing John 19:30.

[3] French: "De Jésus la tête s'incline; / Il met le comble à ses bienfaits," "The head of Jesus inclines / he reaches the height of his benefits."

Dans ses mains que l'amour captive,	In his hands, which love holds captive,
Je trouve un asile chéri;	I find a dear place of safety;
Dans ses pieds sacrés, ma foi vive	and in his sacred feet my living faith
Me découvre un nouvel abri.	Discovers a new refuge for me.
Mais l'heureux centre auquel j'aspire,	But the happy center for which I long
C'est son cœur ouvert sur ce bois;	is his heart, laid open upon the wood;
C'est là que doux est son empire;	it is there that his reign is sweetest:
Oui, le bonheur est dans la croix.	Yes! what happiness is in the Cross.

X. Invocation a l'Esprit-Saint.	**X. Invocation to the Holy Spirit**
Air: Sur cet autel, le Roi de gloire.	*To the tune of "On this altar, the King of glory."*

*[REPRINTED FROM LETTER 3, DATED APRIL 4, 1839. THE LETTER is addressed to Father A***, the parish priest at Saint-Pallais who was reassigned in 1837. The letter refers to the verses below as "the second couplet of the Invocation" and reminds Father A*** that he has the first: "le second couplet d'invocation; vous avez le premier." The melody is unknown.]*

Esprit-Saint, descends dans nos âmes;	Holy Spirit, come into our souls,
embrase-les de tes ardeurs;	enflame them with your passion;
fais-leur goûter ces pures flammes,	let them taste your purest flames,
blesse-les de tes traits vainqueurs.	and wound them with your saving strokes.
eclaire-nous de ta vive lumière,	Light us with your living light,
Divin Esprit consolateur;	Divine Spirit, our Consolation.
viens ranimer l'esprit de la prière	Revive your spirit in our prayers,
dans notre cœur,	in our heart,
dans notre cœur.	in our heart.
O Marie! O notre modèle!	O Mary, O our model!
Epouse de l'Esprit d'amour,	Bride of the Spirit in holy love:
du haut de la gloire éternelle,	from everlasting glory's heights
reçois nos accents en ce jour.	hear our prayers upon this day.
Garantis-nous, ô notre unique asile,	Guard us now, O holy refuge,
des traits de l'Esprit séducteur;	from the wiles of the Seducer.
rends à ton fils, de plus en plus docile,	Bring to your Son, ever more willing,
tout notre cœur,	all our heart,
tout notre cœur.	all our heart.

Xa: A related poem.

Drawn from Letter 80, to Father Briand:

Esprit-Saint, prêtez-lui vos ailes;	Holy Spirit, spread your wings,
Descends, Esprit consolateur,	Descend, O Consoler Spirit,
Et viens, des voûtes éternelles,	Come from the vault of Heaven
Verser tes feux dans notre cœur.	And pour your fires into our heart.
Ah! si, du sein de la lumière,	Ah, if from the bosom of light,
Tu vois, à mon heure dernière,	You see in my last hour,
Pâlir le flambeau de la foi, *(bis.)*	The torch of faith begin to fade, *(repeat)*
Esprit d'amour, éclaire-moi. *(bis.)*	Spirit of love, enlighten my way. *(repeat)*

XI. Fête de l'Assomption.	**XI. On the Feast of the Assumption.**
Dans un transport délicieux	In one singular delicious ecstasy
De respect, d'amour, de tendresse.	Of respect, of love, and of tenderness;
Aujourd'hui, la terre et les cieux	this day do the earth and Heaven
Unissent leur chant d'allégresse.	Unite in one singular hymn of joy.
Si, dans le ciel, les purs Esprits	Just as the pure spirits in Heaven
A Marie offrent des louanges,	offer their praise to Mary our Mother;
Nos transports ont aussi leur prix,	may our own praises be part of her gift
Associés à ceux des Anges.	together with those of the angels.
Quel est ce pompeux appareil	What is this awesome spectacle
D'éclat, d'honneur et de puissance?	of brilliance and honor and might?
O Vierge, rien, sous le soleil,	O Virgin, nothing under the sun
N'égale ta magnificence.	is the equal of your magnificence.
L'indivisible Trinité	The undivided Trinity
Se révèle à toi sans nuage;	reveals to you its true, unclouded self,
L'éternelle félicité	and eternal happiness
Pour toujours devient ton partage.	becomes your righteous portion forever.
Le Père, en ce jour solennel,	The Father, on this solemn day,
Accueille une fille en Marie;	welcomes a daughter in Mary;
L'Esprit-Saint la proclame, au ciel,	and the Holy Spirit proclaims it in Heaven,
Comme son épouse chérie;	as his dear wife.
Jésus, le Roi de l'univers,	Jesus, King of the universe,
Veut que sa mère en soit la Reine;	desires his mother to be its queen;
Son nom fait frémir les enfers;	His name makes the very Hell to tremble
Elle est en tous lieux souveraine.	And she is sovereign everywhere.
Après Dieu, je te dois mon cœur,	After God, I give you my heart,
O Reine du céleste empire!	O Queen of the Heavenly empire!
Je veux partager ton bonheur;	I want to share in your happiness
Nuit et jour, vers lui je soupire.	night and day; towards your Son I sigh.
Pourrais-je être heureux loin de toi?	Could I ever be happy away from you?
Non, c'est au ciel qu'est ce que j'aime.	No: it is Heaven only that I crave.
Fils de Marie, appelez-moi	Son of Mary, call me
A la félicité suprême.	to your supreme happiness.

XII. Invocation à Marie.	XII. Invocation to Mary.
O soleil pur et radieux,	O pure and radiant sun,
Temple sacré du Roi de gloire,	Sacred temple of the King of glory,
Immortelle Reine des cieux,	Immortal queen of Heaven,
Eternise en nous ta mémoire.	Let your memory endure in us forever.
(Refrain.)	*(Refrain.)*
Protège toujours tes enfants,	Companion of your children always,
Du haut des splendeurs éternelles;	from the heights of eternal splendor
Reçois leurs vœux; béuis leurs chants	Receive their wishes, revel in their songs
Ils te seront toujours fidèles.	For they are ever faithful to you.
Ici, loin d'un monde enchanteur,	Here, far from the enchanting world
A l'ombre de ton sanctuaire,	In the shadow of your sanctuary
Nous sentons croître en notre cœur	We feel growing in our heart
L'esprit de grâce et de prière.	The spirit of grace and prayer.
Protège, etc.	*Companion, etc.*
Dans les dangers, dans les combats,	In our dangers, amidst our battles
Tu nous conduis à la victoire,	it is you who lead us to victory.
Et tu daignes guider nos pas	And you deign to guide our steps
Jusques au séjour de la gloire.	Unto the throne of glory.
Protège, etc.	*Companion, etc.*

XIII. Désirs du ciel.	XIII. Desires for Heaven.
Grand Dieu! je languis sur la terre:	Great God! I languish upon the earth:
A mes vœux quand vous rendrez-vous?	When will you give in to my wishes?
Non, rien ne peut me satisfaire	No, there is nothing that can satisfy me
Eloigné d'un objet si doux.	So far away from that object so dear.
(Refrain.)	*(Refrain.)*
Sacré parvis! O ma patrie!	Holy precincts![4] O my true home!
J'appelle ce moment heureux	I call that moment happy
Où, dégagé de cette vie,	when, disencumbered from this life,
Je prendrai mon vol vers les cieux.	I take my flight into the skies.
Vous seul pouvez rompre mes chaînes	You alone can break my chains
Et me rendre la liberté;	and deliver me into liberty.
Vous seul pouvez finir mes peines	You alone can end my pains
Et combler ma félicité.	And fill full my felicity.
Sacré parvis, etc.	*Holy precincts, etc.*
O Jésus, ma douce espérance,	O Jesu, my own sweet hope,
Exaucez mes brûlants désirs:	quench my burning desires;
L'aspect de la divine essence	the face of the divine essence
Peut seul apaiser mes soupirs.	alone can ease my sighs and moans.
Sacré parvis, etc.	*Holy precincts, etc.*
Vous le contemplez,	Think of him,
Vierge sainte,	Holy Virgin,
Ce fils adorable et béni;	Your blessed and adorable Son
Priez qu'en la céleste enceinte,	Pray that, in that heavenly haven
Votre enfant vous soit réuni.	Your child be reunited with you.
Sacré parvis, etc.	*Holy precincts, etc.*

[4] Literally, "sacred square," the open area in front of an important building; cf. Saint Peter's Square.

XIV. Aspiration Improvisée par Eustelle, aux pieds du Saint-Sacrement, Mai 1841.

XIV. Eustelle's improvised prayer at the feet of the Blessed Sacrament, May 1841.

[Reprinted from Letter 38, above.]

O seul ami que j'adore et contemple,
Divin époux, ô Jésus, mon espoir!
Ah! près de toi, que ne puis-je, en ce temple,
Couler mes jours jusqu'à leur dernier soir!

Si ton amour me ravit par ses charmes,
Ah! donne-moi de répondre à ses feux:
Je veux t'aimer dans les croix, dans les larmes,
En attendant de te voir dans les cieux.

O my only friend, whom I adore and contemplate,
Spouse divine, O Jesus, my hope!
Before you in this temple, why can I not
pass my days, until my final night.

If your love so moves me by its charms
Ah, permit me to respond to these fires:
I want now to love you in the crosses, in the tears,
As I wait to see you in Heaven.

XV. Song of Divine Love.

[Reprinted from Letter 124, above.]

Quand votre amour vient m'animer,	When your love came to bring me life,
Mon Dieu! que mon âme est ravie!	My God! how it stirred my soul!
Pourtant, combien, sans vous aimer,	But how many moments of my life
J'ai passé d'instants de ma vie!	I have passed without loving you!
Rien n'est doux loin de vous,	Nothing is sweet if distant from you,
O mon céleste Epoux!	O my Heavenly Spouse!
Adieu, monde, je t'abandonne:	Adieu, world, I leave you behind:
C'est à mon Dieu que je me donne.	It is to my God that I give myself.

GENERAL INDEX

SCRIPTURE INDEX

J. Stephen Russell is professor emeritus of English at Hofstra University, where he taught for over thirty years. He is the author of *The English Dream Vision* (1988), *Chaucer and the Trivium* (1998), and more than thirty articles on medieval and monastic writers from Langland and Dante to Augustine, Aelred of Rievaulx, and Bernard of Clairvaux. Additionally, he is the author of *The Cause* (2009) and *Some Catholic Words* (2026). He has edited or translated works by Richard Challoner, John Gennings, OFM, and Albertanus of Brescia.

www.ingramcontent.com/pod-product-compliance
Lightning Source LLC
LaVergne TN
LVHW100505110826
845146LV00002B/523